# Into Higher Education 2004

**Into Higher
Education**
is now available
online at
**www.skill.org.uk**

into **higher**
education 2004

the **higher education guide**
for people with disabilities

Into Higher Education, the popular annual publication
from Skill, offers invaluable information and advice about
applications and support, grants and benefits in higher
education. The guide also includes profiles written by
disabled students about their experiences in higher education
as well as a list of advice agencies and institutions that
provide higher education courses.

**Into Higher Education can also be accessed online
via Skill's website, www.skill.org.uk.**

Here you can search for the details of the disability policy
and provision in every educational establishment providing
higher education. Individuals can also access a copy of the
institution's disability statement and have direct email access
to the relevant specialist. **It is the easiest way for disabled
people to make that all-important first contact.**

**Many more useful services are also available at
www.skill.org.uk, so visit the site now to make sure
you make the most of what is available.**

**Skill Information Service**
0800 328 5050 (voice) • 0800 068 2422 (text)
info@skill.org.uk • www.skill.org.uk

Registered charity 801971

MAKING KNOWLEDGE WORK

The University of Bradford Disability Office was established over 12 years ago and continues to expand each year as more disabled students make Bradford their first choice of University.

## WHY CHOOSE BRADFORD?

- Dedicated and experienced staff
- Strong commitment to the social model of disability
- Proven track record in successfully supporting disabled students
- Full assessment service for Disabled Students' Allowance (DSA)
- Team of residential Community Service Volunteers to support disabled students
- Free equipment loan service for disabled students who are not eligible for DSA
- Free dyslexia screening of all new students
- Free assessment by chartered educational psychologist of students identified by the screen as possibly having dyslexia
- On site accessible technologies expertise and strong links with national and international suppliers
- Liaison with Social Services and other external agencies

FOR FURTHER INFORMATION, PLEASE CONTACT:

Disability Office
University of Bradford
Tel: 01274 233739    Fax: 01274 235340
Minicom: 01274 235094    Email: disabilities@bradford.ac.uk
Website: www.brad.ac.uk/disability

CONFRONTING INEQUALITY : CELEBRATING DIVERSITY

# Contents

# Acknowledgements

I would like to show my appreciation to all those who took part in the production of this guide, including Rachel Lockhart, Anya Wilson and Erin Milliken at Trotman Publishing, and Juliette Cox at Ecctis.

I would especially like to thank:

Ouch! BBCi's Disability website
Damon Rose, Ouch! Editor
Ruth, Ciaran and Sara – Ouch! diarists
My mother, Arlette Caprez, for directory research
Skill
Oly, Roger Roberts, Lucy Gemma Crane, Giles Donaldson, Bethan West, Jacqueline Fowler, Helen Roocroft, Aneias Martos, Rebecca Atkinson and Amjad Mahboob for contributing their experiences of higher education.

Thank you also to all the staff who contributed their valuable time to giving us the information we needed.

A very big thank you to my family and friends: Peach and Maisie Kazen, Dicky Pool, Sophie Kviman, Mandy Prowse, Linda and Simon Bryer, Lynn Towers, Clare Pace, Sally Dalton, Juliette Preston, Alan Stuart, Jim Bishop, Adrian Mckinney, Leah Montevaldo-Elbourne, Phillip Hawker, Dee Batton, Roz Hawkins, Andy Clare (congratulations!) and Shay Leonard.

And finally:
Thanks to Biba and Suky for being so completely fantastic and to Rook for his inspiration and encouragement.

# About the Editor

Emma Caprez studied for her BA in Design and Media Management at Thames Valley University. For her final-year project she researched, wrote and illustrated a book on the history of the Ealing School of Art. She graduated with First Class Honours in 1993. Emma has worked on several research projects, including one on dramatherapy for people with disabilities, and contributed towards university literature. She has written for two international music papers, *LA Rock Review* and *Rumba*. Emma also wrote *Getting into the Media* (and produced the video of the same name), *Getting into Performing Arts* and *Journalism Uncovered*, all published by Trotman.

# Foreword

### Mabel Davis, BA, BEd

*Mabel Davis is Head Teacher of Heathlands School in St Albans, an all-age special school for deaf children that pioneers inclusion strategies and collaborative partnerships with mainstream schools. She is the first deaf head teacher in the UK. She is also the representative of the Disability Rights Commission on the General Teaching Council for England, and in 1993 she received a RADAR People of the Year Award for services to education. Here she addresses her particular concerns with opening up access to education training for students with a disability and in particular deaf students.*

When I was a disabled student at university in the late 1970s I was regarded as a bit of an oddball. Certainly I appeared to be the only registered disabled person on my BEd course. The university had no idea how to support me as a deaf student and I hesitated to ask for fear of jeopardising my position. It therefore gave me much pleasure to read *The Disabled Students' Guide to University* and realise how much real progress has been made. Higher education has opened its doors with a 'Can do' message in terms of access and supporting students to achieve their potential. It is now expected that people with any disability can aspire to a university education and to full citizenship. Much has been achieved but there is still a great deal to be done.

In my capacity as the Disability Rights Commission's (DRC) representative on the General Teaching Council for England (GTCE) I have sought to keep disability issues high on the agenda. Education is my field of expertise and I have found that, in spite of an ethos of social inclusion, there has been a tendency to pay lip service to equal opportunities, and the subject of disability has not been highlighted as much as it should be. It is my remit to keep it afloat, but as the only disabled member of the GTCE's 64 members, there were times when I felt I had returned to my solitary and isolated position at university. This is not a criticism of the GTCE, but it shows how, when we are in a position of dynamic change, the priorities that vie for attention make it difficult to highlight disability issues that apply to relatively few in the wide educational spectrum.

Within this spectrum, there are people with an equally wide range of disabilities who have either entered or sought to enter teaching as a career. It would appear that access for those with physical disabilities is addressed more positively by the training providers than access for those with sensory disabilities. Deafness does appear to be the least understood of disabilities, even amongst disabled people themselves, as it often involves access to communication and has more social implications. Evidence of this has come to me over the years from prospective deaf students who have expressed concern about their rejection by various teacher training providers. Without exception, all had the relevant entry qualifications, mainly upper second Honours degrees, and would appear to have been prime candidates for PGCE courses or the Graduate Training route. It is not quite that simple. Deaf candidates may have been rejected due to their lack of skill in written English, a prerequisite for anyone who wants to teach. Others may well have demonstrated that ability, but still faced rejection.

Some applicants felt that they had been given unsatisfactory reasons for their rejection while others commented that they were given no explanation at all. It is not known just how many deaf people have been turned down for training via undergraduate courses or employment-based routes, but we need to find this out in order to assess the scale of the problem and the reasons for it, in relation not only to deaf applicants but to applicants of all disabilities. Only then can we discover how far and why certain disability groups may be under-represented in the teaching and other professions.

We may need to investigate further some of the aggregate data – where it exists – on the experiences of applicants with disabilities seeking Initial Teacher Training (ITT) places. The collection of aggregate data may reveal more issues of concern on the part of groups with particular disabilities. We also need to overcome the understandable reticence at the application stage of some applicants to be open about their disability and the support they need.

Given that we are currently experiencing a national recruitment and retention crisis in schools it makes no sense to reject potential teachers without a very good reason. With a national emphasis on social inclusion, one might think that people with a wide variety of disabilities would be actively encouraged to join the teaching profession and act as positive role models for children. This does appear to be happening in some cases, where the Disability Discrimination Act (DDA) has ensured physical access to courses via the required Accessibility Plans in accordance with the Disability Act 2001 amendments to the DDA. However, there appears to be less evidence of providing access for people with sensory impairments such as deafness.

Since no real integration can take place in the classroom until it takes place in the staff room as well, it is important that this matter be placed squarely on every relevant agenda. Questions need to be asked about whether, when careers education or guidance is offered, disabled people are actually being encouraged to consider, or discouraged from considering, applying for teacher training. How many do apply? What percentage are accepted/rejected? What reasons are given for rejection? Is the ratio of disabled teachers currently in training and in the teaching profession known? Data on the ethnicity of teachers and potential teachers is available, so there would appear to be no reason why the same information on disability cannot be found. This data is essential in order to identify the barriers to teaching that still exist for many disabled people. Only then can real efforts be made to remove these barriers.

The GTCE's interest is in clarifying what related work is being carried out by other organisations so that the Council's work on ITT adds value and does not duplicate the work of others. In particular, the 2002 Education Act gives the GTCE responsibility for defining 'suitability to teach' in considering whether to grant provisional or full registration.

The GTCE is aware that some other professional bodies (non-teaching) include medical or physical fitness to practise among their suitability criteria and wanted to take soundings from those who represent/research students with disabilities on this sensitive matter. Concern has been expressed about the misuse of fitness-related suitability criteria and about the tendency to conflate ill health and disability. While there may be very good reasons not to include a medical/physical fitness criterion in assessing suitability for professional registration, it appears that ITT providers may welcome further support and guidance in looking at disability issues at the point of selection.

Sound awareness of the DDA does not make their task less complex. For example, trainees cannot be recommended for Qualified Teacher Status (QTS) without meeting requirements for school-based practice. But what might be considered 'reasonable adjustment' for a higher education institute may not be deemed reasonable for a small partner school, particularly if a trainee is working there for only a number of weeks. It is clear that without further guidance, even well-intentioned ITT providers may struggle to make appropriate decisions about applicants with disabilities. Even so, it is unfair to avoid the complexity of the decision by dismissing applications from disabled candidates who deserve more equitable treatment.

One way to move this situation forward would be to set targets for ITT providers to train a percentage of teachers with disabilities each year. As long as these targets were reasonable and achievable they could encourage providers to develop a strategic approach to making a contribution to a more representative teaching force. In such quotas there would still be the need to determine 'suitability to teach' to ensure that this was not a token gesture for political expediency. The idea is to get capable teachers who happen to have a disability as opposed to 'disabled teachers' *per se*.

Now is a crucial moment to get things right. Education is central to advancement in all other areas and it is to the benefit of all disabled people to get it sorted. It is also in the public interest to enrich the general community with a truly inclusive workforce, and the field of education should be leading the way. It is to be hoped that many young people reading this guide will make sound choices and take equality of access forward to the extent that the need for such a guide will become obsolete.

M G Davis
Head Teacher, Heathlands School, St Albans
Disability Council Representative on
the General Teaching Council for England

# Preface

Welcome to the third edition of *The Disabled Students' Guide to University*. What changes there have been to higher education in the last three years! The introduction of the Disability Discrimination Act (DDA) Part 4[1] is beginning to make a serious impact on institutions throughout the UK, regarding their provision and their awareness. This year we have had more responses than ever to the questionnaires that we routinely send out to all institutions. More and more institutions have units or staff dedicated to supporting students with disabilities, rather than offering services as a sideline. Where structural changes were once impossible due to the age of buildings, physical changes are now being (or soon intended to be) put into place to ensure that all areas are accessible.

Information suggests that the local environment has improved too – public transport (particularly train stations) has become more accessible. I remember speaking to a disability coordinator a couple of years ago who scoffed when I asked if the local train station was accessible: 'Of course it isn't accessible – no train stations are accessible – and trains aren't accessible, so what would be the point?'

Shopping centres, facilities and pavements have been improved in most parts of the country to improve the physical environment and to open up access, giving potential students a wider choice of areas where they study.

Of course some people will question the validity of *The Disabled Students' Guide to University* – shouldn't all institutions of higher education (HE) be accessible, especially now the DDA Part 4 has been introduced and the Quality Assurance Agency (QAA)[2] has a Code of Practice for Students with Disabilities to check up on them? Well, the answer to that is of course they should be, but in reality they are not. Not yet. There is plenty being done, and huge amounts of money are being spent, but there is still a long way to go. Sadly, there are disabled students who face a tough challenge at their place of

---

1  Detailed information from Skill about the DDA Part 4 follows the Introduction.
2  The QAA Code of Practice for Students with Disabilities sets benchmark standards for provision and organisational practice, which are outlined in 24 precepts that identify key areas of provision. The QAA expects the institution to be able to demonstrate compliance with these precepts through its own quality assurance mechanisms.

learning, just trying to get their needs met. While their peers are relaxing at the uni bar, or getting to know each other over coffee, disabled friends are trying to organise a sign language interpreter or ensure the lecture notes distributed to them are in an alternative format. There are institutions that offer a wonderful service to their disabled students – Universities UK (the organisation representing vice-chancellors) has cited 13 flagship case studies, mainly from the newer universities. But there are still places of education that are not living up to what should be expected of them. Consequently some students can't cope and are forced to drop out. There is a feeling that only the most confident and articulate disabled students get through.

Under the DDA, students with disabilities can take legal action if they are treated less favourably than a non-disabled student would be treated. But taking legal action itself requires a huge amount of energy, time and guts, and of course not every disabled student treated less favourably will want to put themselves through that. The student may just choose to put up with it or drop out, the problem will not be remedied, and the university will continue to be ignorant of the changes it should be implementing.

*The Disabled Students' Guide to University* sets out to inform you what is available now. It lets you know how far the institution has got, and how far it will need to go to accommodate your needs. It gives you some initial information to start your shortlist of institution choices. The information given here is no substitute for actually visiting the institutions themselves, but it is a start. And of course, going to university isn't just about studying – you'll want to be able to get out and about and enjoy leisure pursuits or take advantage of the local museums, libraries, shops and nightlife, because being at university or college is also about making new friends. This book aims to give you some of that local information. After all, it might not make sense to study at a university that is itself fairly accessible if the surrounding area is particularly hilly.

The institutions' disability statements vary in length from a small booklet to very thick, highly detailed documents. *The Disabled Students' Guide to University* gives you the edited, essential information all in one book, which means you don't have to wade through piles of disability statements (like I had to!). You will only need to read the full statements once you've made your shortlist of institutions.

This third edition also includes excerpts from the diaries of three freshers who have just embarked on their university careers. Their four-week diaries were published on BBCi's disability website, Ouch! (www.bbc.co.uk/ouch) and provide a hugely valuable insight into what university life is like, particularly for a student with a disability. They are extremely well worth reading.

I hope the institution you eventually study at will meet all your individual needs so that you may enjoy a very happy, and successful, student life.

# Access the Future

The University of Plymouth welcomes and supports students with disabilities including dyslexia and endeavours to meet your specific needs, whilst valuing the special abilities you may have in other areas.

However, you may be feeling unsure about how you would manage your new course of study in relation to your disability but remember:

## You Are Not on Your Own

Many students with disabilities and dyslexia are studying on each of our campuses.

Our resources are improving all the time and broadly they include advice, assessments and support for:

- Admission to particular courses
- Claiming the Disabled Student Allowance
- The identification of dyslexia
- Arrangement of examination provision
- The supply and co-ordination of enablers
- Study skills and computer skills training

The service is confidential; the choice is yours. Call us today.

**DISABILITY ASSIST SERVICES**
Room 8, Babbage Building,
University of Plymouth,
Drake Circus, Plymouth  PL4 8AA.
Telephone: 01752 232278
email: das@plymouth.ac.uk

www.plymouth.ac.uk/disability

# Introduction

Total number of students with disabilities for the year 2001/2:168,760 postgraduate; 649,680 undergraduate; 818,445 in total.

Total number of students with disabilities for the year 1994/5: 140,999 postgraduate; 451,840 undergraduate; 592,839 in total.

This shows that between 1994/5 and 2001/2 there was an increase of 225,606 in the number of students with disabilities studying at higher education level.

*Information from* Students in Higher Education Institutions, *HESA*

Disabled students are significantly under-represented in higher education, but now that universities are being assessed by the Quality Assurance Agency on their provision for disabled students, and with the extension of the Disability Discrimination Act to cover education, it is hoped that access and facilities will continue to improve and student numbers increase.

*The Disabled Students' Guide to University*, now in its third edition, aims to assist you in the process of trying to select the right higher education institution for you, by providing comprehensive information on services, facilities and access, as well as some local information.

### Collection of data
The information for the A–Z entries (well, A–Y actually) was gleaned from several sources. Questionnaires and previous entries (where applicable) were sent to all the universities and higher education institutions in the country, to be filled in by the disability coordinator or the person responsible for students with disabilities. This year we had a record response.

Information was also sought from disability statements that outline what the higher education institution has to offer. These statements vary a great deal in what they reveal and the style in which they are written. Some seem to suggest that disabled students will be 'allowed' to attend their institution providing certain criteria are met, whilst the attitude in others is truly positive – the institution will welcome you with open arms and do anything that they can to accommodate your academic and personal needs. Naturally the latter style of disability statement is far more inviting, but the only real way to find out if the university can live up to its public relations is by going to visit it yourself.

Further information was sought from prospectuses. Some prospectuses will give you a brief outline of what services you can expect from the college or university as a disabled student. Others do not even mention disability, or access and facilities available to meet the needs of disabled students, at all.

Finally, the use of direct communication, whether via email or by phone, was employed. But the end goal was always to get the relevant information that you, the reader, might need. This was no easy task either. I was often passed from department to department, sometimes without even getting a query answered. Information, it seems, is not always readily accessible.

## Questions, questions!

As a pre-entry student you will have many questions to ask before you make your application to your chosen institution. Like all students you will want to be sure that you choose one that offers the course you want to study at an institution you feel comfortable with. The choice of institution may depend on location, or reputation for offering quality-rated courses, or some other influence. But as a student with individual needs you have many additional questions:

➡ Is the campus wheelchair-accessible?
➡ Are induction loops fitted?
➡ Are the toilet facilities accessible?
➡ Is orientation training given?
➡ Will my guide dog be accommodated?
➡ Are extra study support sessions offered?
➡ Does the institution have a policy on alternative study/assessment and examination needs?
➡ What is the institution's policy on meeting the individual needs of students with disabilities?
➡ Will the academic staff be aware of my needs?
➡ Does the institution have a mental health policy?
➡ Do staff and lecturers have mental health training?
➡ Does the institution have specialist software?
➡ Will I receive help with my Disabled Students' Allowances (DSA) application?
➡ Are there computers with specialist software (e.g. text help) available?

➡ Is there accessible accommodation or residences fitted with the Deaf Alerter system?

➡ Does the institution offer provision of personal assistants or support workers?

➡ How will confidentiality be maintained?

➡ Is the students' union bar accessible?

➡ Will I be able to meet other students with disabilities at the institution to discuss their experiences?

➡ What is the local area like in terms of access, facilities and external support?

You will want to know the answers to all these questions and many more. The aim of this guide is to provide you with much of the information you will require to begin your shortlist of institutions to visit. Of course, not all institutions will offer everything you need yet. Don't let this put you off making a visit, because they should be able to make the necessary adjustments you require if you give them enough notice. The best thing you can do is make a list of everything you need to know before you visit the institution and ask all your questions when you get to your pre-application interview.

## Making a visit

If you are interested in a particular institution, you should contact the university or college as soon as possible to discuss what individual needs you have in order to find out how best it can cater for your requirements. The earlier you make contact the better, as it gives the institution more time to arrange any necessary adaptations or personal support, or to ensure you are timetabled into wheelchair accessible lecture theatres or ones with induction loops if necessary. In addition, if you are not happy with the institution for whatever reason, it gives you time to look around and assess the alternatives, or discuss with the institution ways in which it needs to improve.

It is imperative that you visit the institutions you are interested in to see for yourself what the environment is like and to assess the attitude of the personnel you will be in contact with. After all, you will be spending three or more years of your life there and you need to make sure you are confident in making the right decision. Most institutions offer visits and interviews to give you the opportunity to find out what support they can offer you. Naturally you are the best judge of what your needs are, so you can voice these from the outset and get support mechanisms put into action at the earliest possible opportunity. This will prevent delays, or your having to sort out your individual requirements whilst others are busy enjoying themselves at the freshers' ball and making new friends.

## Individual needs
Visiting the institution in person allows you to view the campus and departments you will be using and to see whether the facilities offered meet your requirements. If they don't then you have the opportunity to ensure that they do by the time you arrive to study there, if the institution is able to make the necessary changes. Remember, institutions are obliged to make reasonable adjustments to cater for the needs of disabled students, including the provision of auxiliary aids and services, such as sign language interpreters or providing coursework in an alternative format. It is not a case of 'it would be great if they did', but a case of 'they must'. An institution is not currently obliged to make adjustments to the physical features of premises, but this will change in September 2005. The good news is that many institutions are preparing for this by introducing better access now. This may mean that your physical requirements will be addressed if you give enough advance notice. Disabled students finally have rights. Institutions have to treat students with disabilities and all other students equally; it will be unlawful to do otherwise.

Visiting during term-time allows you to see how the institution really operates and gives you the opportunity to meet other students with disabilities to discuss whether they are receiving adequate support and their needs are being met.

## Disclosure and confidentiality
Of course, not every student with individual needs will want to disclose them. This is entirely a matter of personal judgement and you should do what's best for you. But remember, if you declare your disability your needs will remain confidential if you want, with only the relevant staff being informed – with your permission. However, if a student does not want information on their disability passed on to anyone else, the institution may only be able to make a less satisfactory (or no) reasonable adjustment. Institutions should have a disclosure policy covering what they will do with the information when a student discloses a disability.

## Money matters
For anyone, studying in higher education can be costly, and as a student with individual needs you will probably incur further expenses. Not all support or facilities will be provided free of charge

by the institution, and rent will have to be paid for your accommodation and that of your personal assistant if he or she is residing with you. The Disabled Students' Allowance (DSA) is available to provide financial support for:

➡ non-medical personal assistants, e.g. sign language interpreters and readers;
➡ equipment such as computers and specialist software;
➡ travel and other costs.

People who are eligible include:

➡ full- or part-time undergraduate students (part-time meaning 50 per cent of full-time course);
➡ postgraduate students;
➡ Open University students;
➡ those on undergraduate or postgraduate level courses;
➡ anyone with a minimum of 60 credit points in any one year;
➡ those having UK status;
➡ students settled in the UK for immigration purposes on first day of first academic year of current programme.

The DSA is not affected by previous study or age and is not dependent on income. It is not means-tested, which means your parents' or partner's income will not be taken into account. The Local Education Authority (LEA for England and Wales), the Student Awards Agency for Scotland (SAAS for residents of Scotland) and the Local Education and Library Board (Northern Ireland) must have evidence of your disability in order for you to qualify for this allowance. Your institution will tell you how to obtain this evidence and may be able to assist you in completing the application form.

In addition to the DSA, institutions have funds available to support your financial needs, and some may have specific grants for students with disabilities. If you are unable to access the finance you need to support your studies via the DSA or other institutional funds, you may be able to approach charities or organisations that will pay for your support or living costs. The institution should be able to provide advice on this matter, or you can contact Skill (see Directory), which has an information booklet on this subject. Contact Disability Direct (see Directory) for information on criteria for qualifying for certain state benefits.

## Our apologies in advance

### Terminology
Using the right words is such a tough balancing act. What was an acceptable term last year may be frowned upon today, and terms that are satisfactory today might be rejected next year. We know we cannot please everyone, however hard we try. If anyone is offended by any of the terms used in this publication then we can only apologise profusely – upsetting even a single person was the last thing we intended. We have endeavoured to use the most commonly accepted terms when referring to particular disabilities and hope these are acceptable in the vast majority of cases. Having said this, we are still open-minded and wish to learn together how to move forward with the rights of disabled people, so constructive criticism is always welcome.

### Preferred terms
Please note D/deaf is used to incorporate all types of deafness and to recognise those people who consider themselves to be part of the Deaf community. This term is used alongside hard of hearing, which is also a preferred term.

### Information
ATTENTION: WE NEED YOUR VIEWS. Has anything been omitted from this edition, which you as a prospective student would want to know? We will endeavour to include such information in future editions and welcome any points you have to make on how this guide could be improved. Please remember, though, there is not the space to include absolutely everything!

Although it is sometimes very hard to get institutions to give the information you, the pre-entry student, need to know, you will find details on almost all the HE institutions in the UK within this guide. If there is a higher education institution that is not currently included in this edition, and you feel it should be, please let us know. Again, if you have any particularly positive experiences of the institution you are at or going to be at, please inform us. We can give them credit in the next edition and use your experiences as a case study. Likewise any negative experiences – we want to know about them too. After all, institutions can learn from their own mistakes, so finding out how they are going wrong can make them see how they need to improve.

## Final thought

Every student should be given an equal opportunity to progress effectively and enjoyably in their studies and accomplish their true potential. I wish you every happiness and fulfilment in your future studies.

# Skill
# Information Service

**Open** Monday to Thursday, 1:30pm to 4:30pm

**❝ Skill helped me find out what support I was entitled to.** Before I started my course they sent me information in Braille about access to funding so I could read it myself. What's great about Skill is that they are there for you all the time - **information and advice are just at the other end of the phone. ❞**

Paulette Dale, Marketing and Business Management Student

**Skill's Information Service gives information and advice to disabled people**, and those working with them, about further education, higher education, employment and training. The Information Service also produces information leaflets covering a wide range of topics.

**Individual disabled students, trainee and jobseekers may order up to five information leaflets free of charge.**

Information leaflets are also available free of charge on Skill's website, **www.skill.org.uk**.

**Skill Information Service**
0800 328 5050 (voice) • 0800 068 2422 (text)
info@skill.org.uk • www.skill.org.uk

Registered charity 801971

# Freshers' Diaries

The following excerpts are kindly reproduced from BBCi's Ouch! website (www.bbc.co.uk/ouch).

For four weeks during September and October 2003, Ouch!, the BBC's new website that reflects life as a disabled person, followed three disabled students who were starting university for the first time. Each week they posted diary entries all about their experiences – living away from home, social life and the high and low points of accessibility: on campus, in the accommodation and for study resources.

The three diarists were: Ruth, 18, studying medicine at the University of Leeds; Ciaran, 19, studying English and Creative Writing at Manchester Metropolitan University; and Sara, 18, studying physiotherapy at the University of Birmingham.

## Student profiles

### Ruth
I'm living in catered halls on campus. I've recently had a stomach operation and am still having to eat soft foods. I contacted the refectory catering staff through Student Services, who have gone out and bought a blender to mush my food up for me!

I have asthma and can't socialise in smokey environments – if I did I'd probably end up in hospital for a week. Smoking, and smokey pubs and clubs, is a big part of student culture so I could end up being a pain in the neck to friends. I've heard there is a Wetherspoons nearby with a non-smoking area though.

### Ciaran
I'm now living in halls on campus. My room is the same size as all the others, but I have an en-suite adapted bathroom. The halls have catering, but I've brought along a wide variety of Pot Noodles just in case!

I've bought myself a hideously expensive Yamaha powerchair in preparation for uni. The motors are in the hubs, it's not at all bulky and you can switch between manual and electric easily.

My course is three years long. My ideal job would be working as a music journalist writing for publications like *NME* or *Q* magazine.

## Sara

I'm living on campus in halls. There are four other girls in my house.

I've arrived at university with no access equipment whatsoever, so studying is going to be a little tricky. This is an NHS-funded course and my equipment isn't coming from the usual Disabled Students Allowances (DSA). Every time I called up or sought info I was given a different story. Information was hard to come by and I didn't get my access assessment until two weeks before I started at uni.

I'm studying physiotherapy — I know it's a cliché blind profession, but really that's not why I'm going for it! It's really what I want to do — had I a little more sight I would have wanted to go into medicine, and this is the next best thing.

## Ruth's diary

Ruth has Nail Patella Syndrome (NPS), a rare genetic disorder that affects the nails and bones, and has asthma.

**Week 1**

### Sunday 21 September

I have been allocated a MASSIVE specially adapted room, which I feel a little guilty about as a non-wheelchair user. I will be having a Personal Assistant coming in to wash my hair, and the bathrooms for the other students would be impossible to get two people in. They are tiny!!!

The doors all the way up to my room were really heavy and hard to open. It was a good job my parents were with me ... So I went to see the Housekeeper and she gave me a swipe key, which makes the doors open automatically. Another problem overcome with no fuss at all.

### Monday 22 September

Well, last night was interesting. As students do, everyone was off to bars, nightclubs and pubs, to drink and dance the night away. But little old asthmatic Ruth, having to avoid cigarettes, felt she was rather restricting her companions' choice of activities. I solved the problem by not staying with the same group of people all night. That meant that without being alone for the evening, my new friends could go and explore. You feel like a real thorn in the side, an absolute pain in the neck. Maybe I will schedule nights in, by myself, so that they can all go do what they want.

Set two alarms (just to be sure I woke up! I'm used to having a parent to shake me awake if I sleep through the alarm!) for 7.30am, to be up, dressed and breakfasted by 8.15am, when I had been told my first Personal Assistant (PA) would be around to wash my hair and do my physiotherapy.

Well, the good news is that my PA did come! She was really nice, and it was also really good because no one else was up to ask why she was here. Just made things easier. When people asked tonight why I had this random lady coming to my room, my standard answer was that she was coming to do 'physiotherapy' for me. Not yet ready to share with the world that I need help washing my hair and making drinks.

### Tuesday 23 September
When your mum does all your caring for you she is around a lot more of the time, so it's great, because you can ask for help as and when you need it. It's weird adapting to someone only being around for such a short period every day for pre-arranged appointments. There is no one to ask to do silly little things, like scratch my head when I get an itch. I guess it will be much easier once I get to know people, because that's the kind of thing a good friend wouldn't think twice about being asked to do. But in a new world, where everyone is a stranger, it's not so easy.

### Wednesday 24 September
It was great to meet some of the staff and other students who I will be spending the next five years with. Also, a lovely member of staff gave me some advice – to use my own initiative and tell all the staff who teach me about my problems myself, just in case the message hasn't passed down via the official systems. With about 260 new medical students, you can understand why the lines of communication may not be 100% reliable.

When I got back to halls, the tenth and final room on our corridor had finally been filled! It was the room of a third-year student who is physically disabled. It is so nice to have him there, and not feel at all awkward with him about having personal assistants coming in, because he has them too!

### Thursday 25 September
I can't wait till the actual learning begins. I have wanted to be a doctor for so long, and finally I am in medical school! It's actually quite surreal!

Found the locker area to discover I have been allocated a top locker. Not a problem now, when all I want to do is toss in my gloves and lab coats, but might be hard to reach up to put textbooks in there.

The staff at my hall are so brilliant – the catering staff have been absolute stars! When there is food I can't eat, they either put it in the blender for me or do me a baked potato with cheese. I was really worried about how I would cope, but it all seems to be working out!

### Friday 26 September
Went to the Societies Fair… I signed up to be part of Rev (a Rock Gospel choir) and the Christian Union. All looks very exciting, and I'm looking forward to starting to sing again. Next week is going to be cool.

### Saturday 27 September
I went into town with a friend … This friend is the only person I have told about all of my health problems. I guess it has come out gradually, bit by bit, as we spend more time together. It's quite nice her knowing really. No more awkward moments of being unable to do things, and having to explain why.

### Sunday 28 September
Wow! A week already! It is going so fast! Seven days and five personal assistants later, everything seems to be going pretty well so far – apart from not having heard from the LEA.

When you are at university there is an extra pot of money called DSA or Disabled Students' Allowances, which is there for disabled students to help pay the extra costs incurred in studying due to your disability. Like everything, it takes time to set up, but I was sure it would all be in place ready for when I started uni. They had my medical evidence right from the earliest opportunity (when I handed in my application form for my student loan), and my mum and I have been chasing people up. But due to people being on long-term health leave, holidays, and also less understandably general disorganisation and broken promises, the LEA still hasn't given the go-ahead for buying the equipment that my assessment suggested. Even though they promised that the letter would be sent on Monday.

Luckily for me the university has been able to lend me an Alphasmart – a notetaking machine – because I can't easily use a pen.

My parents have bought me a Minidisc recorder out of their own money, and I have a borrowed PC in my room. There must be loads of disabled students out there whose families can't support them like mine have. The whole system needs to be changed so that students have guaranteed support from day one.

All I can say is that I'm pleased that Social Services have been responsible for organising the funding for my personal care. They have been helpful, swift, and had all the arrangements in place ready for my arrival. I know that every organisation has strong points and weak points, and the help that you receive will vary greatly depending upon who picks up the phone, but it's disappointing when you feel let down and that promises have been broken.

## Week 2

### *Monday 29 September*
Life at Medical School seems to be about two things – hard work and heavy drinking. I have no issues with drinking. The problem is that in Britain it seems almost impossible to find anywhere to go where I can avoid cigarette smoke, a huge problem being asthmatic. Last year, one cigarette resulted in me being ill for three months, including a month completely off college … I am determined to become a doctor, and I can't risk missing work – even if it means I never get to go on a MedSoc social. I have to think about what's important to me.

### *Wednesday 1 October*
My mum seems to have spent most of today on the phone to the LEA … Mum keeps on being given completely different stories every time she rings. You just feel so lied to.

Aside from frustrations with the LEA, today was the first day I have worn clothing that doesn't hide my splints (or rather splint at the moment, as my right splint isn't back from being fixed in Holland yet).

Everywhere I have been today, people have been asking me what I did to my arm. 'Oh no,' I answer, 'I didn't do anything to it. I have a genetic disorder that affects my joints.' I quite like people asking. It's so much better than them just staring.

### *Thursday 2 October*
The letter from the LEA is through! I can go ahead and order my equipment! Yippee!!!

### Saturday 4 October/Sunday 5 October

The last two days have definitely been the best of the week! After the Christian Union meeting on Saturday night, I went out with seven others, taking food and hot drinks to the homeless in the centre of Leeds. It is so great to be able to do something to help other people and make a difference, no matter how small.

One of the girls I was out doing the distribution with invited me back to a friend's party, with the offer of kipping on a floor overnight! Slightly random, but much, much better than going back to an empty room. So after a slight detour to collect a blanket from my room in halls, we wandered off to the party of a person I had only met twice before! Unfortunately we arrived to find the house full of smokers, but my star of a friend removed all the smokers from the kitchen, opened the back door, and made everyone shut the door behind them whenever they came in or out between the two rooms! She even sat out in the freezing night air with me until the kitchen had been completely de-fumed! She has been one of the most lovely and helpful and supportive friends I have made since arriving here. Although I felt really awkward at first about all the fuss, and just wanted to go back to halls because I didn't want people putting themselves out for me, she made me feel so accepted.

Anyway, had a cool night, met lots of new people, got to know one person in particular much better, and just generally escaped from the monotony of evenings in. One and a half hours' sleep later (we did consider just pulling an all-nighter, as so little sleep seems hardly worth having!) Sunday began with a vengeance!

### Week 3

### Monday 6 October

I think Saturday caught up with me today! If I hadn't needed to queue for so long to use a computer in the library then I would have spent that time in bed!

The good thing about the lecture was that we were given pretty comprehensive notes when we came into the lecture theatre, so I didn't have to type or record anything! Much easier, and also nice to not have people giving me odd looks for having my Alphasmart notetaker on my lap. I'm hoping that all the lecturers will be so organised! It will make my life much easier if they are.

This afternoon we got given all the choices of essay titles for our first SSC, or Student Selected Component … If I wanted to make life really easy for myself, there is actually a genetics choice, in which: 'Students will have the chance to investigate the relationships between genetic mutations and the observed characteristics/problems in a disease of their choice'! I already have copies of all the research and background information for my genetic disorder, Nail Patella Syndrome (NPS), and I've taken part in the last two studies! I even have email addresses and am on first-name terms with two geneticists who are studying NPS!

It would kind of defeat the point of doing the project, though.

### Tuesday 7 October
Had an asthma attack at about nine o'clock this evening, and I wasn't even near any cigarettes! Just at choir, singing my heart out. Very annoying, although having said that it was really cool to listen to everyone else singing!

I met my tutor who specialises in biochemistry today. Told him about having difficulty writing for long periods because of having joint problems and it was not an issue. That's how it should be – no fuss, just the reassurance from him to shout if I need help in any way. He said that he provided handouts for most of the sessions he did, which is great. Makes my life tons easier!

### Wednesday 8 October
I got woken at half past seven this morning by a very loud alarm going off … it's a fire drill so at half past seven I was outside in my dressing gown on the front lawn, with several hundred other groggy and unhappy students! At least I was out of bed in loads of time for my PA coming.

### Thursday 9 October
Thursdays on my timetable are officially the longest days on earth! Seven hours timetabled. Yesterday I had a solid three-hour block of 'Amino acids, phenylketonuria and penicillin', working in small groups with no breaks at all! I really struggle to remain interested in peptide bonds for so long!

### Friday 10 October
My splint turned up back from being repaired in Holland today. It felt weird to have the splint back, but a good kind of weird. I know that the more I wear the splints, the more chance my arm will straighten,

the straighter my arm might get, and the quicker it will all happen! It's cool to be symmetrical again too!

### Saturday 11 October
I think I'm coming down with Fresher's Flu (Fresher's Flu being an all-encompassing term used loosely to describe any infectious ailment that a university student suffers from during the first academic term!).

### Sunday 12 October
A lad called Nick asked to look at my knees today. He's a third-year medical student, and we were talking about my genetic disorder – Nail Patella Syndrome (patella meaning kneecap).

I really like talking to other medical students about my genetic disorder. Increasing awareness is really important, and I'm sure it will also mean that fewer cases go undiagnosed. It's not uncommon for NPS to be misdiagnosed.

**Week 4**

### Monday 13 October
My equipment came today! I am still waiting for the disk drive for my laptop (I am getting an external drive of some type, so that it cuts down on the weight of the laptop I am actually carrying around). I feel all set up now, and it was such a lovely feeling to be able to return the Alphasmart to Disability Services! I'm sure they'll be glad to be seeing less of me!

In the Medical School they run a family scheme, where all the first years get second-year 'parents'. The idea is that they form some sort of pastoral support network, having occasional 'family' meals, giving advice, borrowing lecture notes, etc. It's a really nice idea, although I'm not sure I'd want to be related to every single member of the medical school (no matter how distant and convoluted the relationship)!

I couldn't get involved in a lot of the 'getting to know each other' activities arranged in the earlier weeks because of the cigarette smoke, but my 'parents' (I have two mums, as the medical school is about 70% female so lots of people have single-sex-couple parents!) invited me, my 'brother' and an adopted 'sister' around to their house. They have been so lovely and helpful and understanding about everything.

### Tuesday 14 October
Didn't feel well again today; definitely Fresher's Flu. I'm not the only one on my corridor to have succumbed. Slept through lunch, finally waking up only ten minutes after they had finished serving it!

### Thursday 16 October
Today was the day I had been dreading. A 9.00am lecture, followed by a three-hour practical in the labs with no breaks. In fact, it all went much better than expected! The 9.00am lecture was a clinical one, looking at heart attacks. The practical was in pairs, so my lab partner gave me a hand with anything I didn't find easy to do.

And the big news is that the lab practical actually worked! I think both me and my lab partner were pleasantly shocked to get the results we were meant to get! Lab work has never been my strongest point. I reckon I might be able to do the timetabled practicals without support. I know it's there if I need it, but I'm determined to do this as independently as possible. This is excellent!

Nicest bit of the day: a very special friend said today that if I wanted to, I could live with her next year. She knows the problems I have and the help I might need – for instance, with cooking etc. … in studentdom people start searching for houses in January ready for the following year.

### Friday 17 October
Nice day today! Morning lecture was cancelled, and this afternoon I took the IT test that will hopefully exempt me from Friday afternoon IT lessons! It was one of those tests that you can take at any point during the series of sessions, so I took it at the earliest possible opportunity – it will be so good to have free Friday afternoons! I now have a bottom locker, which will be much easier for me.

I had planned to just have a quiet evening in – maybe some work, see a friend – but the lad across the corridor with CP was going out to the cinema, so I ended up going out with him, one of the PAs and another girl from my halls to see *The Italian Job*. It was really nice to go and do something different; I haven't been to the cinema in ages! With the student reduction, it's not too expensive either (I managed to avoid temptation and resist the bags of Minstrels!).

### Sunday 19 October
To any disabled students out there wanting to go to university, and in particular anyone who wants to study medicine – go for it! Find out

what help and support is available, research which universities you apply to carefully, and don't always listen when people tell you no. Find the solutions before you tell people the problems – don't give them any chance to discriminate unnecessarily. Finally, find the people out there who are for you, not against you. They are there, just maybe not that easy to find! Finally, if anyone wants to get in contact with me and ask any questions, that's cool – I'd love to hear from you!

I guess it's time for me to go back to the real world. Four years and twenty-six weeks to go, and I could be treating you when you come into hospital! That's if they let me practise … but I'll cross that bridge when I come to it. I can't wait to get out there and work with people, for people. Better go do some work, I guess!

## Ciaran's diary

Ciaran has cerebral palsy.

### Week 1

#### *Sunday 28 September*
A week can seem really long, sometimes. Especially if, in that particular week, existence as you have known it for the past 19 years changes as completely as is humanly possible

First off, let me say that pretty much everything you hear about the first week of university is a lie. It is billed as a week-long orgy of sex, drugs and booze – but if my student flat is any shining example of typicality, it's more like a week sitting in your room feeling homesick and wondering if you've done the right thing. It's about frequently asking yourself how the hell you could ever have thought that trading in all the comforts of home for a room the size of a shoebox, a stack of watery Pot Noodles and a house full of people who seem to deliberately avoid each other as much as possible was a good idea.

I've been out a fair bit this week, drunk more than my fair share of recreational beverages and heard more names than I'll ever remember.

As far as access in general goes, from what I've seen so far there are definitely some major improvements to be had. To start with, if I remember rightly my room is described by the university as 'adapted accommodation'. If this is true, then in this case adapted clearly does not mean accessible. In the end it comes down to the fact that there simply isn't enough space to function comfortably – I have to keep my en-suite bathroom door open just to turn my chair around in the bedroom. Also many of the doorways aren't that wide.

Going out is a 50/50 experience in that there's drop curbs almost everywhere. It's the same with bars and pubs – of the main drinking holes I've visited this week, one had steps up and another had no steps but a disabled loo with a door so narrow I had to literally 'go' in the doorway.

### Monday 29 September
Had first seminar today. It was all right. My chair can't really fit under the tables though, which is very annoying.

The uni provides Learning Support assistants to help during lectures and seminars, but no help turned up for this seminar.

Am having a meeting tomorrow with my stepdad and my two PAs to discuss how that whole situation is going. It's a very odd thing to have to do, to start organising your own care after being used to having it done for you for so long.

### Tuesday 30 September
Had my second seminar today (as opposed to lecture). Seminars are the smaller classes where you sit and discuss stuff and make various attempts at sounding intelligent. It's nice, but this particular seminar is a straight three hours. Something I'm realising about uni is that you really have to love what you study, because pretty much all your energy is concentrated on that one subject for the entire time you're here, and there's really no time or way to do anything else academically. Once you're in, you're in.

### Wednesday 1 October
Today was my day off so I went and spent a load of cash on all the books I need for this course.

I have noticed that quite a few people I've met have obviously had NO real-life experience of anyone with a disability, and are either extremely patronising or just try and pretend you aren't there. Both are extremely annoying. I think I'm gonna have to work hard whilst I'm here to educate some people and get some opinions changed. I've certainly got my work cut out for me.

### Thursday 2 October
Yesterday I met up with a guy from BBC Manchester who took some photos of me in my natural surroundings (just outside the union bar). The Beeb guy also asked me to write a review of the Radiohead gig I'm off to next month, which is really cool and something I can't wait for. Radiohead rule.

Today was my busiest day, but in the few hours I had off I took a trip to the supermarket and did a fairly big shop. I don't mind admitting that it's the first time I've really done that sort of thing on my own (well, I say 'on my own', but Jo was with me) and it was quite an experience. There's a fair amount of unreachable shelves out there in the big world of corporate supermarkets

### Friday 3 October
I went out to a 'School Disco' night at the union bar, where the head DJ was none other than Mr Pat Sharp. There was a gang of 12 of us – which included me, Matt and (I presume) some of the people who were supposedly too tired to come out with us on Tuesday. After a few drinks one of our group decides we should do our best to get to the front in time for the arrival of Mr S. After a few minutes crowd-negotiating this is, surprisingly, achieved Then all of a sudden, two bouncers on the other side of the stage spot my chair, amble over and simply lift me on stage. Then, when Pat arrives, I rush over to greet him and tell him what a legend he is.

However, the greatest moment of all comes later in the evening when he hands me the mike and asks me what I think of his mullet wig. I tell him I think it looks beautiful and he turns to the entire crowd and says, 'Everybody, Ciaran says it's beautiful!' Needless to say I got a lump in my throat and, as far as I can remember, I spent the rest of last night drinking vodka and apple juice in halls until about 4.00am. I must now go and drink some fluids.

### Saturday 4 October
Today I went to see about joining the rowing club. It was all the way across town at Trafford Rowing Club. I think I'll give it a go as it would be a good way to meet some people

## Week 2

### Monday 6 October
Well, it's been an OK week really. I'm also starting to get to know people on my course a little better now – and in my flat – which is

good. In fact, the girl in the room opposite me has great musical taste that is similar to mine. Which is nice.

I've had no support in any of my lectures or seminars yet. This isn't too bad right now as it's only the beginning, but as things pick up speed I will need notes taking. Access Summit in Manchester rung me up nearly a week and a half ago and told me they'd be in touch to sort something out. They lied.

Second, my room. They've put one grab bar in the bedroom that I needed; now they need to lower the bed so I can actually use the bar effectively, and they need to put another bar in so I can get up from the loo easier. Also, it would be much easier if the bathroom door was a sliding door. I'll get on to all of this.

Third, my equipment hasn't arrived yet. I don't know what's going on, but apparently my LEA hasn't received confirmation that I've started uni yet. God knows why.

### Wednesday 8 October
I'm more than a little bit drunk now and it's actually about one o'clock on Thursday morning, not Wednesday at all. Up until about 5.30pm I was feeling pretty crap as I had a cough/cold/flu thing and it was my day off, so I was basically sitting around feeling ill. Then a fella from the Beeb rings up and says, 'I know it's short notice, but do you fancy reviewing the Thrills at the Academy tonight? There's two tickets on the door reserved and waiting.' Well, how could one refuse? It would just be rude, I thought to myself, not to capitalise on such an opportunity. So I rang my colleague and associate Peter, who was at this point partial to the Thrills, and he agreed to come along.

If you don't mind I'm going to leave this story here for now and continue it tomorrow evening – I know it's cheating slightly, but as I said before I really am rather smashed right now and I (technically) need to be in a lecture in about eight hours. It might be a good idea to at least attempt to get some sleep. Maybe.

### Thursday 9 October
Well, unsurprisingly I missed my nine o'clock lecture this morning. Woke up at 10.00am.

When I first started here I was promised access support for my seminars and lectures for writing notes, etc.; but I'm still getting no help whatsoever! It's getting stupid. I will ring the access provider company in Manchester at some point within the next week and scream at them. I have also decided to buy a dictaphone for lectures.

### Friday 10 October
Today was my other day off, so I did a bit of reading and attempted to start an essay that needs to be in for next Thursday. But it didn't work – I'll do it later. Went out earlier this evening at about nine with a few people from my halls. Started out at a pub called The Pub, which was great except for the huge step at the entrance. Then went on to the Springbok where I was (conveniently) not charged the staggeringly ridiculous entrance fee of a fiver. I thought it was rubbish in there anyway, full of nutters and idiots dancing to abysmal tunes.

One fella who was walking past actually had the ignorance to ruffle and pat my head. That hasn't happened to me since I was about nine years old, and if I hadn't been busy getting hammered I perhaps would have shot him.

After Springbok we went on to a slightly cooler but equally expensive place called M2. That was quite a good bar, although I did feel slightly forgotten when everyone I was with decided to sit (or rather stand) around a high round table. It's hard to strike up conversations with people when you're sat down and they're stood up – and it's a bit more difficult when there's a chunk of table in your face. Eventually though, some seats freed up and everyone moved.

### Week 3

### Monday 13 October
By the way, my bed has been lowered and they've put another grab bar in the bathroom. Now I just need to get the door converted into a sliding one and my room will be pretty much sorted. I found out what's going on with my LEA equipment as well – my computer needs more RAM in it before they can install the stuff. So I'll sort that out for definite this week.

Oh yeah, I never finished the story about what happened at the Thrills gig, did I? We were personally invited backstage to meet the band, and I can honestly say that the Thrills are all genuinely nice guys, especially Daniel and Padraic who bought me beer.

### Tuesday 14 October
Didn't go to my three-hour seminar today – I felt ill, plus I'm working on an essay that needs doing by Thursday. They won't miss me, I'm sure.

One thing I did do was go and buy a dictaphone to help me in lectures – recording the entire thing will mean I have to go back and pick out the relevant notes, effectively twice the work, but I suppose I'll remember more stuff that way

### Wednesday 15 October

Still working on the essay. I have to admit I spent quite a lot of time yesterday playing with my new Dictaphone. As a good way of breaking up essay-writing and efficiently wasting loads of time, you can't beat saying stupid catchphrases from *Bo Selecta* into a Dictaphone and then replaying them at either fast or slow speeds. I highly recommend it.

### Friday 17 October

(Travis) gig was good, the view was quite good and the venue was really good. Getting back was even reasonably straightforward. Getting there was, however, a complete nightmare. The taxi took an hour to arrive, and when it finally turned up the guy said, 'Shall I get the ramps out?' Stupid question as I am, quite unmistakably, in a wheelchair.

### Week 4

### Sunday 19 October

Well, last night was a success in so far as I got myself into bed without assistance for the first time ever whilst at uni. It might seem like a pretty small thing to write about, but really it's a pretty big development (for all the obvious and not so obvious reasons).

Today, I met up with Matt and a guy that he knows who is in his second year doing medicine. He wants to use me for some project or other he's doing, which involves interviewing me and asking me questions about the ol' Cerebral Palsy and how it affects my daily life. I've agreed to it as it seems like it would fit in quite well with this whole diary thing.

### Monday 20 October

So then, I've come to the end of my first month at university – although it seems like a lot longer – and this is my final diary entry for Ouch! It's been a wild ride, without a doubt the longest and busiest four weeks of my life thus far.

Anyway, back to business. How would I sum up uni life so far? The answer is: I can't. There is no epitaph or concise, witty and memorable one-liner that I can drum up to effectively describe or summarise the past month. What I will say is this: you just have to let it happen and dive in at the deep end, because if you spend too much time worrying about the situation you're in – rather than simply accepting it – you'll just go under. I've realised that over the past few weeks.

Everything from getting PAs recruited, through sorting out my room, to meeting the Thrills and Pat Sharp, as well as just getting to know new people and being away from home – it's all been a huge bloody great learning curve. Bearing in mind what has happened in these first few weeks and all the stuff I've got up to, I think that the next three years are going to be very interesting indeed.

### Sara's diary

Sara has albinism and is visually impaired.

### Week 1

*Monday 22 September*
The day before the long-awaited departure into student life, I am feeling a mixture of excitement and anxiety and I can't decide where one ends and the other begins. Excitement as I am about to embark upon what most people say are the best three years of their lives, anxious because I just can't get that feeling of being 'different' out of my head.

*Tuesday 23 September*
I've finally arrived. The halls are great – not too far from campus – and my room has a large desk for all my fabulous computer equipment, when it arrives.

*Wednesday 24 September*
My housemates are all a rather nice bunch of girlies, and I think we are all going to get on rather well.

I also managed to bring up the whole albino thing. It took me ages to finally pluck up the courage and say 'I have albinism, I am visually impaired.' I was desperate not to be judged and defined solely by my disability, yet I didn't want it to go unsaid and for people to give me odd looks as I shove my face in a book or blatantly walk past them in the street. And the amazing thing is that they really don't care; they just said, 'OK, is there anything we can do to help?' and that was it!

All those hours of worry over people running miles in the other direction or freaking out so much they just ignore me – for nothing! Perhaps I should learn to have a little more faith in people.

### Thursday 25 September
Went out last night with the medics, nurses and physios. Had an amazing evening and met loads of people … I think people were really thrown by the concept of why I am OK to wander around in the daytime without too many problems, but am continuously stumbling over steps and have a complete inability to find toilets in a nightclub (flashing lights are not my friends).

I also took time out from my busy schedule of alcohol and clubs to visit the library and check out the facilities available for those of us with 'serious sight loss'. (What is that expression about? I haven't lost any sight – I was born like this!) It turns out that the university's room that usually contains all the adaptive technology has been knocked down and is currently being replaced by individual study booths, which seems like a really good idea. However, this isn't much good to me at the moment, especially as my equipment from Disabled Students' Allowance hasn't come through yet.

### Friday 26 September
Finally got to see the Physiotherapy block today. They have totally re-done the interior for this September so it all looks very impressive – aside from the huge set of unmarked concrete steps outside. I will undoubtedly get closer to these little beauties at some point, and when I say closer I mean arse-step-face-step-arse-step-face-step sort of close.

I also came across the university's love of noticeboards in tiny print.

Despite this it seems that the rest of the facilities are great, and apparently they are putting a large screen monitor and CCTV into the computer cluster, which is nice.

### Saturday 27 September
Damn! My plan to keep my dirty little secret of having been to blind school for the past two years has failed. It appears that many of the students here in Brum come from Hereford, so silly old me jumps in with, 'Oh, I've been at college there for the last two years!' However, it seems that once again my feelings might not be shared by the 'wider community'. It appears that non-disabled people really aren't aware of any of the stigmas surrounding 'special' education that exist amongst us disabled types.

### Sunday 28 September
I have been back in the real world for a week now – and you know what? I love it! I really feel that I am slotting in with everyone else without any problems. As far as the eyesight issues go I'm not bothered, and neither is anyone else.

## Week 2

### Monday 29 September
I had my first lecture today. I was quite impressed one of the lecturers was on the ball enough to give me copies of the sheets she was using on the overhead projector.

I also had the opportunity to meet with my personal tutor. During the meeting we discussed passing information about my sight on to lecturers and getting my own pigeonhole on the end so it's easy to find.

### Tuesday 30 September
Pigeonhole is present and correct, with a nice large-print name label next to it. However, it doesn't appear that any discussions have been had with the lecturers.

Due to the lack of hard copies coming my way, I decided to use that wonderful little creation that any respectable partially sighted person owns – the monocular. Only trouble was that as I was about to remove it from my bag, I realised that I was in a room full of people who had probably never seen one before. In total embarrassment at my close call with looking hideous, I quickly placed the bag back down at my feet with the monocular remaining part of its contents.

I wandered to the laundrette, nice and close to my halls of residence and with plenty of machines (although quite pricey at £1.70 a wash). For some reason the laundry peeps felt the need to position the wonderfully small directions on how to use their fabulous machines on the wall above them in minuscule print. So I did the only reasonable thing I could do – that's right, I got on top of the machine and shoved my face right up against the bloody notice! Unfortunately, I didn't realise that I wasn't alone; as I clambered down from the machine I turned to find a rather amused lad sniggering in the corner – DAMN THIS WORLD.

### Wednesday 1 October
OK, so the monocular situation is getting stupid. Today, I decided to take the big step of placing it on the desk. Admittedly it was still in its

little pouch and so totally unidentifiable, but I feel it is important to introduce people to these things slowly.

Alright, so I might be being pathetic about the telescope, but I was pretty brave today when I took the big step of telling my teaching group for practical sessions that I am partially sighted. (Yes, I know it's dull, but it gets the point across.) I felt that in these particular lectures my eyesight might cause me some hassle, and it would be easier for everyone if 'it' was out in the open right from the start. I deserve a gold star.

### Thursday 2 October
I did it!! I used the monocular and – as with everything else that I have worried about – it was fine. I'm not sure anyone else even noticed it (or perhaps that's just wishful thinking!).

I also came to the conclusion today that I have no choice but to employ a notetaker, as I am totally unable to keep up with the pace – speed handwriting isn't on my list of can do's. I was also extremely aware that there still seems to be no sign of large-print handouts or copies of projector slides … and that I really need some sleep! Unfortunately all the parties are finally catching up with me, to the extent that my eyesight is suffering as my nystagmus has gone crazy!!

### Friday 3 October
Got the chance to have my first lie-in (hallelujah!) so I am feeling a little more human. Decided to go into the city centre to do a spot of shopping. BIG MISTAKE – the place was heaving. I spent my whole time playing the left/right 'dancing game' and being unable to find anything I wanted. However, one plus is that Brum city centre is fairly accessible and easy to navigate, so I didn't get too lost.

### Saturday 4 October
Went to a huge party at the Guild (the Student Union) and lost all my housemates (no, they didn't do it on purpose). Had a bit of a panic and then remembered the wonderful invention of mobile phones and the superb text facility they possess. Located my friends within minutes, and all was well. It's actually given me a little more confidence about going out in the future, as I've realised they're starting to understand that it's difficult for me to find them in busy places.

### Sunday 5 October
I was in an article in the *Sunday Telegraph* magazine today. I wasn't overly impressed with what was said and the way in which people

with albinism were portrayed, but decided to show my housemates anyway. I think the article may have helped them understand albinism a little better and perhaps given them the confidence to ask me questions about it. I was also touched when one of them read the article and said, 'But they haven't mentioned anything positive. What about your A-level results or going to a good uni or about the fact that you're fitting in just like everyone else and everybody loves you?' I can honestly say that made my day!

## Week 3

### *Monday 6 October*
Had another meeting with my personal tutor, which brought with it the good news that the lecturers haven't just been ignoring information about my sight – in fact, they haven't received it yet.

Another heartwarming moment with new friends, as they have now worked out the 'big arm wave' so that I am able to find them in crowded areas, e.g. bars and clubs. It's nice to know that people are ready to help when my usual attempts at total independence fail.

### *Tuesday 7 October*
Had a lecture in 'Basic Life Support' today, and clearly the message about the 'visually impaired student' hasn't reached all corners of the university just yet.

My first 'real' lectures have also highlighted the fact that I am very uncertain about just how much my lecturers are expected to do, and how much is my own responsibility in terms of employing personal notetakers and readers.

### *Wednesday 8 October*
Had my first practical lecture today. It went really well, especially as the lecturer cleverly used me as the model to demonstrate movements to the rest of the class. This would indicate that the message has been received about my seeing issues, which is rather good.

I was further encouraged when I went to check my lovely little pigeonhole (actually it's quite big – just as well under the circumstances) and found lots of nice large-print copies of the overhead projector sheets from the last week of lectures, plus a few handouts ready for the week ahead.

### Thursday 9 October

Have begun to get extremely frustrated at the lack of facilities available to me. Due to the non-existence of computer software and CCTV equipment in the libraries, I was unable to do the research required for one of my lectures. It was a little embarrassing, to say the least. I felt like I was making excuses, even though I know I genuinely couldn't do what was being asked of me due to lack of accessible resources. It was a group learning session, so when I told them of my woeful problems the lovely lecturer said (in his most patronising voice), 'We'll forgive Sara today, seeing as she has extra problems!' I DON'T LIKE BEING PATRONISED!!

I'm also aware of the fact that I am going to have to be very exact when explaining to lecturers about what my 'problem' is. Today I tried to tell one of them that when talking to me he should use my name, otherwise I won't know if he is speaking to me. He interpreted this as, 'I also have a hearing impairment' (yeah, I'm not sure how he got that either).

### Friday 10 October

FANTASTIC NEWS!! The cheque for my DSA has come through, so I can go out and buy all my computer equipment! YAY!!

### Sunday 12 October

I finally got my computer equipment. Admittedly it isn't all here yet (I have still to receive the CCTV and Zoomtext), but thanks to several functions on Windows XP and a large monitor I now have a computer that I am able to access. This is quite a relief.

All in all, my third week of university life has been rather good. Most importantly the social side just keeps getting better and better, and the academic side is also pretty cool – even if the nine o'clock lectures are starting to interfere with my late nights!

### Week 4

### Monday 13 October

Finally given in to the harsh lighting conditions in the practical rooms today and decided to wear my new tinted contact lenses. They really do make all the difference in terms of comfort. Unfortunately, they also take away some of the contrast, thus making reading quite difficult. It also confuses lots of people too – one minute I have blue eyes, and the next minute they're dark brown.

### Wednesday 15 October

Had my first meeting with the university disability coordinator. I know it's quite far into term, but it is partly my own fault as I didn't get my act together to arrange a meeting earlier. The whole thing was rather unproductive – nobody's fault, just the current circumstances. We were trying to arrange note-takers and readers, but because my lectures vary so much and my timetable changes every week it's very hard to put anything in place. The only solution we came up with was for somebody on my course to be my note-taker. Now all I have to do is find someone – I don't want to put pressure on any of my new friends to do it, and I feel a bit weird about asking people.

The one good thing that did come out of the meeting was that I will be able to employ somebody for library assistance. They'll be able to come to the library with me to help find books and do research, which will be really helpful because the libraries here are MASSIVE!!

### Thursday 16 October

The reality of people's memories is finally setting in, and it seems that lecturers especially have selective memory where my visual impairment is concerned. It's strange how they can only apply my 'issues' to certain circumstances and not others. For example, one lecturer understands enough to ask the rest of the class to produce handouts in large print for me, and he can remember to say my name when he is speaking to me, yet he can't remember to produce his own handouts in large print … hmm.

However, all my other lecturers are being fab. I am getting lecture notes in advance in a large font – perhaps not large enough but hey, magnifiers aren't that bad. I am also receiving my own copy of the information from the overhead projectors at the start of each lecture, and they are even learning to describe what they are doing so I can follow it better. I am really impressed by the vast majority of lecturers, and things are far better than I could have ever expected!!

### Saturday 18 October/Sunday 19 October

This weekend has also given me a chance to reflect on my first month at university, and – you know what? – it was a good reflection. Before I arrived here I was so nervous. I had just spent two years in 'special' education and didn't know what the transition back to mainstream would be like, but it couldn't have gone more smoothly.

Socially, I am having a ball and I have made tons of new friends! Academically it isn't bad either – I am definitely meant for mainstream education, not that I regret going to RNC (Royal National College for the Blind) in the slightest.

To be honest, I couldn't be happier. In fact, it's official – I LOVE UNIVERSITY!!

# The Disability Discrimination Act Part 4

Skill: National Bureau for Students with Disabilities, an independent charity, has been working closely with universities and colleges to implement the new Part 4: Education of the Disability Discrimination Act (DDA) and to ensure that disabled students' needs are met in post-16 education. The new law is now in force, except for the requirement to make physical adjustments, which will come into effect on 1 September 2005. However, universities and colleges should already be preparing for this change as well.

The following article by Skill outlines your rights under the new law. Skill hopes that understanding your legal right to equal opportunities will help you to feel confident about going into higher education and accessing any support that you need.

### Will I be protected by the new law?
To be covered by the new Part 4 of the DDA, you will need to fit into the DDA definition of a disabled person and of a student, potential student or applicant.

### 1. How is disability defined by the DDA?
The DDA defines a disabled person as someone who has a physical or mental impairment, which has a substantial and long-term adverse effect on his or her ability to carry out normal day-to-day activities. This is intended to be a fairly wide definition of disability.

Physical or mental impairment includes sensory impairments and also hidden impairments (for example, clinically well-recognised mental health difficulties, learning difficulties, dyslexia and conditions such as diabetes or epilepsy). People who have severe disfigurements are also covered.

A substantial adverse effect is something which is more than a minor or trivial effect and goes beyond the normal differences between people.

A long-term effect of an impairment is one:

➡ that has lasted at least 12 months; or
➡ where the total period for which it lasts is likely to be at least 12 months; or

➡ that is likely to last for the rest of the life of the person affected.

The test of whether an impairment affects normal day-to-day activities is whether it affects one of the broad categories of capacity listed in Schedule 1 of the Act. They are:

➡ mobility;
➡ manual dexterity;
➡ physical coordination;
➡ continence;
➡ ability to lift, carry or otherwise move everyday objects;
➡ speech, hearing or eyesight;
➡ memory or ability to concentrate, learn or understand; or
➡ perception of the risk of physical danger.

### 2. How is 'student, potential student and applicant' defined by the DDA?

The post-16 sections of the DDA protect 'students, potential students and applicants'.

The term 'student' includes anyone enrolled on or attending a course of study, whether:

➡ full- or part-time;
➡ a home or overseas student;
➡ studying in Britain or elsewhere (as part of a registered course at a British higher education institution);
➡ on a taught course or a research degree;
➡ publicly or privately funded;
➡ studying for a qualification or undertaking just part of a course;
➡ enrolled on a one-day course or evening classes.

'Potential students and applicants' includes:

➡ people enquiring about courses;
➡ people attending open days or contacted during recruitment drives;
➡ applicants.

### What activities does the law cover?

The new law gave responsibilities to defined 'responsible bodies' including all further and higher education institutions. The law covers all education and training provided by these bodies, admissions and enrolments, exclusions, and any services provided wholly or mainly for students. This includes not only education, but also, for example:

→ teaching and research facilities;
→ student letting and accommodation services;
→ careers advice;
→ health, welfare and faith services;
→ extracurricular courses for students and employment agency services;
→ leisure and social facilities primarily for students (bars, restaurants, common rooms, clubs and associations and sports facilities);
→ admissions, examination and assessment arrangements;
→ open days and induction events;
→ references for students;
→ graduation services and alumni membership;
→ complaints and appeals.

When an institution arranges for a third party to provide education, training or services on its behalf, the institution is still responsible for ensuring that the provision made by the third party complies with the DDA.

## What counts as discrimination under the DDA Part 4?
According to the Act, discrimination can occur in two ways.

### 1. Less favourable treatment
Firstly, it is unlawful for providers or institutions to treat a disabled person 'less favourably' than they treat, or would treat, non-disabled people for a reason that relates to the person's disability.

An example of less favourable treatment would be: a university makes an offer of a place to a student who is a wheelchair user on the condition that she finds her own living accommodation locally. No other students have this condition placed upon them. This is likely to be unlawful as the student is being treated less favourably than other students because of her disability.

### 2. Failure to make reasonable adjustments
Part of not discriminating is making 'reasonable adjustments'. If a disabled person is at a 'substantial disadvantage', the provider or institution is required to take reasonable steps to prevent that disadvantage. This might include:

→ changes to policies and practices;
→ changes to course requirements or work placements;

➡ changes to physical features of a building;
➡ the provision of interpreters or other support workers;
➡ the delivery of courses in alternative ways;
➡ the provision of materials in other formats.

For example, providing a deaf student with a sign language interpreter so that they can participate in a seminar or producing lecture handouts in large print for a visually impaired student could be reasonable adjustments that a university or college needs to make.

### Should I tell my institution about my disability?

Institutions have a responsibility to do what they can to find out whether individuals have disability-related needs, for example by asking a relevant question on registration forms. It is up to you whether or not you choose to tell the institution about your disability. However, you should think carefully about your decision and its implications. If you have chosen not to disclose your disability or need and your institution has made reasonable attempts to find out whether you have a disability, the institution will not be liable for any failure to make specific individual adjustments.

However, institutions should continually be anticipating the requirements of disabled students and the adjustments they could be making for them. This should mean that the needs of many disabled people will be met automatically. But in other cases, where adjustments need to be made for individuals in response to particular needs, the institution will need to know about the individual's disability in order to make these adjustments. For example, the university should already have an accessible intranet in anticipation of a visually impaired student needing to use it, but individual lecturers may need to be informed when they have a visually impaired student on their course to ensure that they prepare handouts in an alternative format as required.

Institutions do also have a duty to make sure that you are given the opportunity to decide whether you want your disclosure to be kept confidential. So if you are concerned about disclosing your disability because you don't want everyone to know about it, then you can tell the institution that the information you have given them must be kept confidential. This means that the institution will only pass on information to those who need to know, for example, tutors and course lecturers, to ensure that you get the support you need.

## What should I do if I feel I have been discriminated against?

You should first take advice from the Disability Rights Commission (DRC) helpline (contact details below) about your situation. You should first raise your complaint directly with the institution. If you aren't finding the institution complaints process satisfactory, then you should contact the Disability Rights Commission for further advice (contact details below). The DRC is empowered by the law to set up an independent conciliation service for disputes. The conciliation service is able to deal with most complaints in a speedy and effective way. If conciliation cannot resolve a dispute, you may be able to take the dispute to court. You need to take your complaint to court within six months of the date when the alleged discrimination took place (this time period is extended to eight months if the case has first gone to conciliation). Courts will have the power not only to determine the rights of the case, but also to award compensation and impose injunctions or interdicts to prevent the institution from repeating any discriminatory act in the future or to require positive action.

---

### Where can I get further information?

Skill's Information Service can answer enquiries on the DDA and also generally on post-16 opportunities for disabled people in education and employment. Open Monday to Thursday 1.30pm–4.30pm. Tel: 0800 328 5050 (voice), 0800 068 2422 (text), email: info@skill.org.uk, website: www.skill.org.uk.

Skill has also produced a five-step test to help students assess whether disability discrimination has occurred in relation to the provision of further and higher education. The test is available in the form of an information booklet from the Skill Information Service.

The Disability Rights Commission helpline gives advice on your rights under the DDA. Tel: 08457 622 633 (voice), 08457 622 644 (text), email: enquiry@drc-gb.org, website: www.drc-gb.org.

---

# About this Guide

This guide contains information on the provision of services by universities, colleges, schools, institutes and academies within the UK. Each entry gives information on specific details relating to students with disabilities regarding services, facilities and access. The entries are listed in alphabetical order.

### The address
The address given is the general address of the institution and may not be the actual address of the disability coordinator or person responsible for students with disabilities. Check with the institution.

### Contact details
General enquiries contact details are the main switchboard, admissions or course enquiries, not the general enquiries of the disability services department. Information on the disability contact or department is also given. When dialling from outside the UK add 44 at the beginning of the number.

### Courses offered
Fields of study refers to the genres of courses that the institution offers. For smaller institutions a more detailed list of courses may be listed. Information is also given as to whether courses can be studied either part time or by distance learning. Where 'yes' is given for either of these categories it does not necessarily imply that all courses are part-time or can be studied via distance learning. Check with the individual institution to find out further details.

### Background details
General information is given about the institution, on history, background and specialist achievements. Some brief information about the local area may also be given.

### Student numbers
The total number of students at the institution refers to all higher education students studying either full time or part time or via distance learning. In addition the number of disabled students is given. This figure indicates the number of students who have disclosed their disability/ies. As not all students will choose to disclose this information the figure given is probably below the real number of students with disabilities at the institution.

## Disability
Within this guide the term disability has been used to embrace a wide range of individual needs, including physical disabilities, people who are D/deaf or hard of hearing, those with visual impairments, specific learning difficulties (such as dyslexia), medical conditions or hidden disabilities (such as asthma, diabetes or epilepsy), or mental health issues. Any student with individual needs should be able to access support from the person or team of people who are responsible for providing this service at the institution. For some students an individual need or disability may become apparent only during their course of study.

## Specific learning difficulties
In many institutions students with specific learning difficulties, such as those with dyslexia, seem to constitute the main body of students accounted for under the students with disabilities population/community.

## Personnel and support
'Learning support staff and services' lists the staff directly responsible for meeting the individual needs of students with disabilities, with a brief record of the support offered.

## Alternative examination assessment and study arrangements
Alternative examination arrangements refer to the individual needs of the disabled student when completing an exam or an assessment. These alternative arrangements can include: alternative exam paper format such as Braille or large text, additional time, specialist furniture, computer use (with specialist software and hardware), permission to move during exams, to be in a separate room, amanuensis (for dictated answers), questions read, sign language interpreter support, shorter exam and additional coursework, use of specialist equipment, alternatives to coursework, media presentation alternatives (including appropriate colours).

## Auxiliary aids and services
Anything that assists your studies, from the provision of notetakers or computer software to personal assistants and Posturite chairs, is auxiliary aids and services. The institution is obliged to ensure these be made available where reasonable.

## Where do I live?
Home sweet home: to ensure you get suitable accommodation it is necessary for you to make your needs known at the earliest possible time.

## Getting about

'Out and about' and 'Taking it easy' sections give you an idea of what is available and what is accessible within the institution and the local area. The term 'accessible' is used to mean, in brief, accessible by a person who is a wheelchair user. However, wheelchair user access generally means that access has also been improved for others who might not be wheelchair users, for example a person with a visual impairment will also need to accommodate a guide dog in a toilet cubicle. A toilet that is accessible to a wheelchair user will meet these space requirements. Town facilities refer to, for example, shops, libraries, cinemas, theatres, restaurants and bars.

In many cases, where designated places for disabled drivers are available, you will need to apply for a permit.

## More details

'And another thing ...' Other relevant information, not covered by any of the previous sections, is included here, for example details on access, improvement plans or specialist facilities.

## QAA

The QAA (Quality Assurance Agency) has been reporting on provision for disabled people since September 2000. It only reports back 'by exception', in other words when the provision is particularly good or particularly poor. All QAA reports of institutions that have so far been reported on are quoted in their respective entries.

## The Disability Statement/Brochure

Disability statements are usually available in a range of alternative formats such as on the Web, computer disk, tape, large print and Braille.

## External sources of support

The local disability public service provider is a local organisation, charity or council, which can offer you advice, information or support as a disabled person.

## Access and Facilities

Information is given in table form regarding access to lecture theatres, teaching areas, computer rooms, libraries, canteens, Student Union, bar, gym, swimming pool, other sporting facilities, medical, counselling and welfare services. When an area is stated as having access, this means the area is accessible to a person who is a wheelchair user – whether this is achieved because all areas are accessible or through timetabling the student into accessible venues.

Other information contained in this table includes the availability of lifts and whether there are accessible toilet facilities (see 'Getting about', above). Information is also given on whether these areas have been fitted with induction loop systems.

A list of facilities and support workers is given. Please note that institutions do not always have all of these enablers, but employ them as required, or assist the student in obtaining this support, which is funded by the student's DSA.

# Abbreviations

| | |
|---|---|
| Accessible | accessible by a person who is a wheelchair user |
| APEL | accreditation of prior experience and learning |
| BSL | British Sign Language |
| CACDP | Council for the Advancement of Communication with Deaf People |
| C&IT | communication and information technology |
| CCTV | closed-circuit television |
| CSV | Community Service Volunteers |
| DDA | Disability Discrimination Act |
| D/deaf | incorporates all types of deafness and recognises those who consider themselves part of the Deaf community |
| DRC | Disability Rights Commission |
| DSAs | Disabled Students' Allowances |
| DSS | Department of Social Services |
| EASIER | Education Access Support in the Eastern Region |
| FE | further education |
| HE | higher education |
| HEFCE | Higher Education Funding Council for England |
| HMSA | Hypermobility Syndrome Association |
| HNC | Higher National Certificate |
| HND | Higher National Diploma |
| IT | information technology |
| LEA | Local Education Authority |
| LSS | Learning Support Services |
| NFAC | National Federation of Access Centres |
| NUS | National Union of Students |
| NVQ | National Vocational Qualification |
| OU | Open University |
| PA | personal assistant |
| PEALS | Policy Ethics and Life Sciences |
| PG | postgraduate |
| QAA | Quality Assurance Agency |
| RADAR | Royal Association for Disability and Rehabilitation |
| RNIB | Royal National Institute for the Blind |
| RNID | Royal National Institute for the Deaf |
| SA | Student Association |
| SAAS | Student Awards Agency for Scotland |
| SASSA | Study Aids and Study Strategies Assessments |
| SENDA | Special Educational Needs and Disability Act |
| SHEC | Southern Higher Education Consortium |
| SHEFC | Scottish Higher Education Funding Council |
| SU | Student Union |
| SUCCEEDS | Scottish Universities Consortium for Career Planning and Employment Experience for Disabled Students |
| Text | Textphone or minicom |
| UG | undergraduate |
| ULU | University of London Union |
| VDU | visual display unit |

# Case Studies

**Rebecca Atkinson**
**Birkbeck College, University of London**
**BA Politics and Society**

Rebecca Atkinson, who is hard of hearing and partially sighted, is currently in her third year at Birkbeck College.

## What career do you wish to pursue?

'I am currently employed by the BBC as a television producer. I have worked for the BBC for seven years and at present have no plans to change my career. I undertook my part-time degree at Birkbeck out of personal interest rather than in pursuit of a new career. Because all lectures are held in the evening at Birkbeck, I have been able to maintain my career at the same time as acquiring a degree.'

## How have your individual needs been met at Birkbeck College?

'The disability office at Birkbeck helped me to apply for funding from my local education authority for a notetaker, taxis to college and specialist equipment. I was fortunate that my local education authority responded quickly, and have provided me with the financial support that I need to fulfil my studies. My notetaker is paid through the Birkbeck payroll which means I am able to spend more time studying and less time administering payments! This has proved invaluable because when you are studying part time and working you need all the time you can get!'

## What are staff attitudes like at Birkbeck College?

'I have found the disability office to be informative and supportive. Teachers vary on an individual basis but so long as you are clear what you need from them, they are usually very accommodating. Overall, the college has a positive attitude to diversity and I have felt my needs have been met in all areas.'

## What is the general accessibility of Birkbeck currently like?

'Access for me is on the whole good. I have requested that my lectures be held in buildings which are easier for me to get to and from. This request has been honoured.'

**How would you improve the services or access of Birkbeck?**
'The acoustics in some of the larger rooms is not always that good. This could be countered with carpets.'

**How are your social needs at your college met?**
'I have met a number of good friends through my studies at Birkbeck. I would say my social needs have been met. However, when you are studying part time and working there is not always that much time for partying!'

**What is the local area like in terms of access and social life?**
'It's hard for me to say. Birkbeck is located very centrally in London so the area is very busy. There are lots of cars and people, which is not always ideal for disabled people wanting to get about. However, the college is near good bus and tube routes and my local authority have provided funding for taxis home.'

**Advice?**
'I think the best advice I can offer is to be assertive. You need to recognise what your needs are and make sure they are met. Most people are happy to be accommodating but it's your job to tell them what you need. You can't expect everyone to just know. Funding and assistance is out there but only if you take the initiative to ask for it.'

**Jacqueline Fowler**
**Aston University, Birmingham**
**Combined Honours Business Administration**
**and Public Policy and Management**

Jacqueline Fowler is in her final year at Aston University. She has dysexecutive syndrome.

**What career do you wish to pursue?**
'Politics related.'

**How have your individual needs been met at Aston?**
'Ability to record lectures, additional time in exams – also help in arranging a personal assistant.'

**What are staff attitudes like at your university?**
'Understanding and helpful. Also very flexible to needs.'

**What is the general accessibility of the university currently like?**
'Very good – 24-hour access to computers and Internet, good wheelchair access – overall very good.'

**How would you improve the services or access of your university?**
'More information about services available before arrival at university. I was not aware of these services until midway through my course.'

**How are your social needs at Aston met?**
'Small university so good community atmosphere, friendly staff and students, good guild facilities and personal assistant to help with social requirements.'

**What is the local area like in terms of access and social life?**
'Birmingham caters for students as it is home to several universities. Very good nightlife and good access. Aston University also offers clubs, societies and good extracurricular facilities.'

**Advice?**
'Don't let having a disability put you off going to university. You will not be alone and help is available if you need it!'

**Bethan West
University of Wales, Aberystwyth
Law with Spanish**

Bethan West, who has a developmental coordination problem and tendonitis, is in her third year at the University of Wales, Aberystwyth.

**What career do you wish to pursue?**
'A barrister in the Government Legal Service.'

**How have your individual needs been met at Aberystwyth?**
'Excellent support, both pre-arrival and after.'

**What are staff attitudes like at Aberystwyth?**
'I have had problems with one or two insensitive members of staff, but overall people are sympathetic to my needs.'

**What is the general accessibility of Aberystwyth currently like?**
'Aberystwyth is not the best place to go for those with serious mobility difficulties because the main campus is situated on a hill;

however, accessibility is possible and there is a big range of accommodation available that has been adapted for those with special needs.'

## How would you improve the services or access of Aberystwyth?

'Have more ramps, lifts, etc. so that students can access all the buildings more easily. There is already a Disabled Students Officer at the union, but I feel there is a general ignorance as to what duties the officer carries out.'

## What is the local area like in terms of access and social life?

'Aberystwyth is a wonderful place to be in, even for those with mobility problems. I chose to live in the student village last year for this reason and found it an excellent place to be.'

## Advice?

'Don't let the fact that you have a disability put you at any disadvantage – your brain is just as good as everyone else's!! Visit the institutions that you prefer, to see what the access is like, and also try to talk to the disability officer and the subject tutors if you have any particular needs. Also try to ensure that any specific needs, such as exam arrangements, are met well in advance to avoid stress nearer the time. Always stick up for your rights and never be afraid to tell someone that you are having problems. Most of the time the people who help those with disabilities have done the job for years and understand exactly what problems disabled students have. Most of all – have fun!! University years are often the best years of your life and you should try to enjoy them as much as you can once you have all your needs sorted out.

**Aneias Martos**
**University of Birmingham**
**MSc in Advanced Computer Science**

Aneias Martos, who is blind, has come from Greece to study at the University of Birmingham.

## Why did you choose to study in the UK?

'There are many differences between my first university and the University of Birmingham. I chose to study in the UK because I wanted to have the experience of a different country and to share my old one. I chose the University of

Birmingham because I knew that it is one of the most accessible in the UK.'

## What career do you wish to pursue?
'Researcher or employed in a software development company.'

## How have your individual needs been met at your university?
'The Computer Science department is going to make everything accessible, but the available technology is not very efficient.'

## What is the general accessibility of the university currently like?
'The building is accessible; there are also accessible electronic books, Web pages and printing facilities, and the staff are helpful.'

## How would you improve the services or access of your university?
'Using all the available technology and sharing the experience with other UK, EU, US and Canadian universities. Also, adapting the available standards of accessibility technology such as W3C and designing standards for all.'

## How are your social needs at your university met?
'My communication with staff and other students is fine.'

## What is the local area like in terms of access and social life?
'I think that the campus needs to be more accessible. It is a big campus and it is difficult for me to walk around. I think it is important to put in some markpoints to improve accessibility.'

**Helen Roocroft**
**University of Wales College of Medicine**
**Occupational Therapy**

Helen Roocroft is in her third year at the University of Wales College of Medicine. She has dyslexia.

## What career do you wish to pursue?
'I am hopefully going to be an occupational therapist.'

## How have your individual needs been met at UWCM?
'Dyslexia and Disability Service have been great. They have supported me in getting me my laptop, printer and scanner along with money for print cartridges, photocopying and paper to assist me with my studies. My tutors have been very supportive

of my needs and due to the awareness of the dyslexia and disability services available they have been able to give me extra support when I have needed it.'

### What are staff attitudes like at UWCM?

'Occupational therapy tutors are excellent. I have never been made to feel that I could never do the occupational therapy course. They have always been there when I have needed them as have the Dyslexia and Disability Service. I also think it helps that the disability support services actually have awareness courses so that they can understand the problems that I and other dyslexic people face.'

### What is the general accessibility of UWCM currently like?

'The accessibility of the resources I have needed to carry out my degree is good. The Disability Support Service is open five days a week and you can have access to the facilities seven days a week.'

### How would you improve the services or access at UWCM?

'Due to dyslexia becoming more and more recognised, there is beginning to be a small strain on the services, which I feel could be met by having another person employed to assist them in the good work they already do.'

### How are your social needs at your college met?

'Med club is great, that's our Students' Union. There are lots of sporting clubs which you can join.'

### What is the local area like in terms of access and social life?

'The university is two miles outside Cardiff city centre and has a regular bus service into Cardiff. There is lots going on in Cardiff from shopping to clubbing, to cinemas and even ice-skating. Cardiff has lots to do and see.'

### Advice?

'TRY! When I was applying for university I was determined that my disability wouldn't get in the way of my dreams. I thought that it was worth applying for and trying to get in. If you don't try you will never know and you can achieve anything if you put your mind to it. The other advice I would give is never give up and if you don't know, ask. Most people don't judge you, they actually want to assist you to achieve your dreams.'

**Amjad Mahboob**
**Aston University**
**BSc Computer Science**

Amjad Mahboob, who is severely hard of hearing, is in his final year at Aston University.

### What career do you wish to pursue?
'I want to pursue a career in computer science/business.'

### How have your individual needs been met at Aston?
'This year they have been good but not during my previous years.'

### What are staff attitudes like at your university?
'The Disability Unit have been great; unfortunately they did not know about my conditions til late. Generally Computer Science staff could be much better.'

### How would you improve the services or access of Aston?
'More awareness leaflets, signs.'

### How are your social needs at Aston met?
'I am unfortunately not very social because of my hearing loss. I think that at times I lack the confidence to talk to people due to embarrassment.'

### Advice?
'Go and see the DANU (Disability and Additional Needs Unit); they will help make people aware that you have a disability. Never be too ashamed or upset to ask.'

# Tables

It is now unlawful to discriminate against disabled students by treating them less favourably than others. Colleges and universities are now required to provide reasonable adjustments to the provision of education and other services where disabled learners might otherwise be substantially disadvantaged (see Skill's article on the DDA (page xlviii) for more information).

However, given the staggered introduction of this legislation (for example, adjustments to the physical features of premises are not required until September 2005), we thought it would be helpful to produce a quick reference guide to enable you to put together a shortlist of institutions which already meet most or all of your criteria.

Once you've drawn up a shortlist, we would always advise you to contact individual institutions for further information. With institutions constantly improving and expanding on their provision for disabled students, you should contact the relevant disability coordinator to clarify and confirm the exact provision available and whether they will be able to accommodate all your needs.

The tables were compiled from information supplied by those institutions that completed our questionnaires in 2003. When information was not supplied for a particular question a blank has been left. You should also be aware that the tables do not include every institution in the book – only those that filled in the relevant part of our questionnaire.

You will find further information on access and facilities within the individual entries.

## Table 1: Accessibility

This chart represents institutions that completed the table on the questionnaire. It does not cover every institution in the book. Where information was not available a blank has been left. Students interested in applying to a particular college should contact that institution direct to confirm what access they can offer. The publishers would welcome any additional information from institutions to be included in future editions.

| | Aberdeen University | | | | Aberystwyth University of Wales | | | | Arts Institute at Bournemouth | | | |
|---|---|---|---|---|---|---|---|---|---|---|---|---|
| | Wheelchair access | Lifts | WAT | Induction loops | Wheelchair access | Lifts | WAT | Induction loops | Wheelchair access | Lifts | WAT | Induction loops |
| Lecture theatres | ✓ | ✓ | ✓ | | S | S | | S | ✓ | | ✓ | |
| Teaching rooms | ✓ | ✓ | ✓ | | S | S | S | S | S | | ✓ | |
| Libraries | ✓ | ✓ | ✓ | | S | S | S | | S | | ✓ | |
| Computer rooms | ✓ | ✓ | ✓ | ✓ | S | S | ✓ | | ✓ | | ✓ | |
| Canteens | ✓ | ✓ | | | ✓ | ✓ | | | n/a | | ✓ | |
| Student Union | | | | | ✓ | n/a | ✓ | | ✓ | | ✓ | |
| Student bar | | | | | ✓ | ✓ | ✓ | ✓ | n/a | | ✓ | |
| Gym | | | | | | ✓ | ✓ | ✓ | n/a | | ✓ | |
| Swimming pool | | | | | ✓ | ✓ | | | n/a | | | |
| Other sporting facilities | | | | | n/a | n/a | n/a | | n/a | | | |
| Medical facilities | | | | | n/a | n/a | n/a | | ✓ | | | |
| Counselling facilities | | | | | n/a | n/a | n/a | | ✓ | | | |
| Welfare services | | | | | n/a | ✓ | ✓ | | ✓ | | | |

S = Only some of these facilities are currently available – WAT = Wheelchair accessible toilets

A = Talking lifts – T = Tactile controls – W = Lifts that are wheelchair accessible

| | Aston University | | | | Bangor, University of Wales | | | | Bath University | | | |
|---|---|---|---|---|---|---|---|---|---|---|---|---|
| | Wheelchair access | Lifts | WAT | Induction loops | Wheelchair access | Lifts | WAT | Induction loops | Wheelchair access | Lifts | WAT | Induction loops |
| Lecture theatres | S | S | S | | W | W | ✓ | ✓ | ✓ | S | S | Portable induction loops available on request |
| Teaching rooms | S | S | S | | S | S | S | S | ✓ | S | S | |
| Libraries | ✓ | ATW | ✓ | | S | S | ✓ | S | ✓ | ✓ | S | |
| Computer rooms | ✓ | ATW | ✓ | | W | W | ✓ | S | S | ✓ | S | |
| Canteens | ✓ | ATW | ✓ | | W | W | ✓ | | S | n/a | S | |
| Student Union | ✓ | ATW | ✓ | | W | W | ✓ | | S | n/a | n/a | |
| Student bar | ✓ | ATW | ✓ | | W | W | ✓ | | S | ✓ | ✓ | |
| Gym | ✓ | n/a | ✓ | | W | W | ✓ | | ✓ | ✓ | ✓ | |
| Swimming pool | ✓ | n/a | ✓ | | | | | | ✓ | n/a | ✓ | |
| Other sporting facilities | ✓ | n/a | S | | | | | | ✓ | ✓ | ✓ | |
| Medical facilities | ✓ | ATW | ✓ | | ✓ | | | | ✓ | n/a | ✓ | |
| Counselling facilities | ✓ | ATW | ✓ | | ✓ | | | | ✓ | ✓ | ✓ | |
| Welfare services | ✓ | ATW | ✓ | | W | W | ✓ | | S | ✓ | S | |

S = Only some of these facilities are currently available – WAT = Wheelchair accessible toilets
A = Talking lifts – T = Tactile controls – W = Lifts that are wheelchair accessible

| Facility | Bath Spa University College | | | | Birkbeck College University of London | | | | University of Birmingham | | | |
|---|---|---|---|---|---|---|---|---|---|---|---|---|
| | Wheelchair access | Lifts | WAT | Induction loops | Wheelchair access | Lifts | WAT | Induction loops | Wheelchair access | Lifts | WAT | Induction loops |
| Lecture theatres | S | | S | S | ✓ | ✓ | ✓ | S | S | S | S | S |
| Teaching rooms | S | | S | S | ✓ | ✓ | ✓ | S | S | S | S | S |
| Libraries | n/a | | | | ✓ | ✓ | ✓ | | S | S | S | |
| Computer rooms | S | | | | ✓ | ✓ | ✓ | | S | S | S | |
| Canteens | n/a | | | | ✓ | ✓ | ✓ | | ✓ | n/a | S | |
| Student Union | S | | | | | | | | ✓ | ✓ | ✓ | |
| Student bar | | | | | | | | | ✓ | ✓ | ✓ | |
| Gym | | | | | n/a | | | | ✓ | n/a | ✓ | |
| Swimming pool | | | | | n/a | | | | ✓ | n/a | ✓ | |
| Other sporting facilities | | | | | n/a | | | | ✓ | n/a | ✓ | |
| Medical facilities | S | | | | ✓ | ✓ | ✓ | ✓ | ✓ | ✓ | ✓ | |
| Counselling facilities | S | | | | ✓ | ✓ | ✓ | ✓ | ✓ | ✓ | ✓ | |
| Welfare services | S | | | | | | | ✓ | ✓ | ✓ | ✓ | |

S = Only some of these facilities are currently available – WAT = Wheelchair accessible toilets
A = Talking lifts – T = Tactile controls – W = Lifts that are wheelchair accessible

| | Bolton Institute | | | | University of Bradford | | | | British School of Osteopathy | | | |
|---|---|---|---|---|---|---|---|---|---|---|---|---|
| | Wheelchair access | Lifts | WAT | Induction loops | Wheelchair access | Lifts | WAT | Induction loops | Wheelchair access | Lifts | WAT | Induction loops |
| Lecture theatres | S | W | S | ✓ | ✓ | ✓ | ✓ | ✓ | ✓ | WAT | | ✓ |
| Teaching rooms | S | W | S | S | ✓ | ✓ | ✓ | S | ✓ | WAT | | |
| Libraries | ✓ | n/a | ✓ | ✓ | ✓ | ✓ | ✓ | | ✓ | WAT | | |
| Computer rooms | ✓ | n/a | | | ✓ | ✓ | ✓ | | ✓ | WAT | | |
| Canteens | ✓ | W | ✓ | | ✓ | ✓ | ✓ | | | | | |
| Student Union | ✓ | W | ✓ | | ✓ | ✓ | ✓ | | | | | |
| Student bar | ✓ | W | ✓ | | ✓ | ✓ | ✓ | | | | | |
| Gym | ✓ | n/a | n/a | n/a | | | | | | | | |
| Swimming pool | n/a | n/a | | | | | | | | | | |
| Other sporting facilities | | | | | ✓ | ✓ | ✓ | | | | | |
| Medical facilities | n/a | n/a | ✓ | ✓ | ✓ | ✓ | ✓ | | ✓ | WAT | ✓ | |
| Counselling facilities | ✓ | n/a | ✓ | ✓ | ✓ | ✓ | ✓ | | ✓ | WAT | | |
| Welfare services | ✓ | n/a | ✓ | ✓ | ✓ | ✓ | ✓ | | ✓ | WAT | | |

S = Only some of these facilities are currently available – WAT = Wheelchair accessible toilets

A = Talking lifts – T = Tactile controls – W = Lifts that are wheelchair accessible

| | Brunel University | | | | University of Buckingham | | | | Canterbury Christ Church University College | | | |
|---|---|---|---|---|---|---|---|---|---|---|---|---|
| | Wheelchair access | Lifts | WAT | Induction loops | Wheelchair access | Lifts | WAT | Induction loops | Wheelchair access | Lifts | WAT | Induction loops |
| Lecture theatres | ✓ | ✓ | ✓ | | ✓ | ✓ | ✓ | | ✓ | n/a | ✓ | ✓ |
| Teaching rooms | ✓ | ✓ | ✓ | ✓ | ✓ | ✓ | ✓ | | S | S | S | |
| Libraries | ✓ | ✓ | ✓ | ✓ | ✓ | n/a | ✓ | | ✓ | W | ✓ | |
| Computer rooms | ✓ | ✓ | ✓ | ✓ | ✓ | n/a | ✓ | | ✓ | W | ✓ | |
| Canteens | ✓ | ✓ | ✓ | | ✓ | n/a | ✓ | | ✓ | n/a | n/a | |
| Student Union | ✓ | ✓ | ✓ | | ✓ | n/a | ✓ | | S | | ✓ | |
| Student bar | | | | | | ✓ | | | ✓ | n/a | ✓ | |
| Gym | | | | | | | | | | | | |
| Swimming pool | | | | | | | | | | | | |
| Other sporting facilities | ✓ | | ✓ | | ✓ | | | | | | | |
| Medical facilities | ✓ | | ✓ | | | | | | S | n/a | ✓ | |
| Counselling facilities | ✓ | | ✓ | | ✓ | | | | ✓ | n/a | ✓ | |
| Welfare services | | | | | ✓ | | | | ✓ | n/a | ✓ | |

S = Only some of these facilities are currently available – WAT = Wheelchair accessible toilets
A = Talking lifts – T = Tactile controls – W = Lifts that are wheelchair accessible

| | University of Central Lancashire | | | | Central School of Speech and Drama | | | | Chester, University College | | | |
|---|---|---|---|---|---|---|---|---|---|---|---|---|
| | Wheelchair access | Lifts | WAT | Induction loops | Wheelchair access | Lifts | WAT | Induction loops | Wheelchair access | Lifts | WAT | Induction loops |
| Lecture theatres | | | | | ✓ | ✓ | ✓ | | S | | | |
| Teaching rooms | | | | | S | S | S | | S | | | |
| Libraries | | | | | ✓ | ✓ | S | | ✓ | | ✓ | |
| Computer rooms | Please refer to the university's Disability Statement | | | | ✓ | ✓ | ✓ | | S | | | |
| Canteens | | | | | S | S | S | | ✓ | | ✓ | |
| Student Union | | | | | ✓ | ✓ | ✓ | | ✓ | | | |
| Student bar | | | | | ✓ | ✓ | | | ✓ | | ✓ | |
| Gym | | | | | n/a | n/a | | | ✓ | | ✓ | |
| Swimming pool | | | | | n/a | n/a | | | | | | |
| Other sporting facilities | | | | | n/a | | | | | | | |
| Medical facilities | | | | | n/a | | | | ✓ | | | |
| Counselling facilities | | | | | ✓ | ✓ | S | | S | | | |
| Welfare services | | | | | ✓ | ✓ | S | | ✓ | | | |

S = Only some of these facilities are currently available – WAT = Wheelchair accessible toilets

A = Talking lifts – T = Tactile controls – W = Lifts that are wheelchair accessible

| | City University | | | | Conservatoire for Acting and Musical Theatre | | | | Courtauld Institute of Art | | | |
|---|---|---|---|---|---|---|---|---|---|---|---|---|
| | Wheelchair access | Lifts | WAT | Induction loops | Wheelchair access | Lifts | WAT | Induction loops | Wheelchair access | Lifts | WAT | Induction loops |
| Lecture theatres | ✔ | ✔ | ✔ | ✔ | | | | | ✔ | ✔ | | |
| Teaching rooms | ✔ | ✔ | ✔ | ✔ | ✔ | | | | ✔ | ✔ | | |
| Libraries | ✔ | ✔ | ✔ | | ✔ | | | | ✔ | ✔ | | |
| Computer rooms | ✔ | ✔ | ✔ | | ✔ | | | | | | | |
| Canteens | ✔ | ✔ | ✔ | | | | | | | | | |
| Student Union | ✔ | ✔ | ✔ | | | | | | ✔ | ✔ | | |
| Student bar | | | | | | | | | n/a | n/a | | |
| Gym | | | | | | | | | n/a | n/a | | |
| Swimming pool | | | | | | | | | n/a | n/a | | |
| Other sporting facilities | | | | | | | | | n/a | n/a | | |
| Medical facilities | ✔ | | | | | | | | n/a | n/a | | |
| Counselling facilities | ✔ | | | | | | | | ✔ | ✔ | | |
| Welfare services | ✔ | | | | ✔ | | | | ✔ | ✔ | | |

S = Only some of these facilities are currently available – WAT = Wheelchair accessible toilets

A = Talking lifts – T = Tactile controls – W = Lifts that are wheelchair accessible

| | Coventry University | | | | Croydon College | | | | Cumbria Institute of the Arts | | | |
|---|---|---|---|---|---|---|---|---|---|---|---|---|
| | Wheelchair access | Lifts | WAT | Induction loops | Wheelchair access | Lifts | WAT | Induction loops | Wheelchair access | Lifts | WAT | Induction loops |
| Lecture theatres | ✓ | ✓ | ✓ | ✓ | ✓ | | ✓ | | ✓ | ✓ | ✓ | ✓ |
| Teaching rooms | ✓ | ✓ | ✓ | ✓ | ✓ | | ✓ | | ✓ | ✓ | ✓ | |
| Libraries | ✓ | ✓ | ✓ | | ✓ | | ✓ | | ✓ | ✓ | ✓ | |
| Computer rooms | ✓ | ✓ | ✓ | | ✓ | | ✓ | | ✓ | ✓ | ✓ | |
| Canteens | ✓ | ✓ | ✓ | | ✓ | | ✓ | | ✓ | ✓ | | |
| Student Union | ✓ | ✓ | ✓ | | ✓ | | ✓ | | ✓ | | | |
| Student bar | ✓ | ✓ | ✓ | | | | | | n/a | n/a | n/a | |
| Gym | | | | | | | | | n/a | n/a | n/a | |
| Swimming pool | | | | | | | | | n/a | n/a | n/a | |
| Other sporting facilities | | | | | | | | | n/a | n/a | n/a | |
| Medical facilities | ✓ | | ✓ | | ✓ | | ✓ | | n/a | n/a | n/a | |
| Counselling facilities | ✓ | | ✓ | ✓ | ✓ | | ✓ | | ✓ | ✓ | ✓ | |
| Welfare services | ✓ | | ✓ | ✓ | ✓ | | ✓ | | ✓ | ✓ | ✓ | |

*Croydon College Induction loops: Portable induction loop*

S = Only some of these facilities are currently available – WAT = Wheelchair accessible toilets

A = Talking lifts – T = Tactile controls – W = Lifts that are wheelchair accessible

| | De Montfort University | | | | Derby University | | | | University of Dundee | | | |
|---|---|---|---|---|---|---|---|---|---|---|---|---|
| | Wheelchair access | Lifts | WAT | Induction loops | Wheelchair access | Lifts | WAT | Induction loops | Wheelchair access | Lifts | WAT | Induction loops |
| Lecture theatres | ✓ | ✓ | ✓ | S | ✓ | ✓ | ✓ | | S | S | S | |
| Teaching rooms | ✓ | ✓ | ✓ | S | ✓ | ✓ | ✓ | | S | S | S | |
| Libraries | ✓ | ✓ | ✓ | ✓ | ✓ | ✓ | ✓ | | S | S | S | |
| Computer rooms | ✓ | ✓ | ✓ | | ✓ | ✓ | | | ✓ | WT | ✓ | |
| Canteens | ✓ | ✓ | ✓ | | | | | | ✓ | WT | ✓ | |
| Student Union | ✓ | ✓ | ✓ | | ✓ | | | | ✓ | WA | ✓ | |
| Student bar | ✓ | | ✓ | | | | | | ✓ | WA | ✓ | |
| Gym | | | | | ✓ | | ✓ | | ✓ | n/a | ✓ | |
| Swimming pool | | | | | | | | | | | | |
| Other sporting facilities | | | | | | | | | | | | |
| Medical facilities | ✓ | ✓ | ✓ | | ✓ | | | | | | | |
| Counselling facilities | ✓ | ✓ | ✓ | | ✓ | | | | | | | |
| Welfare services | ✓ | ✓ | ✓ | | ✓ | | | | | | | |

S = Only some of these facilities are currently available – WAT = Wheelchair accessible toilets

A = Talking lifts – T = Tactile controls – W = Lifts that are wheelchair accessible

| | Durham University | | | | University of East Anglia | | | | University of East London | | | |
|---|---|---|---|---|---|---|---|---|---|---|---|---|
| | Wheelchair access | Lifts | WAT | Induction loops | Wheelchair access | Lifts | WAT | Induction loops | Wheelchair access | Lifts | WAT | Induction loops |
| Lecture theatres | S | S | S | | ✓ | ✓ | ✓ | ✓ | ✓ | W | ✓ | S |
| Teaching rooms | S | S | S | ✓ | ✓ | ✓ | ✓ | | ✓ | W | ✓ | S |
| Libraries | ✓ | S | S | | ✓ | n/a | ✓ | | W | W | ✓ | S |
| Computer rooms | S | S | S | | ✓ | n/a | | | ✓ | W | ✓ | S |
| Canteens | ✓ | | ✓ | | ✓ | ✓ | | Use portable loop systems – infrared – as and when required | ✓ | W | ✓ | |
| Student Union | | | ✓ | | ✓ | ✓ | | | ✓ | W | ✓ | |
| Student bar | | | ✓ | | ✓ | n/a | ✓ | | ✓ | W | ✓ | |
| Gym | ✓ | | ✓ | | ✓ | n/a | ✓ | | ✓ | W | ✓ | |
| Swimming pool | ✓ | | ✓ | ✓ | ✓ | ✓ | ✓ | | ✓ | W | ✓ | |
| Other sporting facilities | | | ✓ | S | ✓ | n/a | | | ✓ | W | ✓ | |
| Medical facilities | | | ✓ | S | ✓ | n/a | | | ✓ | W | ✓ | S |
| Counselling facilities | | | ✓ | S | ✓ | n/a | | | ✓ | W | ✓ | S |
| Welfare services | | | ✓ | S | ✓ | n/a | | | ✓ | W | ✓ | S |

S = Only some of these facilities are currently available – WAT = Wheelchair accessible toilets
A = Talking lifts – T = Tactile controls – W = Lifts that are wheelchair accessible

| | Edinburgh College of Art | | | | Essex University | | | | Falmouth College of Arts | | | |
|---|---|---|---|---|---|---|---|---|---|---|---|---|
| | Wheelchair access | Lifts | WAT | Induction loops | Wheelchair access | Lifts | WAT | Induction loops | Wheelchair access | Lifts | WAT | Induction loops |
| Lecture theatres | ✓ | ✓ | ✓ | ✓ | ✓ | ✓ | ✓ | ✓ | ✓ | ✓ | ✓ | ✓ |
| Teaching rooms | ✓ | S | ✓ | | ✓ | ✓ | ✓ | | ✓ | | ✓ | ✓ |
| Libraries | ✓ | | | | ✓ | ✓ | ✓ | ✓ | ✓ | ✓ | ✓ | |
| Computer rooms | ✓ | S | | | ✓ | ✓ | | | ✓ | ✓ | ✓ | |
| Canteens | ✓ | ✓ | ✓ | | ✓ | ✓ | | | ✓ | | ✓ | |
| Student Union | ✓ | ✓ | ✓ | | ✓ | ✓ | ✓ | | ✓ | | ✓ | |
| Student bar | ✓ | | | | ✓ | ✓ | ✓ | | ✓ | | ✓ | |
| Gym | | | | | | | ✓ | | | | | |
| Swimming pool | | | | | | | | | | | | |
| Other sporting facilities | | | | | | | | | | | | |
| Medical facilities | ✓ | | ✓ | | ✓ | n/a | ✓ | | ✓ | | ✓ | |
| Counselling facilities | ✓ | | ✓ | | ✓ | ✓ | ✓ | | ✓ | | ✓ | |
| Welfare services | ✓ | | ✓ | | ✓ | ✓ | | ✓ | ✓ | | ✓ | |

S = Only some of these facilities are currently available – WAT = Wheelchair accessible toilets

A = Talking lifts – T = Tactile controls – W = Lifts that are wheelchair accessible

| | Farnborough College of Technology | | | | University of Gloucestershire | | | | Guildford School of Acting | | | |
|---|---|---|---|---|---|---|---|---|---|---|---|---|
| | Wheelchair access | Lifts | WAT | Induction loops | Wheelchair access | Lifts | WAT | Induction loops | Wheelchair access | Lifts | WAT | Induction loops |
| Lecture theatres | ✓ | | | | ✓ | ✓ | ✓ | S | S | | ✓ | |
| Teaching rooms | ✓ | | | | ✓ | ✓ | ✓ | S | S | | ✓ | |
| Libraries | ✓ | | | | ✓ | W | ✓ | S | S | n/a | | |
| Computer rooms | ✓ | | | | ✓ | W | ✓ | | S | | | |
| Canteens | ✓ | | | | ✓ | n/a | ✓ | | | n/a | | |
| Student Union | ✓ | | | | ✓ | n/a | ✓ | | | | | |
| Student bar | ✓ | | | | ✓ | W | ✓ | | | | | |
| Gym | n/a | | | | n/a | n/a | n/a | n/a | | | | |
| Swimming pool | | | | | | | n/a | | | | | |
| Other sporting facilities | | | | | | | | | | | | |
| Medical facilities | | | | | ✓ | n/a | ✓ | | | | | |
| Counselling facilities | | | | | ✓ | W | ✓ | | | | | |
| Welfare services | | | | | ✓ | W | ✓ | | | | | |

*Induction loops (Farnborough College of Technology): Portable hearing loops available*

S = Only some of these facilities are currently available – WAT = Wheelchair accessible toilets
A = Talking lifts – T = Tactile controls – W = Lifts that are wheelchair accessible

| | Heriot-Watt University | | | | University of Hertfordshire | | | | Holborn College | | | |
| --- | --- | --- | --- | --- | --- | --- | --- | --- | --- | --- | --- | --- |
| | Wheelchair access | Lifts | WAT | Induction loops | Wheelchair access | Lifts | WAT | Induction loops | Wheelchair access | Lifts | WAT | Induction loops |
| Lecture theatres | ✓ | | | ✓ | ✓ | n/a | ✓ | ✓ | ✓ | ✓ | ✓ | |
| Teaching rooms | ✓ | ✓ | ✓ | | ✓ | ✓ | S | S | ✓ | ✓ | ✓ | |
| Libraries | ✓ | ✓ | ✓ | | ✓ | ✓ | ✓ | ✓ | ✓ | ✓ | ✓ | |
| Computer rooms | ✓ | ✓ | ✓ | | ✓ | n/a | | | ✓ | ✓ | ✓ | |
| Canteens | ✓ | | ✓ | | ✓ | n/a | | | ✓ | ✓ | ✓ | |
| Student Union | ✓ | | | | ✓ | ✓ | ✓ | | n/a | n/a | n/a | |
| Student bar | ✓ | | | | ✓ | ✓ | ✓ | | n/a | n/a | n/a | |
| Gym | | ✓ | ✓ | | ✓ | n/a | ✓ | | n/a | n/a | n/a | |
| Swimming pool | | | | | ✓ | n/a | | | n/a | n/a | n/a | |
| Other sporting facilities | | | | | ✓ | n/a | | | | | | |
| Medical facilities | ✓ | ✓ | ✓ | | ✓ | n/a | | | ✓ | ✓ | ✓ | |
| Counselling facilities | ✓ | | | | ✓ | n/a | | | | | | |
| Welfare services | ✓ | | ✓ | | ✓ | n/a | ✓ | S | ✓ | ✓ | ✓ | |

S = Only some of these facilities are currently available – WAT = Wheelchair accessible toilets

A = Talking lifts – T = Tactile controls – W = Lifts that are wheelchair accessible

| | Huddersfield University | | | | Imperial College London | | | | Keele University | | | |
|---|---|---|---|---|---|---|---|---|---|---|---|---|
| | Wheelchair access | Lifts | WAT | Induction loops | Wheelchair access | Lifts | WAT | Induction loops | Wheelchair access | Lifts | WAT | Induction loops |
| Lecture theatres | S | S | S | S | S | W | S | S | W | | W | S |
| Teaching rooms | S | S | S | S | S | W | S | S | W | | | S |
| Libraries | W | n/a | S | S | S | W | W | S | W | | | |
| Computer rooms | W | ATW | S | | W | W | W | S | W | | | |
| Canteens | W | ATW | S | | W | W | W | S | W | | | |
| Student Union | | | | | W | W | W | S | W | | | |
| Student bar | | | | | W | W | W | S | W | | | |
| Gym | S | | S | | W | W | W | S | W | | | |
| Swimming pool | | | | | W | W | W | S | n/a | | | |
| Other sporting facilities | | | | | W | W | | S | | | | |
| Medical facilities | W | ATW | S | | W | W | W | S | W | | | |
| Counselling facilities | W | ATW | S | | W | W | W | S | W | | | |
| Welfare services | W | ATW | S | | W | W | W | S | W | | | |

S = Only some of these facilities are currently available – WAT = Wheelchair accessible toilets
A = Talking lifts – T = Tactile controls – W = Lifts that are wheelchair accessible

| | Kent Institute of Art and Design | | | | University of Kent at Canterbury | | | | King Alfred's Winchester | | | |
|---|---|---|---|---|---|---|---|---|---|---|---|---|
| | Wheelchair access | Lifts | WAT | Induction loops | Wheelchair access | Lifts | WAT | Induction loops | Wheelchair access | Lifts | WAT | Induction loops |
| Lecture theatres | ✔ | ✔ | ✔ | ✔ | ✔ | ✔ | ✔ | ✔ | ✔ | | | ✔ |
| Teaching rooms | ✔ | ✔ | ✔ | ✔ | ✔ | ✔ | ✔ | S | ✔ | | | |
| Libraries | ✔ | ✔ | ✔ | | ✔ | ✔ | ✔ | S | ✔ | ✔ | | |
| Computer rooms | ✔ | ✔ | | | S | ✔ | ✔ | | ✔ | ✔ | | |
| Canteens | ✔ | | | | S | ✔ | ✔ | | ✔ | | | |
| Student Union | ✔ | ✔ | ✔ | ✔ | ✔ | | ✔ | | ✔ | ✔ | | |
| Student bar | ✔ | ✔ | ✔ | ✔ | ✔ | ✔ | ✔ | ✔ | ✔ | ✔ | | |
| Gym | ✔ | ✔ | ✔ | ✔ | | ✔ | ✔ | | | | | |
| Swimming pool | | | | | | | | | | | | |
| Other sporting facilities | | | | | ✔ | ✔ | ✔ | ✔ | | | | |
| Medical facilities | ✔ | ✔ | | | S | | ✔ | | ✔ | | ✔ | |
| Counselling facilities | ✔ | ✔ | ✔ | | ✔ | ✔ | ✔ | | ✔ | | ✔ | |
| Welfare services | ✔ | ✔ | ✔ | | ✔ | ✔ | ✔ | ✔ | ✔ | | ✔ | |

S = Only some of these facilities are currently available – WAT = Wheelchair accessible toilets

A = Talking lifts – T = Tactile controls – W = Lifts that are wheelchair accessible

Table 1: Accessibility

| Facility | King's College London | | | | Kingston University | | | | Laban Centre | | | |
|---|---|---|---|---|---|---|---|---|---|---|---|---|
| | Wheelchair access | Lifts | WAT | Induction loops | Wheelchair access | Lifts | WAT | Induction loops | Wheelchair access | Lifts | WAT | Induction loops |
| Lecture theatres | S | S | ✓ | S | S | S | S | S | ✓ | n/a | ✓ | ✓ |
| Teaching rooms | S | S | ✓ | S | S | S | S | | ✓ | ✓ | ✓ | |
| Libraries | ✓ | ✓ | ✓ | | ✓ | ✓ | ✓ | | ✓ | ✓ | ✓ | |
| Computer rooms | ✓ | ✓ | ✓ | | S | S | S | | ✓ | n/a | ✓ | |
| Canteens | ✓ | ✓ | S | | ✓ | ✓ | | | ✓ | ✓ | ✓ | |
| Student Union | ✓ | ✓ | ✓ | | | | | | ✓ | n/a | ✓ | |
| Student bar | | | S | | | | | | | | ✓ | |
| Gym | | | | | ✓ | n/a | ✓ | | | | | |
| Swimming pool | | | | | | | | | | | | |
| Other sporting facilities | | | | | | | | | | | | |
| Medical facilities | ✓ | ✓ | ✓ | | S | n/a | S | | ✓ | ✓ | ✓ | |
| Counselling facilities | ✓ | ✓ | ✓ | | ✓ | n/a | ✓ | | ✓ | ✓ | ✓ | |
| Welfare services | ✓ | ✓ | ✓ | | ✓ | ✓ | ✓ | | ✓ | ✓ | ✓ | |

S = Only some of these facilities are currently available – WAT = Wheelchair accessible toilets
A = Talking lifts – T = Tactile controls – W = Lifts that are wheelchair accessible

| | Lampeter, University of Wales | | | | Lancaster University | | | | Leeds College of Music | | | |
|---|---|---|---|---|---|---|---|---|---|---|---|---|
| | Wheelchair access | Lifts | WAT | Induction loops | Wheelchair access | Lifts | WAT | Induction loops | Wheelchair access | Lifts | WAT | Induction loops |
| Lecture theatres | ✓ | | ✓ | ✓ | ✓ | ✓ | ✓ | ✓ | ✓ | AWT | | |
| Teaching rooms | ✓ | | ✓ | ✓ | ✓ | ✓ | ✓ | ✓ | ✓ | AWT | | |
| Libraries | ✓ | | ✓ | ✓ | ✓ | ✓ | ✓ | | ✓ | AWT | | |
| Computer rooms | ✓ | | ✓ | ✓ | ✓ | ✓ | ✓ | | ✓ | AWT | | |
| Canteens | ✓ | | ✓ | | ✓ | ✓ | ✓ | | ✓ | AWT | | |
| Student Union | ✓ | | ✓ | | ✓ | ✓ | ✓ | | ✓ | AWT | | |
| Student bar | ✓ | | ✓ | | ✓ | ✓ | ✓ | | ✓ | AWT | | |
| Gym | n/a | n/a | n/a | | ✓ | ✓ | ✓ | | n/a | AWT | | |
| Swimming pool | ✓ | n/a | ✓ | | ✓ | ✓ | | | n/a | AWT | | |
| Other sporting facilities | ✓ | | | | ✓ | ✓ | ✓ | | n/a | AWT | | |
| Medical facilities | ✓ | | ✓ | | ✓ | ✓ | ✓ | | n/a | AWT | | |
| Counselling facilities | ✓ | | | | ✓ | ✓ | ✓ | | ✓ | AWT | | |
| Welfare services | ✓ | | ✓ | | ✓ | ✓ | ✓ | | ✓ | AWT | | |

S = Only some of these facilities are currently available – WAT = Wheelchair accessible toilets

A = Talking lifts – T = Tactile controls – W = Lifts that are wheelchair accessible

| Facility | University of Leeds | | | | University of Lincoln | | | | Liverpool Hope | | | |
|---|---|---|---|---|---|---|---|---|---|---|---|---|
| | Wheelchair access | Lifts | WAT | Induction loops | Wheelchair access | Lifts | WAT | Induction loops | Wheelchair access | Lifts | WAT | Induction loops |
| Lecture theatres | ✔ | ✔ | ✔ | ✔ | | n/a | | | ✔ | | ✔ | ✔ |
| Teaching rooms | | | ✔ | | ✔ | n/a | ✔ | | ✔ | ✔ | ✔ | ✔ |
| Libraries | ✔ | ✔ | ✔ | | ✔ | n/a | ✔ | | ✔ | ✔ | ✔ | ✔ |
| Computer rooms | ✔ | ✔ | ✔ | | ✔ | n/a | ✔ | | ✔ | ✔ | ✔ | |
| Canteens | ✔ | ✔ | ✔ | | ✔ | n/a | | | ✔ | | ✔ | |
| Student Union | ✔ | ✔ | ✔ | | ✔ | n/a | ✔ | | ✔ | | ✔ | |
| Student bar | | | ✔ | | ✔ | n/a | ✔ | | ✔ | | ✔ | ✔ |
| Gym | | | | | ✔ | S | ✔ | ✔ | | | ✔ | |
| Swimming pool | | | | | | n/a | n/a | | | | | |
| Other sporting facilities | | | | | ✔ | ✔ | ✔ | | | | | |
| Medical facilities | ✔ | | | | | | ✔ | | ✔ | | | ✔ |
| Counselling facilities | ✔ | | | | ✔ | | ✔ | | ✔ | | | ✔ |
| Welfare services | ✔ | | | | ✔ | n/a | ✔ | | ✔ | | | |

S = Only some of these facilities are currently available – WAT = Wheelchair accessible toilets

A = Talking lifts – T = Tactile controls – W = Lifts that are wheelchair accessible

| | LIPA | | | | Liverpool John Moores University | | | | University of London | | | |
|---|---|---|---|---|---|---|---|---|---|---|---|---|
| | Wheelchair access | Lifts | WAT | Induction loops | Wheelchair access | Lifts | WAT | Induction loops | Wheelchair access | Lifts | WAT | Induction loops |
| Lecture theatres | ✓ | ✓ | ✓ | ✓ | S | W | | S | ✓ | n/a | ✓ | ✓ |
| Teaching rooms | ✓ | ✓ | ✓ | ✓ | S | W | ✓ | S | ✓ | W | ✓ | |
| Libraries | ✓ | ✓ | ✓ | ✓ | W | ✓ | S | ✓ | W | ✓ | ✓ | |
| Computer rooms | ✓ | ✓ | ✓ | ✓ | ✓ | ✓ | S | ✓ | | ✓ | ✓ | |
| Canteens | ✓ | ✓ | ✓ | ✓ | ✓ | n/a | ✓ | | ✓ | n/a | ✓ | |
| Student Union | ✓ | ✓ | ✓ | ✓ | ✓ | W | ✓ | ✓ | ✓ | ATW | ✓ | |
| Student bar | ✓ | ✓ | ✓ | ✓ | ✓ | n/a | ✓ | | ✓ | ATW | ✓ | |
| Gym | | | | | ✓ | n/a | ✓ | | | | | |
| Swimming pool | | | | | | | | | | | | |
| Other sporting facilities | | | | | | | | | | | | |
| Medical facilities | | | | | S | n/a | ✓ | ✓ | | | | |
| Counselling facilities | | | | | S | n/a | | | | | | |
| Welfare services | | | | | ✓ | n/a | ✓ | | | | | |

S = Only some of these facilities are currently available – WAT = Wheelchair accessible toilets

A = Talking lifts – T = Tactile controls – W = Lifts that are wheelchair accessible

| Facility | LAMDA | | | | London Bible College | | | | London Contemporary Dance School | | | |
|---|---|---|---|---|---|---|---|---|---|---|---|---|
| | Wheelchair access | Lifts | WAT | Induction loops | Wheelchair access | Lifts | WAT | Induction loops | Wheelchair access | Lifts | WAT | Induction loops |
| Lecture theatres | | | | | ✓ | ✓ | ✓ | ✓ | ✓ | ✓ | ✓ | ✓ |
| Teaching rooms | S | | | | | | | | ✓ | ✓ | ✓ | |
| Libraries | ✓ | | | | ✓ | | | ✓ | | ✓ | ✓ | ✓ |
| Computer rooms | | | | | ✓ | ✓ | ✓ | | ✓ | ✓ | ✓ | |
| Canteens | ✓ | | | | ✓ | ✓ | ✓ | | | | ✓ | |
| Student Union | | | | | | | | | | | | |
| Student bar | | | | | | | | | | | | |
| Gym | | | | | | | | | | | | |
| Swimming pool | | | | | | | | | | | | |
| Other sporting facilities | | | | | | | | | | | | |
| Medical facilities | | | | | | | | | | | | |
| Counselling facilities | | | | | | | | | ✓ | ✓ | ✓ | |
| Welfare services | | | | | | | | | ✓ | ✓ | ✓ | |

S = Only some of these facilities are currently available – WAT = Wheelchair accessible toilets
A = Talking lifts – T = Tactile controls – W = Lifts that are wheelchair accessible

| | London Metropolitan University | | | | London School of Economics and Political Science | | | | London South Bank University | | | |
|---|---|---|---|---|---|---|---|---|---|---|---|---|
| | Wheelchair access | Lifts | WAT | Induction loops | Wheelchair access | Lifts | WAT | Induction loops | Wheelchair access | Lifts | WAT | Induction loops |
| **Lecture theatres** | ✓ | ✓ | ✓ | ✓ | S | W | S | | S | S | S | S |
| **Teaching rooms** | ✓ | ✓ | ✓ | ✓ | S | ATW | S | | S | S | S | S |
| **Libraries** | ✓ | ✓ | ✓ | ✓ | ✓ | ATW | ✓ | | ✓ | ✓ | S | |
| **Computer rooms** | | ✓ | ✓ | | ✓ | ATW | S | | ✓ | ✓ | ✓ | S |
| **Canteens** | ✓ | ✓ | ✓ | | ✓ | ATW | ✓ | | S | S | ✓ | |
| **Student Union** | ✓ | ✓ | ✓ | | S | W | S | Portable loops available | ✓ | ✓ | ✓ | |
| **Student bar** | ✓ | ✓ | ✓ | | ✓ | n/a | ✓ | | ✓ | ✓ | ✓ | |
| **Gym** | n/a | n/a | n/a | | n/a | n/a | n/a | | n/a | | | |
| **Swimming pool** | | | | | | n/a | | | n/a | | | |
| **Other sporting facilities** | ✓ | | ✓ | | | | | | n/a | | | |
| **Medical facilities** | ✓ | ✓ | ✓ | | ✓ | WT | S | | ✓ | | ✓ | |
| **Counselling facilities** | ✓ | ✓ | ✓ | | ✓ | WT | S | | ✓ | n/a | ✓ | ✓ |
| **Welfare services** | ✓ | ✓ | ✓ | | ✓ | WT | S | | ✓ | n/a | ✓ | ✓ |

S = Only some of these facilities are currently available – WAT = Wheelchair accessible toilets

A = Talking lifts – T = Tactile controls – W = Lifts that are wheelchair accessible

| | Loughborough University | | | | University of Luton | | | | Manchester University | | | |
|---|---|---|---|---|---|---|---|---|---|---|---|---|
| | Wheelchair access | Lifts | WAT | Induction loops | Wheelchair access | Lifts | WAT | Induction loops | Wheelchair access | Lifts | WAT | Induction loops |
| Lecture theatres | W | ✓ | ✓ | S | ✓ | ✓ | ✓ | ✓ | ✓ | S | ✓ | ✓ |
| Teaching rooms | W | ✓ | ✓ | S | ✓ | ✓ | ✓ | | S | S | S | S |
| Libraries | W | ✓ | ✓ | | ✓ | ✓ | ✓ | | ✓ | ✓ | ✓ | |
| Computer rooms | W | ✓ | ✓ | S | ✓ | ✓ | ✓ | | ✓ | S | S | S |
| Canteens | W | S | ✓ | | | | | | ✓ | ✓ | ✓ | n/a |
| Student Union | W | ✓ | ✓ | | | | | | ✓ | ✓ | ✓ | |
| Student bar | W | ✓ | ✓ | | | | | | ✓ | ✓ | ✓ | |
| Gym | W | ✓ | ✓ | | | | | | | | | |
| Swimming pool | | | | | | | | | ✓ | ✓ | ✓ | n/a |
| Other sporting facilities | W | | | | | | | | | | | |
| Medical facilities | W | ✓ | ✓ | ✓ | ✓ | ✓ | ✓ | | ✓ | ✓ | ✓ | ✓ |
| Counselling facilities | W | | ✓ | | | | | | ✓ | n/a | ✓ | n/a |
| Welfare services | W | | ✓ | | ✓ | ✓ | ✓ | | ✓ | ✓ | ✓ | n/a |

S = Only some of these facilities are currently available – WAT = Wheelchair accessible toilets
A = Talking lifts – T = Tactile controls – W = Lifts that are wheelchair accessible

| | Middlesex University | | | | Myerscough College | | | | Napier University | | | |
|---|---|---|---|---|---|---|---|---|---|---|---|---|
| | Wheelchair access | Lifts | WAT | Induction loops | Wheelchair access | Lifts | WAT | Induction loops | Wheelchair access | Lifts | WAT | Induction loops |
| Lecture theatres | S | ✓ | ✓ | S | ✓ | ✓ | ✓ | ✓ | ✓ | ✓ | ✓ | ✓ |
| Teaching rooms | S | | | S | ✓ | S | ✓ | S | ✓ | ✓ | ✓ | |
| Libraries | S | | ✓ | ✓ | ✓ | n/a | ✓ | | ✓ | ✓ | ✓ | ✓ |
| Computer rooms | S | | | ✓ | ✓ | S | ✓ | | ✓ | ✓ | ✓ | |
| Canteens | S | | | | ✓ | n/a | ✓ | | | ✓ | ✓ | |
| Student Union | ✓ | | | | S | | ✓ | | | | | |
| Student bar | ✓ | | | | ✓ | n/a | ✓ | | ✓ | | | |
| Gym | ✓ | | | | ✓ | | ✓ | | | | | |
| Swimming pool | | | | | | n/a | | | | | | |
| Other sporting facilities | ✓ | | | | ✓ | | ✓ | | | | | |
| Medical facilities | ✓ | | | | S | | ✓ | | | | | |
| Counselling facilities | ✓ | | | | ✓ | ✓ | ✓ | | ✓ | | ✓ | |
| Welfare services | ✓ | | | | ✓ | ✓ | ✓ | | ✓ | | | |

S = Only some of these facilities are currently available – WAT = Wheelchair accessible toilets

A = Talking lifts – T = Tactile controls – W = Lifts that are wheelchair accessible

# Table 1: Accessibility

| Facility | National Film and Television School | | | | NEWI | | | | Newman College | | | |
|---|---|---|---|---|---|---|---|---|---|---|---|---|
| | Wheelchair access | Lifts | WAT | Induction loops | Wheelchair access | Lifts | WAT | Induction loops | Wheelchair access | Lifts | WAT | Induction loops |
| Lecture theatres | ✓ | S | S | n/a | ✓ | ✓ | ✓ | ✓ | ✓ | | ✓ | |
| Teaching rooms | ✓ | S | ✓ | n/a | ✓ | S | ✓ | | ✓ | | | |
| Libraries | ✓ | n/a | W | n/a | ✓ | n/a | ✓ | | ✓ | ✓ | ✓ | |
| Computer rooms | ✓ | n/a | W | n/a | ✓ | S | ✓ | | ✓ | | | |
| Canteens | ✓ | n/a | W | n/a | n/a | ✓ | ✓ | | ✓ | | ✓ | |
| Student Union | ✓ | n/a | W | n/a | n/a | | ✓ | | ✓ | | | |
| Student bar | n/a | n/a | n/a | n/a | n/a | | | | ✓ | | | |
| Gym | n/a | n/a | n/a | n/a | | | ✓ | | ✓ | | | |
| Swimming pool | n/a | n/a | n/a | n/a | | | | | ✓ | | | Portable loops available |
| Other sporting facilities | n/a | n/a | n/a | n/a | ✓ | | ✓ | | ✓ | | | |
| Medical facilities | n/a | n/a | n/a | n/a | | | | | ✓ | | | |
| Counselling facilities | n/a | n/a | n/a | n/a | ✓ | | ✓ | | ✓ | | | |
| Welfare services | n/a | W | n/a | n/a | ✓ | | ✓ | | ✓ | ✓ | ✓ | |

S = Only some of these facilities are currently available – WAT = Wheelchair accessible toilets

A = Talking lifts – T = Tactile controls – W = Lifts that are wheelchair accessible

| | University of Northumbria at Newcastle | | | | Norwich School of Art and Design | | | | University of Nottingham | | | |
|---|---|---|---|---|---|---|---|---|---|---|---|---|
| | Wheelchair access | Lifts | WAT | Induction loops | Wheelchair access | Lifts | WAT | Induction loops | Wheelchair access | Lifts | WAT | Induction loops |
| Lecture theatres | ✓ | ✓ | ✓ | S | ✓ | n/a | ✓ | ✓ | S | S | S | S |
| Teaching rooms | ✓ | ✓ | ✓ | S | S | S | S | ✓ | S | S | S | S |
| Libraries | ✓ | ✓ | ✓ | S | S | ○ | ✓ | ✓ | S | S | S | S |
| Computer rooms | ✓ | S | ✓ | S | ○ | ○ | ○ | ○ | S | S | S | S |
| Canteens | ✓ | ✓ | ✓ | ○ | ○ | ○ | ○ | ○ | S | S | S | ○ |
| Student Union | S | ✓ | ✓ | ○ | ○ | ○ | ○ | ○ | S | S | S | S |
| Student bar | ✓ | ✓ | ✓ | S | ○ | ○ | ○ | ○ | S | S | S | S |
| Gym | n/a | n/a | ✓ | n/a | ○ | ○ | ○ | ○ | ✓ | ✓ | ✓ | ○ |
| Swimming pool | ○ | n/a | n/a | n/a | ○ | ○ | ○ | ○ | ✓ | n/a | ✓ | ○ |
| Other sporting facilities | ✓ | ✓ | ✓ | ✓ | ○ | ○ | ○ | ○ | ○ | ○ | ○ | ○ |
| Medical facilities | ✓ | ✓ | ✓ | ✓ | ✓ | ○ | ○ | ○ | ✓ | n/a | ○ | ○ |
| Counselling facilities | ✓ | ✓ | ✓ | ✓ | ✓ | n/a | ○ | ○ | ✓ | ○ | ○ | ○ |
| Welfare services | ✓ | ✓ | ✓ | ✓ | ○ | ○ | ○ | ○ | ○ | ○ | ○ | ○ |

S = Only some of these facilities are currently available – WAT = Wheelchair accessible toilets
A = Talking lifts – T = Tactile controls – W = Lifts that are wheelchair accessible

| | Oak Hill Theological College | | | | Portsmouth University | | | | Queen Mary, University of London | | | |
|---|---|---|---|---|---|---|---|---|---|---|---|---|
| | Wheelchair access | Lifts | WAT | Induction loops | Wheelchair access | Lifts | WAT | Induction loops | Wheelchair access | Lifts | WAT | Induction loops |
| Lecture theatres | ✓ | n/a | ✓ | ✓ | ✓ | ✓ | ✓ | S | S | S | S | S |
| Teaching rooms | ✓ | ✓ | ✓ | | ✓ | ✓ | ✓ | S | S | S | S | S |
| Libraries | ✓ | ✓ | ✓ | | ✓ | ✓ | ✓ | ✓ | ✓ | ✓ | ✓ | |
| Computer rooms | ✓ | | ✓ | | ✓ | ✓ | ✓ | S | S | S | S | |
| Canteens | ✓ | | ✓ | | ✓ | ✓ | ✓ | S | ✓ | ✓ | ✓ | |
| Student Union | | | | | ✓ | ✓ | ✓ | S | ✓ | ✓ | ✓ | |
| Student bar | | | | | ✓ | ✓ | ✓ | | ✓ | ✓ | ✓ | |
| Gym | | | | | | | | | n/a | | | |
| Swimming pool | | | | | | | | | n/a | | | |
| Other sporting facilities | | | | | | | | | S | | | |
| Medical facilities | | | | | ✓ | | | | ✓ | n/a | ✓ | |
| Counselling facilities | | | | | ✓ | | | | ✓ | n/a | ✓ | ✓ |
| Welfare services | | | | | ✓ | | | | ✓ | n/a | ✓ | ✓ |

S = Only some of these facilities are currently available – WAT = Wheelchair accessible toilets

A = Talking lifts – T = Tactile controls – W = Lifts that are wheelchair accessible

| | Ravensbourne College | | | | Robert Gordon University | | | | Royal Academy of Music | | | |
|---|---|---|---|---|---|---|---|---|---|---|---|---|
| | Wheelchair access | Lifts | WAT | Induction loops | Wheelchair access | Lifts | WAT | Induction loops | Wheelchair access | Lifts | WAT | Induction loops |
| Lecture theatres | ✓ | ✓ | ✓ | | ✓ | ✓ | ✓ | ✓ | ✓ | ✓ | ✓ | |
| Teaching rooms | ✓ | ✓ | ✓ | | ✓ | ✓ | | | ✓ | ✓ | ✓ | |
| Libraries | ✓ | ✓ | ✓ | | ✓ | | | ✓ | | ✓ | ✓ | |
| Computer rooms | ✓ | ✓ | ✓ | | ✓ | ✓ | ✓ | | ✓ | ✓ | ✓ | |
| Canteens | ✓ | ✓ | ✓ | | ✓ | | | | ✓ | ✓ | ✓ | |
| Student Union | ✓ | ✓ | ✓ | | ✓ | | | | ✓ | ✓ | ✓ | |
| Student bar | ✓ | ✓ | ✓ | | ✓ | | | | | | | |
| Gym | | | | | n/a | | | | | | | |
| Swimming pool | | | | | n/a | | | | | | | |
| Other sporting facilities | | | | | n/a | | | | | | | |
| Medical facilities | | | | | ✓ | ✓ | ✓ | | | | | |
| Counselling facilities | | | | | ✓ | ✓ | ✓ | | | | ✓ | |
| Welfare services | ✓ | | | | ✓ | ✓ | ✓ | ✓ | ✓ | ✓ | ✓ | |

S = Only some of these facilities are currently available – WAT = Wheelchair accessible toilets

A = Talking lifts – T = Tactile controls – W = Lifts that are wheelchair accessible

Table 1: Accessibility

| | Royal Agricultural College | | | | Royal Northern College of Music | | | | Royal Scottish Academy of Music and Drama | | | |
|---|---|---|---|---|---|---|---|---|---|---|---|---|
| | Wheelchair access | Lifts | WAT | Induction loops | Wheelchair access | Lifts | WAT | Induction loops | Wheelchair access | Lifts | WAT | Induction loops |
| Lecture theatres | ✔ | n/a | ✔ | | S | n/a | ✔ | | ✔ | WA | ✔ | ✔ |
| Teaching rooms | ✔ | n/a | ✔ | | | T | S | | ✔ | WA | ✔ | ✔ |
| Libraries | ✔ | n/a | | | ✔ | n/a | ✔ | | ✔ | WA | ✔ | |
| Computer rooms | ✔ | n/a | ✔ | | ✔ | n/a | ✔ | | ✔ | WA | ✔ | |
| Canteens | ✔ | n/a | | | | n/a | ✔ | | ✔ | n/a | | |
| Student Union | ✔ | n/a | | | | ✔ | | | ✔ | n/a | ✔ | |
| Student bar | ✔ | n/a | | | | ✔ | | | ✔ | WA | | |
| Gym | | n/a | | | | | | | n/a | n/a | | |
| Swimming pool | | n/a | | | | | | | n/a | n/a | | |
| Other sporting facilities | | | | | | | | | n/a | n/a | | |
| Medical facilities | ✔ | | | | ✔ | n/a | n/a | | ✔ | n/a | | |
| Counselling facilities | | | | | | ✔ | ✔ | | ✔ | n/a | | |
| Welfare services | | | | | | ✔ | ✔ | ✔ | ✔ | n/a | | |

S = Only some of these facilities are currently available – WAT = Wheelchair accessible toilets
A = Talking lifts – T = Tactile controls – W = Lifts that are wheelchair accessible

|  | Royal Welsh College of Music and Drama | | | | College of St Mark and St John | | | | St Martins College | | | |
| --- | --- | --- | --- | --- | --- | --- | --- | --- | --- | --- | --- | --- |
|  | Wheelchair access | Lifts | WAT | Induction loops | Wheelchair access | Lifts | WAT | Induction loops | Wheelchair access | Lifts | WAT | Induction loops |
| Lecture theatres | ✓ | S | ✓ | *Portable systems available* | ✓ | ✓ | ✓ |  | ✓ | n/a | ✓ | ✓ |
| Teaching rooms | ✓ | S | ✓ | | ✓ |  |  | ✓ |  |  | ✓ | ✓ |
| Libraries | ✓ | ✓ | ✓ | |  |  |  | ✓ | ✓ | ✓ | ✓ | ✓ |
| Computer rooms | ✓ | ✓ | ✓ | |  |  |  |  | ✓ | ✓ | ✓ | ✓ |
| Canteens | ✓ | n/a | ✓ | | ✓ | ✓ | ✓ |  | ✓ | n/a | ✓ | ✓ |
| Student Union | ✓ | ✓ | ✓ | | ✓ | ✓ | ✓ |  | ✓ | ✓ | ✓ |  |
| Student bar | ✓ | ✓ | ✓ | | ✓ |  | ✓ | ✓ | ✓ | ✓ | ✓ |  |
| Gym | n/a | n/a | n/a | | ✓ |  |  |  | ✓ |  | ✓ |  |
| Swimming pool | n/a | n/a | n/a | |  |  |  |  |  |  |  |  |
| Other sporting facilities | n/a | n/a | n/a | |  |  |  |  | ✓ | n/a | ✓ |  |
| Medical facilities | n/a | n/a | n/a | | n/a | n/a | n/a | n/a | ✓ | n/a | ✓ |  |
| Counselling facilities | ✓ | S | ✓ | | ✓ | ✓ | ✓ | ✓ | ✓ | n/a | ✓ |  |
| Welfare services | ✓ | S | ✓ | | ✓ | ✓ | ✓ | ✓ | ✓ | n/a |  |  |

S = Only some of these facilities are currently available – WAT = Wheelchair accessible toilets

A = Talking lifts – T = Tactile controls – W = Lifts that are wheelchair accessible

| | Salford University | | | | University of Sheffield | | | | Southampton Institute | | | |
|---|---|---|---|---|---|---|---|---|---|---|---|---|
| | Wheelchair access | Lifts | WAT | Induction loops | Wheelchair access | Lifts | WAT | Induction loops | Wheelchair access | Lifts | WAT | Induction loops |
| Lecture theatres | ✔ | ✔ | ✔ | ✔ | S | S | S | S | ✔ | ✔ | | ✔ |
| Teaching rooms | | | | | S | S | S | S | | | | |
| Libraries | ✔ | ✔ | | | S | S | S | S | ✔ | ✔ | ✔ | |
| Computer rooms | ✔ | ✔ | | | S | S | S | S | ✔ | | | |
| Canteens | ✔ | ✔ | | | S | S | S | S | ✔ | | | |
| Student Union | ✔ | | | | ✔ | ✔ | ✔ | ✔ | ✔ | | ✔ | ✔ |
| Student bar | | | ✔ | | ✔ | | ✔ | | ✔ | ✔ | ✔ | ✔ |
| Gym | ✔ | n/a | | | ✔ | | | | | | | |
| Swimming pool | | | | | | | | | | | | |
| Other sporting facilities | | | | | | | | | | | | |
| Medical facilities | ✔ | ✔ | | | ✔ | | ✔ | | ✔ | | | |
| Counselling facilities | ✔ | ✔ | | | ✔ | | ✔ | | ✔ | | | |
| Welfare services | | | | | | | | | ✔ | | | |

S = Only some of these facilities are currently available – WAT = Wheelchair accessible toilets

A = Talking lifts – T = Tactile controls – W = Lifts that are wheelchair accessible

| | University of Southampton | | | | Staffordshire University | | | | University of Strathclyde | | | |
|---|---|---|---|---|---|---|---|---|---|---|---|---|
| | Wheelchair access | Lifts | WAT | Induction loops | Wheelchair access | Lifts | WAT | Induction loops | Wheelchair access | Lifts | WAT | Induction loops |
| Lecture theatres | S | S | S | S | ✓ | ATW | ✓ | ✓ | ✓ | | | |
| Teaching rooms | S | S | S | S | ✓ | ATW | ✓ | ✓ | ✓ | | | |
| Libraries | S | S | S | S | ✓ | ✓ | ✓ | ✓ | ✓ | | | |
| Computer rooms | S | S | S | S | ✓ | ✓ | ✓ | | ✓ | There are lifts where required | See university for details: not in every building | Limited provision |
| Canteens | ✓ | n/a | S | S | ✓ | ✓ | ✓ | | ✓ | | | |
| Student Union | S | ✓ | ✓ | S | ✓ | ✓ | ✓ | | ✓ | | | |
| Student bar | S | S | S | | ✓ | ✓ | ✓ | | S | | | |
| Gym | S | n/a | S | | ✓ | n/a | ✓ | ✓ | S | | | |
| Swimming pool | | | | | ✓ | ✓ | | | | | | |
| Other sporting facilities | S | | | | ✓ | n/a | n/a | | | | | |
| Medical facilities | ✓ | n/a | ✓ | | ✓ | TW | ✓ | ✓ | ✓ | | | |
| Counselling facilities | ✓ | n/a | ✓ | | ✓ | TW | ✓ | ✓ | ✓ | | | |
| Welfare services | ✓ | S | ✓ | | ✓ | | ✓ | ✓ | ✓ | | | |

S = Only some of these facilities are currently available – WAT = Wheelchair accessible toilets
A = Talking lifts – T = Tactile controls – W = Lifts that are wheelchair accessible

| | Surrey Institute of Art and Design | | | | Swansea Institute | | | | Teesside University | | | |
|---|---|---|---|---|---|---|---|---|---|---|---|---|
| | Wheelchair access | Lifts | WAT | Induction loops | Wheelchair access | Lifts | WAT | Induction loops | Wheelchair access | Lifts | WAT | Induction loops |
| Lecture theatres | S | | | | S | S | S | S | ✓ | ✓ | ✓ | ✓ |
| Teaching rooms | S | | | | S | S | S | S | ✓ | ✓ | ✓ | |
| Libraries | | W | ✓ | ✓ | ✓ | ✓ | ✓ | ✓ | ✓ | ✓ | ✓ | ✓ |
| Computer rooms | S | W | | | S | S | S | S | ✓ | ✓ | ✓ | |
| Canteens | S | | | | S | S | S | | ✓ | ✓ | ✓ | |
| Student Union | S | | | | S | S | | | ✓ | ✓ | ✓ | |
| Student bar | S | | | | ✓ | ✓ | ✓ | | | ✓ | ✓ | |
| Gym | | | | | ✓ | n/a | ✓ | | | | | |
| Swimming pool | | | | | n/a (Fitness centre) | n/a | n/a | | | | | |
| Other sporting facilities | | | | | ✓ | n/a | ✓ | | ✓ | ✓ | ✓ | ✓ |
| Medical facilities | | | | | ✓ | n/a | ✓ | | ✓ | ✓ | ✓ | ✓ |
| Counselling facilities | | | | | ✓ | n/a | ✓ | | ✓ | ✓ | ✓ | ✓ |
| Welfare services | | | | | ✓ | n/a | ✓ | | ✓ | ✓ | ✓ | ✓ |

S = Only some of these facilities are currently available – WAT = Wheelchair accessible toilets

A = Talking lifts – T = Tactile controls – W = Lifts that are wheelchair accessible

| | Trinity and All Saints University | | | | Trinity College, Carmarthenshire | | | | Trinity College of Music | | | |
|---|---|---|---|---|---|---|---|---|---|---|---|---|
| | Wheelchair access | Lifts | WAT | Induction loops | Wheelchair access | Lifts | WAT | Induction loops | Wheelchair access | Lifts | WAT | Induction loops |
| Lecture theatres | ✔ | | ✔ | ✔ | ✔ | ✔ | ✔ | S | n/a | n/a | n/a | n/a |
| Teaching rooms | ✔ | | ✔ | ✔ | ✔ | ✔ | ✔ | S | S | S | S | |
| Libraries | ✔ | | ✔ | ✔ | ✔ | n/a | ✔ | S | ✔ | ✔ | ✔ | |
| Computer rooms | ✔ | ✔ | ✔ | | ✔ | n/a | | | ✔ | ✔ | ✔ | |
| Canteens | ✔ | | ✔ | | ✔ | n/a | | | ✔ | ✔ | ✔ | |
| Student Union | ✔ | | ✔ | | | | ✔ | | ✔ | ✔ | ✔ | |
| Student bar | ✔ | | ✔ | | | | | | ✔ | ✔ | ✔ | |
| Gym | ✔ | | ✔ | | | | | | n/a | n/a | n/a | n/a |
| Swimming pool | | | | | | | | | n/a | n/a | n/a | n/a |
| Other sporting facilities | | | | | | | | | n/a | n/a | n/a | n/a |
| Medical facilities | ✔ | ✔ | ✔ | | ✔ | | ✔ | | ✔ | ✔ | ✔ | |
| Counselling facilities | ✔ | ✔ | ✔ | | ✔ | | ✔ | S | ✔ | ✔ | ✔ | |
| Welfare services | | | | | ✔ | | ✔ | | ✔ | ✔ | ✔ | |

S = Only some of these facilities are currently available – WAT = Wheelchair accessible toilets

A = Talking lifts – T = Tactile controls – W = Lifts that are wheelchair accessible

| Facility | University College Chichester | | | | University College Northampton | | | | University of Wales College of Medicine | | | |
|---|---|---|---|---|---|---|---|---|---|---|---|---|
| | Wheelchair access | Lifts | WAT | Induction loops | Wheelchair access | Lifts | WAT | Induction loops | Wheelchair access | Lifts | WAT | Induction loops |
| Lecture theatres | S | WT | ✓ | | ✓ | ✓ | ✓ | S | S | S | S | S |
| Teaching rooms | S | WT | ✓ | | ✓ | ✓ | ✓ | | S | S | S | S |
| Libraries | ✓ | WT | ✓ | | ✓ | ✓ | ✓ | | ✓ | ✓ | S | |
| Computer rooms | ✓ | W | ✓ | | ✓ | | ✓ | | S | ✓ | | |
| Canteens | ✓ | WA | ✓ | | ✓ | ✓ | ✓ | | ✓ | A | S | |
| Student Union | ✓ | W | ✓ | | ✓ | ✓ | ✓ | | ✓ | n/a | ✓ | |
| Student bar | ✓ | W | ✓ | | | | ✓ | | ✓ | n/a | ✓ | |
| Gym | ✓ | W | | | | | | | ✓ | n/a | | |
| Swimming pool | | | | | | | | | ✓ | n/a | | |
| Other sporting facilities | ✓ | n/a | ✓ | | | | | | n/a | n/a | n/a | |
| Medical facilities | ✓ | WA | ✓ | | ✓ | | | | n/a | n/a | | |
| Counselling facilities | ✓ | n/a | ✓ | | ✓ | | | | ✓ | ✓ | ✓ | |
| Welfare services | ✓ | n/a | ✓ | | ✓ | | | | ✓ | ✓ | ✓ | |

S = Only some of these facilities are currently available – WAT = Wheelchair accessible toilets
A = Talking lifts – T = Tactile controls – W = Lifts that are wheelchair accessible

| Facility | UWCN (University of Wales College Newport) | | | | University of Warwick | | | | University of the West of England | | | |
|---|---|---|---|---|---|---|---|---|---|---|---|---|
| | Wheelchair access | Lifts | WAT | Induction loops | Wheelchair access | Lifts | WAT | Induction loops | Wheelchair access | Lifts | WAT | Induction loops |
| Lecture theatres | ✓ | | | ✓ | ✓ | ✓ | ✓ | S | ✓ | | | ✓ |
| Teaching rooms | ✓ | | | | ✓ | ✓ | ✓ | | ✓ | | | |
| Libraries | ✓ | | | ✓ | ✓ | ✓ | ✓ | | ✓ | | | ✓ |
| Computer rooms | ✓ | | | | ✓ | ✓ | ✓ | | ✓ | | | |
| Canteens | ✓ | | | | ✓ | | ✓ | | ✓ | | | |
| Student Union | ✓ | | | | ✓ | ✓ | ✓ | | ✓ | | | |
| Student bar | | ✓ | | | ✓ | ✓ | ✓ | | ✓ | ✓ | | |
| Gym | | | | | n/a | n/a | n/a | | | | | |
| Swimming pool | | | | | | | | | | | | |
| Other sporting facilities | | | | | | | | | | | | |
| Medical facilities | ✓ | | | | ✓ | | | | ✓ | | | |
| Counselling facilities | ✓ | | | | ✓ | | | | ✓ | | | |
| Welfare services | ✓ | | | | ✓ | | | | ✓ | | | |

S = Only some of these facilities are currently available – WAT = Wheelchair accessible toilets

A = Talking lifts – T = Tactile controls – W = Lifts that are wheelchair accessible

| | Writtle College | | | | York St John College | | | |
|---|---|---|---|---|---|---|---|---|
| | Wheelchair access | Lifts | WAT | Induction loops | Wheelchair access | Lifts | WAT | Induction loops |
| Lecture theatres | ✓ | ✓ | ✓ | ✓ | ✓ | ✓ | ✓ | ✓ |
| Teaching rooms | ✓ | ✓ | ✓ | | ✓ | ✓ | ✓ | |
| Libraries | ✓ | ✓ | ✓ | | ✓ | | ✓ | ✓ |
| Computer rooms | ✓ | ✓ | ✓ | | ✓ | ✓ | ✓ | |
| Canteens | ✓ | n/a | ✓ | | ✓ | n/a | ✓ | |
| Student Union | | | ✓ | | | | ✓ | |
| Student bar | ✓ | n/a | ✓ | | ✓ | n/a | ✓ | |
| Gym | ✓ | n/a | ✓ | | ✓ | n/a | ✓ | |
| Swimming pool | n/a | | | | n/a | | | |
| Other sporting facilities | n/a | | | | n/a | | | |
| Medical facilities | n/a | | | | n/a | | | |
| Counselling facilities | ✓ | ✓ | | | ✓ | | | |
| Welfare services | ✓ | ✓ | | | ✓ | ✓ | | |

S = Only some of these facilities are currently available –
WAT = Wheelchair accessible toilets
A = Talking lifts – T = Tactile controls – W = Lifts that are wheelchair accessible

## Table 2: Facilities and services

This chart represents institutions that completed the table on the questionnaire. It does not cover every institution in the book. Where information was not available a blank has been left. Students interested in applying to a particular college should contact that institution direct to confirm what facilities and services they can offer. The publishers would welcome any additional information from institutions to be included in future editions.

| | University of Aberdeen | University of Wales Aberystwyth | ALRA | Arts Institute at Bournemouth | Aston University | University of Bath |
|---|---|---|---|---|---|---|
| Portable induction loops | ✓ | ✓ | | | S | ✓ |
| Video phones | | | | | | |
| Specialist software for students with dyslexia/ visual impairment | | ✓ | | ✓ | S | ✓ |
| Enlarged PC screens | ✓ | ✓ | | | ✓ | ✓ |
| Brailling facilities | | S | | | S | ✓ |
| Colour modification software | | ✓ | | | S | ✓ |
| Sign language interpreters | | ✓ | S | | S | S |
| Lipspeakers | | S | | | S | S |
| Speech-synthesised text | | ✓ | | | S | ✓ |
| Readers/notetakers | ✓ | ✓ | S | | ✓ | ✓ |
| Personal assistants | S | ✓ | S | | S | ✓ |
| Other | | Tactile output | | | Dyslexia support tutors, Visiting teacher service, Mentors | Orientation guides, Access map, Dyslexia tutors |

S = Facilities can be made available if needed.

| | Bath Spa University College | Birkbeck College University of London | University of Birmingham | Blackpool and The Fylde College | Bolton Institute | University of Bradford |
|---|---|---|---|---|---|---|
| Portable induction loops | | ✓ | ✓ | | ✓ | ✓ |
| Video phones | | S | | | | |
| Specialist software for students with dyslexia/visual impairment | ✓ | ✓ | S | ✓ | ✓ | ✓ |
| Enlarged PC screens | ✓ | ✓ | ✓ | ✓ | ✓ | ✓ |
| Brailling facilities | | | ✓ | ✓ | ✓ | ✓ |
| Colour modification software | S | | | | ✓ | ✓ |
| Sign language interpreters | S | S | S | ✓ | S | ✓ |
| Lipspeakers | S | S | | ✓ | S | S |
| Speech-synthesised text | S | ✓ | | ✓ | ✓ | ✓ |
| Readers/notetakers | S | S | ✓ | ✓ | S | ✓ |
| Personal assistants | S | S | S | | S | ✓ |
| Other | | | | | Specialist tutors (dyslexia) | Six support tutors |

S = Facilities can be made available if needed.

| | University of Brighton | British School of Osteopathy | Brunel University | University of Buckingham | Buckinghamshire Chilterns University Col. | Cambridge University |
|---|---|---|---|---|---|---|
| Portable induction loops | | S | ✓ | S | | ✓ |
| Video phones | | | | | | |
| Specialist software for students with dyslexia/visual impairment | ✓ | | ✓ | | ✓ | ✓ |
| Enlarged PC screens | ✓ | | ✓ | | ✓ | ✓ |
| Brailling facilities | S | | ✓ | | S | ✓ |
| Colour modification software | ✓ | | ✓ | S | S | |
| Sign language interpreters | S | S | ✓ | S | S | S |
| Lipspeakers | S | S | ✓ | S | S | S |
| Speech-synthesised text | ✓ | S | ✓ | S | S | S |
| Readers/notetakers | S | S | ✓ | | S | ✓ |
| Personal assistants | S | | | | S | ✓ |
| Other | | | Various support workers | | | |

S = Facilities can be made available if needed.

| | Canterbury Christ Church University College | University of Central England | University of Central Lancashire | Central School of Speech and Drama | Chester, University College | City University |
|---|---|---|---|---|---|---|
| Portable induction loops | ✓ | | | | S | S |
| Video phones | | | ✓ | | | S |
| Specialist software for students with dyslexia/ visual impairment | ✓ | ✓ | | S | S | S |
| Enlarged PC screens | S | | ✓ | S | S | S |
| Brailling facilities | ✓ | ✓ | ✓ | | S | S |
| Colour modification software | ✓ | ✓ | ✓ | | ✓ | S |
| Sign language interpreters | S | ✓ | S | S | S | S |
| Lipspeakers | S | ✓ | ✓ | S | S | S |
| Speech-synthesised text | S | ✓ | S | | S | S |
| Readers/notetakers | ✓ | ✓ | ✓ | S | S | S |
| Personal assistants | S | ✓ | ✓ | S | | S |
| Other | | | | | | |

S = Facilities can be made available if needed.

cv

| | Conservatoire of Acting and Musical Theatre | Courtauld Institute of Art | Coventry University | Croydon College | Cumbria Institute of the Arts | De Montfort University |
|---|---|---|---|---|---|---|
| Portable induction loops | | | ✓ | ✓ | | ✓ |
| Video phones | | | S | | | S |
| Specialist software for students with dyslexia/visual impairment | S | | ✓ | ✓ | S | ✓ |
| Enlarged PC screens | S | | ✓ | ✓ | | ✓ |
| Brailling facilities | | | ✓ | ✓ | | ✓ |
| Colour modification software | S | | ✓ | | | |
| Sign language interpreters | | | ✓ | ✓ | S | ✓ |
| Lipspeakers | | | ✓ | ✓ | | ✓ |
| Speech-synthesised text | | | S | ✓ | | |
| Readers/notetakers | S | | ✓ | ✓ | S | ✓ |
| Personal assistants | S | | ✓ | | S | ✓ |
| Other | | | | | | |

S = Facilities can be made available if needed.

Table 2: Facilities and services

| | University of Derby | University of Dundee | University of Durham | University of East Anglia | University of East London | Edge Hill |
|---|---|---|---|---|---|---|
| Portable induction loops | | | ✓ | ✓ | ✓ | ✓ |
| Video phones | | | S | | | |
| Specialist software for students with dyslexia/visual impairment | S | ✓ | ✓ | ✓ | ✓ | ✓ |
| Enlarged PC screens | S | ✓ | S | ✓ | S | ✓ |
| Brailling facilities | ✓ | ✓ | S | | S | ✓ |
| Colour modification software | | | S | | ✓ | ✓ |
| Sign language interpreters | ✓ | S | S | S | S | |
| Lipspeakers | | S | S | S | S | |
| Speech-synthesised text | S | ✓ | ✓ | ✓ | S | ✓ |
| Readers/notetakers | S | S | ✓ | S | ✓ | ✓ |
| Personal assistants | | S | ✓ | S | ✓ | ✓ |
| Other | | | | | | |

S = Facilities can be made available if needed.

| | Edinburgh College of Art | University of Essex | Falmouth College of Arts | Farnborough College of Technology | Glamorgan University | University of Gloucestershire |
|---|---|---|---|---|---|---|
| Portable induction loops | | S | ✓ | ✓ | ✓ | S |
| Video phones | | | | | | |
| Specialist software for students with dyslexia/visual impairment | ✓ | ✓ | ✓ | S | ✓ | ✓ |
| Enlarged PC screens | ✓ | | ✓ | ✓ | ✓ | ✓ |
| Brailling facilities | S | ✓ | ✓ | ✓ | ✓ | S |
| Colour modification software | S | | ✓ | ✓ | ✓ | |
| Sign language interpreters | S | S | S | ✓ | | S |
| Lipspeakers | S | S | S | S | | S |
| Speech-synthesised text | | S | | ✓ | ✓ | S |
| Readers/notetakers | S | | ✓ | S | ✓ | ✓ |
| Personal assistants | | | ✓ | | ✓ | ✓ |
| Other | | | | | ✓ | ✓ |

S = Facilities can be made available if needed.

| | Goldsmiths University of London | Guildford School of Acting | Harper Adams University College | Heriot-Watt University | University of Hertfordshire | Heythrop College |
|---|---|---|---|---|---|---|
| Portable induction loops | ✔ | | S | ✔ | ✔ | |
| Video phones | | | | | S | |
| Specialist software for students with dyslexia/visual impairment | ✔ | S | S | ✔ | ✔ | |
| Enlarged PC screens | ✔ | ✔ | | ✔ | ✔ | |
| Brailling facilities | | | S | S | S | ✔ |
| Colour modification software | S | S | S | S | ✔ | |
| Sign language interpreters | S | | S | S | S | ✔ |
| Lipspeakers | S | | S | S | S | ✔ |
| Speech-synthesised text | ✔ | | ✔ | ✔ | ✔ | |
| Readers/notetakers | S | | ✔ | ✔ | S | ✔ |
| Personal assistants | S | | S | S | S | |
| Other | | | | | | |

S = Facilities can be made available if needed.

| Facility | Holborn College | University of Huddersfield | University of Hull | Imperial College London | Keele University | Kent Institute of Art and Design |
|---|---|---|---|---|---|---|
| Portable induction loops |  | ✔ | ✔ | S | S | S |
| Video phones |  | S |  |  | ✔ |  |
| Specialist software for students with dyslexia/visual impairment | S | ✔ | ✔ | S |  | S |
| Enlarged PC screens | S | ✔ | ✔ | S | ✔ | S |
| Brailling facilities | S | S | ✔ | S | ✔ | S |
| Colour modification software | S | ✔ | ✔ | S | ✔ | S |
| Sign language interpreters |  | S |  | S | S | ✔ |
| Lipspeakers |  | S |  | S | S | S |
| Speech-synthesised text |  | ✔ |  | S | ✔ | S |
| Readers/notetakers | ✔ | ✔ | ✔ |  | ✔ | S |
| Personal assistants | ✔ | ✔ | ✔ |  | S | S |
| Other |  |  |  |  |  | Dyslexia tutors |

S = Facilities can be made available if needed.

| | University of Kent at Canterbury | King Alfred's Winchester | King's College London | Kingston University | Laban Centre | University of Wales, Lampeter |
|---|---|---|---|---|---|---|
| Portable induction loops | ✔ | ✔ | S | | | ✔ |
| Video phones | ✔ | | S | | | |
| Specialist software for students with dyslexia/visual impairment | ✔ | ✔ | ✔ | ✔ | S | ✔ |
| Enlarged PC screens | S | ✔ | | ✔ | S | ✔ |
| Brailling facilities | S | ✔ | | | S | S |
| Colour modification software | S | S | ✔ | | S | S |
| Sign language interpreters | S | S | S | S | S | S |
| Lipspeakers | S | S | S | S | S | |
| Speech-synthesised text | S | | S | | S | |
| Readers/notetakers | ✔ | ✔ | S | ✔ | S | ✔ |
| Personal assistants | ✔ | S | S | | S | S |
| Other | | | | | | |

S = Facilities can be made available if needed.

| | Leeds College of Music | University of Leeds | University of Lincoln | Liverpool Hope | LIPA | Liverpool John Moores University |
|---|---|---|---|---|---|---|
| Portable induction loops | ✓ | ✓ | S | ✓ | ✓ | ✓ |
| Video phones | S | | | | | |
| Specialist software for students with dyslexia/visual impairment | ✓ | ✓ | ✓ | ✓ | ✓ | ✓ |
| Enlarged PC screens | ✓ | ✓ | ✓ | ✓ | ✓ | S |
| Brailling facilities | S | ✓ | S | S | ✓ | ✓ |
| Colour modification software | S | ✓ | | | ✓ | ✓ |
| Sign language interpreters | S | S | | S | S | S |
| Lipspeakers | S | ✓ | | S | S | S |
| Speech-synthesised text | ✓ | ✓ | ✓ | | ✓ | |
| Readers/notetakers | S | ✓ | S | S | ✓ | ✓ |
| Personal assistants | S | ✓ | S | S | S | ✓ |
| Other | | | | | | |

S = Facilities can be made available if needed.

| | University of London | LAMDA | London Bible College | London Contemporary Dance School | The London Institute | London Metropolitan University |
|---|---|---|---|---|---|---|
| Portable induction loops | | | ✔ | S | S | S |
| Video phones | | | | S | | |
| Specialist software for students with dyslexia/visual impairment | S | | | S | S | ✔ |
| Enlarged PC screens | S | | ✔ | S | S | ✔ |
| Brailling facilities | S | S | | S | S | S |
| Colour modification software | S | | | S | S | S |
| Sign language interpreters | S | S | S | S | S | S |
| Lipspeakers | S | S | | S | S | ✔ |
| Speech-synthesised text | S | | | S | S | ✔ |
| Readers/notetakers | S | S | ✔ | S | S | ✔ |
| Personal assistants | S | S | ✔ | S | S | S |
| Other | | | | | | |

S = Facilities can be made available if needed.

| | LSE | London South Bank University | University of Loughborough | University of Luton | University of Manchester | Manchester Metropolitan |
|---|---|---|---|---|---|---|
| Portable induction loops | S | ✓ | ✓ | S | ✓ | ✓ |
| Video phones | | | | | S | S |
| Specialist software for students with dyslexia/visual impairment | ✓ | ✓ | ✓ | ✓ | ✓ | ✓ |
| Enlarged PC screens | S | ✓ | ✓ | ✓ | ✓ | |
| Brailling facilities | ✓ | | ✓ | S | ✓ | S |
| Colour modification software | S | | | | S | |
| Sign language interpreters | S | S | S | S | S | S |
| Lipspeakers | S | S | S | S | S | S |
| Speech-synthesised text | S | | S | S | ✓ | |
| Readers/notetakers | ✓ | S | ✓ | S | S | S |
| Personal assistants | | | ✓ | | ✓ | S |
| Other | | Dyslexia support tutors | | | | |

S = Facilities can be made available if needed.

| Facility | Middlesex University | Myerscough College | Napier University | National Film and Television School | University of Newcastle | Newman College of HE |
|---|---|---|---|---|---|---|
| Portable induction loops | S | S | ✓ | S | ✓ | ✓ |
| Video phones | S |  | ✓ |  |  |  |
| Specialist software for students with dyslexia/ visual impairment | ✓ | ✓ | ✓ | S | ✓ | T |
| Enlarged PC screens | ✓ | S | S | S | ✓ | T |
| Brailling facilities | ✓ | S | ✓ | S | S | S |
| Colour modification software | S | S |  | S |  | ✓ |
| Sign language interpreters | S | ✓ | S | S | S | S |
| Lipspeakers | S | S | S |  | S | S |
| Speech-synthesised text | ✓ | ✓ |  |  | S | ✓ |
| Readers/notetakers | ✓ | ✓ | S | S | S | ✓ |
| Personal assistants | ✓ | ✓ | S |  | S | ✓ |
| Other |  | Interactive whitescreens |  |  |  | Adjustable tables, Dictaphones, extended arm-rest, Alpha Smart portable WPs |

S = Facilities can be made available if needed.

| | North East Wales Institute of HE | University of Northumbria at Newcastle | Norwich School of Art and Design | University of Nottingham | Oak Hill Theological College | Paisley University |
|---|---|---|---|---|---|---|
| Portable induction loops | ✓ | ✓ | ✓ | ✓ | | ✓ |
| Video phones | | | | S | | |
| Specialist software for students with dyslexia/visual impairment | ✓ | ✓ | ✓ | ✓ | S | ✓ |
| Enlarged PC screens | ✓ | S | | ✓ | | ✓ |
| Brailling facilities | ✓ | S | | ✓ | | ✓ |
| Colour modification software | ✓ | S | | S | | ✓ |
| Sign language interpreters | S | S | S | S | | S |
| Lipspeakers | S | ✓ | S | S | | S |
| Speech-synthesised text | ✓ | S | | ✓ | | ✓ |
| Readers/notetakers | S | ✓ | S | ✓ | | S |
| Personal assistants | S | ✓ | | ✓ | | S |
| Other | | | Library support, personal support | | | |

S = Facilities can be made available if needed.

Table 2: Facilities and services

| | University of Plymouth | University of Portsmouth | Queen Margaret University College | Queen Mary, University of London | Queen's University Belfast | Ravensbourne College of Design |
|---|---|---|---|---|---|---|
| Portable induction loops | ✓ | ✓ | ✓ | ✓ | ✓ | |
| Video phones | | S | | | ✓ | |
| Specialist software for students with dyslexia/visual impairment | ✓ | ✓ | ✓ | ✓ | ✓ | |
| Enlarged PC screens | ✓ | ✓ | ✓ | | ✓ | |
| Brailling facilities | | ✓ | | ✓ | | |
| Colour modification software | ✓ | ✓ | | | | |
| Sign language interpreters | | S | | S | | S |
| Lipspeakers | | S | | S | | S |
| Speech-synthesised text | ✓ | ✓ | ✓ | ✓ | | |
| Readers/notetakers | | ✓ | | ✓ | ✓ | S |
| Personal assistants | ✓ | S | | ✓ | ✓ | S |
| Other | | | | | | |

S = Facilities can be made available if needed.

| | Reading University | College of Ripon and York | Robert Gordon University | Royal Academy of Music | Royal Agricultural College | Royal Holloway, University of London |
|---|---|---|---|---|---|---|
| Portable induction loops | | ✓ | ✓ | | S | |
| Video phones | | S | | | | |
| Specialist software for students with dyslexia/visual impairment | ✓ | ✓ | ✓ | S | S | ✓ |
| Enlarged PC screens | ✓ | | ✓ | S | | ✓ |
| Brailling facilities | ✓ | ✓ | | S | S | |
| Colour modification software | | | ✓ | | | ✓ |
| Sign language interpreters | ✓ | ✓ | | | S | |
| Lipspeakers | ✓ | | | | S | |
| Speech-synthesised text | ✓ | | ✓ | | S | ✓ |
| Readers/notetakers | ✓ | ✓ | S | S | S | ✓ |
| Personal assistants | ✓ | ✓ | S | S | S | ✓ |
| Other | | | | | | |

S = Facilities can be made available if needed.

| | Royal Northern College of Music | Royal Scottish Academy of Music and Drama | Royal Welsh College of Music and Drama | University of St Andrews | St George's Hospital Medical School | College of St Mark and St John |
|---|---|---|---|---|---|---|
| Portable induction loops | | | ✓ | ✓ | | ✓ |
| Video phones | | | S | | | |
| Specialist software for students with dyslexia/ visual impairment | S | ✓ | ✓ | ✓ | | ✓ |
| Enlarged PC screens | | S | ✓ | ✓ | | ✓ |
| Brailling facilities | | S | S | ✓ | | |
| Colour modification software | | S | S | ✓ | | |
| Sign language interpreters | S | S | S | S | ✓ | S |
| Lipspeakers | S | S | S | S | | S |
| Speech-synthesised text | | | ✓ | ✓ | | ✓ |
| Readers/notetakers | S | ✓ | S | ✓ | | ✓ |
| Personal assistants | | S | S | ✓ | | ✓ |
| Other | | | | | | |

S = Facilities can be made available if needed.

The Disabled Students' Guide to University

| | St Martin's College | St Mary's College | University of Salford | University of Sheffield | Sheffield Hallam University | University of Southampton |
|---|---|---|---|---|---|---|
| Portable induction loops | ✓ | | ✓ | ✓ | S | ✓ |
| Video phones | | | | | | S |
| Specialist software for students with dyslexia/visual impairment | | ✓ | ✓ | S | ✓ | ✓ |
| Enlarged PC screens | ✓ | | ✓ | S | ✓ | ✓ |
| Brailling facilities | ✓ | ✓ | ✓ | ✓ | S | ✓ |
| Colour modification software | ✓ | | | S | | ✓ |
| Sign language interpreters | S | | | S | ✓ | S |
| Lipspeakers | S | | | S | S | S |
| Speech-synthesised text | S | ✓ | ✓ | S | ✓ | ✓ |
| Readers/notetakers | ✓ | ✓ | | ✓ | ✓ | S |
| Personal assistants | S | | | ✓ | ✓ | S |
| Other | | | | | Electronic notetakers | |

S = Facilities can be made available if needed.

| | Southampton Institute | Spurgeon's College | Staffordshire University | University of Strathclyde | Surrey Institute of Art and Design | Surrey University, Roehampton |
|---|---|---|---|---|---|---|
| Portable induction loops | ✓ | | ✓ | S | ✓ | ✓ |
| Video phones | | | | S | S | |
| Specialist software for students with dyslexia/visual impairment | ✓ | | ✓ | ✓ | ✓ | ✓ |
| Enlarged PC screens | ✓ | | | ✓ | ✓ | ✓ |
| Brailling facilities | ✓ | | ✓ | ✓ | | |
| Colour modification software | ✓ | | | ✓ | ✓ | ✓ |
| Sign language interpreters | S | | S | S | ✓ | |
| Lipspeakers | S | | S | S | ✓ | ✓ |
| Speech-synthesised text | S | | | ✓ | ✓ | |
| Readers/notetakers | ✓ | | ✓ | S | ✓ | |
| Personal assistants | S | | S | S | ✓ | |
| Other | | | | | Learning mentor | |

S = Facilities can be made available if needed.

| | Sussex University | Swansea Institute of Higher Education | Teesside University | Thames Valley University | Trinity and All Saints | Trinity College, Carmarthen |
|---|---|---|---|---|---|---|
| Portable induction loops | ✔ | ✔ | ✔ | ✔ | ✔ | S |
| Video phones | | S | | | | |
| Specialist software for students with dyslexia/visual impairment | ✔ | ✔ | ✔ | ✔ | ✔ | ✔ |
| Enlarged PC screens | ✔ | ✔ | ✔ | ✔ | | ✔ |
| Brailling facilities | ✔ | S | ✔ | | S | |
| Colour modification software | | S | ✔ | | S | |
| Sign language interpreters | ✔ | S | ✔ | ✔ | S | |
| Lipspeakers | | S | ✔ | ✔ | S | |
| Speech-synthesised text | ✔ | S | ✔ | ✔ | ✔ | ✔ |
| Readers/notetakers | ✔ | S | ✔ | ✔ | S | ✔ |
| Personal assistants | S | S | ✔ | ✔ | ✔ | ✔ |
| Other | | Chairs providing back support can be loaned | | | | |

S = Facilities can be made available if needed.

| | Trinity College of Music | University College Chichester | University College London | University College Northampton | University College Worcester | UWCN |
|---|---|---|---|---|---|---|
| Portable induction loops | S✓ | ✓ | ✓ | S | | ✓ |
| Video phones | | | | | | |
| Specialist software for students with dyslexia/visual impairment | ✓ | ✓ | ✓ | | ✓ | ✓ |
| Enlarged PC screens | ✓ | ✓ | ✓ | | ✓ | ✓ |
| Brailling facilities | ✓ | ✓ | ✓ | ✓ | ✓ | |
| Colour modification software | ✓ | ✓ | ✓ | ✓ | | ✓ |
| Sign language interpreters | S | ✓ | ✓ | S | | ✓ |
| Lipspeakers | S | ✓ | | S | | ✓ |
| Speech-synthesised text | ✓ | ✓ | | ✓ | ✓ | ✓ |
| Readers/notetakers | ✓ | ✓ | | S | ✓ | ✓ |
| Personal assistants | S | ✓ | | S | | ✓ |
| Other | Training in use of specialist equipment | Dyslexia tutors, study skills tutors, video recorders with text readers | | | | |

S = Facilities can be made available if needed.

| | UWIC | University of Wales College of Medicine | University of Warwick | University of the West of England | Wimbledon School of Art | University of Wolverhampton |
|---|---|---|---|---|---|---|
| Portable induction loops | ✓ | ✓ | | ✓ | | ✓ |
| Video phones | | ✓ | | ✓ | | S |
| Specialist software for students with dyslexia/visual impairment | ✓ | ✓ | S | ✓ | | S |
| Enlarged PC screens | ✓ | ✓ | ✓ | S | | |
| Brailling facilities | S | S | S | ✓ | | S |
| Colour modification software | ✓ | S | ✓ | S | | S |
| Sign language interpreters | S | S | S | S | | ✓ |
| Lipspeakers | S | S | S | S | | ✓ |
| Speech-synthesised text | ✓ | | S | S | | ✓ |
| Readers/notetakers | ✓ | ✓ | ✓ | S | | ✓ |
| Personal assistants | ✓ | S | ✓ | S | | ✓ |
| Other | | | | | | |

S = Facilities can be made available if needed.

| | Writtle College | York St John College |
|---|---|---|
| Portable induction loops | ✔ | ✔ |
| Video phones | S | |
| Specialist software for students with dyslexia/visual impairment | S | ✔ |
| Enlarged PC screens | | ✔ |
| Brailling facilities | S | S |
| Colour modification software | S | ✔ |
| Sign language interpreters | ✔ | ✔ |
| Lipspeakers | ✔ | ✔ |
| Speech-synthesised text | ✔ | S |
| Readers/notetakers | ✔ | ✔ |
| Personal assistants | ✔ | ✔ |
| Other | | |

S = Facilities can be made available if needed.

# A–Z of institutions

| University of Aberdeen |
|---|

Regent Walk, King's College, Aberdeen AB24 3FX

*General Enquiries:*
Tel: 01224 272000
Fax: 01224 272576
Email: sras@abdn.ac.uk
Website: www.abdn.ac.uk

**Disability Adviser: Dr Lucy Foley**
**Tel: 01224 273935**
**Fax: 01224 273569**
**Email: l.foley@abdn.ac.uk**

## Fields of study:
Arts and social sciences; divinity; education; engineering; land economy and marine resource management; law; medicine; pure sciences.

➡ Part-time study: **Yes.**
➡ Distance learning: **No.**

## About the university:
Founded in 1495, the University of Aberdeen has two campuses, the main one being located in Old Aberdeen, which is a short bus ride to the bustling city centre and half an hour to the tranquillity of countryside and nearby hills.

| Total number of students: 11,000 full-time<br>Number of disabled students: 750 |
|---|

## Learning support staff and services:
Student Support Officer/Disability Adviser: Dr Lucy Foley.
There are also other staff members within Student Support Services, who provide advice and support for disabled students.
Provision of general support to all students and specifically to students with disabilities. Inform and advise on general issues; answer queries for people considering applying to the university; discuss specific arrangements once the student has been accepted; liaise with academic and non-academic departments to ensure that, where possible, these requirements are met; DSA application assistance.

## Home sweet home:
The university owns and manages a variety of accommodation including traditional halls of residence and self-catering flats. Flashing fire alarms and vibrating pillows have been installed in a number of

rooms for students who are D/deaf or hard of hearing and some of the flats have been adapted for wheelchair users. Further adaptations required may be catered for.

**Out and about:**
University: Dedicated parking spaces near accommodation and study areas.
Public transport: Access varies. Contact Disability Adviser for further information.

**Taking it easy:**
At university: The Sport and Recreation Services Department provides a wide range of facilities. It operates from two buildings: King's Pavilion and Butchart Recreation Centre. Access to all levels and appropriate changing and shower facilities are available in both buildings. Fully qualified and trained staff will assist in planning an exercise or activity programme. New suggestions for additions to what is on offer are welcomed. Safe access to and from the swimming pool is possible through the recent installation of a manually operated hoist system.
Locally: Most leisure facilities in the city are accessible.

**And another thing ...**
➡ Access around the campus will continue to be a high priority for the Estates Department, which has an ongoing programme of improvements.
➡ The university will strive to make all information more accessible, particularly via the Web, and respond to nationwide initiatives to improve accessibility.
➡ Staff training on disability awareness will be a high priority.

## The Disability Statement/Brochure:
Contents include: University policy; registration; disclosure; confidentiality; lectures and examinations arrangements; access; support services; other services and facilities; assessments and additional support; policy on dyslexia; future plans; the student voice; monitoring provision; disclaimer; alternative formats; useful contacts and feedback form.

| University of Abertay Dundee |
| --- |

Bell Street, Dundee DD1 1HG

*General Enquiries:* Information Office
Tel: 01382 308080
Fax: 01382 308081
Email: iro@abertay.ac.uk
Website: www.abertay.ac.uk

**Adviser for Students with Disabilities: John Petrie**
**Tel: 01382 308051**
**Fax: 01382 308118**
**Email: j.petrie@abertay.ac.uk**

## Fields of study:
Computing; business; science and engineering; social and health sciences.

➡ Part-time study: **Yes.**
➡ Distance learning: **Yes.**

## About the university:
The University of Abertay Dundee is located on a city-centre campus, with all of its buildings within a quarter-mile of each other. Dundee is situated at the mouth of the River Tay on Scotland's east coast and is the regional centre for Tayside.

| Total number of students: 6,397 | Number of disabled students: 273 |
| --- | --- |

## Learning support staff and services:
Student Advisory and Counselling Service
Adviser for Students with Disabilities: John Petrie.
Advice and support in claiming DSA; coordination of individual support such as reading and tutoring, notetaker or sign language interpreter; coordination of support at course level (e.g. enlarged lecture handouts, extra time for coursework, exam arrangements); advise relevant staff of personal requirements; support service for dyslexia in initial assessment, and study skills support throughout period of study.

## Home sweet home:
The university has no fully adapted residential accommodation for students with mobility difficulties, although there are two partially adapted residences that are self-catering with adapted en-suite bedrooms. One residence is close to the main campus whilst the other is located 1 mile from the university up a steep hill. Some university accommodation has university wardens whilst others may have a resident student sub-warden. Priority is given to students with disabilities when allocating accommodation. Wherever possible,

requests such as for a city-centre location or one with car parking space will be granted. Accommodation can be guaranteed for duration of student's course.

## Out and about:
University: A small number of dedicated parking spaces for disabled people.
Public transport: Buses, trains and stations are accessible.

## Taking it easy:
At university: There is not an accessible lift to the SA, which is located on the third floor of the Marketgait House. Contact the SA to find out what activities they offer – tel: 01382 227477;
email: a.mill@abertay.ac.uk. A new Student Centre is currently being built and will open in August 2004.
Locally: The local town is easily accessible from the main campus. The town centre is pedestrianised and there is a Shopmobility scheme.

## And another thing ...
➡ Most, but not all, of the university's buildings are wheelchair accessible. Where access is difficult or unachievable, alternative locations or timetables will be arranged wherever possible.
➡ The university is currently looking at networking a range of specialist software packages as well as having specific equipment available for use in the university and for loaning to students for use at home.
➡ A growing number of lecture and course notes are available on the Intranet, allowing easier access to information for all students.
➡ Academic material can be made available in alternative formats: disk; permission to tape lectures; enlarged handouts; copies of overheads; condensed book-lists.
➡ Library staff can obtain books and journals where necessary and concessions on printing charges are also available for visually impaired and dyslexic students.
➡ Future developments include the commissioning of a new Student Centre including a state-of-the-art SA, taking full account of the needs of all students.
➡ Teaching accommodation – access to most parts, and two lifts in the Kydd Building.
➡ Other teaching areas: Marketgait House – three floors and contains the School of Social and Health Studies. No lift.
➡ Library accessible.

## The Disability Statement/Brochure:

*Guide for Students with Disabilities* is available on the university's website.

It covers: Application; accommodation; university campus; facilities and equipment; DSA; student finance; personal support; appeals, grievances and complaints; equal opportunities policy; monitoring provision for disabled students; contacts and further information and future developments.

## Local public disability service providers:

Dundee Society for Visually Impaired People, 10–12 Ward Road, Dundee, 01382 227101.

Tayside Association for the Deaf, 36 Roseangle, Dundee 01382 221124; fax: 01382 200025; text: 01382 227052.

---

### Aberystwyth, The University of Wales

Old College, King Street, Aberystwyth SY23 2AX

*General Enquiries:* Admissions
Tel: 01970 622021
Fax: 01970 627410
Email: ug-admissions@aber.ac.uk
Website: www.aber.ac.uk

**Welfare Coordinator:**
**Gareth Jones**
**Tel: 01970 622955**
**Fax: 01970 621552**
**Email: gaj@aber.ac.uk**
**rha@aber.ac.uk**

## Fields of study:

American studies; biological sciences; computer science; education and lifelong learning; English; European languages; geography and earth sciences; history and Welsh history; international politics; law; management and business; mathematics; physics; rural studies; sport and exercise science; theatre, film and television studies.

➡ Part-time study: **Yes.**
➡ Distance learning: **Yes.**

## About the university:

The University of Wales, Aberystwyth, houses two campuses set in beautiful unspoilt scenery on the shores of Cardigan Bay. The university's Arts Centre is the largest in mid and west Wales. The Centre was recently extended in a £3.5 million project, and its exhibition programme is acknowledged by the Arts Council as a Centre of Excellence. As a major tourist centre, Aberystwyth has a wealth of restaurants and good places to eat and plenty of general activities and facilities.

| Total number of students: 8,749 | Number of disabled students: 663 |
|---|---|

## Learning support staff and services:
Student Support Services
Director, Student Support Services: Gareth Jones; Disability Officer: Rhun ap Harri.
Dyslexia Support Unit – one full-time and four part-time support tutors and postgraduate dyslexic support tutors.
Needs assessment; assistance with DSA applications; provision of auxiliary aids and services; notetaking, interpreting and transcription service; advice and guidance; one-to-one/group tuition for students with dyslexia; alternative examination, assessment and study arrangements; specialist support for students with dyslexia at the Language and Learning Centre, where qualified staff are available for advice and guidance; screening; arrangements of assessment by an educational psychologist; liaison with academic staff and external organisations.

## Home sweet home:
There are two flats in Pentre Jane Morgan (student village) with accommodation for PAs for students requiring 24-hour care. These flats have a choice of bathroom with a hoist or shower room with wheelchair access. The flats are integrated into houses that accommodate non-disabled students. They are equipped with modified working surfaces and electric wheelchair charging facilities. Flashing and vibrator alarm systems can be provided for students who are D/deaf or hard of hearing. Students with disabilities who would experience difficulties in accessing workstations will be given priority for student rooms that have been connected for computer access.
Accommodation can be guaranteed for duration of student's course.

## Out and about:
University: Dedicated parking spaces near both accommodation and study areas.
Public transport: Trains, train stations and some buses and taxis are accessible to people who are wheelchair users.

## Taking it easy:
At university: The policy is integration and inclusion. The SU has a Disabilities Officer elected every year.

Locally: The city centre is hilly and accessible. The pavements are tactile.

## And another thing ...

➡ The campus is situated on an 11% gradient. Many of the campus footpaths contain steps, and the steepness of the gradient in many cases precludes the introduction of simple ramps. Nevertheless progress has been made and work continues on providing better access between key areas by means of ramps or mechanical lifts. Because of the sloping nature of the site, many of the buildings also contain numerous different levels, not all of which are serviced by lifts. Several new buildings have been constructed recently and more refurbishment is planned that will improve access. A full physical access survey of the main Penglais campus has been undertaken by the RNIB and forms the basis for long-term improvements.

➡ Designated ('green card') areas within the main university libraries have a range of equipment to help students with visual impairments or who are D/deaf or hard of hearing.

➡ Specialist software is available on the university computer network to improve access for those with specific learning difficulties.

➡ The university attempts to respond to specific individual needs within academic departments and £10,000 has been made available annually to enable departments to respond to such needs as they arise. For example, the Institute of Biological Sciences has developed facilities over a period of three years to enable students with visual impairments to use their microscopy facilities.

➡ Back-up radio microphones can be provided in cases of emergency. Arrangements are made to record and copy lectures.

➡ Staff from the RNIB and RNID are available to increase awareness of disability issues and advise on individual cases.

➡ The Student Financial Support Office can provide advice and support for students claiming disability benefits including DSA. A small fund is available to provide financial or equipment support for students who are not eligible for support from the Access Fund or DSA. The Office can also provide financial support to qualifying students towards the cost of assessments.

➡ Voluntary groups serving the university include RNIB, RNID, Scope and CSV at a national or local level. The SU supports a 'Dim Prob' group of community volunteers. Prob encourages the participation of students with disabilities who can use their abilities to support people with learning difficulties or the elderly within the community.

## The Disability Statement/Brochure:
Includes: Existing policy; admission; assessments and examinations; accommodation; study support; staff development; finance; medical services; community links; SU; physical access; monitoring provision.

**Local disability public service provider:**
Ceredigion Social Services.

---

| **ALRA: Academy of Live and Recorded Arts** |
| --- |

RVP Building, Fitzhugh Grove, Trinity Road, London SW18 3SX

*General Enquiries:*
Tel: 020 8870 6475
Fax: 020 8875 0789
Email: acting@alra.demon.co.uk
Website: www.alra.demon.co.uk

**Student Support Coordinator:**
**Lee McOwan**
**Tel: Same**
**Fax: Same**
**Email: Same**

**Fields of study:**
Acting; dance and stage management; musical theatre.

➡ Part-time study: **Yes.**
➡ Distance learning: **No.**

**About the academy:**
ALRA is a private college with charitable status specialising in drama. It was founded in 1979 by Sorrel Carson, a professional actress, writer, dancer and teacher. The National Council for Drama Training first accredited the three-year acting course in 1984 and the one-year acting course in 2002. Both courses are validated by Trinity College London. The academy's accommodation includes a variety of teaching/rehearsal spaces, two theatres, purpose-built television and radio studios, a library and a communal café. The academy is a member of the Conference of Drama Schools (CDS) and European League of Institutes of the Arts (ELIA).

| Total number of students: 130 |
| --- |
| Number of disabled students: approx. 10 |

**Learning support staff and services:**
Student Support Coordinator/Registrar (full time): Lee McOwan
One-to-one/group tuition for students with dyslexia and liaison with external agencies.

**Home sweet home:**
ALRA does not provide student accommodation.

**Out and about:**
Academy: No dedicated parking spaces.
Public transport: Contact Access and Mobility (see Directory).

**Taking it easy:**
At academy: No specific social support.
Locally: The city centre is flat but not very accessible. The pavements are *not* tactile. Contact Wandsworth Council for further information, and Artsline (see Directory).

**And another thing ...**
➡ The academy says: 'We are always willing to try to accommodate students with disabilities, but our buildings and the nature of the courses make this difficult.'
➡ As a government dance and drama award provider the academy has access to disability funds for award students, who so far have mostly been students with dyslexia.

## The Disability Statement/Brochure:
No disability statement.

| Anglia Polytechnic University |
| --- |

East Road, Cambridge CB1 1PT

*General Enquiries:*
Tel: 0845 271 3333
Fax: 01225 417701 ext: 2598
01245 493131 ext: 3298
Email: answers@apu.ac.uk
Website: www.apu.ac.uk

**Student Adviser: Iain Hood/**
**Penny Baldwin**
**Tel: 01223 363271**
**Fax: 01223 417719**
**Email: i.i.hood@apu.ac.uk**
**p.baldwin@apu.ac.uk**
**Text: 01245 25915**

**Fields of study:**
Applied sciences; arts and letters; business; community health and social studies; design and communication systems; education; health care practice; language and social sciences; law.

➡ Part-time study: **Yes.**
➡ Distance learning: **Yes.**

## About the university:
Anglia Polytechnic University is located on three campuses: one at Cambridge and two at Chelmsford. A new business and management centre, the Michael A Ashcroft Building, opened in 2003. This state-of-the-art building is located at the Rivermead campus in Chelmsford.

| Total number of students: 28,000   Number of disabled students: 900 |
| --- |

## Learning support staff and services:
There is a learning support centre on both the main campuses. In each case this comprises student advisers, dyslexia and disability advisers, IT and study skills services.

The university funds an Access Centre as a member of the National Federation of Access Centres. There are seven members of staff here who will recommend equipment, provide training in its use, and continue to be available to advise students on more complex applications and upgrades. A system of disability coordinators is established in most fields and departments, who liaise between their colleagues, students and members of the Learning Support Team. There is also a Student Support Scheme.

## Home sweet home:
On-campus rooms will be adapted as necessary, providing the accommodation office has enough notice. Accommodation can be guaranteed for duration of student's course.

## Out and about:
University: Dedicated parking spaces near accommodation, but demand often exceeds supply. Parking in the Cities of Cambridge and Chelmsford is difficult for everyone.

Public transport: The local rail transport is not accessible, though a fleet of accessible buses now covers Cambridge.

## Taking it easy:
At university: The university's gym is accessible.

Locally: Cambridge is pedestrianised and the area is very flat. Cambridge County Council provides an access guide.

## And another thing …
➡ Access varies at the three campuses. See www.apu.ac.uk/stu_services/.
➡ The university now has a fully functional Regional Transcription Centre, which is able to provide key documents in a range of alternative formats for visually impaired and dyslexic students.

The Centre also conducts awareness training for academic and support staff both internally and externally on a consultative basis.

➡ The Learning Support Team and many of the policies it has recommended have been embedded in the university following the team's successful completion of the HEFCE-funded 'Learner Support and Support for Learning Project.' The EASIER project aims to extend the expertise gained by Access Centre staff and members of the team to other universities and further education institutions in the region.

## The Disability Statement/Brochure:

Brief document containing information on: Current policy; admissions; teaching; assessment and examinations; current provision; services; planned developments in provision, information and contacts.

## Local disability public service providers:

Cambridge County Council.
Essex County Council.

---

| The Arts Institute at Bournemouth |
| --- |

Wallisdown, Poole, Dorset BH 13 5HH

*General Enquiries:*
Tel: 01202 533011
Fax: 01202 537729
Email: general@aib.ac.uk
Web: www.aib.ac.uk

**Disability Coordinator: Carolyn Atherton**
**Tel: 01202 363291**
**Fax: 01202 537729**
**Email: catherton@aib.ac.uk**

### Fields of study:

Art; art and events; costume; design; fashion; film and animation; garden design; graphic design; illustration; information technology; model making; new media; performing arts; photography.

➡ Part-time study: **Yes.**
➡ Distance learning: **No.**

### About the institute:

The Arts Institute at Bournemouth focuses exclusively upon contemporary art, design and media. The Library and Learning Resource Centre, which houses a number of paintings and sculptures that form part of the Arts Council Reserve Collection of British Art, won the Poole Pride of Place Award in 2000. Bournemouth, which has a large, cosmopolitan student population with a vibrant club scene, is situated on the south coast within the county of Dorset. Dorset is an area of outstanding natural beauty with miles of sandy beaches, quaint villages and beautiful countryside.

| Total number of students: 3,208 | Number of disabled students: 575 |
| --- | --- |

## Learning support staff and services:
Learning Support
Full-time staff: Learning Support Coordinator: Brian Long; Lecturers/Tutors: Ludmila Machura and Ann Meacher.
Part-time staff: Lecturers/Tutors: Louise Higgs and Rose Smith; Administrator: Angela Bastable.
Needs assessment carried out on the premises by Southampton CELT (Centre for Enabling and Learning Technologies); assistance with DSA applications; provision of auxiliary aids and services; advice and guidance; one-to-one/group tuition for students with dyslexia; alternative examination, assessment and study arrangements; liaison with external organisations; DAST (Dyslexia Adult Screening Test); support of FE students and international students.

## Home sweet home:
There are five adapted bedrooms with wheelchair access, adapted kitchen and lift within the halls of residence.
Accommodation *cannot* be guaranteed for duration of student's course.

## Out and about:
Institute: Dedicated parking spaces near both accommodation and study areas.
Public transport: Some buses, trains, train stations and taxis are accessible to people who are wheelchair users or who have visual impairments. Look on the institute's website for information about local transport and the relevant contacts.

## Taking it easy:
Institute: There is no gym, swimming pool or sporting facilities at the institute. The student bar is wheelchair accessible.
Locally: City centre is hilly but accessible. Some of the town's facilities are accessible and there is a ShopMobility scheme. The pavements are tactile.

## Aston University

Aston Triangle, Birmingham B4 7ET

*General Enquiries:*
Tel: 0121 359 3611
Fax: 0121 359 6350
Email: prospectus@aston.ac.uk
Website: www.aston.ac.uk

**Student Services Adviser: Sian Howarth**
**Tel: 0121 359 3611 ext: 5432**
**Fax: 0121 359 0985**
**Email: s.l.howarth@aston.ac.uk**

### Fields of study:
Business; engineering and applied science; languages and European studies; life and health sciences.

➡ Part-time study: **Yes.**
➡ Distance learning: **Yes.**

### About the university:
The compact, flat Aston campus is characterised by trees, water and plenty of green space. All teaching, residential, accommodation and most recreational facilities are on one site at Aston Triangle. It is set in the heart of Birmingham, a major centre for entertainment, business, culture and sport. Birmingham is conveniently central to an extensive network of motorways and railways.

Total number of students: 7,420     Number of disabled students: 263

### Learning support staff and services:
Disability and Additional Needs Unit (DANU)
Full-time Disability Coordinator: Sian Howarth; Full-time Disability Assistant: Keren Mousley.
Advise and support students and coordinate all aspects of academic and pastoral welfare; orientation on arrival; needs assessments; assistance in DSA applications and access funds; liaison with departments; arrange tests for dyslexia on site; provision of auxiliary aids and services (some services are subject to availability and successful application of funding); coordination of study support, BSL interpreters, dyslexia support tutors, Visiting Teacher Service, etc.; support service for students with mental health issues; liaison with residences regarding accessible accommodation; information and liaison with other support services, e.g. social services, counselling; alternative examination arrangements.

**Home sweet home:**
Rooms with a vibrating emergency alerter system and visual
doorbells; en-suite bathrooms with adaptations; larger rooms with
wheelchair user access; mobility-related equipment such as hoists,
grab rails and adapted beds and general adaptations for wheelchair
users are available. Rooms for PAs can be provided. Lifts with audible
announcements and tactile buttons.
Accommodation can be guaranteed for duration of student's course.

**Out and about:**
University: Dedicated parking spaces near both accommodation and
study areas. Students living off campus may arrange for car parking
space by contacting Security.
Public transport: Some buses are accessible. The local train system is
accessible to people who are wheelchair users and people who have
a visual impairment. The nearest train station is New Street,
Birmingham, which is fully accessible. Contact Travel West Midlands
for further information. TOA have taxis that are accessible for
wheelchair users.

**Taking it easy:**
At university: The Students' Guild has six floors (including a
basement) with lift access to all but the top floor. Access to all the
offices, shops, society meeting rooms, music venues, cafés, and bars
is possible by wheelchair. The main front entrance of the Guild has
two steep flights of steps. During the day wheelchair access is
possible directly from the main building of the university via a bridge.
During the evening this is closed and access is possible through the
basement entrance. The non-academic facilities on Aston Triangle
campus are generally accessible. The Woodcock Sports Centre
(which houses a swimming pool, sports halls and gym) is wheelchair
accessible. The male and female changing rooms are tricky to
access for wheelchair users, however, as the doorways are narrow in
places. An audible fire alarm is fitted and the pool area has flashing
lights and a horn to alert swimmers to leave the pool. Access to the
Gem Sports Centre (sports halls and courts) is flat, the weights room
on the upper level is not wheelchair accessible.
Locally: The city centre is now almost totally pedestrianised and
reasonably flat. The town facilities are accessible and there is a
Shopmobility scheme, which operates from Snow Hill station. The
pavements are tactile. There is a local area access guide called *The
Disability Access Charter*.

## And another thing ...

➡ All floors of the library are accessible by lift and there is a RADAR toilet on the first floor.

➡ The library is able to send books to you by post and offers a photocopying service, e-journals and can provide extended book loans by arrangement.

➡ Aston University in conjunction with Birmingham University and the University of Central England runs the Birmingham Universities PA Scheme (BUPAS), which recruits and trains student to provide a variety of support for students with disabilities and individual needs, including: notetakers; help with lab work; library assistance and amanuensis.

➡ A focus group is being established via the Students' Guild. This comprises student members who pass on the issues or complaints raised at their meetings to the Disability Working Party (a formal university committee).

## The Disability Statement/Brochure:

*Guide for Students with Disabilities and Specific Learning Difficulties*
Available on disk, enlarged, in Braille and on the university website:
www.Aston.ac.uk/welfareservices/disability

## Local disability public service providers:

BID (Birmingham Institute for the Deaf) 0121 246 6100.
Focus (Birmingham) 0121 428 5000.
Disability West Midlands 0121 414 1616; email: disabilitywm.org.uk.

---

| **Barnsley College** |
| --- |

PO Box 266, Church Street, Barnsley S70 2YW

*General Enquiries:* Admissions
Tel: 01226 216216
Fax: 01226 216613
Email: admissions@barnsley.ac.uk
Website: www.barnsley.ac.uk

**Additional Support Coordinator:**
**Darren Ruse**
**Tel: 01226 216192**
**Fax: 01226 216465**
**Email: d.ruse@barnsley.ac.uk**

## Fields of study:

Business; cultural studies; health and social science; humanities and science; service industries.

➡ Part-time study: **Yes.**
➡ Distance learning: **Yes.**

## About the college:
Barnsley College is now one of the largest tertiary colleges in the country, with a national and international reputation for innovation. The college's teaching sites are all within easy reach of each other and the town centre. Barnsley is in the centre of the UK, just off the M1 motorway, between Sheffield and Leeds.

## Learning support staff and services:
Additional Support Service
Additional Support Coordinator: Darren Ruse.
Additional Support and Additional Learning Support are cross-college processes that offer guidance, assessment and support to students with individual learning requirements. The service includes: ongoing assessment of needs; technical, targeted provision; provision to assist students with numeracy and literacy requirements; access to assistive IT equipment and training; provision of specialist tuition for dyslexic students; arrangement of curriculum and communication support for students with sensory impairments; alternative examination arrangements; adaptation of learning materials in the learner's preferred medium; enable tutors to modify the planning and delivery of their teaching programmes; provision of support for short-term injuries or health concerns; provision of learning support assistants to assist students with mobility requirements and/or personal needs. The service aims to equalise opportunities.

## Home sweet home:
The list of accommodation is available on the college Website. Accommodation can be guaranteed for duration of student's course.

## Out and about:
College: Dedicated parking spaces on each major site.
Public transport: Local transport is not accessible.

## Taking it easy:
At college: Several tables in the refectories on the Old Mill Lane and the Huddersfield Road sites have been adapted for wheelchair user access. All refectories are accessible. The college has recently built an accessible single storey multi-function hall on the Honeywell site for use by sports, performing arts and music departments. Contact the SA (tel. 01226 216445) for information on the facilities and activities it offers.
Locally: Old Mill Lane, Eastgate House and Church Street sites are situated in the town centre with easy access to many banks and shops.

## And another thing …

- ➡ Many sites are fully accessible. Site access sheets are available from all receptions.
- ➡ Relocation of classes to accessible venues is possible when prior notice is given.
- ➡ The college employs sign language interpreters from the RNID on a lease basis.
- ➡ Support workers to help with mobility are available, as are personal readers/writers and proofreaders.
- ➡ Computer software/hardware with ergonomic mouse facilities and ergonomic keyboard.
- ➡ Support may extend to practical work, field trips and placements.
- ➡ The Learning Information Service can help with welfare rights advice and information on money matters, including DSA.
- ➡ The college does not have its own medical team. There are a number of trained first aiders. There is a room on each of the major sites where you can rest or take medication.
- ➡ Brailling facilities.
- ➡ LUNAR software for enlarging text on screen for people with visual impairments and CCTV system, VDU enhancement and add-on magnification screens.
- ➡ Software Texthelp for students with dyslexia.
- ➡ Voice activation systems such as 'Dragondictate'.
- ➡ Lip readers, notetakers and sign language interpreters for students who are D/deaf or hard of hearing.
- ➡ Communicators; induction loops in major areas including the large lecture theatre, but not across the college; mobile radio amplification systems; hearing aid; textphone in main reception; video reader.
- ➡ The libraries and computers located at the Old Mill Lane and Honeywell sites are accessible.
- ➡ There are accessible toilet facilities at all sites except at the Shambles Street site (Ashion Innovation Centre).

## The Disability Statement/Brochure:

*Breaking Barriers*
Includes: Policy; admissions; education, facilities and support; other support; assessment and examinations; physical access by site; complaints; future policy; useful telephone numbers. A4, ten pages.

## Local disability public service provider:

DIAL, Disability Information and Advice Line, Barnsley 01226 240273.

| University of Bath |
|---|

Claverton Down, Bath BA2 7AY

*General Enquiries:*
Tel: 01225 383019
Fax: 01225 386366
Email: admissions@bath.ac.uk
Website: www.bath.ac.uk

**Student Advisers: Philippa Kerin
and Adrienne Miles
Tel: 01225 383241
Fax: 01225 386709
Email: learningsupport@bath.ac.uk**

**Fields of study:**
Engineering and design; humanities and social sciences;
management; science.

➡ Part-time study: **Yes.**
➡ Distance learning: **Yes.**

**About the university:**
Founded in 1966, the modern University of Bath is a purpose-built
development. The university is compact, with all major facilities
located close to a central pedestrian parade set in its 200-acre
greenfield site. The city of Bath was first exploited by the Romans,
who were attracted to the hot springs. The city was rediscovered by
eighteenth-century society who chose to incorporate 'taking the
waters' as part of their social routine. Construction of the elegant
Pump Rooms and Assembly Rooms, the Circus and Royal Crescent
and the unique Puleney Bridge all began during this period. Today the
historic city of Bath still attracts many visitors.

| Total number of students: 6,287 Number of disabled students: 560 |
|---|

**Learning support staff and services:**
Learning Support Service
One Learning Support Manager, full time: Morag Kiziewicz; one full-
time and one part-time Student Adviser: Philippa Kerin and Adrienne
Miles; two full-time and one part-time admin staff: Kathy Miller,
Michelle Czechak and Sandra Jefferies; three part-time, one-to-one
tutors; two part-time IT staff; up to 30 notetakers/academic
assistance staff.
Advice; support for open day and interview visits; guidance on
access around the campus; ongoing support; academic support;
alternative examination arrangements; liaison with academic
departments; arrangement of DSA; running of a CSV project to
support students' personal needs in and around campus.

All support is provided for. However, in order to ensure full appropriate support, students are required to contact the Learning Support Service, email: learningsupport@bath.ac.uk or visit the Website: www.bath.ac.uk/learningsupport.

## Home sweet home:
Integrated accommodation block on campus with adapted rooms – adapted kitchen, bathroom, wheelchair access room for charging electric wheelchairs. Extra room for PAs. Adaptation for students who are D/deaf or hard of hearing.

Accommodation can be guaranteed for duration of student's course for medical conditions. For information please contact Del Davis in Accommodation Services on: 01225 386550.

## Out and about:
University: Dedicated parking spaces near both accommodation and study areas. Lift access to university buildings and ramp access on to the main level of the university. Access Audit has been recently completed.

Public transport: Local bus services to town centre and shops are accessible (call Local Authority for details: 01225 477000). The university is at the top of a steep hill. There is no taxi scheme for disabled people operating in the area.

## Taking it easy:
At university: All services are available. There is good access to most social areas, including cafés, bars, sports and arts facilities. The access to the SU Venue Bar is limited for those with mobility disabilities.

Locally: The local town is relatively flat and accessible, but the roads leading to the city centre are on a steep hill. Some of the town facilities are accessible. There is a Shopmobility scheme and some pavements are tactile. Please contact Bath and North East Somerset (B&NES) Council for details (see below).

## And another thing …
➡ A detailed access map for students with disabilities is available.
➡ Weekly IT 'drop-in' for enabling technology.
➡ There is a pool of equipment available for loan to students not in receipt of DSA.
➡ Alternative furniture, including adjustable-height desks and stools, available for use in the library and Learning Centre and during exams.
➡ There is a Students' ACCESS group for students with disabilities and specific learning difficulties.

- ➡ AWARE: Academic and Student Welfare Advice and Representation is available to provide support.
- ➡ Learning Support is a member of Skill.
- ➡ The university funds educational psychologist assessments for registered students and discretionary funding for support services where needed.
- ➡ Members of staff not already mentioned above who are designated to support students with disabilities are as follows: Admissions: Leslie Currie 01225 826826 ext 6800, email: L.L.Currie@bath.ac.uk; Careers Advice: Diane Hay 01225 826009, email: D.Hay@bath.ac.uk; Computing Services: Chris Carr 01225 8268226 ext 6112, email: bush@bath.ac.uk; Library and Learning Centre: Sheila Page 01225 826826 ext 6835, email: S.D.Page@bath.ac.uk
- ➡ Liz Davies, Counsellor and Chris Mills, Assistant Counsellor can be contacted in Counselling Services on 01225 825461 or emailed: E.V.Davies@bath.ac.uk; C.A.Mills@bath.ac.uk.

## The Disability Statement/Brochure:
*Information for Students with Disabilities*
Contents include: Applications; facilities and equipment; campus access; support systems; sources of support; examinations and assessments; disabled students learning at a distance; financial support; monitoring; future developments.

## Local disability public service providers:
Sharon Brookes, Access Officer, 01225 477670.
B&NES Council 01225 477000.

---

### Bath Spa University College
Newton Park, Newton St Loe, Bath BA2 9BN

| | |
|---|---|
| *General Enquiries:* | **Disability Officer: vacant** |
| Tel: 01225 875875 | **Tel: 01225 875541** |
| Fax: 01225 875444 | **Fax: 01225 875857** |
| Email: enquiries@bathspa.ac.uk | **Email: disability@bathspa.ac.uk** |
| Website: www.bathspa.ac.uk | |

## Fields of study:
Applied sciences; art and music; education and human sciences; humanities.

➡ Part-time study: **Yes.**
➡ Distance learning: **Yes.**

## About the university:

Bath Spa University College is located on two campuses at Newton Park and Sion Hill. The grounds of the main campus at Newton Park were designed by Capability Brown in the eighteenth century, and are currently being restored to their original design. This site is located 4 miles from the lively city centre of Bath whilst Sion Hill is within walking distance. Bath is England's only World Heritage City and is famous for its Roman Baths, romantic riverside and elegant Georgian architecture.

| Total number of students: 4,500 | Number of disabled students: 312 |
| --- | --- |

## Learning support staff and services:

Disability Office
Assistance with DSA applications; provision of auxiliary aids and services; advice and guidance; one-to-one/group tuition for students with dyslexia; alternative examination, assessment and study arrangements; support service for students with mental health problems; liaison with external organisations.

## Home sweet home:

There are six rooms adapted for disabled students with accessible kitchens with lowered work surfaces, sink, etc. and bathrooms adapted with handrails and alarmed. Accommodation can be guaranteed for duration of student's course.

## Out and about:

College: Most of the college's main buildings have nearby car parks with dedicated parking spaces for drivers with disabilities. Advice on the most convenient places to park and the best level routes into accessible buildings can be given by the Estates Surveyor (see below). Alison Cox, the Transport Officer, can discuss and arrange all aspects of your transport requirements. This can include free travel between the two campuses and/or college trips (tel: 01225 875461; email: a.cox@bathspa.ac.uk).
Public transport: Local transport is not accessible to people who are wheelchair users, but is accessible for people with visual impairments – contact Alison Cox for further information (see above). Triple A, the taxi scheme for disabled people, operates in the area.

## Taking it easy:
At college: The SU office and shop at Newton Park are accessible, as are the refectory and snack bar. The student bar is inaccessible. Locally: The city centre is hilly but accessible as are the town facilities. There is a Shopmobility scheme and the pavements are tactile.

## And another thing …
➡ The Newton Park campus is mostly on fairly flat and level ground with many new buildings. The Sion Hill campus is on very hilly ground and includes a listed Georgian crescent.
➡ Wheelchair users should note that some buildings on campus (in particular the historic listed buildings) are currently not wheelchair accessible. Nevertheless most of the premises are accessible to people with a mobility impairment, and the college is able to take additional actions, such as retimetabling classes, or providing office services (such as registry) in accessible locations.
➡ The college is committed to maximising access for all disabilities and has an improvement plan that includes a full access audit and an ongoing schedule of adaptations (contact Estates Surveyor, tel: 01225 875631; email: m.Osborn@bathspa.ac.uk).
➡ Bath Spa is actively seeking to increase the number of its disabled students. Other future developments include increased provision of assistive technology and increased provision for students with mental health difficulties, sensory disabilities, dyslexia and other learning difficulties.
➡ The college has links with Bath Dyslexia Institute, the Bristol Centre for the Deaf, the Bath Association for Mental Health, RNIB and the Equal Opportunities Higher Education Network.
➡ The ground floor of the library at Newton Park is accessible to wheelchair users.

## The Disability Statement/Brochure:
The university no longer produces one as 'it has been superseded by the new law'.

## Local disability public service providers:
RNID.
Centre for Visual Impairment.

## Birkbeck College, University of London

Malet Street, Bloomsbury, London WC1E 7HX

*General Enquiries:*
Tel: 020 7631 6000
Fax: 020 7631 6270
Email: admissions@bbk.ac.uk
Website: www.bbk.ac.uk

**Disability Coordinator: Mark Pimm**
**Tel: 020 7631 6315**
**Email: m.pimm@bbk.ac.uk**
**Fax: 020 7631 6307**

### Fields of study:
Arts and cultural studies; biological and chemical sciences; computer science and information systems; crystallography; earth sciences; economics, mathematics and statistics; English and humanities; geography; history, classics and archaeology; history of art, film and visual media; languages, linguistics and culture; law; management and organisational psychology; philosophy; politics and sociology; psychology; social and natural sciences.

➡ Part-time study: **Yes.**
➡ Distance learning: **Yes.**

### About the college:
On 2 December 1823 some 2,000 people flocked to the Crown & Anchor Tavern on the Strand to witness George Birkbeck and his supporters launch London's first ever Mechanics' Institution dedicated to the education of working people. From radical beginnings Birkbeck has developed into one of the country's leading specialists in part-time higher education. In 1996 it launched one of the first tutor-assisted, university-level courses to be taught entirely over the Internet. Since then further online courses have enabled students in economically emerging regions to study at Birkbeck for a fraction of the cost of coming to Britain. Students are divided into tutorial groups according to their time zones, illustrating the truly global nature of the courses.

Total number of students: 6,000     Number of disabled students: 360

### Learning support staff and services:
Disability Office
Two full-time and two part-time staff, including: Disability Coordinator: Mark Pimm; Disability Administrative Assistant: Elizabeth Maingay, tel: 020 7631 6336, email: e.maingay@bbk.ac.uk.
Assistance in application to the college; assistance with enrolment

and registration; support and advice with travel, parking, physical access and financial support including assistance in DSA applications; assistance with obtaining college funds and access funds; arranging and conducting needs assessment; advice and assistance with the purchase of special equipment; recruiting, supporting and paying PAs, dyslexia tutors and mental health mentors; support in arranging specialist computer training; support in arranging individual practical support; liaise and act as an advocate with college staff and external agencies on the student's behalf; alternative examination arrangements; involve the students and the SU in the development of policy and support services for students with disabilities; provision of basic screening and study skills advice for students with specific learning difficulties such as dyslexia and dyspraxia; arrangement of a dyslexia assessment by an educational psychologist; arrange specialist one-to-one dyslexia tutorial support; arrange orientation for guide dog or long cane users; liaison with staff throughout the college; support service for students with mental health issues. Each School has a disability liaison officer who can assist you with arranging support in lectures, tutorials and laboratories as well as liaising with lecturers on your behalf. The Disability Office (Room G057) is open from 10am to 6pm.

**Home sweet home:**
Students on full-time postgraduate courses can apply for accommodation from the University of London, which has limited accommodation. Accommodation for full-time postgraduate students can be guaranteed.

**Out and about:**
College: Residents of the boroughs of Hammersmith and Fulham, Kensington and Chelsea, Westminster and Camden can make use of the central London 'Dial-a-Ride' scheme for regular door-to-door journeys. Students can ask an attendant at reception to ring externally for a taxi to travel home. Parking for disabled drivers is very limited at college buildings, but Orange Badge holders may apply for a Green Badge from Camden Council that will entitle them to park without charge in the numerous residents' parking bays and pay-and-display zones in the area. The college has a system whereby students can telephone main reception for assistance to access a wheelchair from their car, if they are parked near the college, and be assisted to their classroom. There is also dedicated parking near the accommodation areas.
Public transport: Nearest tube stations are all approximately half a mile from the various college buildings and are accessible to people with visual impairments but not accessible to wheelchair users. The

trains and buses are accessible to people who are wheelchair users and those who have a visual impairment. Some buildings are better served by bus services. Contact the Disability Coordinator for details of accessibility and Access and Mobility (see Directory). Metro cabs are accessible to wheelchair users.

**Taking it easy:**
At college: The senior common room is wheelchair accessible but the junior one is not. A new building has recently been completed, which has a number of new teaching rooms with improved wheelchair access and hearing loop facilities. It is planned to have a refectory on the ground floor and it is hoped the junior common room will be relocated there too. Locally: The city centre is flat and accessible with tactile pavements and accessible town facilties. Students can use University of London (ULU) facilities, which are next door to the university. ULU is about to be refurbished and will include a new swimming pool. Local area access guides are available, contact Camden Council and Artsline (see below and Directory).

**And another thing ...**
➡ Disability access appraisal was most recently carried out in January 2000 using the published guidance of the Centre for Accessible Environments. A rolling programme of improving access provisions for people with physical disabilities has been developed.
➡ Contrasting colours are used for fixtures and backgrounds when redecorating, and the needs of persons with visual impairment are taken into account when new lighting or signage is being planned.
➡ Relocation of classes to accommodate wheelchair users, and whether an induction loop facility was required, would be explored when necessary.
➡ Arrangements can be made for new students with visual impairments to be accompanied from a nearby tube station or bus stop to the college and also on routes within the college until the student has become familiar with these journeys.
➡ Rest rooms are available.
➡ Details of induction loops are available on www.bbk.ac.uk/so/loops.htm.
➡ The Disability Alliance is an SU society and is run by students with disabilities and open to all students.
➡ The college is a member of Skill and an associate member of the Computer Centre for People with Disabilities, based at the University of Westminster.
➡ There are toilet facilities for wheelchair users.

➡ Lifts provide access to most areas of the major buildings.
➡ Induction loops are fitted at the reception desk of the main building and in several college lecture theatres.
➡ The Malet Street library is on the first floor of the main college building and is accessible via lifts and stairs.
➡ The Gresse Street library is located on the ground floor and in the basement. With advance notice, access via the fire escape can be arranged; this is suitable for wheelchair users. Staff will collect material that is not readily accessible in both libraries.
➡ Most of the SU offices are accessible by wheelchair. The bar can only be accessed via seven steps and it does not have a minicom.
➡ Students with disabilities receive financial assistance from the 'access fund' and, where ineligible for this, through the disability premium funding.

**QAA Report: Paragraph 66, October 2002**
The *Account* explained that support for students with disabilities was part of the college's 'commitment to widening participation and access'. This aspect of student support struck the audit team as being particularly well developed, offering an extensive range of facilities supported by a specialist Disability Office, with an impressively vigorous and proactive approach. Development of this area of support is underpinned by the activity of a Working Group of the Teaching Committee.

**The Disability Statement/Brochure:**
*Information for Students with Disabilities*
Includes: Applications; access and facilities; support services; examinations and assessments; financial support; monitoring and evaluation of support; future plans and disclaimer.

**Local disability public service providers:**
London Borough of Camden 020 7278 4444.
London Borough of Westminster 020 7641 6000.
Royal National Institute for the Blind 020 7388 1266.

---

**Birmingham College of Food, Tourism and Creative Studies**

Summer Row, Birmingham B3 1JB

*General Enquiries:*
Tel: 0121 604 1000
Fax: 0121 608 7100

**Specific Learning Needs Coordinator:**
**Clive Davies**
**Equal Opportunities Coordinator:**

Email: marketing@bcftcs.ac.uk
Website: www.bcftcs.ac.uk
Mini: 0121 604 4007

**Godfrey Henry**
**Tel: 0121 604 1000 ext: 243**
**Fax: 0121 604 1144**
**Email: c.davies@bcftcs.ac.uk;**
**g.henry@bcftcs.ac.uk**

### Levels of study:
The college is a specialist vocational and business and management centre offering programmes ranging from NVQ craft skills to HNC, HND, degree and postgraduate (to Master's level).

### Fields of study:
Business management; childcare and social care management; culinary arts; food and consumer management; food and retail management; hair and beauty; hospitality management; leisure and sports management; tourism management.

➡ Part-time study: **Yes.**
➡ Distance learning: **No.**

### About the college:
The Birmingham College of Food, Tourism and Creative Studies is an accredited college of the University of Birmingham. In 1998 the college won the Queen's Anniversary prize for Further and Higher Education, in which it was described as a 'Centre of Excellence'. The college is accredited to use the Employment Service – Positive about Disabled People symbol. The college is also a Hospitality Assured institution, and a Department for Education and Skills 'Centre of Vocational Excellence for Catering and Hospitality' (COVE). Birmingham is a progressive, lively and dynamic city.

| Total number of students: 7,058 | Number of disabled students: 376 |
|---|---|

### Learning support staff and services:
Study Support Unit; Student Services Unit
Equal opportunities coordinator; specific learning needs coordinator; college nurse; and counsellors.
Loan of personalised equipment; provision of specialist assistance wherever possible; alternative examination arrangements; proofreading for students with dyslexia; study skills; initial dyslexia assessment; referral of students to nominated educational psychologist for assessment for students with specific learning needs; liaison with a range of external agencies including the LEA, British Dyslexic Organisation and the Birmingham Institute for the Deaf.

Where it is not possible for the college to provide specific items of equipment, help will be given to identify, and apply to, a range of other agencies for finance or equipment support.

## Home sweet home:

The college's halls of residence provide a secure accommodation environment, with some rooms designed with mobility and sensory support. Nine rooms are specifically designed to support students with physical disabilities and have adjacent PA room facilities. Accommodation can be guaranteed for duration of student's course.

## Out and about:

College: There are dedicated parking spaces near both accommodation and study areas. A limited number of dedicated bays in front of building, due to small number of general on-site parking facilities.

Public transport: Access is good. New Street train station is only ten minutes' walk from the college. Several buses stop outside the college. The city also operates a 'Ring and Ride' service.

## Taking it easy:

At college: There are plenty of accessible leisure facilities, including the college's Spa (health, fitness and beauty centre). The Guild of Students has recently been allocated refurbished ground-floor space for offices and a common room. In addition there is use of local facilities such as the National Indoor Arena – all fully accessible for disabled users.

Locally: Birmingham is accessible and has a pedestrianised centre with a Shopmobility scheme. The college is a city-centre site, in close proximity to Birmingham Central Library, art gallery, theatres and cinemas, and a busy entertainment environment, Symphony Hall at the International Convention Centre, and the National Indoor Arena. There is a local area access guide – contact the Specific Learning Needs Coordinator for further information.

## And another thing ...

➡ The college has staff members who are qualified and experienced in supporting disabled students, including those with a visual impairment, who are D/deaf or hard of hearing, with mobility difficulties, dyslexia and mental health difficulties. The college provides mandatory equal opportunities training for all staff. It currently schedules a number of events to provide awareness and understanding for both staff and students' disability.

**Local disability public service provider:**
Birmingham City Council. Social Services Department 0121 303 4125.

---

| Birmingham Conservatoire |
|---|

Paradise Place, Birmingham B3 3HG

*General Enquiries:*
Tel: 0121 331 5901/5902
Fax: 0121 331 5906
Email: conservatoire@uce.ac.uk
Website: www.conservatoire.uce.ac.uk

**Head of Welfare Services:**
**Mark Ellerby**
**Email: mark.ellerby@uce.ac.uk**

**Fields of study:**
Music; music and jazz and music technology.

➡ Part-time study: **Yes, postgraduate only.**
➡ Distance learning: **No.**

**About the conservatoire:**
Birmingham Conservatoire, located in the city centre of Birmingham, is a leading music college where students are able to take part in external performance engagements. Ground-floor rooms are all accessible to people with mobility disabilities and there is a lift to the remaining floors. Staff will discuss your requirements.
Total number of students: 400

**Learning support staff and services:**
Please refer to the University of Central England in Birmingham for further information and contact details of the Disability Adviser who is responsible for setting up support arrangements for students with disabilities.

---

| University of Birmingham and the University of Birmingham, Westhill |
|---|

(For further details on Westhill, see following entry)
Edgbaston, Birmingham B15 2TT

*General Enquiries:*
Tel: 0121 414 3344
Fax: 0121 414 3971

**Disability Coordinator: Sue Green**
**Tel: 0121 414 2897**
**Fax: 0121 414 5133**

University of Birmingham and the University of Birmingham, Westhill

Email: admissions@bham.ac.uk    **Email: disability@bham.ac.uk**
Website: www.bham.ac.uk

## Fields of study:
Arts; business; commerce and economics; government and politics; languages; literacy and history; social sciences.

➡ Part-time study: **Yes.**
➡ Distance learning: **Yes.**

## About the university:
The University of Birmingham is a campus university where practically all the academic buildings and most of the residences are on one self-contained site just 3 miles from the city centre. Most schools/departments are located in one specific building, although the campus is very large. The architecture of the campus is varied, ranging from the grand traditional redbrick buildings that include the Great Hall, built in 1900, to the 1960s architecture of the Muirhead Tower and the more domestic-scale buildings of the 1980s and 1990s. According to a study by the *Guardian* and independent consultants, the university is one of the top four universities in the country in the judgement of employers.

| Total number of students: 24,500   Number of disabled students: 800 |
| --- |

## Learning support staff and services:
Student Support and Counselling Service
One full-time disability coordinator; one full-time learning support coordinator and one learning support adviser.
Assistance with DSA application and other allowances; needs assessments on campus; arrangement of support, e.g. dyslexia tuition; operation of a notetaking scheme and a limited Brailling service; advice and guidance; alternative examination, assessment and study arrangements; liaison with external organisations; loan of equipment, e.g. Dictaphones, electronic scooter, laptops, reading edge scanner; mentoring for Asperger's syndrome; Adaptive Technology Project.

## Home sweet home:
Jarratt Hall, new in 2001, is a purpose-built self-catering hall with adapted en-suite bathrooms and lowered kitchen units. It is very close to campus. The Vale has new accommodation with accessible rooms from 2003. In some cases, accommodation can be guaranteed for the duration of the student's course.

## Out and about:
University: Dedicated parking spaces near both accommodation and study areas, and more can be provided on demand. The university will assist with providing transport in some cases.
Public transport: Some 'kneeling' buses are accessible, as are 'Ring and Ride' taxis with wheelchair ramps. Ring and Ride provide adapted minibuses, and all black cabs are wheelchair accessible.

## Taking it easy:
At university: Munrow Sports Centre and swimming pool are accessible to students with physical disabilities – information sheet available. The Guild of Students has a Students with Disabilities Committee and a peer support group for students with dyslexia that runs if enough volunteers come forward.
Locally: Accessibility is fairly good and improving all the time, with lots of new wheelchair-accessible buildings. Some pavements are tactile and there are some Shopmobility schemes in the surrounding towns.

## And another thing ...
The main library has assistive technology study booths with specialist equipment and software for visually impaired or dyslexic students. There is a visual impairment resource room.

➡ There is a Disability Forum with wide membership.
➡ A mobility map is available detailing most accessible routes on the campus and there is also an audio/tactile model in the main library. Mobility training on campus can possibly be arranged.

## The Disability Statement/Brochure:
Covers: Equal opportunities; access; admission; exams and assessments; support services; financial services; confidentiality; staff; careers services; the Guild of Students; academic services and support; IT provision; physical environment; miscellaneous facilities; future activity and future policy development.
An information pack is available from the Student Support and Counselling Service for disabled students, which includes the Disability Statement. The information pack can also be viewed on the Web: www.sscs.bham.ac.uk/disability.

## Local disability public service providers:
Birmingham City Council Social Services Department 0121 303 4125.
Community Service Volunteers 0121 643 8080.

| University of Birmingham, Westhill |
|---|

Weoley Park Road, Selly Oak, Birmingham B29 6LL

*General Enquiries:*
Tel: 0121 472 7245
Fax: 0121 414 2969
Email: westhill-info@bham.ac.uk
Website: www.westhill.ac.uk

**Fields of study:**
Community, play and youth studies; counselling; humanities; Islamic studies; PGCE; theology.

➡ Part-time study: **Yes.**
➡ Distance learning: **No.**

**About the university:**
Westhill was founded in 1907 with the support of George Cadbury, who donated the land. It is situated on an 80-acre garden site, containing a mix of old buildings and more modern structures including the state-of-the-art Orchard Learning Centre. Westhill has a Muslim prayer room for use by Muslim members of the Westhill community. Within 20 minutes of leaving Westhill by bus or car you can be in the centre of Birmingham – a cosmopolitan city in the heart of England. Its history and industrial heritage, combined with major redevelopment in recent years, have created one of the most modern and diverse cities in Europe.

| Total number of students: 1,500 | Number of disabled students: 80 |
|---|---|

**Learning support staff and services:**
Please refer to the University of Birmingham entry as all services are administered through their disability coordinator.

**And another thing ...**
➡ The Orchard Centre has facilities for visually impaired and dyslexic students.
➡ There is a variety of teaching rooms on the ground floor, and the Learning Resources Centre has a lift that is accessible to wheelchair users.
➡ Computer rooms and refectories are accessible to wheelchair users.
➡ Some lecture rooms have induction loops and there is a portable system.
➡ Support workers employed when necessary.

## Blackpool and The Fylde College

Ashfield Road, Bispham, Blackpool, Lancashire FY2 0HB

*General Enquiries:*
Tel: 01253 352352
Fax: 01253 356127
Email: visitors@blackpool.ac.uk
Website: www.blackpool.ac.uk

**Disability Coordinator:**
**Tel: 01253 504358**
**Fax: 01253 356127**
**Email: lw@blackpool.ac.uk**

### Fields of study:
Art and design; business and computing; leisure and hospitality; maritime; tourism.

➡ Part-time study: **Yes.**
➡ Distance learning: **No.**

### About the college:
Blackpool and The Fylde College has recently completed a £3 million upgrade of its central Blackpool campus, creating a new venue with a strong emphasis on visual and performing arts. The campus, which is situated in the heart of the town, also saw the refurbishment of the library and refectory. Sir Bobby Charlton opened the college's new all-weather Astroturf pitch, which cost over half a million pounds to construct. Blackpool as a town has plenty to offer students, both day and night.

Total number of students: 1,500 HE
Number of disabled students: 75 HE

### Learning support staff and services:
As a primarily FE college, HE support taps into resources already set up in FE. There are approximately 40 learning support tutors and 50 education support workers. The service is able to provide sign language interpreters up to level 3 and lipspeakers. Materials can be adapted into various formats and assistive technology is available.

### Home sweet home:
The college uses guesthouses, holiday flats, etc. from surrounding areas, which are vetted and have various levels of access. Accommodation can be guaranteed for duration of student's course.

### Out and about:
College: Dedicated parking spaces near both accommodation and study areas.

Public transport: There are various specialist buses run by the local bus company and specialist transporters such as Dial-a-Ride.

**Taking it easy:**
At college: Leisure facilities are for all students.
Locally: Contact Blackpool Borough Council for information about accessibility in Blackpool (see below).

**Local disability public service provider:**
Blackpool Borough Council, Progress House, Clifton Road, Blackpool, Lancashire.

---

| **Bolton Institute** |
|---|

Deane Road, Bolton BL3 5AB

*General Enquiries:*
Tel: 01204 900600
Fax: 01204 399074
Email: enquiries@bolton.ac.uk
Website: www.bolton.ac.uk
Text: 01204 903081

**Disability Adviser**
**Katie Jennings**
**Tel: 01204 903086**
**Fax: 01204 903809**
**Email: kj2@bolton.ac.uk**
**Textphone on order**

**Fields of study:**
Arts; business and technology; science and education.

➡ Part-time study: **Yes**
➡ Distance learning: **No**

**About the institute:**
Bolton Institute currently operates on two main sites, Chadwick and Deane, approximately 1 mile apart. The institute is situated within easy reach of the Lake District, West Pennine Moors and the Yorkshire Dales and has good motorway and rail links. Manchester with its nightlife and big city amenities is a short train ride away.

| Total number of students: 8,000+   Number of disabled students: 500 |
|---|

**Learning support staff and services:**
Student and Residential Services
Full-time Disability Adviser: Katie Jennings.
Advice and guidance; assistance with DSA applications; arrangement of assessments; provision of auxiliary aids and services; alternative

examination, assessment and study arrangements; liaison with academic departments and external bodies.
Additional support is provided by various members of staff at the institute, throughout other departments and faculties. Nominated staff provide extra support, advice and a guide to service provision for students with disabilities and individual needs. Learning Support and Development (LS&D) has nominated certain staff in a coordinating role:
LS&D IT liaison officer and LS&D team leader/subject librarian.

### Home sweet home:

Two accessible en-suite rooms in both halls of residence that are adapted for students with disabilities. These are allocated on a first come, first served basis. In order to maintain their inclusive policy all residential staff regularly attend training sessions on awareness and support issues. The emphasis is that all students are able to maintain their independence, within an inclusive and supportive environment. Accommodation can be guaranteed for duration of student's course.

### Out and about:

Institute: Limited dedicated parking spaces near both accommodation and study areas.
The local public transport service provides buses that are accessible for wheelchair users. The local train station is adapted for wheelchair users. There is a taxi scheme for disabled people operating in the area, the Ring a Ride Service.

### Taking it easy:

Institute: The sports hall, situated at Deane campus, currently has limited access for wheelchair users. The catering facilities on both sites are fully accessible.
Locally: The city centre is mainly flat, and accessible. Town facilities are accessible, and there is a Shopmobility scheme. The pavements are tactile.

### And another thing ...

➡ A road divides the Deane campus. At times access within this site may give rise to difficulties for wheelchair users, so wherever possible and with prior consultation alternative arrangements may be made, such as alternative venues and the use of video/audio-taped lectures.
➡ There are enabling technology rooms containing specialised IT facilities and equipment within the learning support centres situated on both campuses.

Bournemouth University

➡ In order to support students who do not qualify for DSA the institute also provides a limited bank of resources, including items such as PC systems, Franklin Language Masters and Dictaphones. Various departments also provide specialised loan equipment.
➡ Financial assistance may be given to fund dyslexia assessment.
➡ Bolton Institute has many local links with external bodies as well as national links, such as with RNIB, RNID, Access centres (NFAC), Dyslexia Institute, and the Students with Disabilities Committee of the NUS.
➡ Accessible toilet facilities are available on both sites.
➡ The main lecture theatres have been fitted with induction loop systems.

## The Disability Statement/Brochure:
Currently being reviewed.

## Local disability public service providers:
Bolton Social Services and the Greater Manchester Coalition of Disabilities.
Chamber Health Centre, Ashboumer Street, Bolton.
Town Hall, Bolton.
Bolton Deaf Society 01204 521219.
Visual Aid 01204 531882.

| Bournemouth University |
| --- |

Fern Barrow, Poole, Dorset BH12 5BB

*General Enquiries:*
Tel: 01202 524111
Fax: 01202 702736
Email: marketing@bournemouth.ac.uk
Website: www.bournemouth.ac.uk

**Additional Learning Needs Adviser: James Palfreman-Kay**
**Tel: 01202 595327**
**Fax: 01202 595475**
**Email: jmpkay@ bournemouth.ac.uk**
**Text: 01202 595475**

## Fields of study:
Business; conservation sciences; design, engineering and computing; finance and law; health and community studies; media; service industries.

➡ Part-time study: **Yes.**
➡ Distance learning: **Yes, but very few courses offered.**

## About the university:

Located on the sheltered south coast of England, Bournemouth is almost surrounded by sea and has its fair share of sun. The university incorporates two main campuses, Talbot and Bournemouth. The larger of the two, Talbot, is 2¹/₂ miles from Bournemouth town centre. The buildings here are new and lie on an extremely level campus so are easy to access, as is the Bournemouth campus. Placements are a key feature of many of the courses at Bournemouth, with over 70 per cent of degree programmes offering a placement period.

Total number of students: approx. 14,000
Number of disabled students: 800+

## Learning support staff and services:

Dr James Palfreman-Kay: Additional Learning Needs Adviser; Jean Blake: Administrative Assistant; Patricia Ware: Dyslexia Support Tutor; Keith Hayward: IT Support Technician.

Advise on technical or human support; assist with DSA applications; liaise with tutors on the students' behalf; offer advice and support for students on placements by phone or by email; initial assessment of dyslexia and ongoing support for students who require additional assistance with study techniques on either an individual or group basis; alternative assessment and examination arrangements; assistance and information on specialist software and support for students who have obtained a computer through their DSA.

## Home sweet home:

Six houses within the student village adjacent to the Talbot campus have a purpose-built unit with en-suite bathroom facilities for those with physical disabilities. These units may be adapted to suit individual needs. There are also some adapted units available in Cranborne House. The university can also provide accommodation for PAs at the student rate. Other forms of accommodation may be available.

Accommodation can be guaranteed for duration of student's course subject to discussion.

## Out and about:

University: The university provides several double-decker bus services at a minimal fare to both campuses from various parts of the town, for staff and students, although there is no wheelchair lift on this service. Any student requiring accessible transport should contact the Additional Learning Needs Adviser. Dedicated parking spaces near both accommodation and study areas on the Talbot

Campus. Parking at the Bournemouth campus is extremely limited but can be arranged. Parking can also be provided at the Cranborne House residence (close to the centre of Bournemouth).

## Taking it easy:
At university: Access to SU buildings, catering and sports facilities is good.
Locally: Contact Disability Bournemouth Information Service or Bournemouth Borough Council for information on the area.

## And another thing ...
➡ Bournemouth and Talbot campuses are fully accessible to wheelchair users.
➡ All buildings are served by modern lifts, a number of which are talking lifts, and many entrances have automatic door openers and access ramps. Access to and within all buildings, including the libraries, SU buildings, catering and sports facilities, is good.
➡ The university will endeavour, wherever reasonable, to make any necessary adaptations around the campus to meet the specific requirements of individual students.
➡ The Learning Support Team within Academic Services provide general guidance on study skills. They run workshops and also provide times when they are available for short individual consultations on a 'drop-in' basis.
➡ The university has links with RNIB, RNID and Adult Dyslexia Organisation.
➡ Induction loop in Talbot House main hall.
➡ PA systems/radio microphones in some lecture theatres.
➡ Notetakers or BSL interpreters provided at students' expense or from other funding source.
➡ Specialised IT equipment for visually impaired and dyslexic students.

## The Disability Statement/Brochure:
Includes: Policies on access and confidentiality; support staff; admissions; financial assistance; specific facilities; physical environment; accommodation; transport; academic support; student services; SU; monitoring and evaluation; staff development; links and contacts.

## Local disability public service providers:
Disability Bournemouth Information Service, open Tuesday and Friday, 01202 300230.
Bournemouth Borough Council.

| Bradford College |
|---|

Great Horton Road, Bradford, West Yorkshire BD7 1AY

*General Enquiries:*
Tel: 01274 753004
Website: www.bilk.ac.uk
Email: maxinea@bilk.ac.uk

**Head of Department and Coordinator for Equal Opportunities: Louise Hart**
**Tel: 01274 753446**
**Fax: 01274 420441**

## Fields of study:
Applied human studies; applied social science and humanities; art, design and textiles; business studies; computing and business administration; engineering and construction, management, hospitality and leisure studies; pure and applied science; teacher education.

➡ Part-time study: **Yes.**
➡ Distance learning: **Yes.**

## About the college:
Bradford College is the largest 'mixed economy' college in the country. The city of Bradford has had a college since 1832, and with its rich and diverse culture has much to offer the student.

| Total number of students: 32,000    Number of disabled students: 794 |
|---|

## Learning support staff and services:
The Department of Learning Support is a central department based at the Sue Carroll Centre, Westbrook building. There are over 20 full-time and 141 part-time teaching and non-teaching staff within the department, who assess and deliver additional learning support for disabled students on FE and HE programmes across the college. For a full list of all staff please contact Learning Support.
Needs assessments; assistance with DSA applications; provision of auxiliary aids and services; advice and guidance; one-to-one/group tuition for students with dyslexia; alternative examination, assessment and study arrangements; support service for students with mental health issues and liaison with external organisations.

## Home sweet home:
The McMillan Halls of Residence are predominantly for HE students. Some rooms already have adaptations for students who are D/deaf or hard of hearing, and in addition four rooms have adaptations for physically disabled people. The college will adapt rooms to meet

individual requirements provided sufficient notice is given. Accommodation can be guaranteed for duration of student's course.

## Out and about:
College: The college provides specialist transport for disabled students between college sites and on educational visits. Dedicated parking spaces near both accommodation and study areas.
Public transport: Accessibility to local transport is mixed. Accessible taxis can be funded by the LEA for FE students (full-time and under 25) and by the DSA for HE students.

## Taking it easy:
At college: College students can access Bradford University Sports Hall. Most refectories are accessible. The SU bar on the main campus is accessible.
Locally: The city centre is hilly, but accessible. The town facilities are accessible and there is a Shopmobility scheme. Pavements are tactile. There is a disability guide to the area, *Bradford Access Guide* – ask the Department of Learning Support for further information.

## Local disability public service providers:
Access Officer, Bradford Council.
Leeds City Council.

---

| **University of Bradford** |
| --- |

Richmond Building, Richmond Road, Bradford, West Yorkshire
BD7 1DP

*General Enquiries:*
Tel: 01274 233081
Fax: 01274 236260
Email: enquiries@bradford.ac.uk
Website: www.bradford.ac.uk

**Head of Disability Services: Liz Clarke**
**Tel: 01274 235156**
**Fax: 01274 235340**
**Email: e.m.clarke@**
**bradford.ac.uk**

## Fields of study:
Archaeological and environmental sciences; engineering; health studies; informatics; life sciences; management; science foundation; social and international studies.

➡ Part-time study: **Yes, a few courses.**
➡ Distance learning: **Yes, in some subjects.**

## About the university:

The University of Bradford received its Royal Charter in 1966, but its origins date back to the 1860s. The university recently invested more than £2 million, modernising and upgrading lecture theatres and teaching facilities throughout the campus. The university's single campus, which is surrounded by countryside, is just ten minutes' walk from the city. Bradford is one of the ten largest cities in Britain and has all the facilities of a thriving, modern city. The Yorkshire Moors and Dales are close by.

| |
|---|
| Total number of students: 9,800 |
| Number of disabled students: approx. 650 |

## Learning support staff and services:

Disability Office

One full-time head of disability services; one part-time assistant disability officer, with responsibility mainly for dyslexic students; one full-time IT officer for disabled people and a full-time administrator in the Disability Office; a team of six full-time CSVs and some part-time notetakers, all of whom provide support to students with disabilities. There are also six support tutors, one of whom works with students with mental health difficulties.

The Disability Office was established 12 years ago and has set up an equipment demonstration room for disabled students, with IT equipment that includes voice recognition systems. There is also an increasing range of assistive technology available on loan. The Disability Office works closely with the library and computer centre with regard to access to information, and liaises closely with academic departments to meet the support needs of disabled students. The website receives 1,000+ enquiries per month – www.brad.ac.uk/disability.

## Home sweet home:

Eight en-suite rooms, which are suitable for wheelchair users. Other adaptations can be made on an individual basis as and when required. The university's accommodation booklet contains a detailed questionnaire, which asks relevant questions about access needs. Half of the halls of residence are covered by the Deaf Alerter system fire alarm. Accommodation can be guaranteed for duration of student's course by negotiation and if the student wishes to stay in halls.

## Out and about:

University: Local taxis can be paid for through DSA. For disabled students who are not wheelchair users there is some limited free

transport run by the SU in the evenings and at weekends. Dedicated parking spaces near both accommodation and study areas.
Public transport: Trains are accessible, as are buses.

## Taking it easy:
At university: Disabled students use the same facilities as all other students.
Locally: Some of the town is accessible and is constantly being improved although it is hilly. Most of the town facilities are accessible and there is a Shopmobility scheme. Some pavements are tactile. There is a publication called the *Bradford Access Guide*, published by Bradford Access Action, which gives useful information about the main buildings in Bradford.

## And another thing ...
➡ The Disability Office team lends equipment when possible to students who are not eligible for DSA, e.g. international students with disabilities.

## Local disability public service provider:
Bradford Social Services, Olicana House, Chapel Street, Bradford.

| University of Brighton |
| :---: |

Mithras House, Lewes Road, Brighton BN2 4AT

*General Enquiries:*     **Disability Coordinator: Kirsty Mackenzie**
Tel: 01273 600900     **Tel: 01273 643799**
Fax: 01273 642825     **Fax: 01273 642622**
Email: admissions@bton.ac.uk     **Email: disability@bton.ac.uk**
Website: www.brighton.ac.uk     **Text: 01273 683552**

## Fields of study:
Arts and architecture; business; education and sport; health; IT; science and engineering.

➡ Part-time study: **Yes.**
➡ Distance learning: **No.**

## About the university:
Graduate employment from Brighton University is amongst the highest in the UK and it is the fourth largest provider of teacher education. There are four main campuses providing on-site amenities

however, the building stock is varied and there are some sites that may prove inaccessible for some students. Brighton itself has a rich and diverse cultural life and is situated on the south-east coast of England.

| Total number of students: approx. 20,000 |
|---|
| Number of disabled students: approx. 850 |

### Learning support staff and services:
Disability Team
Full-time staff: Learning Support Officer.
Part-time staff: Sensory Impairment Support Officer; Disability Team Assistant; IT Student Support Officer; Learning Support Tutor.

Assistance with DSA applications and Hardship Fund; provision of auxiliary aids and services; advice and guidance; one-to-one/group tuition for students with dyslexia; alternative examination, assessment and arrangements; support service for students with mental health issues and liaison with external organisations. The Disability Service also coordinates a pool of support workers for disabled/dyslexic students (paid from DSA), loans equipment and supports nursing students who do not qualify for DSA.

### Home sweet home:
All halls of residence have accessible accommodation with en-suite facilities and accessible kitchens with extra room for a PA if desired. There are residential advisers and caretaking staff on call seven days a week. Adaptation to halls' units can be made to suit individual requirements, although this is not generally possible where major structural adaptations are necessary. Accommodation can be guaranteed for duration of student's course.

### Out and about:
University: There are dedicated parking spaces for disabled drivers near the accommodation and study areas.
Public transport: The majority of Brighton and Hove buses are now accessible to wheelchair users, as are some trains. An accessible taxi service operates in the area.

### Taking it easy:
At university: There are a number of facilities for sport and recreation on all sites except Grand Parade, but accessibility is poor. Brighton Health and Racquet Club and Eastbourne: Hillbrow are fully accessible to those with mobility disabilities – reception staff can

offer advice and assistance regarding the use of the swimming pool. The Sport and Recreation Office on the Falmer Site hosts the regional manager of the English Federation for Disability Sport. D/deaf or hard of hearing students should note there is no minicom facility within the department or induction loops at reception points. All staff are trained in disability awareness.

Locally: The city centre is both flat and hilly. Some of the local town facilities are accessible and the city centre is generally accessible. Some pavements are tactile. There is a local area disability guide available called *disabledgo.info* – contact the Disability Team for more details. For information on town accessibility see: www.brighton-hove.gov.uk.

### And another thing ...

➡ The university has completed an access audit, which has informed the long-term programme of alterations to building stock to ensure better accessibility. Induction loops are planned for all the issue and enquiry desks in the libraries; most are already in place. Many of the library staff have learnt basic BSL.

➡ There is specialist software for students with dyslexia/visual impairment within all libraries.

➡ The university is able to arrange for support workers, such as sign language interpreters, lipspeakers and PAs as recommended by an Access Centre and funded by DSA.

### The Disability Statement/Brochure:

Comprehensive formal document covering equal opportunities, exams and assessments; funding available; support and useful contacts. Information regarding disability access and support can be gained from individual departments.

### Local disability public service provider:

Brighton and Hove Federation of Disabled People 01273 203016.

| University of Bristol |
|---|

Senate House, Tyndall Avenue, Bristol BS8 1TH

*General Enquiries:*
Tel: 0117 928 9000
Fax: 0117 928 1424
Email: admissions@bristol.ac.uk
Website: www.bristol.ac.uk

**Disability Services Manager: Lin Reynolds**
**Tel: 0117 954 5727**
**Fax: 0117 923 8546**
**Email: anna.lickley@bristol.ac.uk**
**Text: 0117 954 5728**

**Fields of study:**
Arts; engineering; law; medicine; science; social sciences.

➡ Part-time study: **No.**
➡ Distance learning: **No.**

**About the university:**
University College, Bristol, founded in 1876, was the first institution in the UK to offer places to women on the same footing as men. The Bristol Medical School, founded in 1833, soon became associated with the college, and became part of it in 1893. The college became a university in 1909. Until the early nineteenth century Bristol was the most important city in England after London. Today Bristol is an important financial centre. There is a rich legacy of buildings as well as the famous suspension bridge across the Avon Gorge. From Bristol there is easy access to Bath, Wells and the countryside of the west of England and Wales.

| Total number of students: 12,168    Number of disabled students: 652 |
|---|

**Learning support staff and services:**
Access Unit for Deaf and Disabled Students
Disability Coordinator: Lin Reynolds.

Assessment of student needs; information and advice regarding DSA; arrangement of practical assistance for temporarily disabled students; liaison with academic departments, student services and facilities and the SU; advice and information to university staff, other universities and external agencies regarding students and support services; provision of a counsellor for D/deaf or hard of hearing students.

**Home sweet home:**
Some university accommodation has been adapted for D/deaf and hard of hearing students, and some accommodation is accessible for wheelchair users and visually impaired students. These rooms are in catering and self-catering halls of residence.
Accommodation cannot be guaranteed for duration of student's course.

**Out and about:**
University: There are some dedicated parking spaces near accommodation and study areas.
Public transport: Local transport is not accessible.

**Taking it easy:**
At university: For information on the SU visit www.ubu.org.uk
Locally: For information about Bristol city and its accessibility contact
Bristol City Council (see below).

**And another thing ...**
➡ Induction loops in some lecture rooms.

**Local disability public service provider:**
Bristol City Council www.bristol-city.gov.uk.

---

| British School of Osteopathy |
| :---: |

275 Borough High Street, London SE1 1JE

*General Enquiries:*
Tel: 020 7407 0222
Fax: 020 7089 5300
Email: admin@bso.ac.uk
Website: www.bso.ac.uk

**Disability Coordinator: Patricia Costall**
**Tel: 020 7089 5300 ext: 261**
**Email: patc@bso.ac.uk**

**Field of study:**
Osteopathy.

➡ Part-time: **Yes.**
➡ Distance learning: **Yes. Three years part-time with distance learning, then two final full-time years.**

**About the school:**
Dr Mark Littlejohn founded the British School of Osteopathy in 1917.
In 1983 HRH the Princess Royal became the School's patron. The
School is the oldest and largest full-time school of osteopathy in the
UK, and the clinic sees over 700 patients a week and provides
around 38,000 treatments a year. The School's degrees are validated
by the Open University.

**Learning support staff and services:**
Educational Development and Welfare Services
One full-time member of staff; one part-time counsellor with support
tutors brought in as appropriate.
Advice and assistance in securing support to both prospective and
new students and throughout a student's time at the school.

## Home sweet home:
There is no school accommodation, only private contracts. Accommodation *cannot* be guaranteed for duration of the student's course.

## Out and about:
School: There are dedicated parking spaces near to study areas.
Locally: Borough underground station has a lift. For information on London's public transport services contact Access and Mobility (see Directory).

## Taking it easy:
At School: The SU and bar are currently not wheelchair accessible.
Locally: The city centre is flat and accessible. Most of the local town facilities are accessible. There is a Shopmobility scheme, but the pavements are not tactile. Artsline publishes a number of access guides on the city of London (see below).

## And another thing...
➡ All applicants are given equal consideration, irrespective of any disability, provided they comply with the 'Standard 2000 Areas of Capability', laid down by our professional registration body the General Osteopathic Council.
➡ Whilst the School would wish to be supportive of students with disabilities and provides assistance for those with specific learning difficulties, the physical aspects of osteopathic practice require physical agility and manual dexterity. The requirement for confidentiality in dealing with patients would make the presence of a third-party practitioner assistant inappropriate.

## Local disability public service providers:
Access and Mobility (see Directory).
Artsline (see Directory).

---

### Brunel University
Uxbridge, Middlesex UB8 3PH

*General Enquiries:*
Tel: 01895 274000
Fax: 01895 232806
ext: 4886/3708/2910
Email: admissions@brunel.ac.uk
Website: www.brunel.ac.uk

**Head of Service: Martin Smith**
**Tel: 01895 274000 ext: 4886**
**Fax: 01895 816260**
**Email: disability@brunel.ac.uk**
**Text: 01895 816246**

## Fields of study:
American studies and history; biological sciences; business and management; design; economics and finance; education; electronic and computer engineering; English; foundation courses; geography and earth sciences; government; health studies; human sciences; information systems and computing; languages; law; mathematical sciences; mechanical engineering; performing arts; social work; sport sciences; systems engineering; London Bible College.

➡ Part-time study: **Yes.**
➡ Distance learning: **Yes.**

## About the university:
Brunel, which dates back to 1798, has four traffic-free campuses at Uxbridge (the main and largest site), Osterley, Twickenham and Runnymede. Located on the western edge of the capital, Brunel is near both to city life and to many parks and places of local interest, offering the Brunel student a cultural and cosmopolitan life. The university has a good graduate employment record.

Total number of students: 13,000    Number of disabled students: 650

## Learning support staff and services:
Disability Service
Full-time staff: Head of Service: Martin Smith, who is a qualified state registered occupational therapist and does some assessments; Disability Adviser: Susannah Morgan and Bryan Coleman; Service Administrator; Publicity/Information Officer; and Mental Health Mentor Scheme Manager.
Part-time staff: Dyslexia Adviser: Amanda Shaw; Support Workers Scheme Coordinator; 14+ support workers; Assistant Administrator: Debbie Reader.
Advice and information; dyslexia screening assessments; one-to-one tuition for students with dyslexia; assistance with DSA applications and other funding (Hardship Fund and European Social Fund (ESF) Disability Funding); provision of auxiliary aids and services; liaison with academic departments and external agencies; alternative examination, assessment and study arrangements; support service for students with mental health issues; employs range of support workers such as notetakers, BSL communicators, dyslexia study skills tutors and study mentors.

## Home sweet home:
Uxbridge campus: New bedrooms are en-suite with showers. Fire alarm sounds are augmented by vibrators under pillows and by visual

means in some student bedrooms. The number of rooms fitted with this facility will be increased to meet demand. Extra rooms will be made available to PAs if possible (rental costs need to be covered by students, SS, etc.). Wheelchair accessible en-suite rooms; extra rooms for PAs; flashing beacons and vibrating pillows. Runnymede campus: No wheelchair accessible rooms, but large rooms available and adaptations can be made if necessary (flashing beacons and vibrating pillows can be provided). Osterley campus: Wheelchair-accessible rooms, (flashing beacons and vibrating pillows can be provided). These rooms are not en-suite. Twickenham campus: No wheelchair accessible rooms but some large rooms available and adaptations can be make (flashing beacons and vibrating pillows can be provided).

Accommodation can be guaranteed for duration of student's course at all campuses if agreed by the University Medical Officer.

## Out and about:
University: dedicated parking spaces near both accommodation and study areas.
Local transport: Uxbridge: Good accessibility; Uxbridge tube station has wheelchair access.
Osterley: Local underground and rail stations have no wheelchair access.
Twickenham: Satisfactory access by bus. Rail and underground stations are some distance away.
Runnymede: Access difficult and all approaches to the campus involve steep hills.
Hillingdon Borough Taxi Card Scheme provides an accessible service for disabled people in the area. Contact Access and Mobility for further information (see Directory). Dial-a-Ride taxi scheme operates in the area.

## Taking it easy:
At university: The Union of Brunel Students has generally good access, and activities are available to all students. The sports centre/gym is on the ground floor.
Locally: Uxbridge is pedestrianised and flat with a Shopmobility scheme in Uxbridge. The local town facilities are accessible on most sites and the pavements are tactile. The local association of disabled people, DASH, also provides advice (see below). Other campus sites are further from their towns. Artsline (see Directory) provides access information for London.

**And another thing ...**

➡ The Disability Service welcomes and encourages students to make contact prior to the start of their course, to discuss individual needs and concerns.

➡ The university is working hard to improve accessibility but there are some limitations with a number of campus buildings. Wherever possible, scheduled classes are moved to accessible rooms if necessary. Developments continue to be undertaken on access issues throughout the university. There is a programme of work to comply with the DDA scheduled over the next three to five years. As part of the redevelopment programme, lecture theatres are being fitted with induction loops and full wheelchair access. New lifts are being installed throughout and entrances are being fitted with automatic doors.

➡ The Disability Service/Publications are in the process of producing a map highlighting access, lifts, ramps and car parking.

➡ There are a number of accessible toilet facilities available throughout the campus.

➡ Brunel offers a Support Workers' Service to students, which includes notetakers, readers, sign language interpreters, typists, scribes in exams and study skills support.

➡ The library has two study carrels that house two PCs, scanner, Jaws Kurzweil 1000/3000. A Braille embosser is available for visually impaired students. The majority of monitors are 17", but there are also a number of 19" and 21" monitors. Texthelp! Read and Write and Inspiration is available on all PCs campus-wide. CCTV is available in all libraries.

➡ The university has recently initiated the Brunel Access Group for staff with disabilities and is hoping to extend this to students in 2004/5. The Disability/Special Needs service are continually striving to raise awareness of disability issues and maintain a positive learning environment for disabled students through publicity, staff development training programmes and departmental talks.

➡ There are plans to establish a Mental Health Mentoring Service.

## The Disability Statement/Brochure:

*Handbook for Disabled Students and those with Special Needs.*
Available from Disability Service or on the Brunel Website.
Includes: Vice-Chancellor's welcome; introduction; the team; current policy and practice; admission arrangements; sites accessibility; facilities; resources and equipment; pastoral care and support services; specific learning difficulties; special study and assessment arrangements; financial support; quality; monitoring feedback and

complaints procedure; appendices: useful contacts, computer equipment, travel information and maps.

## Local disability service providers:
DASH (Disablement Association Hillingdon).
HBADP (Hounslow Borough Association of Disabled People), 12 School Road, Hounslow, Middlesex TW3 1QZ; 020 8577 3226; minicom 020 8572 3923.
RAID (Richmond Advice and Information on Disabilities) Disability Action and Advice Centre, 4 Waldegrave Road, Teddington TW11 8HT; 020 8831 6070.
Hillingdon, Hounslow and Richmond Councils cover the four campus sites.

---

## University of Buckingham
Hunter Street, Buckingham MK18 1DW

*General Enquiries:*
Tel: 01280 814080
Fax: 01280 822245
Email: admissions@buckingham.ac.uk
Website: www.buckingham.ac.uk

**Student Support Adviser: Jenni Beard**
**Tel: 01280 820348**
**Fax: 01280 820267**
**Email: jenni.beard@**
**buckingham.ac.uk**

## Fields of study:
Accounting and finance; business studies (management); economics (international studies); English language and literature; history; history of art and heritage management; information systems; international studies; law; politics and psychology.

➡ Part-time study: **Yes.**
➡ Distance learning: **No.**

## About the university:
The small University of Buckingham is the only private university in the UK and according to its prospectus has one of the highest IT spends per student of any UK university (better than Oxford or Cambridge). Buckingham was also the first university to introduce Honours degree programmes that are run on a four terms per year basis, with degree courses completed over two years. Buckingham is a thriving market town, which has grown rapidly over the last 25 years and is within easy reach of major academic and artistic centres such as Oxford and London.

University of Buckingham

| Total number of students: 780 | Number of disabled students: 45 |
| --- | --- |

## Learning support staff and services:
One full-time Student Support Adviser: Jenni Beard; one full-time secretary.
Screening of students who feel they have individual needs; arrangement of educational assessment by an educational psychologist for students who feel they may have educational needs; personal tuition for students with dyslexia who need support organising and carrying out their academic work; alternative examination arrangements; liaison with academic and administrative staff regarding disability needs.

## Home sweet home:
Wheelchair access, adapted rooms and showers and possible extra room for PAs.
Accommodation can be guaranteed for duration of student's course.

## Out and about:
University: The university can possibly arrange specialist transport for its disabled students to a limited degree. Dedicated parking spaces near both accommodation and study areas.
Public transport: Some buses are accessible. There is a taxi scheme operating in the area for disabled people.

## Taking it easy:
At university: The normal facilities for students are on the ground floor and thus available to disabled students.
Locally: Buckingham is flat and moderately accessible but there is no access guide to the town. The sports facilities are accessible.

## And another thing ...
➡ The university is on a split site and has many old buildings that may pose access difficulties for students with mobility disabilities. The newer buildings have been designed with the needs of physically disabled people in mind.

## The Disability Statement/Brochure:
*Policy for Disabled Students*
Admissions; access; accommodation; facilities; identification of needs; examinations and confidentiality.

## Local disability public service provider:
AVDC (Aylesbury Vale District Council).

## Buckinghamshire Chilterns University College (BCUC)

Queen Alexandra Road, High Wycombe, Bucks HP11 2JZ

*General Enquiries:*
Tel: 01494 603015
Fax: 01494 471585
Email: marketing@bcuc.ac.uk
Website: www.bcuc.ac.uk

**Head of Disabilities Support Services: Anne Peters**
**Tel: 01494 605049**
**Fax: 01494 603189**
**Email: anne.j.peters@bcuc.ac.uk**
**Text: 01494 605049**

### Fields of study:
Arts and media; business; design; health studies; human sciences; leisure and tourism and technology.

➡ Part-time study: **Yes.**
➡ Distance learning: **No.**

### About the university college:
There are three campuses at Buckinghamshire Chilterns University College – Chalfont, High Wycombe and Wellesbourne. Buckinghamshire is a county steeped in history while offering the best of modern facilities. The train station is just a ten-minute walk away from the High Wycombe Campus, and London is just a 35-minute train ride away.

Total number of students: 9,022    Number of disabled students: 354

### Learning support staff and services:
Disability Support Services Team open Monday–Friday 9am–5pm.
Full-time staff: Head of Disabilities Support Services: Anne Peters; Student Disabilities Adviser: Julia Oldham.
Part-time staff: Student Disabilities Adviser – Dyslexia (Thursdays and Fridays): Emily Coote; Disabilities Administrator (term-time only): Margy Appleton.
Assistance with DSA applications; provision of auxiliary aids and services; advice and guidance; assistance arranging specialist equipment; support in accessing dyslexia support specialists, communicators, sign language interpreters, notetakers, technical and personal support; one-to-one/group tuition for students with dyslexia; counselling service; development of policies and provision to enhance awareness of disability issues and liaison with external organisations and agencies.

## Home sweet home:

There are four rooms providing wheelchair access for students with disabilities on the High Wycombe site and two on the Chalfont site. Work is currently in progress to increase this number. Kitchens with adapted work-benches and sink areas are also available. Accommodation can be guaranteed for duration of student's course.

## Out and about:

University college: The university college will pay for transport on open days. Dedicated parking spaces near both accommodation and study areas.

Public transport: The railway station, and some trains, buses and taxis are accessible to people who are wheelchair users. Some buses, trains, train stations and taxis are accessible to people with visual impairments. There is a taxi scheme for disabled people operating in the High Wycombe area.

## Taking it easy:

At university college: The gym is accessible.

Locally: High Wycombe is hilly, but flat in the central area, and is an accessible town. The town centre is flat and some of the town's facilties, including the Swan Theatre, are fully accessible. The cinema is also accessible, but seating for wheelchair users is available only at the front. A Shopmobility scheme operates in and around High Wycombe, and the central area has tactile pavements at key crossing points. There is a local area disability guide which at the time of writing was being updated. Please contact the Disabilities Support Service for further information.

## And another thing ...

➡ Access to some of the university college's buildings is difficult for those people with mobility difficulties and/or for wheelchair users. BCUC is currently improving access for students with disabilities.

➡ The three campuses vary considerably in terms of age, use and quality. Queen Alexandra Campus is accessible to wheelchair users. Chalfont Campus has buildings with limited access for wheelchair users. Wellesbourne Campus has limited access for wheelchair users and there are no lift systems to areas above the ground floor. Prospective students are advised and welcome to visit BCUC and the surrounding town in order to make an informed decision.

➡ The university college hopes to relocate to new accessible premises in High Wycombe in 2006/7.

➡ The university college has a Disability Steering Group, which monitors the implementation of the action agreed under the QAA's *Code of Practice*, Section 3: Students with Disabilities. Representation is encouraged from all parts of the BCUC, including students with disabilities.

## QAA Report: Paragraphs 95 and 96, August 2002

The *Account* noted that the university college had appointed a full-time Disabilities Adviser, and that Disabilities Support Services provides advice and guidance for prospective and current students with disabilities. Arrangements for students with special needs, including dyslexia, are made by the Disabilities Adviser. The audit team discussed the university college's response to the QAA *Code of Practice* on students with disabilities and to the Disability Discrimination Act 1995. As with other published elements of the QAA *Code of Practice*, the team noted that the university college had carefully checked its own procedures against the advice in the *Code* and had taken steps to amend the former in the light of the latter. As part of its response, the university college had established a Disabilities Steering Group (DSG), which is drawing up a Disability Development Plan. DSG reports to the Student Affairs Committee of the Council.

Reviewing the work undertaken and in progress in the university college to support students with disabilities, the audit team noted that while not having received earmarked funding under the HEFCE Disabilities Initiative, the university college had nonetheless taken positive steps to support current and prospective students with disabilities.

## The Disability Statement/Brochure:

*Disability Statement 2001*
Includes: Current policy; contacts; education facilities and support; enquiries and applications; examination and assessments; access and accommodation; students with disabilities at the university.

## Local disability public service providers:

Alan Switzalkie, Access Officer, High Wycombe Council
01494 461 000.
Town Access Group, BCUC 01494 522141.
Priory Centre 01494 523440.

## Camberwell College of Arts, The London Institute

Peckham Road, London SE5 8UF

*General Enquiries:*
Tel: 020 7514 6302
Fax: 020 7514 6310
Email: enquiries@camb.linst.ac.uk
Website: www.camb.linst.ac.uk

**Disability Representative: Eve Graves**
**Tel: 020 7514 6422**
**Fax: 020 7514 6405**
**Email: e.graves@**
**camb.linst.ac.uk**

### Fields of study:
Art and design; conservation; design; graphic design; visual arts – ceramics/drawing/painting/sculpture/silversmithing and metalwork.

➡ Part-time study: **Yes, some.**
➡ Distance learning: **No.**

### About the college:
Camberwell College of Arts, in south London, is at the heart of a remarkable artistic community. The college, which is part of the London Institute, was endorsed as one of the top colleges in the country when the QAA awarded Camberwell 23 out of 24 in its Subject Review of Art and Design. In addition, the college has previously been recognised by the Queen's Anniversary Prize for Further and Higher Education for its work in paper conservation. Camberwell is near to central London and to Tate Modern, the South Bank Centre and the Design Museum. The London Institute is Europe's largest centre for education in art, design and communication. It brings together five of the world's most distinguished art and design colleges: Camberwell College of Arts, Central St Martins College of Art and Design, Chelsea College of Art and Design, London College of Fashion and London College of Printing.

Total number of students: 1,435     Number of disabled students: 180

### Learning support staff and services:
Disability Representative and Dyslexia Coordinator: Eve Graves.
See London Institute entry for further information and contact details of the Disability Team who are responsible for setting up support arrangements.

## Camborne School of Mines

University of Exeter, Redruth, Cornwall TR15 3SE

*General Enquiries:*
Tel: 01209 714866
Fax: 01209 716977
Email: admissions@csm.ac.uk
Website: www.ex.ac.uk/CSM/

**Fields of study:**
Geology; minerals engineering; minerals surveying and resource management; mining/mine and quarry engineering; surveying and environmental management and environmental science and technology.

**About the school:**
Cornwall is an ideal location for the practical training of students from the Camborne School of Mines in all aspects of Earth resources. The region has a tradition of being used to study geology, mining engineering, surveying, minerals engineering and environmental issues. In fact Cornwall is the most important area for the extraction and processing of industrial and metalliferous minerals in the UK. All CPD (continuing professional development) modules are offered in flexible, distance-learning format. Students receive email and telephone support from their tutors.

**Learning support staff and services:**
Please refer to the University of Exeter's entry for further information and contact details of the Disability Coordinator, who is responsible for setting up support arrangements at Camborne School of Mines.

## University of Cambridge

Cambridge CB2 1TN

*General Enquiries:* Admission
Tel: 01223 742710
Fax: 01223 332332
Website: www.cam.ac.uk
Email: admissions@cam.ac.uk

**Disability Adviser: Judith Jesky**
**Tel: 01223 332301**
**Fax: 01223 766863**
**Email: jmj28@cam.ac.uk or**
**ucam-disability@lists.cam.ac.uk**
**Text: 01223 764083**

University of Cambridge

## Fields of study:
Anglo-Saxon, Norse and Celtic; archaeology and anthropology; architecture; chemical engineering; classics; computer science; economics; education studies; engineering; English; geography; history; history of art; land economy; law; linguistics; management studies; manufacturing engineering; mathematics; medicine; modern and medieval languages; music; natural sciences; oriental studies; philosophy; social and political sciences; theology and religious studies; veterinary medicine.

➡ Part-time study: **No.**
➡ Distance learning: **No.**

## About the university:
Cambridge University is one of the oldest universities in the world and one of the largest in the UK. Cambridge is a collegiate university, and students are members of a college, live within their college base and attend seminars and supervisions within college. Students then attend lectures, do lab work, etc. at the appropriate university faculty and take the university examinations. There are 31 colleges and over 100 departments, faculties and schools and a central administration. All prospective students should refer to the university's access guide available on www.ca.ac.uk/cambuniv/disability/.

| Total number of students: 16,500   Number of disabled students: 645 |
| --- |

## Learning support staff and services:
The Disability Resource Centre (DRC)
Disability Adviser: Judith Jeskey and team are based at Keynes House, Trumpington Street, Cambridge CB2 1QA
Information and advice at any stage of application; assistance with DSA applications; dyslexia support; assistance in recruiting note-takers and readers; Access technology training sessions and liaison across the university regarding student support and disability awareness.

## Home sweet home:
All of the colleges are responsible for providing accommodation, and facilities vary in their accessibility. Most have some rooms accessible to wheelchair users (most en-suite), and some colleges are able to accommodate a PA. Guide dogs can be accommodated in many colleges. Rooms can be adapted where required to suit the needs of students who are D/deaf or hard of hearing. The university's access guide gives an overview of each college.

Accommodation can be guaranteed for duration of student's course.

## Out and about:
University: Dedicated parking spaces near both accommodation and study areas are limited and subject to application procedures.
Public transport: Dial-a-Ride and Taxicard scheme. Low-floor buses. There is a bus pass scheme providing free travel for blind/visually impaired people and half-price travel for those with mobility difficulties, tel: 01223 358977. The train station is a mile from the centre of town.

## Taking it easy:
At university: Fenner's, the university's physical education centre, is accessible to people who are wheelchair users and has a fitness room with some equipment specifically designed for the use of people with disabilities.
Locally: Cambridge is a historic, small and compact city centre. The town centre is pedestrianised from 10am to 4pm Monday to Saturday.

## And another thing ...
➡ The university's access guide gives an overview of accessibility to help you in shortlisting colleges you wish to consider – for more information contact the college admissions office or the disability adviser. The access guide can be viewed on the university Website: www.cam.ac.uk/cambuniv/disability/accguide/.
➡ For more information contact the DRC website.

## The Disability Statement/Brochure:
Available online at: www.cam.ac.uk/cambuniv/disability/hefce.html
Includes: Application; facilities and equipment – general; facilities and equipment by disability; accessibility; personal care; accommodation; sources of help; teaching and examinations; financial support; monitoring provision; future developments; contact name and disclaimer.

## Local disability public service providers:
Directions Plus, Orwell House, Cowley Road, Cambridge.
Cambridge City Council, The Guildhall, Cambridge.
CAMREAD, 167 Green End Road, Cambridge CB4 1RN; 01223 424220. Reading service for visually impaired people.
Lifecraft, The Bath House, Gwydir Street, Cambridge CB1 2LW; 01223 566957. Drop-in and information centre about mental health difficulties, treatments and local resources.

## Canterbury Christ Church University College
North Holmes Road, Canterbury, Kent CT1 1QU

*General Enquiries:*
Tel: 01227 767700
Fax: 01227 470442
Email: Admissions@cant.ac.uk
Website: www.cant.ac.uk

**Disability Adviser: Margaret Scott**
**Tel: 01227 782842**
**Fax: 01227 767279**
**Email: m.a.scott14@**
**canterbury.ac.uk**
**Text: 01227 782842**

**Fields of study:**
American studies; animal science; art; business; business mathematics; continuing professional development for teachers; early childhood studies; English; English in international communication; French; geography; health studies; heritage conservation; history; initial teacher training; information technology; leisure studies; marketing; mathematics; media studies; music; psychology; public health; radio, film and television studies; science (environmental); science (natural); social science; sport science; statistics; TESOL; theology and religious studies; tourism studies.

➡ Part-time study: **Yes.**
➡ Distance learning: **Yes, but only for MA, TEFL and TESOL.**

**About the college:**
Canterbury Christ Church University College was founded by the Church of England in 1962 and welcomes students of all faiths and none. The Canterbury campus was built on what was once the old orchard ground of St Augustine's Abbey and is still largely surrounded by the medieval abbey wall and the buildings of St Augustine's that are next to the college. The city of Canterbury is only five minutes' walk from the college. Canterbury is a tourist attraction, famous for its cathedral, and not far from the seaside. A new higher education campus has recently been built in the heart of Thanet, in east Kent, designed and built with twenty-first-century HE needs in mind. The Salomaos campus near Tunbridge Wells provides programmes in clinical psychology, careers guidance and teacher training. .

Total number of students: 13,000
Number of disabled students: approx. 700

**Learning support staff and services:**
Student Support Department
Full-time staff: Director: Geoff Haworth; Secretary: Pam Wall; Senior

Counsellor: Margaret Simpson.
Part-time staff: Disability Adviser: Margaret Scott; Study Support Unit Secretary: Sissy Dewhirst; Disabilities Adviser's Secretary: Lauren Lunsford.
Assistance with DSA applications, Hardship Funds, grants and trusts; provision of auxiliary aids and services; advice and guidance; one-to-one/group tuition for students with dyslexia; dyslexia screening; support for students with mental health issues; orientation training; alternative examination arrangements and liaison with external organisations.

**Home sweet home:**
There are two rooms suitable for students who are wheelchair users and their PAs, and two rooms accessible for wheelchair users who do not require a live-in PA. The rooms are on the ground floor and are en-suite. These rooms are in catered and self-catering halls. A guide-dog relief area is provided by a hall on campus. Accommodation can be guaranteed for duration of student's course.

**Out and about:**
College: At the moment, the SU minibuses are not wheelchair accessible. The Disability Adviser is able to provide information on other local accessible transport. Dedicated parking spaces near both accommodation and study areas.
Public transport: Some buses, trains and taxis are currently accessible to wheelchair users. Trains and taxis are accessible for people with a visual impairment. Lynx Taxis, which are accessible for wheelchair users, operate in the area.

**Taking it easy:**
At college: The SU has level access to the ground floor where most events take place, and has wheelchair accessible toilet facilities. The student bar is accessible. The St George's Fitness Centre is not accessible to wheelchair users or those with mobility difficulties. There is a recently formed Focus Group for disabled students. The college has connections with the local PHAB club.
Locally: Due to its age, the local city is not very accessible: it is flat with hills to the north and has cobbled streets. Some of the town's facilities are accessible and there is a Shopmobility scheme. Some pavements are tactile. The Disability Adviser holds a database of accessible facilities in the area, including sporting venues, and there is an access map to Canterbury as well as an access guide.

**And another thing ...**

➡ Although the college surroundings are very attractive and interesting this brings with it some real problems in terms of access for physically disabled people. The most recent buildings are accessible for wheelchair users and people with mobility difficulties, but some of the older buildings have not yet been adapted. Some disabled people may find difficulty in moving easily from one part of the campus to another due to changes in level and the mixture of old and new buildings. The new campus at Thanet is accessible to disabled people.

➡ There has been a multimillion-pound development programme over recent years that has included many parts of the college.

➡ Lifts and ramps have been installed and accessible toilet facilities are available in most of the college buildings.

➡ The college tries to ensure that accessible lecture theatres and classrooms are available to students who require this and to provide induction loops for students who are D/deaf or hard of hearing.

➡ Amongst the range of programmes offered by the college are those that are specifically designed to develop skills and understanding for supporting people with disabilities, including: BSc in Occupational Therapy; programmes in special educational needs; accreditation of programmes for the Royal London Society for the Blind; and sign language courses. The college is able to draw on this in-house expertise in its commitment to supporting students with disabilities.

➡ A relief area is provided for guide dogs at Canterbury campus.

➡ The college will arrange for communication support for D/deaf or hard of hearing students for interviews and open days.

## The Disability Statement/Brochure:
*Information for Disabled Students 2000–2003*
Includes: College; support; admissions; information by disability; accommodation, medical care and personal support; examination and assessments; sporting and leisure facilities; services; monitoring and complaints; future plans and further information.

## Local disability public service providers:
DIAL UK 01302 310123; email: dialuk@aol.com.
The Student Services Department holds a database of 3,000 organisations and providers of services in Kent, produced by Kent Information Federation: 0808 808 5050.

## Cardiff University – Prifysgol Caerdydd
46 Park Place, Cardiff CF10 3AT

*General Enquiries:*
Tel: 029 2087 4404
Fax: 029 2087 4130
Email: info@Cardiff.ac.uk
Website: www.cardiff.ac.uk

**Adviser for Disabilities/Special Needs:**
**Simon Phillips**
**Tel: 029 2087 4610**
**Fax: 029 2087 4947**
**Website: www.cardiff.ac.uk/ssd**
**Mini: 029 2087 4610**
**Email: phillipss3@cf.ac.uk**

### Fields of study:
Architecture; biosciences; business; chemistry; city and regional planning; computer science; dentistry; earth sciences; engineering; English communication and philosophy; European studies; history and archaeology; Japanese studies; journalism, media and cultural studies; law; mathematics; medicine; music; optometry and vision sciences; pharmacology and therapeutics; pharmacy; physics and astronomy; psychology; religious and theological studies; social sciences; Welsh/Cymraeg.

➡ Part-time study: **Yes.**
➡ Distance learning: **Yes.**

### About the university:
The university is based in and around Cardiff's civic centre, alongside the National Museum and Gallery, the Welsh Assembly's offices and other civic buildings. The university is currently ranked 15th out of 102 UK universities for research, according to the most recent independent assessment of research. Cardiff has recently been hailed as the most desirable city in the United Kingdom in which to work and live.

Total number of students: 15,500    Number of disabled students: 400

### Learning support staff and services:
Student Advisory Services
Adviser for Students with Disabilities/Special Needs: Simon Phillips.
Coordination of arrangements for the admission of students with disabilities; alternative examination/assessment arrangements; information and advice on setting up and funding personal support workers; advice on DSA, finance, car parking, accommodation, equipment and study needs; the administration of the Dyslexia

Resource Centre, which includes arrangement of assessment by an educational psychologist; advice and support given on computing skills, study skills, purchase of equipment and applications to LEAs.

## Home sweet home:
Wheelchair accessible accommodation is available in five halls of residence – some catered and some self-catering. For students who are D/deaf or hard of hearing, study bedrooms are available with flashing/vibrating fire alarms, if required. Accommodation, at the usual fee paid by students, can be made available for PAs if necessary. It may be possible to arrange minor adaptations, e.g. grab rails, cool storage for medication, safe disposal of syringes and extra power points. Contact Jan Keelan at the Residences Office (tel: 029 2087 4849). Accommodation can be guaranteed for duration of student's course.

## Out and about:
University: Dedicated parking spaces near both accommodation and study areas, but not all halls of residence have parking facilities.
Public transport: Buses and trains are accessible.

## Taking it easy:
At university: The university is seeking ways of making the sports and recreation facilities accessible for as many students as possible. Contact the sport and recreation manager on 029 2087 4045. The SU annually elects a non-sabbatical officer for students with disabilities.
Locally: Cardiff is an accessible town.

## And another thing ...
➡ In excess of £140 million has been invested in recent years to provide students with modern and well-equipped facilities. Work has been carried out to provide ramps, escape chairs, automatic entrance doors, wider corridor doors, motorised doors to lifts, alarms and disabled toilet facilities. However, some of the older buildings present problems of access for students with mobility difficulties.
➡ Access to and facilities within the 13 libraries vary. Library staff will be pleased to make arrangements to provide a full range of services and facilities – contact Linda Kelly (tel: 029 2087 4795).
➡ A CCTV (shared between libraries) is available to enlarge text for students who are visually impaired.
➡ Future plans include installing loop systems to selected lecture rooms.

➡ The university liaises with Disability Wales, RNIB, RNID, the Equal Opportunities Higher Education Network and CSV.

## QAA reports:
'Students met by the team stated that the prospectuses and other publications (such as that dealing with disabled access) gave a fair and honest depiction of the university', paragraph 58, October 2001.

## The Disability Statement/Brochure:
Includes: Existing policy; existing provision – including accommodation and study support; future plans and further information.

## Local disability public service provider:
Disability Wales.

---

| University of Central England in Birmingham |
| :---: |

Perry Barr, Birmingham B42 2SU

*General Enquiries:*
University Marketing Unit
Tel: 0121 331 5000
Fax: 0121 331 6740
Email: prospectus@uce.ac.uk
Website: www.uce.ac.uk

**Disability Team**
**Tel: 0121 331 6265/5128**
**Fax: 0121 331 6569**
**Email: disability@uce.ac.uk**
**Website: www.ssv.nce.ac.uk**

## Fields of study:
Art and design; built environment; business; computing, information and English; computing, multimedia and engineering; education; health and community care; law and social sciences; music.

➡ Part-time study: **Yes.**
➡ Distance learning: **No.**

## About the university:
Although a modern university, UCE is steeped in history, having evolved over some 150 years through the amalgamation of various institutes, colleges and schools in the Birmingham area. UCE consists of eight campuses including the Birmingham Conservatoire. This development is reflected in the buildings on the university's different sites and campuses, providing an interesting mix of styles, which range from modern accommodation at Perry Barr to the Grade I listed Venetian Gothic building at Margaret Street.

University of Central England in Birmingham

| Total number of students: 25,000 |
| Number of disabled students: 2,000 |

## Learning support staff and services:

Three Disability Advisers; Dyslexia Support Coordinator; Transition and Diversity Coordinator; Healthy Minds Project Coordinator; PA Scheme Coordinator.

The Disability Team aims to meet students' needs on an individual and confidential basis. The PA scheme recruits students and graduates to act as support workers in a variety of capacities and also organises support such as BSL interpreters.

The Disability Advisers arrange support for students and liaise with academic departments to arrange individual support within faculties. The Advisers have some basic signing skills.

The Transition and Diversity Coordinator arranges individual transition programmes for disabled applicants and liaises with local college of FE on transition issues.

The Healthy Minds Project aims to promote a programme of awareness of mental health issues amongst lecturers and students and to develop support systems for students who may be mental health service users.

The Dyslexia Support Coordinator works with a team of experienced and qualified dyslexia support tutors to provide one-to-one tuition to dyslexic students.

For further information about the PA scheme, log on to: www.personalassistancescheme.org.uk.

For information and support for transition from FE to HE, log on to the Think Uni website: www.thinkuni.info.

## Home sweet home:

There are a number of rooms available for students with disabilities at Cambrian Hall, The Coppice and Oscott Gardens.

Accommodation can be guaranteed for duration of student's course.

## Out and about:

University: Dedicated parking spaces near both accommodation and study areas on main sites.

Public transport: Bus service accessible to wheelchair users and has audible information. Local train stations are accessible to wheelchair users, but UCE recommends that wheelchair users travel via Birmingham International station, which has a good passenger lift to all platforms. Some access is possible at Birmingham New Street station, but only via goods lifts. Accessible taxis are available from ranks outside both of these stations.

## Taking it easy:
At university: SU.
Locally: Birmingham city centre has been and still is undergoing substantial refurbishment to provide attractive, varied and accessible entertainment, shopping, etc.

## And another thing ...
➡ The Disability Advisers may be able to arrange the loan of equipment to students who do not qualify for DSA funding.
➡ With one or two exceptions, most university buildings are accessible.

## The Disability Statement/Brochure:
*Students with Disabilities: A guide to support*
Contents: Applications; support; access; accommodation; exams; finance; monitoring and complaints; future plans and what to do next.

## Local disability public service provider:
Birmingham City Council.

---

| **University of Central Lancashire** |
| --- |

Preston PR1 2HE

*General Enquiries:* Admissions Office
Tel: 01772 201201
Fax: 01772 892911
Email: cenquiries@uclan.ac.uk
Website: www.uclan.ac.uk

**Senior Adviser:
Catherine Badminton
Tel: 01772 892593
Fax: 01772 892939
Email: disability@uclan.ac.uk
ccolcomb@uclan.ac.uk**

## Fields of study:
Art, design and technology; business; cultural; health; land-based and environmental studies; legal and social studies; science.

➡ Part-time study: **Yes.**
➡ Distance learning: **Yes, a few courses.**

## About the university:
Preston and Cumbria are the two campuses of the University of Central Lancashire. The university is a blend of historic and hi-tech architecture. Six months after graduation, 95 per cent of UCLAN students are either in work or in full-time study. The university is

University of Central Lancashire

located right in the centre of Preston, Lancashire's administrative and commercial centre.

> Total number of students: 20,000
> Number of disabled students: 1,000

## Learning support staff and services:
Student Services
Senior Adviser for Students with Disabilities and/or learning difficulties: Catherine Badminton; Chris Colcomb (Cumbria Campus). Academic assessment of need; assistive technology; examinations; training/technical services; liaison with tutors; additional support workers; support with daily living; funding your requirements; residential accommodation; welfare matters; career guidance.

## Home sweet home:
A number of rooms in halls of residence have adapted facilities on the Preston campus.
Accommodation can be guaranteed for duration of student's course.

## Out and about:
University: Dedicated parking spaces near both accommodation and study areas.
Public transport: The Preston campus is near the town centre and is convenient for public transport. There is a taxi scheme for disabled people operating in the area.

## Taking it easy:
At university: A new outdoor sports facility, the Preston Sports Arena, has recently been opened 2 miles from the main campus. The facilities are accessible to disabled users. Indoor facilities, which are still located on the main campus, are not quite as accessible.
Locally: Preston has a pedestrianised city centre and is both flat and hilly. There is a Shopmobility scheme and some pavements are tactile.

## And another thing ...
➡ The university belongs to NFAC.
➡ The majority of buildings are accessible with lifts.
➡ There is a Specialised Learning Resource Unit that offers a transcription service; access to personal readers; provision of equipment; coordination and day-to-day management of volunteer readers and registers of educational interpreters, notetakers, readers and audio typists.
➡ There is an elected disability officer in the SU.

➡ Support organisations and links include: RNIB; RNID; British Deaf Association and Council for Advancement of Communication with Deaf People.
➡ The university is working towards meeting the QAA guidelines, 'Students with Disabilities', and the anticipated legislation, which should end discrimination in education.
➡ If you have no source of funding you may be eligible for certain in-house services.
➡ Effort is made to support students who are not in receipt of DSA.

## The Disability Statement/Brochure:
*A Guide for Students with Disabilities @uclan*
Includes: Application; support; learning; confidentiality; living; student services; assistance with daily living; leisure; money matters; Cumbria campus; case studies; future developments and useful contacts.

## Local disability public service provider:
Lancashire County Council 01772 261743.

---

| **Central School of Speech and Drama** |
| --- |

Embassy Theatre, Eton Avenue, London NW3 3HY

*General Enquiries:*
Tel: 020 7722 8183
Fax: 020 7722 4132
Email: enquiries@cssd.ac.uk
Website: www.cssd.ac.uk

**Disability Coordinator: Keith Silvester**
**Tel: 020 7559 3933**
**Email: k.silvester@cssd.ac.uk**

## Fields of study:
Acting; media education with English; musical theatre, voice studies, drama and movement therapy; theatre – practice and circus, drama and education.

➡ Part-time study: **Yes, some courses.**
➡ Distance learning: **No.**

## About the school:
The Central School of Speech and Drama is currently located on two London sites: the main site at Swiss Cottage and a second site at Oval, Kennington. The Swiss Cottage site has as its centre the large turn-of-the-century Embassy Theatre. The Oval site building does not form part of the school's longer-term site development strategy.

| Total number of students: 653 | Number of disabled students: 40 |
|---|---|

## Learning support staff and services:
Student Counselling and Advisory Services
Full-time staff: Head of Student Counselling and Advisory Service:
Keith Silvester.
Part-time staff: Varies according to need for assessment and tuition;
Disability Support Officer
Assistance with DSA applications and other funding; advice and
guidance; one-to-one/group tutition for students with dyslexia;
dyslexia assessment testing; alternative examination, assessment and
study arrangements; support for students with mental health issues;
liaison with external organisations.

## Home sweet home:
The school has no student accommodation. Students are helped to
find accommodation through the counselling and advisory service
and (in summer) an accommodation officer. The school would try to
assist with any specific needs.
Accommodation cannot be guaranteed for duration of student's
course.

## Out and about:
School: There are *no* dedicated parking spaces near accommodation
or study areas.
Public transport: There is no lift at Swiss Cottage tube station but buses
are mostly accessible. Contact Access and Mobility (see Directory).

## Taking it easy:
At school: Student Union and bar.
Locally: Reasonably accessible. The town centre is flat and the
facilities are accessible. The pavements are not tactile. Information is
provided on entry via the school's *Student's Companion*. Artsline
publish a number of guides about access in London (see Directory).

## And another thing ...
➡ The Embassy Theatre is now fully wheelchair accessible. Much of the
   ground, first and second floors are fully accessible, with links to two
   adjoining new buildings. Unfortunately, however, a small area of the
   'core' central building remains currently unsuitable for wheelchair
   access, where staircases are too narrow for wheelchair lifts.
➡ All new parts of the school's site, built during the 1990s, have
   wheelchair access including lifts. The first of these new buildings,
   opened in 1992, includes workshops, theatre and design studios

as well as lecture and tutorial rooms. The second new building, opened in 1997, houses the library, the student bar and common room, as well as a number of administrative offices.

➡ There are a decreasing number of inconvenient and generally inaccessible Portakabin-style buildings on the rest of the site, which the school now owns and can fully develop. These will eventually disappear as future building phases are realised. However, such developments are heavily dependent on funding.

➡ The Oval site is a converted space which is all on one level, with wheelchair access and – where necessary – an alternative access point. The site has disabled facilities throughout, but is a temporary site and does not form part of the school's longer-term strategy.

➡ Students undertaking the BA(Hons) Theatre Practice (Circus) course are taught at the Circus Space, a converted former power station in Hoxton, north London. Disabled access to training spaces on this site is limited. Contact the Circus Space direct to discuss your needs.

➡ The majority of disabled students at the Central School of Speech and Drama are students with dyslexia.

➡ The school maintains active links with: Skill; the Adult Dyslexia and Skills Development Centre; the Adult Dyslexia Organisation; the Computer Centre for People with Disabilities at the University of Westminster; the Centre for Deaf People at the City Literary Institute; NIACE, the national organisation for adult learning; AMOSSHE (Association of Managers of Student Services in Higher Education; Graeae Theatre Company and Razor Edge Theatre Company.

## The Disability Statement/Brochure:
Available on the school's website.

---

| **Central St Martins College of Art and Design** |
| --- |

Southampton Row, London WC1B 4AP

*General Enquiries:* Lisa Armstrong
Tel: 020 7514 7022
Fax: 020 7514 7024
Email: applications@csm.linst.ac.uk
Website: www.csm.linst.ac.uk

**Disability Representative:**
**Malcolm Johnston**
**Tel: 020 7514 7127**
**Fax: 020 7514 7127**
**Email: m.johnston@csm.linst.ac.uk**

Chelsea College of Art and Design

## Fields of study:
Art and design; ceramic design.

- ➡ Part-time study: **Yes, postgraduate only.**
- ➡ Distance learning: **No.**

## About the college:
Central St Martins is the largest of the London Institute art colleges, yet it combines the benefits of size with the establishment of smaller study communities. Students are encouraged to engage in art and design as a collective and negotiated process, as well as an individually oriented enquiry. The college is also the home of the independently refereed *Journal of Contemporary Art*, after all. The London Institute is Europe's largest centre for education in art, design and communication. It brings together five of the world's most distinguished art and design colleges: Camberwell College of Arts, Central St Martins College of Art and Design, Chelsea College of Art and Design, London College of Fashion and London College of Printing.

## Learning support staff and services:
College Disability Representative: Malcolm Johnston; Dyslexia Coordinators: Claire Lofting (Southampton Row), Bill Henderson (Charing Cross), Tom Beggs (Southampton Row), Judy Johnson (Eagle Court).
See London Institute for further information and contact details of the Disability Team who are responsible for setting up support arrangements.

---

### Chelsea College of Art and Design
Manresa Road, London SW3 6LS

*General Enquiries:* College Office
Tel: 020 7514 7755
Fax: 020 7514 7778
Email: enquiries@chelsea.linst.ac.uk
Website: www.chelsea.linst.ac.uk

**Disability Representative:
Anne Smith
Tel: 020 7514 7750
Fax: 020 7514 7849
Email: a.smith@chel.linst.ac.uk**

## Fields of study:
Fine art – painting/sculpture/fine art media; interior design; practice and theory of visual art; textiles.

➡ Part-time study: **Yes.**
➡ Distance learning: **No.**

## About the college:
Chelsea College of Art and Design, which is part of the London Institute, has an international reputation for innovation and experiment. The School of Art has built its reputation over more than a century, and the recently created School of Design has quickly established itself in the forefront of innovations based on a sound understanding of technique. The college encourages its students to challenge orthodoxies both old and new in the belief that the renewal of art and design is fundamental to human society at a personal and public level. Both Schools of Art and Design are supported by a modern art and design library of international significance. The London Institute is Europe's largest centre for education in art, design and communication. It brings together five of the world's most distinguished art and design colleges: Camberwell College of Arts, Central St Martins College of Art and Design, Chelsea College of Art and Design, London College of Fashion and London College of Printing.

## Learning support staff and services:
College Disability Representative: Anne Smith; Dyslexia Coordinators: Pauline Courtenay (Hugon Road), Freya Purdue (Manresa Road).
See London Institute entry for further information and contact details of the Disability Team, who are responsible for setting up support arrangements.

---

### Chester, University College
Parkgate Road, Chester CH1 4BJ

*General Enquiries:*
Tel: 01244 375444
Fax: 01244 392820
Email: enquiries@chester.ac.uk
Website: www.chester.ac.uk

**Disability and Specific Needs Support Worker: Martha Broughton**
**Tel: 01244 375444 ext: 3601**
**Fax: 01244 392806**
**Email: disability@chester.ac.uk**
**Text: 01244 392870**

## Fields of study:
Art and technology; biology; business; computer science/information systems; criminology; dietetics; drama and theatre; English literature; geography; health and community studies; history; journalism;

languages; mathematics; media studies; nursing and midwifery; PE and sports science; psychology; radio and TV production; religious studies; teacher training; theology.

➡ Part-time study: **Yes, in some areas of study.**
➡ Distance learning: **No.**

### About the college:
Chester University College (Chester Campus) is a self-contained campus located in the historic town of Chester. Founded in 1893 by, among others, 19th-century prime minister William Gladstone, Chester College is only ten minutes' walk from the city centre and less than an hour's drive from the mountains and coastline of north Wales.

| Total number of students: approx. 8,000 |
| :---: |
| Number of disabled students: 385 |

### Learning support staff and services:
Learning Support Unit
Full-time staff: Assistant Director (TLSS): Carol Thomas, Disability and Specific Needs Worker: Martha Broughton; Tutors: Jane Taylor, D. Scott and I. Scott.
Part-time staff: R. Wilson.
Needs assessment; assistance with DSA application and Hardship Fund; provision of auxiliary aids and services; advice and guidance; one-to-one/group tuition for students with dyslexia; alternative examination, assessment and study arrangements; support service for students with mental health issues (via the medical centre(s)); liaison with external organisation; advise academic and support staff; develop institutional policy and provision and enhance awareness of disability issues.

### Home sweet home:
The campus at Chester is relatively flat and quite compact, therefore all the adapted rooms are located quite close to most of the teaching blocks. The college has adapted four ground-floor rooms for wheelchair users; all have modified en-suite bathroom facilities but none support self-catering. The college owns a single flat that has been modified for a person with physical disabilities and which supports self-catering. In addition to the above, the college has two ground-floor rooms fitted with vibrating fire alarms for the benefit of students who are D/deaf or hard of hearing. Warrington Campus is also flat and largely accessible. The College is currently making improvements to the facilities at the campus in order to enhance physical access and accommodation for people with disabilities.

Accommodation can be guaranteed for duration of the student's course only by agreement with the accommodation manager.

### Out and about:
College: Dedicated parking spaces near both accommodation and study areas. Six spaces close to library, one next to the accommodation block.
Public transport: The train station is accessible for wheelchair users and there are some wheelchair accessible buses. The Motability taxi scheme operates in the area.

### Taking it easy:
At college: There is a swimming pool, which is accessible, but there is no hoist and the tiles are slippery. An access audit has recently been conducted and these issues are to be addressed. The new gym and sports hall are accessible, as are the SU and bar.
Locally: Chester is fairly flat and its facilities' accessibility is variable. There is a Shopmobility scheme and some of the pavements are tactile. DIAL House, Chester, has undertaken a survey to determine the accessibility of a number of venues in Chester (cinemas, restaurants, theatres, pubs, etc.). Its findings have been published in a booklet entitled *A Young Disabled Person's Guide to Chester*. Chester City Council has produced a general access guide.

### And another thing ...
➡ An access guide for Chester Campus is available.
➡ There is also an Interact Mentoring Project/Careers Enhancement Project, which has been going since 1999.

## The Disability Statement/Brochure:
Sources of support and guidance; contact names and numbers; the college's approach to supporting students with disabilities or specific needs; management of application details; academic support by disability; academic support by service; physical access; personal care support systems; specific arrangements for studying; assessment and examinations; financial support; procedures for monitoring provision for students with disabilities; proposed disability-related developments; social life; additional reading; appendix.

### Local disability public service providers:
DIAL House, Hamilton Place, Chester; 01244 315025; www.dial housechester.org.uk.
Chester Tourist Information Centre, Town Hall, Northgate Street, Chester; 01244 402385; g.tattum@chestercc.gov.uk.

Chester City Council.
Vision Support Service, Liverpool Road.

---

## City College Norwich

Ipswich Road, Norwich NR2 2LJ

*General Enquiries:* Information Centre
Tel: 01603 773311
Fax: 01603 773301
Email: none
Website: www.ccn.ac.uk

**Disability Support Team**
**Manager: Marie Rought**
**Tel: 01603 773058**
**Fax: 01603 773535**
**Email: mrought@ccn.ac.uk**
**Text: 01603 773509**

**Fields of study:**
Arts; business; childhood studies; computing; construction;
engineering; environmental health; hospitality, travel, tourism, leisure;
media and multimedia; sciences.

➡ Part-time study: **Yes.**
➡ Distance learning: **Outreach but not at home.**

**About the college:**
City College, Norwich is just a few minutes' walk from the heart of
this cathedral city. It is a campus institution that was established 100
years ago and is a partner college of Anglia Polytechnic University.
City College provides FE and HE courses. Norfolk boasts an unspoilt
coastline and the famous Norfolk Broads.

Total number of students: 15,000 Number of disabled students: 1,320

**Learning support staff and services:**
Disability Support Team
Disability Support Team Manager: Marie Rought; Student Advisers:
Gareth Cronin, Karen Burridge, Sue Herring (for students who are
D/deaf or hard of hearing); senior facilitator; communication support
workers; sign language communicators; facilitators; communication
support assistant; administrative assistant.
Identify needs; organise additional support required; draw up the
Student Support Plan; arrange informal visits to the college; liaise with
external agencies; referral to educational psychologist for dyslexia
assessment; monitor and make recommendations on access and
inclusiveness; one-to-one classroom support; additional support with

English for D/deaf and hard of hearing students; assistance with getting around college; personal assistance; support in exams as appropriate; clarification of assessment criteria; production of copies of publications in alternative formats.

The Learner Centre offers learning support to all college students. The staff here can offer advice on study skills, assessment procedures and exam support. A Learner Centre facilitator will provide one-to-one classroom support.

## Home sweet home:

Six rooms have been adapted for use by disabled students. Accommodation can be guaranteed for duration of student's course.

## Out and about:

College: An accessible minibus is available for field trips, visits or work placements. Dedicated parking spaces near both accommodation and study areas.

Public transport: There are two buses that service the college, only one of which is accessible to wheelchair users.

## Taking it easy:

At college: The SU is on the top floor, which is accessed via a ramp to the main entrance and a lift. The SU bar is located on the ground floor. The gym is accessible, with one-to-one tuition for students with visual impairments and individual support programmes arranged. The annual membership is very cheap, approx. £5 per year. All the refectories are accessible.

Locally: Norwich shopping mall is accessible and has a Shopmobility scheme.

## And another thing ...

➡ The Disability Support Team continues to grow and develop to provide support for a full range of disabilities to include students with visual impairment and those who are D/deaf or hard of hearing, physical disabilities, autistic spectrum disorders, mental health issues, etc. Foundation Studies Centre has the responsibility for students with general learning difficulties, and the Learner Centre for those with specific learning difficulties.

➡ Many college programmes include field trips, visits or work placements. Wherever possible, arrangements will be made to ensure all students are able to participate fully.

➡ The college has a laptop computer loan scheme. Other items for loan include talking calculators, portable loops and Dictaphones.

➡ Facilities: text reader; CCTV text enlarger; text enlargement software; voice activated software; large screen monitors; word prediction software; alpha smart laptop notetakers.
➡ Sign language communicators, hearing support assistants, readers/notetakers and facilitators are available to students who require them.

## The Disability Statement/Brochure:
Available in all accessible formats on request.
Includes: Disability Support Team; heads of centres; policy; legislation; joining a programme; support; educational facilities; other facilities and support; student services; access; college committees; complaints; college campus plan.

### Local disability public service provider:
Social Services, Norfolk Health Authority.

---

| City University, London |
| --- |

Northampton Square, London EC1V 0HB

*General Enquiries:*
Tel: 020 7040 5060
Fax: 020 7040 5070
Website: www.city.ac.uk

**Disability Officer**
**Tel: 020 7040 0246**
**Fax: 020 7040 8592**
**Email: disability@city.ac.uk**
**dyslexia@city.ac.uk**
**Text: 020 7040 5080**

### Fields of study:
Arts and media; business management; computing; engineering; health sciences; law; mathematical, actuarial and statistical sciences; social and behavioural sciences.

➡ Part-time study: **Yes.**
➡ Distance learning: **Yes.**

### About the university:
City University – the university for business and the professions – is in the top 10 per cent of UK universities for graduate employment. The university is located in central London (Islington) on the borders of the City – one of the world's leading financial centres – and the West End with its social and cultural riches. Some 40 per cent of students are studying at postgraduate level.

| Total number of students: 13,000 | Number of disabled students: 238 |

## Learning support staff and services:
Disability Services and Dyslexia Support Unit
Full-time staff: Disability Services Assistant: Duncan Crawford
Part-time staff: Dyslexia Support Coordinator: Ellen Morgan
Provision of information, support and advice on a wide variety of issues including access and grants (including DSA application assistance); referral to local Access centres or arrangement of assessment on site; arrangement of sign language interpreters, lipspeakers, notetakers (provided by third party); advise academic and administrative staff including the timetabling service; alternative examination and assessment arrangements; advice and demonstration of adaptive technology; orientation sessions; support service for students with mental health issues; Disabled Student Networking (see below) is also facilitated by Disability Services.
The Dyslexia Support Unit offers: screening and diagnostic services for students with dyslexia; psychologist diagnostic assessment arrangements; study support programmes; examination preparation; training and advice to academic departments.
Non-medical support assistance may be sought with the help of the Student Employment Service within the Career Development Centre.

## Home sweet home:
The university has wheelchair accessible accommodation available in two of the residential halls: Walter Sickett Hall and Francis Rowley Court. Specialist needs should be arranged by prior negotiation with Disability Services and the Accommodation and Welfare Service. PA accommodation can be arranged. All study bedrooms have direct dial telephone links with voicemail and connection to the university's central computing facilities. The various halls are all within approximately half a mile of Northampton Square. Accommodation can be guaranteed for duration of student's course when necessary.

## Out and about:
University: Vehicle parking on the Northampton Square site can be arranged. The City of London (Barbican site) operates a Red Badge scheme similar to the Blue Badge scheme. The London Borough of Islington makes most controlled parking available to Blue Badge holders. Contact Disability Services for more information. There are dedicated parking spaces near accommodation and study areas.
Public transport: Some buses, trains, train stations and taxis are accessible to wheelchair users and people with a visual impairment. Information on public transport is held by Disability Services. The

nearest underground stations are Angel, Barbican and Farringdon. Contact Access and Mobility (see Directory).

## Taking it easy:

At university: university catering facilities and the SU buildings are fully accessible to wheelchair users. The SU has a representative of students with disabilities on its executive committee. Only the ground floor of the sports centre is currently accessible. There are plans to provide and complete wheelchair access to the sports centre playing courts and changing rooms by 2005.

Locally: City University is based in central London adjacent to the vibrant social centres of Angel and Clerkenwell. The city centre is flat and facilities are accessible. There is a Shopmobility scheme and the pavements are tactile. Disability Action Islington (see below) can provide information on the local area, and Artsline (see Directory) on art and culture venues. See also *Access all areas: disability, technology and learning* publication.

## And another thing …

➡ All new and refurbished teaching space and lecture theatres are wheelchair accessible with in-built induction loops, but some rooms in older parts of the estate are not. The Timetabling Service will allocate student groups to appropriate teaching accommodation.

➡ Large monitors are standard in public computing services, departmental facilities and the Open Learning Centre. The library is accessible. There are plans to ensure that all central student support services are relocated into accessible accommodation over the next two years. The university's access map can identify best routes around the university.

➡ There is large, clear signage throughout the university, new lifts with floor announcements, and important doors have signs, such as to toilet facilities, in Braille.

➡ Audio Visual Services have radio induction microphones for hearing aid users. There are plans to recruit and arrange training for notetakers. There is subtitled material in the library catalogue.

➡ The Open Learning Centre offers study skills and IT support.

➡ The university works with specialist employment agencies when organising student placements and employment.

➡ Particular emergency evacuation procedures will be confirmed for all buildings that students with disabilities are likely to access.

➡ The university has links with City Lit Support Unit.

➡ The university facilitates a Disabled Students Network that provides a focus for social networking and self-help amongst students with disabilities.

## QAA Report: Paragraph 64, September 2000

In July 1998 the Welfare Committee and its Disability Sub-committee, which reported to Council, were replaced by the Student and Staff Services Development Group (SSSDG), which reports jointly to the University Council and Senate. In the Account it was claimed that, 'the project-based approach adopted by SSSDG facilitates collaboration between professional heads of central services, academic staff and the students union, focusing on issues that cut across service divisions'. The audit team considered the support offered to students with disabilities in particular. It noted that the university's commitment to this group of students is evident from its conversion of a part-time disability officer into a full-time post supported by a new part-time administrator's post. Sections devoted to the admission and support of disabled students appear in both undergraduate and postgraduate prospectuses, as does reference to recent improvements in disabled access to the students union and the library. The team learnt from its meeting with students that some work remained to be done, for example on access to the sports centre and improved communication with the SU on matters related to disability. Nonetheless it was clear to the team that the university had undertaken planning and committed resources towards meeting the needs of its disabled students. The university also appeared to be well placed to meet the precepts of the section of the QAA *Code of Practice* on students with disabilities when it addresses these later in the current year.

## The Disability Statement/Brochure:

*Handbook for Students with Disabilities or Dyslexia at City University: A guide to provision and facilities.* Available online at www.city.ac.uk/disability/s
Includes: Student support and guidance; application; accessibility; facilities and equipment; support by disability; accommodation; examinations; careers; other sources of support; planned future developments; feedback and further information.

## Local disability public service providers:

Disability Action in Islington (DAI), 90–92 Upper Street N1 0NP; 020 7226 0137; Text: 020 7359 1891; Fax: 020 7359 1855; email: daii@compuserve.com.
Islington Access Group 90–92 Upper Street, London N1 0NP.
City of London Access Officer, Social Services Department, Milton

Colchester Institute

Court, Moor Lane, London EC2Y 9BI; 020 7332 1995;
Text: 020 7332 3929.
Access and Mobility (see Directory).

---

## Colchester Institute

Sheepen Road, Colchester, Essex CO3 3LL

*General Enquiries:*
Tel: 01206 518000
Fax: 01206 763041
Email: info@colch-inst.ac.uk
Website: www.colch-inst.ac.uk

**Disability Coordinator:**
**Christine Cottingham**
**Tel: 01206 518733**
**Fax: 01206 518643**
**Email: Christine.cottingham**
**@colch-inst.ac.uk**

**Fields of study:**
Art, design and media; business, management and computing;
engineering, construction and science; health and social care; music
and performance arts.

➡ Part-time study: **Yes.**
➡ Distance learning: **No.**

**About the college:**
As a partner college of Anglia Polytechnic University, Colchester
Institute is part of a federation of educational establishments
providing higher education in this region. The Colchester campus is
situated just outside the old Roman walls and in close proximity to
both the town centre and the railway station. Colchester, once the
Roman capital of Britain, and Britain's oldest recorded town, is a
blend of ancient and modern with its Norman castle and museums
and a multimillion-pound sports and leisure centre.

Total number of students: 10,000
Number of disabled students: approx 400

**Learning support staff and services:**
Four full-time and six part-time members of staff; teacher for people
who are D/deaf or hard of hearing.
LSA (Learning Support Assistant) support for disabled students;
dyslexia support; assistance with application for the DSA.

**Home sweet home:**
There is no student accommodation. The institute uses rented accommodation if necessary.

**Out and about:**
Institute: 12 dedicated parking spaces near study areas.
Public transport: Anglia Railways is accessible to wheelchair users but the local buses are not.

**Taking it easy:**
At institute: As the institute is predominantly FE there is no bar or any other leisure facilities. A common room is in the process of being refurbished and this is accessible.
Locally: The area is accessible

**Local disability public service provider:**
Essex Disability Team, Park Road, Colchester.

---

| **Conservatoire for Acting and Musical Theatre** |
| :---: |

Millmead Terrace, Guildford, Surrey GU2 4YT

*General Enquiries:*                            **Jilly Hawksfield**
Conservatoire Coordinator              **Tel: 01483 734805**
Tel: 01483 560701                            **Fax: 01483 535431**
Fax: 01483 535431
Email: enquiries@conservatoire.org;
coco@conservatoire.org
Website: www.conservatoire.org

**Fields of study:**
Acting; stage management and musical theatre.

➡ Part-time study: **No.**
➡ Distance learning: **No.**

**About the conservatoire:**
The Conservatoire for Acting and Musical Theatre provides vocational training for actors and technicians in all areas of theatre and recorded media with nationally recognised qualifications.

| Total number of students: 240 | Number of disabled students: 12 |
| :--- | :--- |

**Learning support staff and services:**
There are no specific staff for students with disabilities.
Needs assessments; assistance with DSA applications; advice and guidance; alternative examination, assessment and study arrangements and support service for students with mental health issues.

**Home sweet home:**
The conservatoire has no halls of residence. It would try to find suitable accommodation for students with disabilities within its network of landlords in the town. Accommodation could therefore *not* be guaranteed for duration of student's course.

**Out and about:**
School: There are Dial-a-Ride facilities. There are no dedicated parking spaces near study areas.
Public transport: The train station and some buses, trains and taxis are accessible to wheelchair users and people with visual impairments.

**Taking it easy:**
At school: The SU is accessible. The conservatoire operates a pastoral care system for all students, where each one has a pastoral tutor for the duration of their course. This facility is extended to everyone, and disabled students may receive more support if necessary. Each new student is also allocated a second-year student for additional help and support.
Locally: The town centre is hilly but accessible. Some of its facilities are accessible and there is a Shopmobility scheme. The pavements are not tactile. There is a local accessibility guide called the *Access Guide to Guildford*.

**Local disability public service provider:**
Guildford Borough Council: 01483 505050.

---

| **Courtauld Institute of Art** |
| --- |

Somerset House, Strand, London WC2R ORN

*General Enquiries:*
Tel: 020 7848 2649
Fax: 020 7848 2410
Email: pgadmissions@courtauld.ac.uk
Website: www.courtauld.ac.uk

**Academic Registrar: Sarah West**
**Tel: 020 7848 2649**
**Fax: 020 7838 2410**
**Email: sarah.west@**
**courtauld.ac.uk**

**Field of study:**
History of art.

➡ Part-time study: **Yes, PhD/MPhil only.**
➡ Distance learning: **No.**

**About the institute**
The Courtauld Institute of Art, founded in 1932, is the major centre in Britain for the study of the history of western art. The Institute is located in the Strand Building of Somerset House, built in 1776–80 and the most famous neo-classical building in central London. The institute is part of the federal University of London and thus enjoys access to its broad-ranging support services.

| Total number of students: 389 | Number of disabled students: 10 |
|---|---|

**Learning support staff and services:**
There are no staff or services specifically for students with disabilities. The academic registrar is the member of senior management who is responsible for students with learning difficulties and/or disabilities. The institute aims to provide personal attention for applicants and will take reasonable steps to make adjustments and provide necessary facilities. Support is offered by: personal tutor system, welfare officer, Central Institutions Health Service and careers advice.
Needs assessment; assistance with DSA applications and HEFCE grants; advice and guidance; alternative examination, assessment and study arrangements; support service for students with mental health problems and liaison with external organisations.

**Home sweet home:**
The institute does not have its own residential accommodation, but its students are eligible to apply for places in the University of London intercollegiate halls of residence where there is adapted accommodation. It may then be possible to direct them towards suitable accommodation. The University of London accommodation office also has details of outside organisations that can provide housing advice for students with disabilities.

**Out and about:**
Institute: There are very limited dedicated parking spaces near study areas.
Public transport: Buses, the train stations, taxis and some trains are accessible to wheelchair users. All are accessible to people with

visual impairments. Contact Access and Mobility regarding access to public transport in London (see Directory).

**Taking it easy:**
At institute: The SU and refectory are accessible. Students can use the ULU (University of London Union) facilities.
Locally: Access in central London is mixed. The area is flat, with accessible facilities and tactile pavements. Artsline publish a number of guides about access in London (see Directory).

**And another thing ...**
➡ Facilities for disabled students in the Grade I listed building are generally good, as there is a lift in both wings. This gives access to the lecture theatre, to most of the galleries, to most seminar rooms, to the SU and the refectory and to the book and photographic libraries. Access within the libraries is limited, as not all changes of level can be managed with the aid of ramps, but staff provide special delivery services for students who require them.
➡ Some teaching takes place in the study rooms of individual members of staff; not all of these are accessible by lift, but teaching is relocated to accommodate students with disabilities whenever this is possible.
➡ The institute is reviewing its provision for students with disabilities in the light of the Disability Discrimination Act. Through the University of London the institute has access to the Royal Association for Disability and Rehabilitation (RADAR) as consultants on disability issues, and a new building audit will be carried out to ascertain where improvements can be made to ensure full participation by people with disabilities.

**The Disability Statement/Brochure:**
Covers: Current policy; current provision; academic services; physical environment and future activity and policy.

| Coventry University |
|:---:|

Priory Street, Coventry CV1 5FB

*General Enquiries:*
Tel: 024 7688 7688
Fax: 024 7688 8638
Email: education.cor@coventry.ac.uk
Website: www.coventry.ac.uk

**Disabilities Officer: Helen Bogusz**
**Tel: 024 7688 8029**
**Fax: 024 7688 8029**
**Email: disoff.ss@**
**coventry.ac.uk**
**Mini: 024 7688 8742**

## Fields of study:

Art and design; business; engineering; health and social sciences; international studies and law; mathematical and information sciences; science and the environment.

➡ Part-time study: **Yes.**
➡ Distance learning: **Limited.**

## About the university:

Coventry became a university in 1992, but its roots can be traced as far back as Coventry College of Design in 1843. Coventry University is a single city-centre campus that boasts a new, state-of-the-art £16 million library, which is almost wholly naturally ventilated, cooled and lit. Coventry is a lively, multicultural city, which recently celebrated opening the Sky Dome – a £33 million entertainment and leisure complex in the city centre. Coventry is just minutes from 750 square miles of Warwickshire countryside.

| Total number of students: 16,500+ |
| Number of disabled students: 424 |

## Learning support staff and services:

Disabilities Office
Disabilities Officer: Helen Bogusz; Mental Health Coordinator; Learning and Study Support Coordinator/Dyslexia Support: Sarah Williams and seven other members of staff in the Disabilities Office. Advise on welfare benefits and other entitlements including DSA; liaise with LEAs and social services departments; provision of auxiliary aids and services; advice and guidance; one-to-one/group tuition for students with dyslexia; alternative examination, assessment and study arrangements; support service for students with mental health issues; organise appropriate accommodation; coordinate schemes that provide both academic and personal support (including orientation of the campus); operate an equipment loan service that includes specialist items such as laptop computers, spellcheckers, radio hearing aids/portable loop systems, Dictaphones and wheelchairs; work closely with Careers Guidance and liaison with external organisations.

## Home sweet home:

There are adapted catered single bedrooms in Priory Hall in the heart of the campus, and a large number of self-catering bedrooms in the Singer Hall of Residence have been designed for students with disabilities. Features include: adapted bathrooms with overhead hoists; work and cooking surfaces and equipment at a practical height for wheelchair users; wheelchair battery charging facilities; flashing alarms; telephones in rooms; intercoms for students who require support from personal assistants. In addition, the housing officers are always looking for suitable properties in the Coventry area for students with disabilities to rent in order to broaden the choice of accommodation. A large house has also been adapted for wheelchair access. Accommodation can be guaranteed for the duration of the student's course.

## Out and about:

University: Dedicated parking spaces near both accommodation and study areas. The Disabilities Office has a fully adapted minibus available for students to borrow for field trips and social purposes.

Public transport: Train stations and some buses, trains and taxis are accessible to people who are wheelchair users. All modes of transport are accessible by people with visual impairments. Coventry is well served by public transport. Coventry Pool Meadow bus station is only a short distance from the main campus.

## Taking it easy:

At university: The SU has access to all areas of its buildings, including access to sports and societies, and regularly checks to see if improvements can be made. The Alma Sports Centre in Raglan Street has all its facilities on the ground floor. The equipment can be used by all, and all instructors have experience in instructing disabled people. The new Coventry University Sport and Recreation Centre, due to open in January 2004, will offer facilities for disabled users. There is also a mentoring/volunteer scheme in operation.

Locally: The city centre is flat and the facilities are accessible. There is a Shopmobility scheme and the pavements are tactile. A local area access guide is available; contact the Disabilities Office for further information. Through investment in physical access improvements Coventry is becoming an accessible city. A Disabled People's Working Group meets monthly at the Council House to address improvements and access issues in Coventry. The University Disabilities Office has a representative on this group to put forward the views of its students. Coventry Leisure Services offer a range of sports, arts and recreational facilities, from sports centres to museums, libraries, parks and theatres. For more information refer to *Access to Leisure for Disabled People*, available from the Disabilities Office. The Midlands Sports Centre in Coventry caters for all disabilities and has an extensive range of specially adapted equipment. A *Coventry Disability*

*Information Guide* is available from the Social Justice Team (see below).

## And another thing ...

➡ The university has developed an Independent Living Scheme with Community Service Volunteers, which can provide up to 24-hour personal support and/or academic and social support for students with disabilities. The duties that each volunteer undertakes depend solely on the requirements of the student for whom they are recruited.

➡ Within each school a learning support coordinator is assigned to coordinate disability provision.

➡ There is a non-sabbatical 'students with disabilities officer' elected on to the SU executive committee on a yearly basis to ensure that all members of the student body are given equal opportunities, access and privileges.

➡ Only a handful of rooms are inaccessible, and teaching staff work closely with the Disabilities Office to ensure that classes which students with disabilities are required to attend are not held in these rooms.

➡ Main teaching facilities have lifts and suitable entrances for wheelchair users.

➡ A number of teaching rooms are equipped with hearing loops.

➡ Many of the lifts have recorded voice announcements and Braille buttons.

➡ With all new buildings and major maintenance work, the Estates Department is standardising facilities for students with disabilities including toilets with additional handrails, wider doors and easier locks, etc.

➡ Careers Guidance offers a series of workshops on making applications for employment or postgraduate courses.

## The Disability Statement/Brochure:

*You're Not Alone!* the handbook for students with disabilities including: information about the university; accommodation; physical accessibility; special equipment and computing services; support services and facilities; leisure; funding; future developments; useful publications and map. Contact the Disabilities Office at the university for a copy.

## Local disability public service providers:

Phil Woodcock, Corporate Equality Adviser, Coventry City Council. Employers' Network on Disability.
Social Justice Team, City of Coventry, Room 13, Council House, Earl Street, Coventry CV1 5RR.

| Croydon College |
|---|

College Road, Croydon CR9 1DX

*General Enquiries:*
Tel: 020 8760 5914
Fax: 020 8760 5880
Email: info@croydon.ac.uk
Website: www.croydon.ac.uk

**Learning Support Manager: Roy Jenkins**
**Tel: 020 8686 5700 ext: 3129**
**Fax: 020 8760 5880**
**Email: jenkir@croydon.ac.uk**
**Text: 020 8760 5914**

**Fields of study:**
Art and design; business; education and law; information technology, engineering and construction; leisure and service studies; professional and management studies.

➡ Part-time study: **Yes.**
➡ Distance learning: **Yes.**

**About the college:**
Croydon College is one of the largest providers of further and higher education programmes in the country and has two campuses – Fairfield and Barclay Road – that are adjacent to the Fairfield Halls concert venue in the heart of the town centre. Most HE courses are based in the Barclay Road site, known as the Croydon Higher Education Centre (CHEC). Croydon is a multicultural centre with strong African, Caribbean and Asian influences and links with many other ethnic communities; it is located relatively close to London.

| Total number of students: 14,000    Number of disabled students: 600 |
|---|

**Learning support staff and services:**
Learning Support Service
Student Support Team, eight full-time and two part-time lecturers; two support assistants.
Assessment of individual support needs – seeking specialist advice where necessary; assistance with DSA applications; support for dyslexia including individual tutorials; alternative examination arrangements; provision of notetakers and scribing; low-vision assessments, tutorials and advice and assistance with materials and equipment for visually impaired students; mobility training; bank of equipment for loan; enabling technologies.
For students who are D/deaf or hard of hearing, assessments and support will be offered from a specialist team who come into the college from outside agencies. Support includes sign language

interpreters, communicators, notetakers and specialist tutorial support.
In addition, two members of the college staff are trained notetakers, and Margaret O'Connor, one of the student support assistants, has the CACDP stage 2 Certificate in BSL.

## Home sweet home:
There is no student accommodation.

## Out and about:
College: Parking spaces are available for disabled students in the college car park.
Public transport: East Croydon train station is two minutes away and has full access for wheelchair users. Tramlink is fully accessible and is an ideal mode of transport for people with visual impairment, as all stations are announced automatically. The college is one minute from a bus stop, which is serviced by accessible buses. Dial-a-Ride taxi scheme for disabled people operates in the area.

## Taking it easy:
At college: The SA bar on the ground floor is accessible to wheelchair users.
Locally: The town centre is flat, pedestrianised and accessible. There is a Shopmobility scheme, but the pavements are not tactile.

## And another thing …
➡ Major building works took place in 1997/8. As a result the college now has a greatly improved library, situated on the ground floor of the Fairfield building. This currently houses the flexible learning areas, IT and CD-ROM areas, traditional library services and media services. The college started a major refurbishment programme in 2003.
➡ The facilities and access in the Barclay Road building have been improved to enable wheelchair access. There are wheelchair accessible toilet facilities on the ground floor, a ramp to the students' entrance and two passenger lifts. Contact the Learning Support Service or Information Centre for further access information.
➡ StudyScan, an innovative computer-based assessment for use by students with dyslexia. The college is liaising with the designers of the system, and feedback from students and tutors in the college will contribute to its development.
➡ The college plans to continue to train more students with disabilities in the use of enabling technology to further facilitate independent learning.

➡ Magnilink CCTV and Lunar software for use by visually impaired students.
➡ Software for dyslexic students.
➡ Screen filters, individual loop systems, Text Help software, hoist with sling and voice recognition software are some of the equipment available to borrow.
➡ The College has a Braille embosser.

## The Disability Statement/Brochure:
*A Guide to College Services for People with Learning Difficulties and/or Disabilities.*
Includes: Policy; admissions; educational facilities and support; facilities by disability; complaints and appeals; examination arrangements; other support; physical accommodation and access.

### Local disability public service providers:
Croydon Council.
Croydon Disability.

---

### Cumbria Institute of the Arts
Brampton Road, Stanwix, Carlisle, Cumbria CA3 9AY

*General Enquiries:*
Tel: 01228 400300
Fax: 01228 514491
Email: info@cumbria.ac.uk
Website: www.cumbria.ac.uk

**Disabilities Officer:**
**Bridget Barling/Loretta Anenghan**
**Tel: 01228 400317**
**Fax: 01228 514491**
**Email: bbarling@cumbria.ac.uk**
**Lheneghan@cumbria.ac.uk**

### Fields of study:
Craft; design; digital multimedia; fine arts; heritage and humanities; media; performing arts.

➡ Part-time study: **Yes.**
➡ Distance learning: **Can be negotiated.**

### About the institute:
The main campus of the Cumbria Institute of the Arts overlooks the River Eden and Rickerby Park, 1 mile from Carlisle's city centre. The college has comprehensive and up-to-date media production facilities. Much of Cumbria is designated as the Lake District National Park, and the northern boundary of Cumbria forms the border with Scotland.

| Total number of students: 812 | Number of disabled students: 73 |

## Learning support staff and services:
Student Advice Centre
Personal progression and development tutor; student counsellors.
Identify needs and arrange support mechanisms; work with the
student to establish an individual action plan; tutorial support with
specialist tutor, usually on a one-to-one basis; provision of specialist
equipment, such as IT; provision of personal support workers, e.g.
notetakers, sign language interpreters; identify any relevant sources
of funding; individual alternative examination and assessment
arrangements.

## Home sweet home:
There are three self-contained bedsits with en-suite bathrooms for
wheelchair users. Rooms can possibly be made available for PAs.
Provision is made according to need, e.g. Deaf Alerter system.
Accommodation can be made available for duration of student's
course if necessary.

## Out and about:
College: There are dedicated parking spaces near both
accommodation and study areas. However, there is currently gravel
on the ground that the disability officer is pressing to have removed.
Public transport: There is no accessible public transport, although
some taxis are wheelchair accessible.

## Taking it easy:
At college: The college is small, but there is a wheelchair accessible
recreational student area with television. There is no bar. Students can
use the Northumbria University SU facilities, which are accessible.
There are also three other colleges in town to which students can be
linked.
Locally: Carlisle city centre is pedestrianised, flat and accessible. Its
facilities are accessible and there is a Shopmobility scheme. The
pavements are tactile. For further access information contact the
access officer at Carlisle City Council.

## And another thing ...
➡ The main college buildings are predominantly accessible for
   wheelchair users, with lifts and ramps, etc. The library is on two
   levels and access improvements are needed. The college has
   accessible toilet facilities.
➡ There are induction loops in the lecture theatres.

- Specialist software and equipment is generally obtained by students via their DSA or other funding source.
- The individual action plan is established to ensure necessary support is provided and to promote academic development. The action plan will be monitored on at least a termly basis.
- The college resource areas – computer resources, audio visual, library and workshops – may be able to provide specialist equipment and support.

## The Disability Statement/Brochure:
Includes: Disability officer; admissions; educational facilities and support; complaints; examination and assessment and counselling and welfare.

### Local disability public service providers:
Access Officer, Carlisle City Council.
Council for Voluntary Service, 27 Spencer Street, Carlisle CA1 1BE
01228 512513; fax: 01228 597761.
Social Services 01228 606060.

---

| **Dartington College of Arts** |
| --- |

Totnes, Devon TQ9 6EJ

*General Enquiries:*
Tel: 01803 862224
Fax: 01803 861666
Email: registry@dartington.ac.uk
Website: www.dartington.ac.uk

**Disability Officer: Larry Harding**
**Tel: 01803 840636**
**Email: l.harding@**
**dartington.ac.uk**

### Fields of study:
Art and performance; arts management and research; music; music composition; music performance; performance arts; performance writing; theatre; visual performance.

- Part-time study: **No.**
- Distance learning: **No.**

### About the college:
Dartington College of Arts is set on an estate in the Dart Valley close to Dartmoor and the coast. Practising artists have been visiting Dartington for more than 50 years including Hindemith, Michael Chekhov and Stravinsky.

Total number of students: 450      Number of disabled students: 73

## Learning support staff and services:
Disability Officer: Larry Harding.
Support people with accessing the campus – accessibility of some buildings and the impact of the physical demands of the programme.

## Home sweet home:
Accommodation can be guaranteed for duration of student's course.

## Taking it easy:
At college: Union accessible, main concert venues accessible, no looping.
Locally: No pedestrianised area; very steep roads; social areas (e.g. pubs) generally inaccessible.

## De Montfort University
The Gateway, Leicester LE1 9BH

*General Enquiries:*
Tel: 0116 255 1551
Fax: 0116 257 7515
Email: enquiries@dmu.ac.uk
Website: www.dmu.ac.uk

**Disability Coordinator: Tina Sharpe**
**Tel: 0116 257 7593**
**Fax: 0116 257 7609**
**Email: tsharpe@dmu.ac.uk**
**Text: 0116 257 7593**

## Fields of study:
Applied sciences; art and design; business and law; computing sciences and engineering; education and sports science; health and community studies; humanities and social science.

➡ Part-time study: **Yes.**
➡ Distance learning: **Yes.**

## About the university:
De Montfort University is one of Britain's largest universities and is based at Leicester and Bedford. Bedford has two campuses, at Lansdowne and Polhill, and Leicester has three – City, Scraptoft and Charles Frears. Bedford is a pleasant riverside town situated near London, Oxford and Cambridge. Leicester is at the heart of the Midlands.

Total number of students: 17,000    Number of disabled students: 600

## Learning support staff and services:
Student Learning Advisory Service
Full-time staff: Two Advisers; Administrator.
Pre-entry visits; student induction; needs assessments; assistance with DSA applications and benefit advice; provision of auxiliary aids and services; PA scheme; advice and guidance; one-to-one/group tuition for students with dyslexia; alternative examination, assessment and study arrangements; specialist assessment of dyslexia; individual learning support programmes; support service for students with mental health issues and liaison with external organisations.

## Home sweet home:
Some wheelchair accessible accommodation in new halls – accessible kitchens, flashing doorbells and flashing and vibrating alarms.
Accommodation can be guaranteed for duration of student's course.

## Out and about:
University: Dedicated parking spaces near both accommodation and study areas.
Public transport: Some wheelchair accessible buses and taxis. There is a taxi scheme for disabled people operating in the area, called Mobility.

## Taking it easy:
At university: Contact SU for entertainment and other social activities.
Locally: Both campus towns are accessible for wheelchair users. Town facilities are accessible, there is a Shopmobility scheme and the pavements are tactile.

## And another thing ...
➡ WorkBank – independent employment agency on the university campus offering vacation and term-time work (Leicester only).

## The Disability Statement/Brochure:
Pre-applications; support; services; mobility around the university; SU; catering; residential buildings; funding; organisations and future plans.

## Local disability public service providers:
Mosaic, The Guild Hall, Colton Street, Leicester, 0116 2517051.
Centre for Integrated Living.

| University of Derby |
|---|

Kedleston Road, Derby DE22 1GB

*General Enquiries:*
Tel: 01332 622222
Fax: 01332 294861
Website: www.derby.ac.uk

**Disability Support Coordinator:**
**Ben Bailey/Cheron Stevenson**
**Tel: 01332 591311**
**Fax: 01332 597742**
**Email: b.bailey@derby.ac.uk**
**Text: 01332 6227711**

### Fields of study:
Art and design; business; computing and technology; education and social science; environmental and applied sciences; health and community studies; humanities; language and law; tourism and hospitality management.

➡ Part-time study: **Yes.**
➡ Distance learning: **Yes.**

### About the university:
Derby became a university in 1992. There are five campuses: Kedleston Road, Mickleover, Britannia Mill, Green Lane and Buxton. Derby is situated in the middle of England – the Peak District National Park is 30 minutes away by train, bus or car and only two hours from London.

| Total number of students: 25,000 |
|---|
| Number of disabled students: approx. 450 |

### Learning support staff and services:
Specialist Support
Coordinators of Support and Advisory Services: Ben Bailey and Cheron Stevenson; student advisers. There are four full-time and three part-time members of staff.
Needs assessments; assistance with DSA applications and Hardship Funds; provision of auxiliary aids and services; advice and guidance; one-to-one/group tuition for students with dyslexia; alternative examination, assessment and study arrangements; support service for students with mental health issues; in-class support workers (readers or notetakers); Access Centre support; liaison with departments and external agencies.
Specialist Support can offer support to D/deaf students including notetaking; language tutorials; study skills; examination support;

technical equipment. Interpreting services cannot be guaranteed due to demand.

## Home sweet home:
On most sites the halls of residence are able to offer rooms specifically designed for students with disabilities on most sites. Some include adjacent or en-suite bathrooms. Some of the accommodation has visual fire alarm systems for D/deaf students. Students requiring this sort of accommodation will be given priority. Those students who require assistance with their daily needs will be provided with accommodation for their PA in adjacent rooms.
Accommodation can be guaranteed for duration of student's course where necessary.

## Out and about:
University: Dedicated parking spaces near both accommodation and study areas.
Public transport: Trains, train stations, taxis and some buses are accessible to people who are wheelchair users and/or with visual impairments.

## Taking it easy:
At university: The entrance for wheelchair users into the SU building is not the main one, but once inside there is access to the bar, etc. The swimming pool is accessible for wheelchair users.
Locally: Derby is relatively flat and has good access. The city centre is pedestrianised and the town's facilities are accessible. Pavements are tactile and there is a local area guide, *Derby City Access Guide*. Contact Disability Direct (see Directory) for access guide.

## And another thing ...
➡ The university houses an Access Centre (NFAC).
➡ Most students get funding for specialist software as there is no software for students with dyslexia or visual impairment.
➡ The university has the following facilities: portable hearing loops, video phones, enlarged PC screens – in the Learning Centre, Specialist Support and in computer labs – a Brailling embosser, sign language interpreters, a lip speaker, and readers and notetakers. There is also an amanuensis for examinations.

## The Disability Statement/Brochure:
Includes: Support and advice; pre-entry advice; disability policy; examinations; dyslexia support; access centre; DSA; admissions; support and advice; accommodation and useful contacts.

**Local disability public service provider:**
Disability Direct.

| University of Dundee |
|---|
| Perth Road, Dundee DD1 4HN |

*General Enquiries:*
Information Centre
Tel: 01382 344000
Fax: 01382 201604
Email: srs@dundee.ac.uk
Website: www.dundee.ac.uk

**Disability Coordinator: Di Shaw**
**Tel: 01382 345091/345402**
**Fax: 01382 345403**
**Email: d.z.shaw@dundee.ac.uk**
**Text: 01382 345403**

**Fields of study:**
Art and design; arts and social sciences; education and social work; law and accountancy; medicine, dentistry and nursing; science and engineering.

➡ Part-time study: **Yes.**
➡ Distance learning: **Yes.**

**About the university:**
At the heart of the City of Discovery, the University of Dundee offers the widest range of courses in Scotland and is the only one offering both Scots and English law. The university has won a coveted Queen's Anniversary Prize for its outstanding contribution in the area of minimal access therapies – popularly referred to as 'keyhole surgery'. The university was also rated top in the UK for the teaching of English, and in the top five for art and design, biosciences, anatomy and physiology and pharmacology (the *Guardian*). The university's location is between hills to the north and several miles of sandy beaches to the south, as well as some 1,300 acres of parkland.

| Total number of students: 11,951    Number of disabled students: 231 |
|---|

**Learning support staff and services:**
Disability Support Centre
Full-time Disability Coordinator: Di Shaw; Full-time Department Secretary: Anne Gosling.
Individual and confidential support relevant to the student's disability; coordinate services for students with disabilities; liaise with all other relevant departments; support and training for staff; production of

information leaflets and equipment for loan or purchase; study support recruitment – peer tutoring, graduate tutors, readers and scribes; assistance with DSA and trust applications; functional needs assessments with specialist organisations arranged (e.g. RNIB, RNID, educational psychologists and occupational therapists and HE Access Centre).

The Disability Support Centre houses the Visually Impaired Unit and the Dyslexia Unit, both with specialist resources.

Each academic department and large central service units such as the library and Information Technology Service have a member of staff who acts as a disability support officer.

## Home sweet home:

There is a range of purpose-built and adapted residential accommodation for students with disabilities. West Park Villas offer 21 single ground-floor rooms with en-suite shower and toilet facilities suitable for residents with mobility difficulties. Five of these rooms have an interconnecting door with an adjacent room allowing a PA to stay nearby. Two of the ground-floor kitchens have lowered work surfaces. Seabraes Hall offers four rooms that have en-suite shower and toilet facilities suitable for residents with mobility difficulties. Students may elect to remain in halls for the duration of their course.

## Out and about:

University: Dedicated parking spaces near main teaching areas and accommodation.

Public transport: Trains are accessible for wheelchair users. Some buses are accessible and there is one taxi that is accessible by a wheelchair user.

## Taking it easy:

At university: The SA building, including the bars, discos and the sports centre, are fully wheelchair accessible and most have accessible toilet facilities.

Locally: The city of Dundee is flat and accessible. Many of its facilities are readily accessible to people with disabilities and there is a Shopmobility scheme. The pavements are tactile. Information about access to local services and facilities can be obtained from the Disability Coordinator. There is also a local area disability guide called *Accessible Dundee.*

## And another thing ...

➡ The main campus is compact and on a gentle incline. University buildings are a mixture of old and new. Every effort to provide access for all students is made by relocation of classes, or the physical adaptation of buildings; however, wheelchair access is not universally available. Whilst 12 main buildings are fully accessible, access to the remaining ones is central to the estates strategy. Many of the older buildings have lifts but some are not fully accessible to wheelchair users. Steps have white-lined edges and many ramps have been installed.

➡ There are two study units for students with individual needs, each of which can accommodate 12 students.

➡ Equipment in the Visually Impaired Unit includes a scanner, Braille embossers, CCTV and a permanent workstation for users. The Dyslexia Unit consists of a quiet room and a computer room.

➡ Induction loop systems are fitted in most large lecture theatres.

➡ The main library has a lift available for disabled users to access the upper floor and there is a wheelchair accessible toilet.

➡ The university also houses the HE Access Centre for Tayside and Fife – Centre Manager: Shirley Hill; tel: 01382 345407; email: s.hill@dundee.ac.uk.

## The Disability Statement/Brochure:
Contents include: Admissions; the campus; halls of residence; individual needs and provision; DSA; HE Access Centre; external links; library and IT provisions; study support; careers; SA; research; policy and practice; future provision; and staff contacts.

## Local disability public service providers:
Dundee City Council, Tayside House, Crichton Street, Dundee.
Dundee Access Group.
The Red Cross.

---

### University of Durham
Old Shire Hall, Durham DH1 3HP

*General Enquiries:*
Tel: 0191 334 2000
Fax: 0191 334 6250
Website: www.dur.ac.uk

**Director of Service: Margaret P Collins**
**Tel: 0191 334 8115**
**Fax: 0191 334 8113**
**Email: margaret.collins@durham.ac.uk**
**Text: 0191 334 8115**

## Fields of study:
Anthropology; archaeology; arts; biological sciences; business management; chemistry; classics and ancient history; computer

science; East Asian studies; economics and finance; education; engineering; English studies; geography; geological sciences; history; law; linguistics and English language; mathematical sciences; Middle Eastern and Islamic studies; modern languages; music; natural sciences; philosophy; physics; politics; psychology; social sciences; sociology and social policy; sport; theology; youth work.

- ➡ Part-time study: **Yes.**
- ➡ Distance learning: **Yes.**

**About the university:**
Durham is a collegiate university served well by both road and rail, lying on the main rail route from London to Edinburgh and bypassed by the A1(M). The administration, teaching and residential premises of the university are spread around the small, compact city of Durham. The streets are narrow, cobbled, often steep and lined with historic buildings including the Norman cathedral, reputed to be one of the most beautiful Gothic churches in the world. Queen's Campus is at Stockton-on-Tees, 25 miles away.

Total number of students: 13,500    Number of disabled students: 700

**Learning support staff and services:**
Durham University Service for Students with Disabilities (DUSSD) Pelaw House, Leazes Road, Durham DH1 1TA (this address for all disability enquiries).
Two full-time advisers; two part-time advisers; one part-time admin adviser; two part-time secretaries; two part-time support tutors; one full-time IT support technician and one part-time assistant.
Needs assessment; assistance with DSA applications and small funds often available; provision of auxiliary aids and services; advice and guidance; one-to-one/group tuition for students with dyslexia; alternative examination, assessment and study arrangements; support service for students with mental health issues; liaison with external organisations and support in lectures, lab, field or placements.

**Home sweet home:**
Durham Campus: Most of the colleges now have new accommodation suitable for disabled people, including en-suite rooms adapted for physically disabled students and rooms adapted for D/deaf or hard of hearing students. Wheelchair users are usually placed in a college near to their academic department for easier access.
Stockton Campus (Queen's): Wheelchair access, adapted kitchen; double room for PA and flashing light/vibrating pillow for fire alarm.

Accommodation can be guaranteed for duration of student's course if needed.

## Out and about:
University: There is no specific transport for disabled students but some arrangements are in place for travel between Durham and Stockton campuses. There are dedicated parking spaces near accommodation and some near study areas, but the nature of the university means that driving and parking in Durham city is not easy for anyone. Queen's Campus, Stockton, is a purpose-built campus on a flat site and is readily accessible to disabled people.
Public transport: Durham Campus: Some buses, trains, train stations and taxis are accessible to people who are wheelchair users and/or who have a visual impairment. Queen's Campus: The trains, train station, taxis and some buses are accessible to wheelchair users. All are accessible to people with a visual impairment. Dial-a-Ride taxi scheme operates in the area.

## Taking it easy:
At university: DUSSD have a weekly newsletter, open house and open surgery event. The colleges and SU organise social events. There are no ramps into the SU, which is located on a very steep hillside, although there is a lift inside.
Locally: Durham is very hilly and not in general accessible, although some central shops and sports facilities, etc, are. There is a Shopmobility scheme operating in the area, and some pavements are tactile. An access guide is available. Stockton is flat and the city centre is accessible. The town's facilities are accessible and there is a Shopmobility scheme. The pavements are tactile.

## And another thing ...
➡ Durham is a hilly city, making wheelchair use difficult. Ramps, handrails and better signs are being introduced, where appropriate, to improve access.
➡ There may be small sources of funding available, possibly within the student's college, for particular circumstances.
➡ The education and welfare officer of the SU can give advice on student matters to those with disabilities.
➡ The Stockton campus is purpose-built and much more accessible to those with physical disabilities.
➡ The college system ensures a network of pastoral care exists in Durham – there is good liaison between departments, colleges and DUSSD staff and other student services. Personal support is very important.

## The Disability Statement/Brochure:
Covers: Policy and practice; general university provision; specific university provision; student support services; special provision; future development. Other information literature is available.

## Local disability public service providers:
Durham County Council Social Services Department 0191 383 1010.
Durham City Access Group 0191 386 6111.
Disability Information Centre 01642 827471

| University of East Anglia |
|:---:|

Norwich NR4 7TJ

*General Enquiries:*
Tel: 01603 456161
Fax: 01603 458553
Email: admissions@uea.ac.uk
Website: www.uea.ac.uk

**Disability Coordinator: Pat Ramsey**
**Tel: 01603 893693**
**Fax: 01603 893454**
**Email: p.ramsey@uea.ac.uk**
**Text: 01603 593873**

## Fields of study:
Biological sciences; Business; chemical sciences; development studies; economic and social studies; English and American studies; English language and British studies; environmental sciences; history; information systems; IT and computing; language, linguistics and translation studies; law; management; mathematics; medicine; music; occupational therapy and physiotherapy; social work and psychological studies; world art studies and museology.

➡ Part-time study: **Yes.**
➡ Distance learning: **No.**

## About the university:
The University of East Anglia is situated in parkland on the outskirts of the medieval city of Norwich and is less than two hours from London by train. UEA has welcomed students with disabilities since it was established in 1963. The university has 19 schools of study organised into three groups. Teaching for nursing students takes place in hospitals in Norwich and King's Lynn as well as on the main campus. The city centre is a 15-minute bus ride away

| Total number of students: 10,000 UG<br>Number of disabled students: 500 |
|:---:|

**Learning support staff and services:**
Disability Coordinator: Pat Ramsey.
Pre-application visits; assessment of equipment and other support needed; DSA applications; arrangement and payment of non-medical assistants (notetakers, support tutors, etc.) and the PAs; liaison with relevant academic staff; alternative individual examination. A range of leaflets is available.

**Home sweet home:**
Adapted accommodation for wheelchair users and PAs is available in Waveney Terrace. Minor changes can be made to adapt other accommodation to the individual needs of students with disabilities. Rooms for students with visual impairments include additional electrical sockets, wide shelving for large-print material. Rooms for students who are D/deaf or hard of hearing have flashing-light fire alarms and vibrating under-pillow pads. The university has considerable experience in supporting students who require personal assistance, including 24-hour care and different levels of part-time care. The Disability Coordinator provides supervision and training and arranges accommodation for resident assistants.
Accommodation can be guaranteed for duration of student's course.

**Out and about:**
University: Dedicated parking spaces near both accommodation and study areas. The university has wheelchair accessible buses.
Public transport: Local transport is accessible to wheelchair users and people with visual impairment. Most local taxi firms have accessible taxis.

**Taking it easy:**
At university: The SU building has lift access to the upper floor but the lift is very small and the controls can be difficult to access. All catering outlets and the UEA Studio are accessible, as are shops and banks. Banks have one cashier's window with a loop system. The Sportspark encourages disabled students to participate in sport. The new £17.5 million building offers a comprehensive range of indoor facilities including a 50m swimming pool. The Sportspark facilities are fully accessible.
Locally: The city centre is hilly, but accessible. Most facilities are accessible and there is a Shopmobility scheme. The pavements are tactile. NAG (see below) has published a revised edition of its *Guide to the City*, which includes over 650 detailed entries.

## And another thing ...

➡ The university is built on a large campus on a sloping site. The campus's walkway has several different levels, linked by steps, therefore sloping points have been built to provide access to all main buildings; however, some are steeper than the preferred maximum. The step-free routes may also involve a detour.

➡ An access audit was undertaken in 1997, the recommendations of which are gradually being implemented. Over the next few years all the university's older lifts will be refurbished to make them fully accessible to wheelchair users and visually impaired people.

➡ The library has level access through an automatic door and a lift, which serves all floors. There are wheelchair user accessible toilets.

➡ All schools of study are accessible to wheelchair users, with the exception of the School of Law.

➡ The Computing Service has three floors but no lift. The lower and upper floors are accessible. The student IT area on the middle floor is not accessible to wheelchair users, but the equipment and software on this level are available elsewhere on campus.

➡ The campus is reasonably well provided with accessible toilets.

➡ White paint is used to highlight the top and bottom steps of all outdoor flights.

➡ Increasingly, staff post lecture notes on the UEA Intranet.

➡ PC and software for students with visual impairments including Jaws screen reader.

➡ Library staff provide user support. One member of part-time library staff is qualified in BSL to level 1.

➡ Careerlink puts current UEA students in touch with recent working graduates and there are a number of disabled graduates.

➡ UEA has links with RNID, and local organisations.

## The Disability Statement/Brochure:

*Information for Students with Disabilities*
Includes: Admission; supporting study needs; examinations; physical access; accommodation; personal assistance; financial help; student support services; national and local links.
There are other leaflets with more detailed information for students with: dyslexia; unseen disabilities; visual impairments or those who are D/deaf or hard of hearing.

## Local disability public service providers:

Norfolk and Norwich Association for the Blind.
Norwich Access Group (NAG).

## University of East London

Barking Campus, Longbridge Road, Dagenham, Essex RM8 2AS

*General Enquiries:*
Tel: 020 8223 3000
Fax: 020 8223 2978
Email: admiss@uel.ac.uk
Website: www.uel.ac.uk
Text: 020 8223 2853

**Coordinator for Students with Disabilities: Simon Jarvis**
**Tel: 020 8223 4337**
**Fax: 020 8223 2882**
**Email: s.jarvis@uel.ac.uk**
**Text: 020 8223 2853**

### Fields of study:
Accounting, finance and economics; architecture; art and design; business management; computing; conservation and environment; engineering; geography and land management; health and sports studies; humanities; IT studies; law and criminology; life sciences; media and communications; psychology; social and political studies.

➡ Part-time study: **Yes, some courses.**
➡ Distance learning: **Yes, some courses.**

### About the university:
There are three campuses at the University of East London – Barking, Docklands and Stratford. The Docklands Campus opened in 1999, right on the waterfront – and is the first university campus to be built in London in the last 50 years. All the campuses are within easy reach of central London and all the amenities the capital city has to offer.

Total number of students: 14,000 Number of disabled students: 1,000

### Learning support staff and services:
Disability Service and Access Centre
Disability Service
Full-time staff: Disability Advisers: Simon Jarvis and Beverley Gull (Stratford and Barking); Disability Administrator: Fozya Sharif; Dyslexia Coordinator: Jenny Summerton.
Part-time staff: Disability Coordinator: Viv Parker; Disability Adviser: Michele Farmer (Docklands); Dyslexia Administrator: Debbie Moseley; dyslexia support tutors.
Access Centre (NFAC)
Full-time staff: Technology Manager: Din Wong
Part-time staff: Access Centre Administrator: Anu Dorasaimy
Needs assessment; assistance with DSA applications and other

funding including support from mainstream HEFCE funding; provision of auxiliary aids and services; advice and guidance; one-to-one/group tuition for students with dyslexia; alternative examination, assessment and study arrangements; support service for students with mental health issues; liaison with external organisations and keep students informed and ensure they are treated with consideration and respect.

## Home sweet home:
A number of purpose-built study bedrooms are available at each residential location, and priority is given to students with disabilities. Any additional equipment can be arranged via the Disability Service. Accommodation *cannot* be guaranteed for duration of student's course.

## Out and about:
University: Dedicated parking spaces near both accommodation and study areas.
Public transport: Some buses, trains, train stations and taxis are accessible to wheelchair users and people with visual impairments but private transport is usually arranged for disabled students. Contact Access and Mobility (see Directory) for information on London's public transport.

## Taking it easy:
At university: The sports centre is accessible for wheelchair users. The accessibility of facilities and services for the social support of disabled students is currently under review to extend and improve.
Locally: The local city centre is flat and facilities are accessible. Pavements are tactile in Stratford. Artsline (see Directory) produces a number of publications on access in London.

## And another thing ...
➡ The RNIB Physiotherapy Support Service is based at the Stratford campus. This is a national service for all visually impaired students on physiotherapy degree courses. The service is able to offer support to other UEL students with visual impairment if it has spare capacity.
➡ Barking and Dagenham Disablement Association provides transport and various kinds of personal support services to students.
➡ The university will help with the recruitment of personal support. Where possible the university will arrange to employ and manage the support.

➡ The university also has links with the Adult Dyslexia Organisation.
➡ All students with dyslexia or disabilities will be offered financial assistance for assessment of needs, advice, guidance and some support.
➡ The Education Development Service offers staff development on disability and dyslexia to all staff and departments.

## The Disability Statement/Brochure:
At the time of writing, the disability statement was being revised to meet SENDA.

## Local disability public service provider:
Barking and Dagenham Disablement Association.

| Edge Hill |
|---|

St Helens Road, Ormskirk, Lancashire L39 4QP

*General Enquiries:*
Tel: 01695 575171
Fax: 01695 579997
Email: enquiries@edgehill.ac.uk
Website: www.edgehill.ac.uk

**Disability Coordinator:**
**Tel: 01695 584746**
**Fax: 01695 579997**
**Email: devereuh@edgehill.ac.uk**

### Fields of study:
Biology; business and management; computer studies; critical criminology; disability and community studies; drama; early childhood studies; education; English; environmental sciences; film studies; geography; history; information systems; journalism; leisure management; marketing; mathematics; media and communication; multimedia; psychology and social sciences; race and equality studies; social work studies; sociology; sport; teaching and learning support; women's studies.

➡ Part-time study: **Yes.**
➡ Distance learning: **Yes.**

### About the college:
Edge Hill is set on a green 75-acre campus, just outside the historic market town of Ormskirk in Lancashire and within easy reach of the cities of Liverpool and Manchester and the seaside resort of Southport. Edge Hill has campuses at Ormskirk, Aintree, Chorley, Knowsley and Skelmersdale.

| Total number of students: 8,100+ Number of disabled students: 320 |
| --- |

## Learning support staff and services:
There is not a 'Disability Unit', but the inclusive philosophy of Edge Hill means that identified staff in Teaching and Learning Development and the Student Information Service are working with disability issues. There are two full-time staff and three with part-time duties. Learning Support Officer for Students with Specific Learning Difficulties: Sheila Blankfield; Disability Adviser: Hazel Devereux; Admin Support: Amanda Boult and Kathy Guilpain; Admissions: Adrienne Ibison; and Disability Coordinator: David Johnstone. There are currently 25 learning facilitators.
Advice and guidance on DSA applications; assessment of needs.

## Home sweet home:
Many halls are accessible by wheelchair and there are five purpose-built, en-suite rooms, fully equipped for wheelchair users' access. Adapted bedrooms will be provided on a first come, first served basis. Accommodation can be guaranteed for duration of student's course.

## Out and about:
College: Dedicated parking spaces near both accommodation and study areas.
Public transport: Taxis and bus service are accessible. Students who are wheelchair users do travel on the Merseyrail network.

## Taking it easy:
At college: Clubs (including the Disability Support Group), societies, volunteer activity and sports facilities are available for social support. The main focus for students is the Venue, where there is a bar and activities organised by the SU take place. It is generally accessible to wheelchair users and there are adapted toilet facilities. Many off-campus events are organised, and accessible transport is available. The Sporting Edge is a new leisure complex and has a high standard of facilities accessible to disabled students. There is also a swimming pool on site, though this is inaccessible to wheelchair users at present. There is an accessible pool in Ormskirk that has a hoist. Locally: The town is half a mile away and is flat and largely accessible. An access guide is available.

## And another thing ...
➡ The Ormskirk site, where most undergraduate programmes are taught, is flat and largely accessible.
➡ Recently invested £20 million in information technology and

infrastructure as well as a 25-acre, £3.7 million sports and recreational facility.

➡ Students with disabilities or other support needs (such as those with dyslexia) can receive additional support from the Teaching and Learning Development Unit.

➡ In 1994 Edge Hill was the first institution to introduce a degree subject involving the detailed study of all aspects of disability – political, cultural and environmental.

➡ Edge Hill encourages all applicants to visit and view facilities in order that specific adaptations can be tailored to individual needs.

➡ Future activities include: developing links with local mental health service to improve practical support to students with mental health needs; to further develop opportunities for disabled students to participate in international exchanges.

## The Disability Statement/Brochure:
*Information for Students with Support Needs*
Includes: Applications; life at Edge Hill; study at Edge Hill; more information and checklist.

## Local disability public service providers:
West Lancashire Association of Disabled People.
Disability Helpline, Skelmersdale.

| Edinburgh College of Art |
|---|

Lauriston Place, Edinburgh EH3 9DF

*General Enquiries:*
Tel: 0131 221 6000
Fax: 0131 221 6001
Website: www.eca.ac.uk

**Learning Support/Disability Coordinator: Jay Kirkland**
**Tel: 0131 221 6202**
**Email: j.kirkland@eca.ac.uk**

## Fields of study:
Design and applied arts; drawing and painting; sculpture; visual communications; architecture; landscape architecture; planning and housing.

➡ Part-time study: **Yes.**
➡ Distance learning: **No.**

## About the college:
Edinburgh College of Art is one of Europe's oldest and largest art schools. The College offers students studio-based one-to-one tuition

from practitioners across a wide range of disciplines in art, design and environmental studies. Situated at the heart of one of Europe's finest cities, Edinburgh College of Art is only a short distance from the national museum, galleries, library, universities, theatres and gardens.

> Total number of students: approx. 1,500
> Number of disabled students: 204

## Learning support staff and services:
Full-time staff: Learning Support/Disability Tutor.
Part-time staff: Learning Support/Disability Tutor; two Language Support Tutors; and Additional Learning Support Tutors
Needs assessments arrangements; assistance with DSA applications; advise on appropriate technical support; liaison with college staff; initial dyslexia assessments; referrals to an educational psychologist; advise on study skills, essay-writing and organisation of work and alternative examination and assessment arrangements.

## Home sweet home:
While ECA does not have its own accommodation an arrangement with the University of Edinburgh is in place. Some of this accommodation is suitable for students with a variety of disabilities. For further information please contact Student Services (0131 221 6023).
Accommodation *cannot* be guaranteed for duration of student's course.

## Out and about:
College: There are dedicated parking spaces near study areas.
Public transport: There are buses accessible to wheelchair users on some routes. Taxicard and Handicabs provide accessible taxis for disabled users.

## Taking it easy:
At college: Agreements to use facilities of Edinburgh University are currently being negotiated.
Locally: The city centre is hilly and accessible in some parts. Local town facilities are accessible; there is a Shopmobility scheme and pavements are tactile. The Central Library, which has a Resource Centre, is fully accessible.

## And another thing ...
➡ Because the college is spread over different sites and incorporates older buildings, not all classrooms and studios currently have wheelchair access.

➡ The Lauriston Campus is mostly wheelchair accessible with the exception of most of the Architecture Building.

➡ The Grassmarket Campus is situated up a steep cobbled slope. It is best to drive up or be dropped off in the main parking area. Entry to most buildings is level or ramped, with lift access to the library only. There are two toilets which are accessible to people who are wheelchair users.

➡ Schools/departments will ensure that all classes and tutorials are undertaken within an accessible space.

➡ The Grassmarket library is accessible via a lift and has some specialist seating, Posturite chairs and an adjustable desk.

➡ The main library on the Lariston Campus is wheelchair accessible, and seating for students with mobility disabilities is being improved. Some specialist seating and an adjustable table with a sloping reading/writing board are available and an adjustable desk. The library is on the first floor, with access via a lift.

➡ The lecture theatres have an induction loops system. Portable systems are available for seminars or individual sessions.

➡ There is a deaf alerter fire alarm.

➡ Fee discounts may apply: for further information please contact Sherrey Landles on 0131 221 6254 or s.landles@eca.ac.uk.

➡ Information can, usually be provided on request in large print, on disk or in Braille.

## The Disability Statement/Brochure:

*ECA Welcomes Students with Disabilities*
Includes: Student welfare; accommodation; disability and learning support; examinations and assessments; financial support; support by disability; health and safety; contacts; library facilities and disclaimer.
Local disability public service provider:
Lothian Coalition for Disabled People, Norton Park Centre, 57 Albion Road, Edinburgh EH7 5QY 0131 475 2360.
Scottish Dyslexia Association, Unit 3 Stirling Business Centre, Wellgreen, Stirling FK8 2DZ 01786 446650 Fax: 01786 471235
Email: info@dyslexia-in-scotland.org.
Disabled Persons' Housing Service 0131 225 7788.

| University of Edinburgh |
| --- |

Old College, South Bridge, Edinburgh EH8 9YL

*General Enquiries:*                                    **Disability Coordinator:**
Registry                                                       **Marnie Roadburg**

University of Edinburgh

Tel: 0131 650 1000          **Tel: 0131 650 6828**
Fax: 0131 651 1236          **Fax: 0131 650 6677**
Email: Registry@ed.ac.uk    **Email: Disability.Office@ed.ac.uk**
Website: www.ed.ac.uk    **Website: www.disability-office.ed.ac.uk/**

## Fields of study:
Arts; divinity; education; law; medicine; music; science and engineering; social sciences; veterinary medicine.

➡ Part-time study: **Yes, some.**
➡ Distance learning: **No.**

## About the university:
The University of Edinburgh was founded over 400 years ago, its first student, in arts and divinity, being enrolled in 1583. The university's buildings, both historic and modern, are some of the city's best-known landmarks and architectural features. The majority of university departments are grouped in and around the Central/George Square area. Edinburgh is a green and architecturally beautiful city, attracting over 2 million visitors, and is host to the Edinburgh International Arts, Fringe, Film, TV and Science Festivals as well as the home of the new Scottish Parliament.

| Total number of students: 20,333 |
|---|
| Number of disabled students: 700+ |

## Learning support staff and services:
Disability Office, within Student Services
Receptionists/Secretaries: Jane Robinson and Alistair Knock; Disability Coordinator: Marnie Roadburg; Dyslexia Advisers: Jane Kirk and Kathy Smith; Disability Advisers: Rosie Addis and Lorna Thomas. Pre-application visits for prospective students; assistance in identifying what support and technology may be appropriate to students' needs; help with applications for financial assistance; assistance with finding PAs, readers, notetakers or interpreters; liaising with members of academic staff in relation to access to the curriculum; assistance given to students who wish to acquire their own specialist equipment; alternative exam arrangements and drawing on expertise of specialist agencies.
Screening and assessment for students with dyslexia; individual study skills advice.
The Disability Office works closely with the university's Disability Committee.

**Home sweet home:**
There is a range of accessible full-board residences and accessible self-catering flats for students with a mobility disability.
Accommodation is available at Pollock Halls for students who have a guide dog. Accommodation Services will help students who wish to live as independently as possible and do not wish to take up places in residences. Priority, where possible, is given to students with a motor or sensory disability.
Accommodation can be guaranteed for duration of student's course.

**Out and about:**
University: Dedicated parking spaces near both accommodation and study areas.
Public transport: Some buses are accessible.

**Taking it easy:**
At university: The SA services are based in university buildings of various ages – not all are wheelchair accessible. The SA provides bars, catering and entertainment in a variety of locations that, where it has been deemed possible, have been made accessible.
Arrangements to ensure access will be made if prior notice is given. The 160 societies are open to all students and meet in university property and city locations. Contact the Edinburgh University Student Association for further details.
Locally: Edinburgh is a compact and historic city with many hills and cobbled streets. A comprehensive guide on access to public buildings, cinemas, theatres and public toilets in the Edinburgh and Lothian area, entitled *Access in Lothian*, together with a range of other information on facilities and resources for disabled people, is available from Grapevine – see below.

**And another thing …**
➡ Access for people who are wheelchair users: most lecture theatres and teaching rooms have access, and arrangements can be made through central booking systems to provide access to lecture theatres and teaching areas where required. There is an ongoing programme of improvements.
➡ Access and facilities in the main libraries, refectories, SA and bars: majority of refectories are wheelchair accessible and have local facilities.
➡ Most auditoriums open to the general public have induction loops. Some other areas have infrared hearing devices that are available through central booking systems. Current improvement programme includes centre loops for reception areas. Ongoing

improvements under way to install lifts and improve access for disabled people where required.
➡ There is a range of specialist technological provision (e.g. Brailling facilities, CCTV, specialist hardware and software).
➡ One of the university's commitments is to spend a minimum of £100,000 per annum on projects aimed at improving access to teaching facilities, especially major lecture theatres.

## The Disability Statement/Brochure:
The statement covers the period from 2003 to 2005 and includes: Disability policy; the Disability Office; student experiences; admissions and regulations; academic support; library; examinations and assessments; equipment and technology; financial assistance; physical environment; accommodation; student services; Centre for Continuing Education; SA; developing policy and provision and useful contacts.

### Local disability public service providers:
Grapevine 0131 475 2370.
Lothian Coalition of Disabled People, Norton Park Centre, 57 Albion Road, Edinburgh EH7 5QY; 0131 475 2360.

---

| University of Essex |
|---|

Wivenhoe Park, Colchester, Essex CO4 3SQ

*General Enquiries:*  **Disability Coordinator: Angela Jones**
Tel: 01206 873333  **Tel: 01206 872366**
Fax: 01206 873598  **Fax: 01206 872367**
Email: admit@essex.ac.uk  **Email: disab@essex.ac.uk**
Website: www.essex.ac.uk

### Fields of study:
Accounting and finance; American studies; biochemistry; biology; business management; computer science; drama; economics; electronic systems; English language and linguistics; European studies; film studies; health studies; history; history of art; humanities; human rights; Internet science; Latin American studies; law; literature; mathematics; modern languages; philosophy; politics; psychology; sociology; sports science.

➡ Part-time study: **Yes, some courses.**
➡ Distance learning: **No.**

## About the university:

The University of Essex is located on one main campus 2 miles from the centre of Colchester – the oldest recorded town in Britain. The university is surrounded by countryside as it is situated on the Essex and Suffolk borders and near to the East Anglian coastline. The university has entered into partnership with the South East Essex College, located in the heart of Southend on Sea. Here there are two main sites, which are a very short distance apart.

---

Total number of students: approx. 6,000
Number of disabled students: 410

---

## Learning support staff and services:

The Disability Team in the Student Support Office
Full-time staff: Disability Coordinator: Angela Jones; Learning Support Coordinator: Shirley Dow; Disability Support Coordinator: Lunn Bowman Burns.
Part-time staff: Access Coordinator: Louise Ward.
Needs assessment; assistance with DSA applications; provision of auxiliary aids and services; advice and guidance; one-to-one/group tuition for students with dyslexia; alternative examination, assessment and study arrangements; support service for students with mental health issues and liaison with external agencies.

## Home sweet home:

Residences have 12 self-catering rooms designed for wheelchair users (which won an Access Award from Colchester Borough Council). Each room has an en-suite shower and toilet and adapted kitchen. Rooms are available for PAs. Some rooms have visual and vibrating fire alarms. Hearing dogs and guide dogs can be accommodated. Accommodation can be guaranteed for duration of student's course.

## Out and about:

University: The SU minibus has a tail lift. Dedicated parking spaces near both accommodation and study areas.
Public transport: The buses are not accessible for wheelchair users, but the Borough Council subsidises wheelchair accessible taxis through a token scheme. The trains and train stations are accessible to both wheelchair users and people with a visual impairment. Some taxis are accessible to wheelchair users.

## Taking it easy:

At university: There is a Disabled Students' Society that is part of the SU. Students with disabilities are encouraged to participate in activities at the sports centre, the SU, and all its clubs and societies, etc., which are all accessible. Colchester Leisure World is accessible for wheelchair users, and transport is provided by the SU minibuses. A wheelchair users' basketball team is based near Colchester. Locally: The town centre is flat and accessible. The sports centres, cinemas and theatres are accessible. There are signed performances at the theatre. There is a Shopmobility scheme and some pavements are tactile. Colchester Borough Council produces a guide for people with disabilities.

### And another thing ...
➡ SU bar has a drop-level counter ensuring ease of access.
➡ The university has the status of assessor for the East Anglia Regional Access Centre.
➡ Essex is known for its research into supporting students with disabilities, e.g. Professor Arnold Wilkins helped to develop coloured overlays and coloured lenses specifically to help with reading, and Dave Lyons has led a research and development programme in computer-aided education for people with severe learning difficulties.

## The Disability Statement/Brochure:
Useful booklet covering: Application and admission; sources of advice and information; academic support; funding arrangements; personal assistance; buildings and facilities; monitoring and developing services; information on local and national provision; research into disability; specific information for students with different disabilities; student profiles; statistics; further information and contact details.

### Local disability public service providers:
Disability Access Officer, Environmental Services, Building Central, Lexden Grange, 127 Lexden Road, Colchester CO3 3RJ; 01206 282436; text: 01206 282266; Website www.colchester.gov.uk. Essex Disabled People's Association 01245 287177.

| University of Exeter |
| :---: |

Northcote House, The Queen's Drive, Exeter EX4 4QJ

*General Enquiries:*      **Disability Coordinator: Emma Shelton**
Tel: 01392 263035      **Tel: 01392 264150**
Fax: 01392 263108      **Fax: 01392 264150**

Email: prospectus@exeter.ac.uk
Website: www.exeter.ac.uk

**Email: E.L.Shelton@
exeter.ac.uk**

## Fields of study:
Arab and Islamic studies; biological sciences; business and economics; Camborne School of Mines (CSM); chemistry; classics, ancient history and theology; drama and music; education; engineering and computer science; English; geography and archaeology; historical, political and sociological studies; law; mathematical sciences; modern languages; medicine and health sciences; physics; psychology.

➡ Part-time study: **Yes.**
➡ Distance learning: **No.**

## About the university:
Exeter University has three main sites – two in Exeter and CSM, Cornwall. The main campus is Streatham, which is built around a country estate overlooking Exeter. The high street is only a 15-minute walk away. Probably the best-known building in Exeter city is the cathedral, which was consecrated in 1133. Exeter University is set in a city surrounded by the beaches, moorland and countryside that rank Devon and Cornwall among Europe's top tourist destinations.

| Total number of students: 11,000 Number of disabled students: 350 |
| --- |

## Learning support staff and services:
Student Advice Centre
Disability Coordinator: Emma Shelton; special needs adviser; two dyslexia tutors; IT tutor.
Information on DSA and other financial support; diagnostic assessment; technical needs assessments; alternative examination arrangements and staff training.

## Home sweet home:
There are a number of en-suite rooms in the halls and flats, which are suitable for students with a disability, and some rooms in the older residences have been converted to provide suitable facilities. The university is currently constructing a new building to address the needs of disabled students.
Accommodation can be guaranteed for duration of student's course.

## Out and about:
University: A free minibus operates from the train station up the hill to the Streatham campus, but it is currently not accessible for

wheelchair users. Dedicated parking spaces can be viewed on the website map.

Public transport: There are some low-loading buses available.

**Taking it easy:**
At university: The Guild of Students has a disability representative. The university is working towards having an accessible sports centre and swimming pool. The SU and bar are wheelchair user accessible. Locally: A guide is available from Devon County Council called *Access Guide to Exeter: Independent living in the city.*

**And another thing ...**
➡ The Streatham campus is hilly.
➡ Some lecture theatres are not wheelchair accessible; please check with subject department. It is possible to timetable students into accessible areas.
➡ Many of the lecture theatres and other teaching rooms have induction loops fitted and mobile units are also available.
➡ There are no video phones nor is there colour modification software.
➡ The university has specialist software for dyslexia/visually impaired students; enlarged PC screens; Brailling facilities; sign language interpreters; lipspeakers; speech-synthesised text; readers/notetakers; guides for visually impaired students.
➡ Since January 2002 the university's Website has shown accessibility of the campus.
➡ The main library has a 'special needs zone' with special IT equipment available to those students for whom it is appropriate.
➡ Diagnostic assessments may be paid for out of the hardship fund.
➡ There is a quarterly magazine for people with physical and sensory disabilities in Devon called *Devon Link.*

**The Disability Statement/Brochure:**
Statement includes: Applications; facilities and equipment available; access; personal assistance; sources of support; studying, assessments and exams; financial support; monitoring provision; proposed developments; disclaimer and contacts.

**Local disability public service provider:**
Sue Kelley, Devon Disability Officer 01752 785890.

| Falmouth College of Arts |
|---|

Woodlane, Falmouth, Cornwall TR11 4RH

*General Enquiries:*
Tel: 01326 211077
Fax: 01326 211205
Email: admissions@falmouth.ac.uk
Website: www.falmouth.ac.uk

**Disability Coordinator: Cindy Curtis**
**Tel: 01326 213759**
**Fax: 01326 213738**
**Email: cindycurtis@**
**falmouth.ac.uk**
**Text: 01326 213836**

## Fields of study:
Broadcasting; creative advertising; English with media studies; film studies; fine art; graphic design; history of modern art and design; illustration; interactive design; interior and landscape; journalism; photographic communication; photography and professional writing; spatial design; studio ceramics; 3D design; textile design; visual culture.

➡ Part-time study: **Yes.**
➡ Distance learning: **No.**

## About the college:
Falmouth College of Arts was originally founded as an art school in 1902. The college is now a leading specialist university sector college. In 1999 it received 24 out of 24 in the QAA's national Subject Review of art and design. The college is located in an area of outstanding natural beauty in west Cornwall. Flanked by the Fal Estuary, the castles of St Mawes and Pendennis and the Gulf Stream of the Atlantic Ocean, Falmouth College has two campuses – at Woodland and Tremough.

| Total number of students: 2,200 | Number of disabled students: 400 |
|---|---|

## Learning support staff and services:
Disability Service
Full-time staff: Disability Coordinator: Cindy Curtis; Disability Administrator: Melanie Dove; English Support Tutor; three Student Counsellors and a Registered General Nurse.
Needs assessments; assistance with DSA applications and Hardship and Access Funds; provision of auxiliary aids and services; advice and guidance; one-to-one/group tuition for students with dyslexia; alternative examination, assessment and study arrangements; support service for students with mental health issues; dyslexia and

study skills screening for all first-year undergraduates; arrangement of assessments by an educational psychologist; IT training; study skills and strategy assessments; bank of support workers; support to meet individual requirements and liaison with external organisations.

**Home sweet home:**
There are six designated rooms for disabled students, three of which are wheelchair accessible flats within halls of residence with adapted kitchens and bathrooms. There is also a Deaf Alerter fire system. Priority is given to students with disabilities who apply for college accommodation.
Accommodation can be guaranteed for duration of student's course.

**Out and about:**
College: Dedicated parking spaces near accommodation but not study areas. The college does provide some specialist transport for its disabled students.
Public transport: Some buses, trains, train stations and taxis are accessible to people who are wheelchair users and/or who have visual impairments. Dial-a-Ride taxi scheme for disabled people operates in the area.

**Taking it easy:**
At college: Main facilities are accessible. The SU arranges events and there is a dedicated sport/leisure organiser.
Locally: The town centre is hilly and cobbled and accessible with some difficulty. Local library, shops and banks are accessible and there is a Shopmobility scheme. There are some tactile crossings. Sports facilities for wheelchair users are poor, but improving.

**And another thing ...**
➡ The hilly terrain of Falmouth may cause difficulties for students who are wheelchair users or those with mobility difficulties; however, a range of students with disabilities have studied successfully at Falmouth.
➡ The college will cover the cost of students requiring a Psychological Report where necessary.
➡ The college liaises with agencies such as RNID, RNIB and British Dyslexia Association to encourage recruitment of disabled people.
➡ The college is a member of Skill.
➡ Falmouth College has been awarded 'Investors in People' status.

**Local disability public service providers:**
Cornwall County Council, County Hall, Truro, Cornwall TR1 3AY;
01872 322000; www.cornwall.gov.uk; enquiries@cornwall.gov.uk.
RNIB.
RNID.
Link into Learning.
British Dyslexia Association.

| **Farnborough College of Technology** |
| --- |

Boundary Road, Farnborough, Hampshire GU14 6SB

*General Enquiries:* Information
Tel: 01252 407040
Fax: 01252 407041
Email: info@farn-ct.ac.uk
Website: farn-ct.ac.uk

**Disability Adviser: Sally Cox**
**Tel: 01252 407129**
**Fax: 01252 407041 Attn: S. Cox**
**Email: s.cox@farn-ct.ac.uk**

**Fields of study:**
Applied health and science; business administration; computing;
education and humanities; engineering; leisure, health and fitness;
management and finance; media and visual arts.

➡ Part-time study: **Yes, generally.**
➡ Distance learning: **Yes, generally.**

**About the college:**
Farnborough College of Technology, founded in 1957, is an
accredited College of the University of Surrey. The college is located
on one main site in Farnborough and has over ten partner sites. It
offers a variety of courses including Access, further and higher
education.

| Total number of students: 12,172 | Number of disabled students: 535 |
| --- | --- |

**Learning support staff and services:**
Two full-time and two part-time members of staff, a voluntary tutor
and support staff as well as tutors and other staff as required.
Needs assessment; advice and guidance; one-to-one/group tuition
for students with dyslexia; alternative examination, assessment and
study arrangements; support service for students with mental health
issues and liaison with external organisations.
Disability adviser is available to staff and students. Website offers

advice on aspects of disability and extensive links to other sites. Technability arranges pre-entry-level courses that are run part-time and full-time in addition to the specialist courses for people who are visually impaired or who are D/deaf or hard of hearing, those with physical disabilities and people with mental health issues.

## Home sweet home:
There is one room in the student village that has an adapted bathroom and ramp and an adjoining room for a PA. Accommodation is adapted as required. No student has been refused entry on the grounds of lack of access.
Accommodation can be guaranteed for duration of student's course.

## Out and about:
College: For certain students on specific courses the college runs a tailgate minibus. Dedicated parking spaces near both accommodation and study areas.
Public transport: Some buses, trains, train stations and taxis are accessible to wheelchair users and all are accessible to people with visual impairments. Contact the college for up-to-date information. Rushmore accessible taxi scheme for disabled people operates in the area.

## Taking it easy:
At college: Mallards sports club is accessible.
Locally: The town centre is fairly flat and accessible, but the town's facilities are not accessible. A new cinema is planned locally. There is a Shopmobility scheme and some pavements are tactile. Local Access group can be contacted for information concerning access to the local community. Shopmobility runs in the local centre of Farnborough and the pavements are tactile.

## And another thing ...
➡ Despite the college priority of continually improving access, some rooms can at present only be reached by stairs. The college will endeavour to accommodate wheelchair users in accessible rooms if informed. Unfortunately, some specialist rooms are not easily transferred to more convenient locations.
➡ There are lifts in three blocks for ease of access.
➡ There is a variety of specialist software for students who are visually impaired, and arrangements can be made for Mobility Officers to provide orientation training around the college.
➡ The college has a variety of specialist equipment including a Braille embosser, portable induction loops and voice recognition software.

➡ Students are encouraged to discuss their specific requirements with their personal tutor/course tutor and accommodation officer if relevant, in order that provision may be planned at the earliest opportunity.

## Disability Statement/Brochure:
*Disability Statement 2003*
Covers: Admissions; support; contacts; medical needs; counsellors; careers; access; specialist equipment; examination arrangements; financial support and where to look for course information.

## Local disability public service provider:
Access Officer, Council Offices, Rushmore Borough Council 01252 398722 text: 01252 371233 fax: 01252 398726.

---

### The University of Glamorgan
Llantwit Road, Treforest, RCT, South Wales CF37 1DL

*General Enquiries:*
Tel: 01443 480480
Fax: 01443 480558
Email: enquiries@glam.ac.uk
Website: www.glam.ac.uk

**Disability Coordinator: Val Norris/
Sharon Jones
Tel: 01443 483663/01443 482494
Fax: 01443 482084
Email: vnorris@glam.ac.uk;
sjones12@glam.ac.uk**

## Fields of study:
Applied sciences; business; care services and technology; computing; electronics; humanities and social sciences; law.

➡ Part-time study: **Yes.**
➡ Distance learning: **Yes.**

## About the university:
The University of Glamorgan is just 20 minutes from Cardiff, the capital city of Wales, and is located on a safe, single campus. The university has good links with local and national employers and was the first university in Wales to be awarded the prestigious Investor in People standard. The campus is based in Treforest in the Taff Valley close to entertainment and social venues and the National Museum and Gallery, Museum of Welsh Life and Cardiff Castle.

---

Total number of students: 8,000
Number of disabled students: 527 currently registered

## Learning support staff and services:

Student Services

Four full-time staff: Sharon Jones, Val Norris, Dilys Pritchard and Delyth Morgan.

Discussion of university provision; discussion of students' individual needs and how these can be met by the university; bank of information leaflets; providing opportunities for students to meet; accommodation arrangements; support arrangements; alternative teaching, assessment and examination arrangements; negotiating and providing a Learning Support Partnership Agreement between the university and the student; monitoring and review of the Agreement; staff development for teaching and support staff and for student support workers; maintenance of a comprehensive network of non-medical assistant support through the staff coordinators in each academic and support department, student readers, student mobility assistants as well as assisting in the selection and employment of the student's own non-medical assistants if required.

## Home sweet home:

Some accommodation has been modified for wheelchair access; other considerations – flashing/vibrating alarms – as necessary.
Larger rooms for students who have guide dogs, and extra rooms set up for use by PAs, etc.
Accommodation can be guaranteed for duration of student's course.

## Out and about:

University: Dedicated parking spaces near both accommodation and study areas.
Public transport: Buses are not wheelchair accessible. Most train stations are wheelchair accessible and help can be provided as long as it is pre-booked.

## Taking it easy:

At university: Sport and recreation centre on campus, with adapted showers and toilets for disabled people, also a lift between floors and help available via a booking system. SU available for the social support of all students. PAs provided for social support where necessary.
Locally: Information available from VisitWales including a guide.

## Local disability public service provider:

Local council.

| Glasgow Caledonian University |
| :---: |

70 Cowdaddens Road, Glasgow G4 0BA, UK

*General Enquiries:*
Tel: 0141 331 3000
Fax: 0141 331 3005
Email: StudentServicesEnquiries
@gcal.ac.uk
Web: www.gcal.ac.uk

**Disability Team: Gillian McLeish,**
**Margaret McShane, Gwen Gibb**
**Tel: 0141 331 3878**
**Fax: 0141 331 3877**
**Email: disability@gcal.ac.uk**

**Fields of study:**
Built and natural environment; business; computing and mathematical science; engineering science and design; health and social care; law and social sciences; life sciences; nursing, midwifery and community health.

➡ Part-time study: **Yes.**
➡ Distance learning: **No.**

**About the university:**
The university began as a small college in 1878 and has since grown and diversified into one of the largest universities in Scotland. The Caledonian Business School is based here. The university is located in a modern, purpose-built campus in the city centre and has recently invested £45 million in the development of new facilities including state-of-the-art leisure facilities. A recent survey rated Glasgow Caledonian as one of the leading universities for teaching and research. Glasgow Caledonian is also one of the first universities to fulfil the Scottish Parliament's policy on social inclusion regarding improving access and widening participation in HE through non-traditional routes and sectors.

| Total number of students: 14,000    Number of disabled students: N/A |
| :--- |

**Learning support staff and services:**
Disability Team in Learner Support
Gillian McLeish: G.Mcleish@gcal.ac.uk; Margaret McShane: M.McShane@gcal.ac.uk and Gwen Gibb: G.Gibb@gcal.ac.uk. Assessment of needs; support information and guidance; advice to relevant staff; liaison with external agencies; contribution to policy and procedures relevant to the recruitment and welfare of disabled students; establishment of system of support for students with disabilities in academic departments; contribution to the university's Staff Development Programme including tailored disability awareness-

raising for academic and central departments; development and quality of the disability service; alternative examination and assessment arrangements.

There are also departmental disability coordinators.

Each school has a named disability adviser who provides advice to disabled students and staff.

The Effective Learner Support, located in the Caledonian Learning and Information Centre, provides study support for all students including those with specific needs, including dyslexia. There is also a technician in Learner Support available to provide support for students with disabilities.

Assessment of needs will be the responsibility of the central Disability Team in liaison/partnership with admissions tutor, module leader, year leader and School disability coordinators.

**Home sweet home:**
There are some flats that are specially equipped and adapted for students with disabilities.

**And another thing …**
- In November 2000 a SHEFC Disability Needs Analysis of Policies and Procedures was undertaken. The audit report has established a range of key recommendations the university is advised to carry forward to ensure compliance with the QAA Code.
- Pre-entry students with disabilities may visit the university and establish convenient and accessible routes with Disability Support, Academic and Estates staff or with the assistance of external organisations. In addition, tours of the campus, shadowing a class for the day, experiencing lab work and meeting with existing students is offered.
- With the student's agreement, the university recognises it is essential that information about disabled students' needs is given to academic staff in a timely and efficient manner.
- The university recognises that schools may have individual students with disabilities who require support where a cost is likely to be incurred that the DSA cannot meet. Consequently it is the department's responsibility to ensure that it can provide the necessary funding to meet any such costs.
- Timetabling to ensure teaching locations are accessible will also ensure there is sufficient time to travel between locations.
- The university will ensure that all central publications are available in alternative formats.
- All new staff have disability awareness training and all staff will be provided with appropriate development in equal opportunities.

- The university has a joint Special Needs Group that comprises ICT, Disability Support and library staff.
- The Website is being designed to accommodate the needs of disabled users, following the World Wide Web Consortium's Accessibility Guidelines.

## The Disability Statement/Brochure:
*University Code of Practice: Students with Disabilities*
The information includes: Aims and scope of code; legislative framework; quality framework; language; physical environment; information for students with disabilities; registration; learning and teaching; examination and assessments; staff development; specialist support services; monitoring; complaints and appendix.

| Glasgow School of Art |
|---|

167 Renfrew Street, Glasgow G3 6RQ

*General Enquiries:*
Tel: 0141 353 4562
Fax: 0141 353 4746
Email: s.falconer@gsa.ac.uk
Website: www.gsa.ac.uk

**Disability Coordinator: Jill Hammond**
**Tel: 0141 353 4527**
**Fax: 0141 353 4746**
**Email: j.hammond@gsa.ac.uk**

### Fields of study:
Architecture; design; fine art and product design engineering.

- Part-time study: **Yes, in architecture.**
- Distance learning: **No.**

### About the school:
Glasgow School of Art (GSA) is housed in a building designed by the Glasgow architect Charles Rennie Mackintosh. It has up-to-date studios and laboratories, including computer-aided design facilities. The school is one of the few independent art schools in Britain and continues to have a central role in the education of artists, designers and architects. GSA is an associated institution of the University of Glasgow.

| Total number of students: 1,400   Number of disabled students: 10%+ |
|---|

### Learning support staff and services:
Disability Coordinator and Student Counsellor: Jill Hammond; dyslexia support tutor.

Learning needs assessments and personal support; assistance in arranging support needs such as readers and lipspeakers; arrangement of dyslexia assessments with an educational psychologist; individual and group work with dyslexic students offering course support; assistance in DSA applications; counselling; contact with a wide range of external agencies.

## Home sweet home:
The residence is located on the same hill as the rest of the campus and currently offers one place suitable for a wheelchair user in a shared, mixed-gender flat. There have been problems with supporting students in this domestic environment, and this would need to be discussed in detail with a student wishing to move in. Contact the Student Residence Manager for further information: Fiona Sloan, tel: 0141 332 7683; email: f.sloan@gsa.ac.uk. The Estates Department has expressed a willingness to meet the needs of disabled students wherever possible – contact Bill Mason, tel: 0141 353 4548; email: w.mason@gsa.ac.uk.
Accommodation can be guaranteed for duration of student's course.

## Out and about:
School: Dedicated parking spaces near accommodation, and permit-holder-only spaces near to study areas.
Public transport: Call Transcentre on 0141 332 7133 for information on buses and the tube.

## Taking it easy:
At school: The SU offers the Victoria Café Bar and supports a range of student-organised clubs and societies. There is an active Dyslexic Students Group.
Locally: GSA is located in the centre of Glasgow, a major city with all the leisure and recreation facilities this implies. Details about sports and recreational facilities in Glasgow are also available from the Student Services office, tel: 0141 353 4509; email: student.services@gsa.ac.uk.

## And another thing ...
➡ The campus is situated on a steep hill and most of the buildings are accessible to wheelchair users only with assistance and/or by circuitous routes. The school's buildings are not fully wheelchair accessible. The Estates Office is currently developing a strategic approach to improving physical access.
➡ All undergraduate courses are studio-based with 'workshop' elements. The studio is the main teaching/learning environment.

There are a wide variety of teaching methods including lectures, seminars, tutorials, group critiques and reviews of work, placements, visits to exhibitions and industry.

➡ The nature of creative practice and studio learning can present problems for some students with mobility or sensory disabilities. The physical environment in studios changes constantly as students' work develops. Students also need to move quite regularly between buildings.

➡ All courses have a wide range of technical equipment and workshop machinery appropriate to the specialism. Use or adaptation for use by students with physical or sensory disabilities is assessed on an individual basis. In situations where equipment or processes have not been adapted, the school has been able to make use of additional technical support – such as readers, PAs, scribes and lipspeakers.

➡ Access to the Visual Impairment Units of the University of Glasgow and Glasgow Caledonian University can be negotiated for visually impaired students.

➡ The school's Library and Information Services are not fully wheelchair accessible, and this is under review. Library staff will assist where necessary.

➡ Counselling service is available and those students who use BSL can be referred to the local counselling service provided by RNID.

## The Disability Statement/Brochure:
*Information for Students with Disabilities*
Includes: Courses; applications; facilities and equipment; information services; physical environment; leisure and recreation; financial support; sources of assistance; further information; monitoring; future activities and contacts.

| University of Glasgow |
|---|

Glasgow G12 8QQ

*General Enquiries:*
Tel: 0141 330 2000
Fax: 0141 330 4045
Email: specialneeds@gla.ac.uk
Website: www.gla.ac.uk

**Special Needs Adviser: Shona Robertson**
**Tel: 0141 330 5497**
**Fax: 0141 330 5497**
**Email: specialneeds@**
**admin.gla.ac.uk**

### Fields of study:
Agriculture; arts, divinity; education; engineering; law and financial studies; medicine; science; social sciences; veterinary medicine.

➡ Part-time study: **Yes.**
➡ Distance learning: **Yes.**

**About the university:**
Founded in 1451, the University of Glasgow is the second oldest
university in Scotland and the fourth oldest in the UK. The university
has a compact campus in the West End of Glasgow – the city's busy
area. The main Gothic building is one of the city's best-known
landmarks. The Faculty of Veterinary Medicine is located at Garscube,
4 miles from the university, and the Crichton campus is located in
Dumfries to the south-west of Glasgow. The Glasgow School of Art
and the Scottish Agricultural College are associated institutions of the
University of Glasgow. The university overlooks Kelvingrove Park and
the impressive Kelvingrove Museum and Art Gallery. Glasgow,
Scotland's largest city, is situated in the west of Scotland, an hour
away from Edinburgh. The Highlands are to the north and the Borders
to the south.

| Total number of students: 22,638   Number of disabled students: 920 |
| --- |

**Learning support staff and services:**
Special Needs Adviser: Shona Robertson; five Learning Advisers: Iain
Allison; Margery McMahon; Barbara Weightman and Grace Wink (who
deal with different facilities within the university) and Peter Dreghorn
at the Crichton campus.
Provision of practical and academic support; liaison with academic
departments regarding study needs; alternative examination
arrangements; liaison with external agencies; assessment and
purchase, maintenance and training on special PCs and software.
All undergraduate students are assigned an adviser of studies who
can help with advice about course selection, academic progress and
other pastoral matters.

**Home sweet home:**
Most of the halls of residence have facilities for those with disabilities,
and rooms for students with specific needs were incorporated into
the design of Cairncross House, one of the newer halls.

**Out and about:**
University: There are dedicated parking spaces for drivers with
disabilities. Intersite minibus, which is free but not accessible by
wheelchair users.

## And another thing ...

➡ Many of the principal buildings on the main university campus date from the late nineteenth century and are not accessible to some with physical disabilities. However, the university is committed to improving access for everyone. The recently refurbished facilities at the Crichton campus are fully accessible to wheelchair users. The campus terrain is flat, although facilities are spread out.

➡ There are adapted laboratories and computers and automatic doorways to some major facilities, e.g. the library. There are access aids such as stair climbers.

➡ There are installed and portable induction loops in lecture rooms and tutorial rooms.

➡ There are lifts in all the large buildings on the main campus (but not the Modern Languages Building).

➡ The university has its own museum and art gallery on campus. The Hunterian Art Gallery contains works by Charles Rennie Mackintosh.

➡ The university is currently involved in a collaborative project, funded by the Scottish Higher Education Funding Council (SHEFC). The project aims to adapt the curriculum to accommodate a wider range of students, particularly those with a disability and individual need.

➡ Future developments include the establishment of a Disabilities and Special Needs Forum and to make the university, which is built on a hill, more accessible and user friendly.

### The Disability Statement/Brochure:

Includes: Pre-entry advice; current provision; learning support; student support; practical support; future plans and developments and contacts.

| University of Gloucestershire |
|---|

PO Box 220, The Park, Cheltenham GL50 2QF

*General Enquiries:*
Tel: 01242 532700
Fax: 01242 532810
Email: webmaster@glos.ac.uk
Website: www.glos.ac.uk

**Disability Adviser: Anna Donough**
**Tel: 01242 543416**
**Fax: 01242 543341**
**Email: adonough@glos.ac.uk**

## Fields of study:

Accountancy; art, media and design; business and computing; community nursing; education; environment; humanities; languages; leisure, tourism, hospitality and sport; social sciences; theology and social work.

➡ Part-time study: **Yes.**
➡ Distance learning: **Yes (religious studies only).**

## About the university:

The University of Gloucestershire is easily accessible from many major cities – London, Bristol, Birmingham and Oxford – with the M5 and A40 close by. There are three main campuses situated in Cheltenham: Park, Pittville and Francis Close Hall, with a fourth, Oxstalls, in the heart of Gloucester. A new Learning Centre was opened in 2001 at Francis Close Hall. West of Gloucester is the Royal Forest of Dean and close to Cheltenham is the Cotswold Way.

| Total number of students: 8,000 | Number of disabled students: 810 |
| --- | --- |

## Learning support staff and services:

Student Development Centre
Disability Advisers: Anna Donough and Kate Gregory; part-time Administrator: Nicky Smith; counsellors.
Assistance with DSA applications and benefits, trusts and internal funds; provision of auxiliary aids and services; advice and guidance; one-to-one/group tuition for students with dyslexia; alternative examination, assessment and study arrangements; support service for students with mental health issues; liaison with external organisations; advisory interview prior to application/registration; information on disability access and promoting physical access in liaison with Facilities Services; advice on diagnostic and needs assessment (dyslexia) and liaison with relevant academic departments.

## Home sweet home:

Each hall of residence has rooms for use by students with disabilities; this includes: wheelchair access, remote control automatic doors on two campuses, flashing fire alarms, adapted en-suite bathrooms, hoist and shower chair. The halls are two minutes away from the main teaching areas. Accommodation may be guaranteed for duration of student's course.

## Out and about:

University: The university bus, which connects all four campuses throughout the day, is accessible to wheelchair users. Dedicated parking spaces near both accommodation and study areas.

Public transport: Some accessible buses locally. Contact the Cheltenham Disability Advice Centre (see below). The train and train stations are accessible to wheelchair users. Some buses, trains, train stations and taxis are accessible to people with a visual impairment. The Dial-a-Ride taxi scheme for disabled people operates in the area.

## Taking it easy:

At university: The SU works for and on behalf of all students. It has a Sport for All policy. The vice-president of the SU is particularly responsible for ensuring that students with disabilities have an adequate voice on the committees and working groups of the university.

Locally: Cheltenham has a relatively flat centre that is accessible and mainly pedestrianised. Some of the town facilities are accessible. Disability Action Cheltenham (see below) operates a Shopmobility scheme. Most pavements are tactile. Cheltenham is a Regency town – many buildings are unable to change their façade as they are listed buildings, but most services offer alternatives. Contact the Cheltenham Disability Advice Centre (see below).

## And another thing ...

- ➡ The four campuses vary in terms of physical accessibility due to the listed nature of some buildings, although most teaching areas are accessible. If students are unable to access a teaching area alternative provision will be provided.
- ➡ Access details to learning centres for wheelchair users are published in *Guide to Learning and Information Services*.
- ➡ Academic/personal tutors are assigned to all students, who should refer to them if they are encountering any particular difficulties.
- ➡ Each learning centre has a member of staff identified as having a responsibility to assist students with disabilities.
- ➡ Special provision is made within modules requiring placements/field trips/studio work/laboratory work to ensure that all students can address learning outcomes appropriately.
- ➡ The Student Development Centre is responsible for a Special Needs Resources Area, which holds a wide range of magazines and leaflets covering many areas of disability, and provides information on disability benefits and the Disability Discrimination Act. The notice boards within the Centre are regularly updated with information on disability issues.

➡ To make an appointment with one of the counsellors contact the SDC Administrator, Nicky Smith, on 01242 543341 or email: counselling@glos.ac.uk

➡ Learning and Information Services assists students who require special equipment for study purposes – team manager tel: 01242 532980.

➡ There is a low-level photocopier at each site and a dedicated bookable workstation with software designed for students with visual impairments and specific learning difficulties.

➡ The university's Website has text-only alternatives for every page. Specific pages detailing provision for students with disabilities can be found at www.glos.ac.uk/uog/content.asp?pid=5.

## The Disability Statement/Brochure:
*Statement for Students with Disabilities and Special Needs*
Includes: Pre-registration and admission; registration, induction and progression; post-experience, postgraduate and research degree students; assessment; support departments; SU; partnerships; responsibilities and monitoring; contacts.

### Local disability public service providers:
Cheltenham Disability Advice Centre 01242 243030.
GUiDE Information Service 01452 331131.
Disability Action Cheltenham 01242 273292.
Gloucestershire Deaf Association 01452 372999; text: 01452 372600.
Gloucestershire Dyslexia Association 01242 704431; email: info@gda-dyslexia.org.uk.
Cheltenham Assessment Centre 01452 331131; email: enquiries@guide-information.org.uk.

| Goldsmiths, University of London |
| :---: |

New Cross, London SE14 6NW

*General Enquiries:*
Tel: 020 7919 7766
Fax: 020 7717 2240
Email: admissions@gold.ac.uk
Website: www.goldsmiths.ac.uk

**Disability Coordinator:**
**Mary Brown**
**Tel: 020 7717 2292**
**Fax: 020 7919 7241**
**Email: disability@gold.ac.uk**

### Fields of study:
Anthropology; art history; community work; cultural studies; design; drama and theatre arts; education; fine art; history; languages

(French, German, Spanish); mathematical and computing sciences; media and communications; music; psychology; social policy and politics; sociology; textiles.

➡ Part-time study: **Yes.**
➡ Distance learning: **No.**

## About the college:
Goldsmiths, which has been part of the University of London since 1904, is located in an urban area of south-east London and in close proximity to central London. The college is even nearer to Blackheath's open spaces and the Thames waterfront at Greenwich. Goldsmiths plays a specialist role within the university, concentrating on the study of creative, cultural and social subjects.

| |
|---|
| Total number of students: approx. 9,000<br>Number of disabled students: 458 |

## Learning support staff and services:
Disability Office and Language Unit (see information below*)
Full-time staff: Disability Coordinator: Mary Brown; Lecturer in Learning Support: Julia Lockheart.
Needs assessments at the Assistive Technology Centre; assistance with DSA applications and other sources of funding; provision of auxiliary aids and services; advice and guidance; one-to-one/group tuition for students with dyslexia; timetable teaching in accessible areas; alternative examination arrangements; liaison with external organisations.

## Home sweet home:
A number of rooms in college accommodation have been adapted to assist either those with mobility disabilities or visually impaired or D/deaf or hard of hearing students. Rooms in halls can be adapted to accommodate your needs. Contact the Disability Coordinator for more information.
Accommodation can be guaranteed for duration of student's course.

---

* Study support is available through the English Language Unit, which has a member of staff responsible for supporting students with dyslexia. Contact Julia Lockheart, tel: 020 7919 7197; email: englang-unit@gold.ac.uk; www.gold.ac.uk/studentservices/disability.

## Out and about:

College: Dedicated parking spaces in college grounds near to accommodation and study areas.

Public transport: Taxis and some buses, trains and train stations are accessible to people who are wheelchair users. Buses, taxis and some trains and train stations are accessible to people with visual impairments. The college is located in the Borough of Lewisham, south-east London, ten minutes from New Cross and New Cross Gate rail and tube stations with regular connections to and from central London. Contact Access and Mobility for further information (see Directory).

## Taking it easy:

At college: The SU is not wholly wheelchair accessible. The bar is not accessible.

Locally: The city centre is both hilly and flat. The local town facilities are not accessible. Pavements are tactile.

## And another thing ...

➡ The campus is made up of a variety of buildings, from the Victorian main building to new, purpose-built facilities. Access to some areas of the college is restricted for those with mobility difficulties. The college will, in consultation with you, make reasonable adjustments to facilitate your needs.

➡ The majority of the college buildings do not have lifts.

➡ The major lecture theatres have loop systems for those with hearing difficulties. There is also a portable loop, which can be made available.

➡ All new buildings are built with accessibility in mind (including the Rutherford Information Services Building; contact Jon Fox, tel: 020 7919 7504; email: j.fox@gold.ac.uk).

➡ The college is currently planning a major independent audit of access to the campus buildings.

➡ As part of the college's ongoing commitment to improving standards in all areas of college life, provision for students with disabilities is constantly being audited by the Disability Steering Group. Disabled students are invited to play an active role.

➡ Students can work in conjunction with staff to organise for course materials and handouts to be produced in suitable formats. Scanning equipment is available in the College Information Services department.

➡ The college has built an Assistive Technology Centre for students with disabilities.

➡ Colour-coded maps that contrast physical accessibility to the site are being developed, as is a comprehensive staff development programme to raise awareness of disability-related needs.

## The Disability Statement/Brochure:
Includes: Applications; accessibility; facilities and equipment by disability; examinations; finance; monitoring; future developments; useful contacts; declared disability figures. A4, nine pages.

## Local disability public service provider:
Lewisham Council 020 8314 6000.

| University of Greenwich |
| --- |

Old Royal Navy College, Park Row, Greenwich, London SE10 9LS

*General Enquiries:*
Tel: 0800 005 006
Fax: 020 8331 8145
Email: courseinfo@greenwich.ac.uk
Website: www.greenwich.ac.uk

**Disability Coordinator:**
**Tel: 020 8331 7875**
**Fax: 020 8331 8604**
**Email: d-centre@gre.ac.uk**

## Fields of study:
Architecture and landscape; business; chemical and life sciences; computing and mathematical sciences; earth and environmental sciences; education; engineering; health; humanities; land and construction management; languages; law; post-compulsory education and training; social sciences.

Part-time study: **Yes.**
Distance learning: **Yes.**

## About the university:
The University of Greenwich was founded as an independent institution in 1890 and soon began teaching at degree level. Custodian of 17 listed buildings, the University of Greenwich is the leading new university for research and consultancy income according to the Higher Education Statistics Agency. There are five campuses at Greenwich.

| Total number of students: 17,123 | Number of disabled students: 639 |
| --- | --- |

## Learning support staff and services:
The Disability and Dyslexia Centre based in Student Services
Two full-time dyslexia advisers and one full-time administrator; eight part-time disability advisers; eight part-time IT advisers; five part-time dyslexia tutors.
Pre-course advice; assistance with DSA applications; and arranging support such as notetakers, PAs; equipment loans and other support. There is a disability named contact in each school and department who is the first point of contact.

## Home sweet home:
The university gives top priority to disabled students when allocating places in halls of residence and in other university-managed housing. There are several wheelchair accessible rooms at all campuses as well as rooms suitable for visually impaired and D/deaf or hard of hearing students. The university has a policy and a budget to adapt accommodation to disabled students as required.
Accommodation can be guaranteed for duration of student's course.

## Out and about:
University: There is inter-site transport but it is not accessible to wheelchair users. Dedicated parking spaces near both accommodation and study areas.
Public transport: In general the local transport is not wheelchair accessible. Local accessible taxis are available. Contact Access and Mobility for information on London's public transport services (see Directory).

## Taking it easy:
At university: Wheelchair accessible gyms, sports halls, squash courts and SU bars.
Locally: The cinemas and sports centre are accessible. Artsline publishes a number of guides on access in London (see Directory).

## And another thing ...
➡ A disability resource room has been set up that contains a range of equipment designed to make studying easier for disabled students.
➡ The Disability and Dyslexia Centre has a limited range of equipment that can be loaned to disabled students including 4-track (four times usual recording time) cassette recorders and Alpha Smart 2000 keyboards.
➡ The Disability Working Group is integrated into the management structure of the university and there is a steering group for development of the Disability and Dyslexia Centre.

## The Disability Statement/Brochure:
Includes: Pre-application and application procedures; the Disability and Dyslexia Centre; DSA; campus accessibility; accommodation; current provision; examination and assessment; support for students by disability; other support services; future plans; action plan; and appendices – useful contacts, examples of disabled and dyslexic students at the university; list of disability named contacts; disclaimer. A4, 36 pages.

## Local disability public service provider:
Greenwich Association of Disabled People (GAD), Christchurch Forum, Trafalgar Road, London SE10 9EQ; 020 8305 2221; text: 01208 858 9307.

---

| **Harper Adams University College** |
| --- |

Newport, Shropshire TF10 8NB

*General Enquiries:*
Tel: 01952 820280
Fax: 01952 814783
Email: admissions@harper-adams.ac.uk
Website: www.harper-adams.ac.uk

**Head of Student Service: Ian Robson**
**Tel: 01952 815222**
**Fax: 01952 815241**
**Email: ibrobson@**
**harper-adams.ac.uk**

## Fields of study:
Agriculture; agri-food marketing; animal health and welfare; business; engineering and design; food; land, countryside and environment; leisure and landscape.

➡ Part-time study: **Yes.**
➡ Distance learning: **No.**

## About the college:
Harper Adams University College was founded in 1901. Set in rural Shropshire it is in the centre of an intensive and progressive mixed farming area and within easy access of hill and upland farms. Harper Adams was inspected by the Higher Education QAA, which assessed the quality of education in agriculture, land management and food institutions throughout the university sector. The college was awarded 23 out of a maximum of 24, which is the top score gained by any institution in this subject area.

| Total number of students: 1,570 | Number of disabled students: 103 |
| --- | --- |

## Learning support staff and services:
Student Services
There is no specific disability unit. Services for students with disabilities are given by Student Services. One part-time support tutor for disabled students.
Deal with pre-application enquiries; needs assessments through a local assessment centre; educational psychologist assessment arrangements; DSA application assistance; alternative examination arrangements; provision of PAs, notetakers and assistance with computers when required; continual communication with students to react quickly to any problems that have been identified.
The college's Learning and Teaching Strategy contains plans for the development of its programme of initial screening and diagnosis of dyslexia and other learning difficulties. The college also plans to review and extend learning support for students with learning difficulties through a central support service.

## Home sweet home:
There are seven self-catering rooms for students with disabilities at the Harris and Gloucester halls. These rooms have purpose-built facilities that include en-suite rooms with a level-access shower. Harris Hall has a lift to each floor. Student wardens are trained in first aid.
Accommodation can be guaranteed for duration of student's course.

## Out and about:
College: Dedicated parking spaces near both accommodation and study areas.
Public transport: Due to its rural nature the area is not well served by public transport, but buses are available from the college to Newport (and vice versa) at the beginning and end of the day. This transport is not accessible to students with mobility difficulties.

## Taking it easy:
At college: There is a swimming pool and equipped weights room in the SU. There are plans to install a lift in the SU building.
Locally: The local town is accessible for wheelchair users.

## And another thing ...
➡ The college is a single-site campus through which a minor but busy road passes. There is no great distance between buildings and all are easily accessible via the road and path network.
➡ The courses at Harper Adams are vocational in nature and usually involve student placements in industry or commerce. The college

does its best to place students with organisations that provide an appropriate educational experience, but it may not be possible to arrange a placement opportunity, in the case of some disabilities, if the work is of a physical nature. In such cases the college has been able to identify placements within the college so that the requirements of the programme of study can be met.

➡ The college is a member of Skill.

## The Disability Statement/Brochure:
*Information for Applicants with Disabilities*
Includes: Getting to and from the college; accommodation; catering; social activities; academic facilities; applications; support; student placements; examinations; careers; financial support; postgraduate students; travel; health and safety and other organisations.

## Local disability public service provider:
Telford and Wrekin Council.

---

| Heriot-Watt University |
| --- |

Edinburgh EH14 4AS

*General Enquiries:*
Tel: 0131 449 5111
Fax: 0131 449 5153
Email: enquiries@hw.ac.uk
Website: www.hw.ac.uk

**Disability Adviser: Sandra Sabiston**
**Tel: 0131 451 3509**
**Fax: 0131 451 3612**
**Email: s.sabiston@hw.ac.uk**

### Fields of study:
Accountancy, finance, economics and management; arts; combined studies; engineering; environmental management; information technology; languages; mathematics; ocean science and technology; science; sport and exercise science; textiles.

➡ Part-time study: **Yes.**
➡ Distance learning: **Yes.**

### About the university:
Heriot-Watt University boasts up-to-date teaching and learning methods and is a pioneer in the use and implementation of educational technology and distance learning. Ninety-four per cent of graduates enter directly into work, further study or training, placing the university close to the top of the employment league tables for UK universities.

| Total number of students: 6,300 | Number of disabled students: 212 |

## Learning support staff and services:
Disability Service
Part-time staff: Disability Adviser: Sandra Sabiston; Dyslexia Adviser:
Sarah Carley; Technology Adviser: Stuart Misson.
Needs Assessment; assistance with DSA applications and Disability
Premium Funding; provision of auxiliary aids and services; advice and
guidance; one-to-one/group tuition for students with dyslexia;
alternative examination, assessment and study arrangements; service
for students with mental health issues (referred to Student
Counsellor); arranging visits for prospective students; funding PAs;
screening for dyslexia; study skills advice; arranging assessments;
assessment of technology requirements and ongoing technical
support and liaison with external organisations.

## Home sweet home:
On the Riccarton campus, 24 bedrooms are equipped for students
with mobility difficulties or students who are wheelchair users. Most
have en-suite facilities, telephone and Internet access. The majority of
these rooms are equipped with a doorbell warning light system
(linked with the fire alarm system) and vibrating pillow for students
who are D/deaf or hard of hearing. Help alert pull cords have also
been installed. Resident wardens are based on site and available to
the residents in their hall as necessary. The Scottish Borders campus
has some self-catering flats, which have been adapted for wheelchair
users. Every effort is made to ensure the needs of any individual are
met as far as possible. All adapted rooms are integrated within
campus accommodation.
Accommodation can be guaranteed for duration of student's course.

## Out and about:
University: Transport for disabled students is provided if required.
Dedicated parking spaces near both accommodation and study
areas.
Public transport: Only trains and some taxis are wheelchair
accessible.

## Taking it easy:
At university: Support from the Student Association, which has an
elected disabled students' officer. The Centre for Sport and Exercise
at Riccarton is accessible by wheelchair users on the ground floor,
but to access the second floor requires the negotiation of eight steps.
The majority of the facilities are on the ground floor, including a toilet

and shower suite fully equipped for wheelchair users. Accessible sports facilities at the Borders campus SU. The swimming pool at Napier University is accessible to wheelchair users and is available to students with disabilities or specific needs who are matriculated students at Heriot-Watt.

Locally: Being an established city with many listed buildings, Edinburgh cannot claim to be fully accessible; it is both hilly and flat, though the main shopping area on Princes Street is flat. However, most of the public service areas are accessible. There is a Shopmobility scheme and the pavements are tactile. A local area disability guide is available.

### And another thing ...

➡ The advisers can provide certain items of equipment on loan, e.g. spellcheckers, PCs, TV magnifying screen, hearing helper/radio aid and small fridges for insulin storage.

## The Disability Statement/Brochure:

Includes: University policy; applications and admissions; access, exams and assessment; students with disabilities and special needs; special needs advisers; general student welfare; financial assistance; medical services; careers support; facilities and equipment for students by disability; staff development and training; student complaints and appeals; accommodation; sports facilities; Student Association; library; links with other organisations; plans for the future.

### Local disability public service provider:

Edinburgh Committee for the Coordination of Services for People with Disabilities, 0131 453 2418.

---

| University of Hertfordshire |
|---|

Hatfield, Herts AL10 9AB

*General Enquiries:*
Tel/Text: 01707 284451
Fax: 01707 285094
Email: admissions@herts.ac.uk
Website: www.herts.ac.uk

**Disability Officer: Lena Kloos**
**Tel/Text: 01707 284454**
**Fax: 01707 285094**
**Email: L.J.Kloos@herts.ac.uk**
**Website: www.herts.ac.uk/equality**

### Fields of study:

Art and design; business; engineering and information sciences; health and human sciences; humanities, languages and education; interdisciplinary studies; law and natural sciences.

→ Part-time study: **Yes.**
→ Distance learning: **Yes, but limited options.**

## About the university:
The university has two main campuses at Hatfield and St Albans, and an Observatory Station between Hatfield and Hertford. All campuses have good access for disabled people.

| Total number of students: 21,000 |
|---|
| Number of disabled students: 1,000 |

## Learning support staff and services:
The Equality Unit
Full-time staff: Disability Officer; Lena Kloos; Head of Equality Unit: Marcella Wright.
Part-time staff: Disability Support Officer: Ruth Cohen-Rose; Administrative Secretary: Sue Ryan.
The university also has 11 faculty disabled students' coordinators and a disability network with a further 17 members of staff providing support in faculties and departments.
Assistance with DSA applications and the University Disability Fund; provision of auxiliary aids and services; advice and guidance; one-to-one/group tuition for students with dyslexia; alternative examination, assessment and study arrangements; liaison with external organisations; facilitate work of Disabled Students' Network including the Faculty of Disabled Students' Coordinators.
The Faculty of Disabled Students' Coordinators can help to facilitate and support any adjustments required, including completion of Study Needs Agreements, which determine, for example, support needs in lectures and exams. The Disability Support Officer can help with use of assistive technologies in the university's learning resources centres.

## Home sweet home:
The university has 27 fully adaptable rooms accessible for wheelchair users. Adaptations can also be made to other rooms should they be required, e.g. providing vibrating pillow alarms or fridges.
Accommodation can be guaranteed for duration of student's course, for disabled students with specific requirements.

## Out and about:
University: Dedicated parking spaces near both accommodation and study areas. There is an accessible university bus. The university has good links with local transport services specifically for disabled people.

Public transport: Some buses and taxis are accessible to wheelchair users. Dial-a-Ride operates in the area and there is a Hertfordshire Mobility Helpline. Contact the disability officer for more information.

**Taking it easy:**
At university: All SU facilities are wheelchair accessible. Students should note: these areas can be smoky and noisy. The extensive sports facilities are accessible. The university and SU aims to fully support disabled students who would like to form social groups with their peers, and all existing groups and societies are accessible for disabled people.
Locally: Most students visit St Albans or Stevenage. The town centre, Hatfield, is flat and its facilities are generally accessible. There is a Shopmobility scheme.

**And another thing ...**
➡ The campus at Hatfield College Lane is hilly.
➡ The pavements are tactile.
➡ There is a small internal fund for those outside all other funding sources.
➡ The university provides extensive information on disability support and access via its Equality Unit and website: www.herts.ac.uk/equality.
➡ All the campus learning resource centres provide a wide range of disability support equipment and assistive technology.
➡ The university's email discussion forum for disabled students offers the opportunity to get to know other disabled students via email. Visit SPIREnetStudentTalk/listbot.com.
➡ Textphones are available at all campuses and the Typetalk service is available to all staff.

**QAA Report: Paragraph 85, August 2001**
Student Services provide specialist advice and services for students with special needs and there is a full-time disabled student officer. A support network, which works across the university, includes representatives from the faculties as well as other central service providers such as the Admissions Office, Careers and the Department of Estates. The annual report of the disabled student officer provides the university with evidence with which to assess the effectiveness of these arrangements.

**The Disability Statement/Brochure:**
Can be found on the Equality Unit's website: www.herts.ac.uk/equality

**Local disability public service providers:**
DISH (Disability Information Service Hertfordshire) 0800 181067.
PASS (Hertfordshire's PA Support Service), 23b Weltech Centre,
Ridgeway, Welwyn Garden City, Hertfordshire AL7 2AA; 01707
321442; fax: 01707 327100; email: pass@hertspass.com.
Hertfordshire Action on Disability, Woodside Centre, The Commons,
Welwyn Garden City, Hertfordshire AL7 4DD; 01707 324581;
fax: 01707 371297 email: information@hadnet.co.uk.

| Heythrop College, University of London |
|:---:|

Kensington Square, London W8 5HQ

*General Enquiries:*
Tel: 020 7795 6600
Fax: 020 7795 4200
Email: r.bolland@heythrop.ac.uk
Website: www.heythrop.ac.uk

**Fields of study:**
Church history and historical theology; combined studies; New
Testament; pastoral studies; philosophy; systematic theology;
Testament and Intertestamental.

➡ Part-time study: **Yes.**
➡ Distance learning: **No.**

**About the college:**
Heythrop College, as a Jesuit foundation, is part of the University of
London, and specialises in philosophy and theology. It is a small
college located in central London, off Kensington High Street near
Kensington Gardens. Heythrop welcomes students and scholars of all
faiths and none.

| Total number of students: 500 | Number of disabled students: 0 |
|---|---|

**Learning support staff and services:**
No specific staff or services for students with disabilities.

**Home sweet home:**
No particular provision for students with disabilities although first-year
students will usually be offered a place at one of the University of
London's intercollegiate, catered halls of residence.

**Out and about:**
At college: There is no current transport provision or dedicated parking space for students with disabilities.
Public transport: Contact Access and Mobility for information on London and its public transport services (see Directory).

**Taking it easy:**
Locally: Access guides to London are available from Artsline (see Directory).

**And another thing ...**
➡ The college is aware of its complete lack of provision for students with physical disabilities. Some work is in hand to improve access on the ground floor, e.g. a toilet for wheelchair users.

## The Disability Statement/Brochure:
Does not have one.

| Holborn College |
|---|

Woolwich Road, Charlton, London SE7 8LN

*General Enquiries:*
Tel: 020 8317 6000
Fax: 020 8317 6001
www.holborncollege.ac.uk

**Student Services Officer: Sharon Bolton**
**Tel: 020 8317 6212**
**Fax: 020 8317 6008**
**Email: Sharon.Bolton@**
**holborncollege.ac.uk**

**Fields of study:**
Business and law

➡ Part-time study: **Yes.**
➡ Distance learning: **Yes.**

**About the college:**
Holborn College has been established since 1969. It is an independent college located on a campus in central London, with more than 70 per cent of students being from outside Europe.

| Total number of students: approx. 13,000 |
|---|
| Number of disabled students: 0 |

**Learning support staff and services:**
There are no specific staff to support students with disabilities.

**Home sweet home:**
There is currently no accommodation which is accessible to students with disabilities, but assistance would be offered in finding suitable accommodation.
Accommodation *cannot* be guaranteed for duration of the student's course.

**Out and about:**
College: There are dedicated parking spaces for students with disabilities near the study areas.
Locally: Buses, trains, train stations and taxis are accessible to people who are wheelchair users. Buses and some trains are accessible to people who are visually impaired. There are wheelchair accessible buses which come to the college. Contact Access and Mobility for information on London's public transport services (see below).

**Taking it easy:**
At college: Waterfront leisure centre, Woolwich and college events provide social support.
Locally: The city centre is flat and accessible. The town facilities are accessible and there is a Shopmobility scheme. Artsline publishes a number of guides on the city of London (see below).

**And another thing …**
➡ Although there are no disabled students currently at the Holborn, the College would welcome applications from disabled people and would take all possible steps to accommodate their needs.

**Local disability public service providers:**
Access and Mobility (see Directory).
Artsline (see Directory).
Greenwich Council.

---

| **The University of Huddersfield** |
| :---: |

Queensgate, Huddersfield HD1 3DH

*General Enquiries:*      **Disability Support Manager**: Claire Shanks
Tel: 01484 422288          **Tel: 01484 473724 or 472339**
Fax: 01484 516151              **Fax: 01484 472560**

Email: admissions@hsd.ac.uk
Website: www.hud.ac.uk

**Email: c.l.shanks@hud.ac.uk**
**Text: 01484 473689**

## Fields of study:
Applied sciences; business; computing and mathematics; design technology; education and professional development; engineering; human and health sciences; music and humanities.

- ➡ Part-time study: **Yes.**
- ➡ Distance learning: **No.**

## About the university:
Founded in the 1840s and a university since 1992, Huddersfield has strong links with industry, commerce and the arts. The University of Huddersfield has two main sites, the academic campus on Queensgate in the town centre and its main residential site at Storthes Hall Park. Easily accessible by road, rail and air, the university lies at the heart of the transpennine corridor, which links Humberside to Merseyside. Huddersfield town is close to the rugged South Pennines, Peak District, Brontë Country and the Yorkshire Dales.

Total number of students: 17,000   Number of disabled students: 1,100

## Learning support staff and services:
Student Services, Welfare Support Department
Full-time staff: Disability Manager: Claire Shanks; Student Support Adviser: Rachel Rogers. Another full-time member of staff is yet to be appointed.
Part-time staff: Student Support Adviser: Nancy Morson
Assistance with DSA applications and Hardship Fund; provision of auxiliary aids and services; advice and guidance; one-to-one/group tuition for students with dyslexia; alternative examination, assessment and study arrangements; support service for students with mental health issues and liaison with external organisations.
Support workers can be provided through the Support Workers Service.

## Home sweet home:
At Storthes Hall 20 rooms are purpose-built for students with disabilities.
Accommodation can be guaranteed for duration of student's course.

## Out and about:
University: Dedicated parking spaces near both accommodation and study areas.

Public transport: There are some kneeling buses and accessible taxis. Trains and train stations are wheelchair accessible. Some buses, trains and taxis are accessible for people with visual impairments. The train station is accessible to people with visual impairments. Kirklees Metropolitan Council runs the Taxi Voucher Scheme.

### Taking it easy:
At university: The SU building, Milton Hall, has limited access for students with mobility difficulties.
Locally: The city centre, which is hilly, is pedestrianised and there are plenty of places to park. Only some facilities are accessible. There is a Shopmobility scheme and the pavements are tactile.

### And another thing …
➡ A detailed access guide is provided for all students with disabilities.
➡ Limited access to: the Student Union; music block – courses run by the School of Music and Humanities; Ramsden building – courses run by the School of Human and Health Sciences; St Peters building – courses run by the School of Music and Humanities.
➡ Induction loops are available in two lecture theatres, Ramsden building Room 17, St Paul's Hall and workshop block.
➡ The university has a trust fund for students with disabilities, which aims to offer additional support in the event of unforeseen circumstances.
➡ There is an ongoing programme of refurbishment and new building work. Disabled access takes a high priority within this programme.
➡ As well as receiving the Investors in People accreditation, the university has received the Kickstart Award for eliminating discrimination and inequality in employment, and the Way Ahead Award for access for disabled people.

## The Disability Statement/Brochure:
Statement includes: Current policy; current provision; academic support; teaching and assessment; general support mechanisms; physical environment; future activity and development and contacts.

### Local disability public service providers:
Kirklees Social Services 01484 223028.
Social Services Information Points 01484 223000.

| **University of Hull** |
|---|

Cottingham Road, Hull HU6 7RX

*General Enquiries:*
Tel: 0870 126 2000
Fax: 01482 442290
Email: admissions@hull.ac.uk
Website: www.hull.ac.uk

**Disability Officer: Emma Coyne**
**Tel: 01482 466833/**
**01723 362392**
**Fax: 01482 466669**
**Email: disability-services@**
**hull.ac.uk, r.laidlaw@hull.ac.uk**
**Text: 01482 466692**

**Fields of study:**
American studies; biological science; business; chemistry; computer science; economics and social history; engineering; English; European studies; fine art; gender studies; geography; history; law; mathematics and statistics; modern languages; music, drama and dance; nursing and midwifery; philosophy; physics; psychology; social policy and criminology; social work and social studies; sport science; teaching and theology.

➡ Part-time study: **Yes.**
➡ Distance learning: **Yes.**

**About the university:**
The University of Hull was founded in 1927. Two miles north of the city centre, Hull is a flat and compact campus. Over 70 years on it has a second, Scarborough campus, which is located on a hilly site. The university is green, both in terms of its campuses and environmentally.

| Total number of students: 15,000  Number of disabled students: 700+ |
|---|

**Learning support staff and services:**
Disability Services
Hull campus: Full-time staff: Disability Officer: Emma Coyne; disability coordinator; IT technician; two dyslexia tutors.
Part-time staff: disability coordinator (sensory impairments)
Scarborough campus: Part-time staff: disability support adviser; dyslexia tutor.
Assistance with DSA applications and other funding; provision of auxiliary aids and services; advice and guidance; one-to-one/group tuition for students with dyslexia; alternative examination, assessment and study arrangements; support service for students with mental

health issues; arranging training in the use of equipment and software; referring students with suspected dyslexia for screening and psychological assessment; advising and providing staff development for disability tutors within the faculties; advising the Accommodation Office about individual needs of students with disabilities; advising the university's Disabilities Committee on policy and procedures for supporting students with disabilities and liaison with external organisations.

### Home sweet home:

The university is guide dog friendly and has adapted student accommodation to take account of the needs of guide dog users. Most of the student accommodation is covered by deaf alerter systems. There are also rooms adapted for students with mobility difficulties. For students with musculo-skeletal difficulties the Miriam Hebron Disability Resource Centre has a range of ergonomic equipment for use in the Centre. Given sufficient notice, further alterations to suit the special requirements of individual students will be made.

Accommodation can be guaranteed for duration of student's course.

### Out and about:

University: Dedicated parking spaces throughout the campus.

Public transport: Trains, train stations, taxis and some buses are accessible to wheelchair users. All are accessible to people with visual impairments. Contact the transport department of Hull City Council. There is a Dial-a-Ride taxi scheme for disabled people operating in the area.

### Taking it easy:

At university: The SU building has level ground-floor access. It provides a range of catering and refreshment facilities throughout the day, and diverse entertainment in the evenings and at weekends. All the SU facilities are accessible by students with disabilities. The SU also manages its own sports and fitness centre, which is accessible to people with mobility disabilities.

Locally: Parts of Hull are pedestrianised. The city centre is flat and accessible and the local facilities are generally accessible. There is a Shopmobility scheme and the pavements are tactile.

### And another thing ...

➡ The university has initiated a programme that will adapt most of its major buildings to facilitate better access.

➡ Steps are being replaced or augmented with access ramps of appropriate gradient and doors widened.

- Level or ramped access is available to academic and academic-support buildings.
- WC facilities for disabled users are being built, and suitably sited car parking spaces are being allocated specifically for people with mobility disabilities.
- Induction loops are being installed in many teaching rooms.
- Access to academic buildings on the university's Scarborough campus is currently under review.
- The Department of Psychology offers an assessment service for students who wish to be assessed or reassessed for dyslexia.
- Regular dyslexia support group and individual tutorial support for study skills are also available to students on all campuses. Tutorial support is adapted according to the demands of participants' courses and individual requirements.
- The Miriam Hebron Centre was established to provide a wide range of IT and learning support facilities such as specialist computer software, scanners and CCTV.
- There are various publications relating to disability that may prove useful available from Disability Services.
- The university's Disabilities Committee provides a forum in which student representatives as well as academic, administrative and support staff can discuss issues, monitor provision and shape policy.
- The university has links with RNIB and the local Hearing Impaired Service.

### QAA Report: Paragraph 46, January 2001

The account drew attention to the particular efforts that have been made to meet the requirements of students and staff with special needs. Of particular note was the Miriam Hebron Centre, which provides a range of IT resources designed for use by students with a variety of special needs, and the Dyslexia Service, which offers a screening programme and a range of course-related and technology-based methods of support. The range of student support services, the account stated, is augmented by a programme of training events for staff offered by the IFL Staff Development Programme, under its Supporting Students Programme. The audit team noted that those involved in this work undertake regular monitoring and evaluation of their provision, and would wish to commend the university's continued commitment to supporting students and staff with special needs.

### The Disability Statement/Brochure:
*Opportunities and Support for Students with Disabilities*

Disability Services; other support services; campuses and accommodation; examinations; other information; case histories; other useful documents.

**Local disability public service providers:**
Hearing Impaired Service.
Disability Choices and Rights, Arthur Richardson Centre, Savoy Road, Hull HU8 0TX; 01482 788668; fax: 01482 719591; website www.choicesandrights.org.uk; email: info@choicesandrights.demon.co.uk.

| Imperial College London |
|---|

London SW7 2AZ

*General Enquiries:*    **Disabilities Officer: Loretto O'Callaghan**
Tel: 020 7589 5111    **Tel: 020 7594 8935**
Fax: 020 7594 8004    **Fax: 020 7594 9050**
Email: admissions@ic.ac.uk    **Email: l.ocallaghan@imperial.ac.uk**
Website: www.ic.ac.uk

**Fields of study:**
Aeronautics; biochemistry; biology; chemical engineering and chemical technology; chemistry; civil and environmental engineering; computing; electrical and electronic engineering; environment, earth sciences and engineering; management; materials; mathematics; mechanical engineering; medicine; physics.

➡ Part-time study: **Yes.**
➡ Distance learning: **Yes.**

**About the college:**
Imperial College London has its main campus in South Kensington, an area in central London that is home to the Science Museum, Natural History Museum and the Victoria and Albert Museum as well as Hyde Park and Kensington Gardens. The college's other London-based campuses are at Charing Cross, Chelsea and Westminster, Hammersmith, Royal Brompton and St Mary's – all within a short distance of South Kensington. The college also has special facilities at Silwood Park, near Ascot, and at Wye, a rural campus near Ashford, Kent. Imperial College London is recognised as one of the top three UK university institutions for research quality and in the media league tables came second overall in *The Times Good University Guide* (14 April 2000).

Total number of students: 10,500    Number of disabled students: 120

## Learning support staff and services:
Disablities Office
Full-time staff: Disability Officer: Loretto O'Callaghan.
Needs assessments are arranged with an external agency; assistance with DSA applications; advice and guidance; alternative examination, assessment and study arrangements; support service for mental health issues; available to discuss matters such as access, accommodation, financial entitlement or other concerns; works closely with academic departments as appropriate; advises staff on dyslexia; advises on where students should seek personal assistance (PAs are not provided by the college); offers initial assistance in getting around the college's various London sites; can visit students in their area of work or hall of residence at South Kensington, the medical campuses, Silwood Park or Wye and liaison with external organisations.
Admission tutors in departments will offer advice to applicants and discuss how best to meet any individual needs to assist students on courses including field trips, vocational placements and study abroad.

## Home sweet home:
Within Linstead Hall there is one self-contained flat and one study/bedsitting room with en-suite bathroom that are suitable for some disabled students. However, only one is wheelchair accessible. Guide dogs are welcome in the college. In Weeks Hall there is one study/bedsitting room with en-suite bathroom that has been designed for wheelchair users. Students with disabilities share the communal cooking facilities with other students on the same landing. Leisure facilities are shared with students from other floors and are accessible by lift. In Beit Hall there are en-suite rooms that have been adapted for students with disabilities and are accessible for wheelchair users. Imperial College at Wye has two en-suite rooms suitable for wheelchair users. On the Withersdane site are two more rooms suitable for some disabled students that are not wheelchair accessible.
Accommodation can be guaranteed for duration of student's course if needed.

## Out and about:
College: There is a limited number of dedicated parking spaces near both accommodation and study areas.
Public transport: Contact Access and Mobility for information on London's public transport services (see Directory).

## Taking it easy:

At college: The SU welcomes students with disabilities and encourages participation in activities, which are accessible. Refurbishment of the union at South Kensington has meant that more areas are now wheelchair accessible. The sports centre at South Kensington, also open to the public, is accessible by stair lift. Most catering outlets are accessible for wheelchair users.

Locally: London is a flat city with accessible town facilities. Artsline publish a number of guides on access in London (see Directory).

## And another thing ...

➡ Because of the size and nature of some buildings (parts of Wye College, for example, date back to the fourteenth century) the college will be undertaking an audit of accessibility both to and within buildings and of courses run. The central library at Wye is, however, accessible to wheelchair users.

➡ Many of the academic departments at South Kensington are accessible to wheelchair users, and hearing loops have been installed in some areas of the college.

➡ Many of the college lifts have tactile controls and speech.

➡ Central library facility at South Kensington is accessible with assistance and has hearing loops in key areas.

➡ Guide dogs and hearing dogs for deaf people are welcome.

➡ Awards ceremonies take place in the Royal Albert Hall, adjacent to the South Kensington campus, which is accessible.

➡ Personal evacuation plans are prepared for individual students who will be supplied, if required, with vibrating pagers, and where necessary flashing light and other types of alarms will be installed.

➡ D/deaf or hard of hearing students tend to use the services of the City Lit (see Directory) and pay direct for sign language interpreters and notetakers.

➡ In certain circumstances the college may pay for an assessment for dyslexia.

➡ There is no dedicated dyslexia support unit in the college.

## The Disability Statement/Brochure:

*Information for Applicants with Disabilities*

Includes: The college estate; equal opportunities; admission procedures and provision; disability officer and other support staff; SU; library provision; health care and safety; counselling; careers; centre for educational development and future activity and policy development.

| Keele University |
| --- |

Newcastle-under-Lyme, Staffordshire ST5 5BG

*General Enquiries:*
Tel: 01782 584003
Email: undergraduate@keele.ac.uk
Website: www.keele.ac.uk

**Disability Coordinator: Toni Middling**
**Tel: 01782 584105**
**Fax 01782 584105**
**Email: disabilityservices**
**@keele.ac.uk**
**Text: 01782 583271**

## Fields of study:
Business; criminology; English and American literature; environmental studies; European studies; finance; history; information technology; law; marketing; medicine; midwifery; modern languages; music; nursing; physiotherapy; politics; psychology; Russian history and culture; science.

➡ Part-time study: **No.**
➡ Distance: **No.**

## About the university:
Keele is a mix of old architecture (nineteenth-century Keele Hall and the Clockhouse) and new (teaching blocks and accommodation). The university is set in 600 acres of landscaped parkland, fields, woodlands and lakes.

| Total number of students: 9,000 | Number of disabled students: 500 |
| --- | --- |

## Learning support staff and services:
Disability Services
Two full-time and one part-time members of staff.
Needs assessments; assistance with DSA applications; provision of auxiliary aids and services; advice and guidance; one-to-one/group tuition for students with dyslexia; screening and testing for dyslexia; alternative examination, assessment and study arrangements; support service for students with mental health issues and liaison with external organisations.

## Home sweet home:
There is one accessible suite with a room for a PA. If this is in use, alternative arrangements will be made. Further effort will be made to meet individual needs. Guaranteed accommodation for the duration of the student's course.

**Out and about:**
University: Dedicated parking near both accommodation and study areas.
Public transport: Some buses, trains and taxis are accessible to wheelchair users. The train station is currently being refurbished.

**Taking it easy:**
At university: Accessible leisure centre on campus.
Locally: The city centre is hilly and some facilities are accessible. There is a Shopmobility scheme and some pavements are tactile.

**And another thing ...**
➡ Staffordshire Regional Access Centre can give disabled students a professional assessment of assistive technology, study strategy and your human academic support needs.
➡ Students can make use of the equipment in the resource centre, which includes Braille embosser; tactile diagram machine and scanner.

## The Disability Statement/Brochure:
*Services and Facilities for Disabled Students and Applicants*
Access on campus; services and facilities; Disability Services; accommodation; careers; examination and records; information services; SU Independent Advice Unit; learning support; leisure centre; medical and dental practice; public transport and finance.

**Local disability public service provider:**
Staffordshire Assist – county service for students with a sensory disability.

| Kent Institute of Art and Design |
| --- |

Fort Pitt, Rochester, Kent ME1 1DZ

*General Enquiries:*
Tel: 01634 830022
Fax: 01634 820300
Email: info@kiad.ac.uk
Website: www.kiad.ac.uk

**Disability Coordinator: David A. Kirk**
**Tel: 01634 820314**
**Fax: 01634 820300**
**Email: dkirk@kiad.ac.uk**

**Fields of study:**
Architecture; design; fine art; photography and fashion; visual communications.

➡ Part-time study: **Yes, on fine art course.**
➡ Distance learning: **No.**

## About the institute:

The Kent Institute has three campuses around Kent, in Maidstone (visual communication), Rochester (design, fashion and photography) and Canterbury (fine art and architecture). Each has a unique portfolio of courses and specialist facilities whilst also benefiting from being part of the larger institute.

| Total number of students: 2,700 | Number of disabled students: 483 |
| --- | --- |

## Learning support staff and services:

Part-time Disability Coordinator: David A. Kirk; part-time dyslexia adviser.

Supports students from the time they make a first application to the completion of their course. The disability coordinator regularly visits each campus. Help is given to students with a range of disabilities on such issues as claiming additional allowances and, where appropriate, receiving additional support.

The dyslexia adviser visits the campuses on a weekly basis to provide advice and support for students with dyslexia.

## Home sweet home:

There are adapted flats with adapted kitchens for wheelchair users. There are no extra rooms for PAs.

Accommodation can be guaranteed for duration of student's course.

## Out and about:

Institute: Dedicated parking near both accommodation and study areas.

Public transport: None of the three campuses is near a railway station.

## Taking it easy:

At institute: Access to the SU, bar and sports facilities. The sports facilities are run by the local authority. They are some distance from the campuses.

Locally: Rochester town centre is hilly, Maidstone town centre is both flat and hilly and Canterbury city centre is flat, but all are accessible. There are Shopmobility schemes and the pavements are tactile.

## University of Kent at Canterbury

The Registry, Canterbury, Kent CT2 7NZ

*General Enquiries:*
Tel: 01227 827272
Fax: 01227 827077
Email: recruitment@ukc.ac.uk
Website: www.ukc.ac.uk

**Disability Support Coordinator:**
**Andy Velarde**
**Tel: 01227 823158**
**Fax: 01227 823119**
**Email: inclusive_learning@ukc.ac.uk**
**Text: 01227 823158**
**Website: www.ukc.ac.uk/guidance/
disabiltysupport.htm**

**Fields of study:**
Humanities; science; social sciences; technology and medical studies.

➡ Part-time study: **Yes.**
➡ Distance learning: **No.**

**About the university:**
The University of Kent is based on a collegiate system composed of four college – Rutherford, Keynes, Eliot and Darwin. It was built in the period after the Second World War when universities were moving away from redbrick buildings and is situated in the Kent countryside on a hill above the medieval cathedral city of Canterbury.

Total number of students: 13,000    Number of disabled students: 700

**Learning support staff and services:**
Disability Support Unit
Full-time staff: Disability Coordinator: Andy Velarde
Part-time staff: Assistant Coordinator: Tom Sharp; Secretaries: Gill Campbell and Joanna Yeadon.
Needs assessments; assistance with DSA applications and Hardship Fund; provision of auxiliary aids and services; advice and guidance; one-to-one/group tuition for students with dyslexia; alterative examination, assessment and study arrangements; support service for students with mental health issues; negotiating with academic departments; arranging for dyslexia screening; organising support from dyslexia tutors, notetakers, library assistants and mentors, and liaison with external organisations.
Each faculty has a disability officer whose role is to promote disability issues in their own faculty and offer support and information to staff and individual students.

**Home sweet home:**
There are currently eight rooms adapted for wheelchair users/students with mobility difficulties, with six more rooms available in 2004. There are also four rooms with additional equipment for students who are D/deaf or hard of hearing.
Accommodation can be guaranteed for duration of student's course if applied for.

**Out and about:**
University: Dedicated parking spaces near both accommodation and study areas.
Public transport: Buses are not wheelchair accessible. Train stations and some trains and taxis are wheelchair accessible. The train station and some buses, trains and taxis are accessible to people with visual impairments. A taxi scheme for disabled people operates in the area.

**Taking it easy:**
At university: The sports centre is accessible to wheelchair users and is used extensively by disability groups from the local community. The staff there can help in designing exercise programmes tailored to individual needs. The student centre, a multipurpose building, is also accessible.
Locally: Canterbury is flat and accessible for wheelchair users. Some of the town facilities are accessible, there is a Shopmobility scheme and the pavements are tactile.

**And another thing ...**
➡ The main campus is set on a hill about a mile outside Canterbury. Much of the site is fairly flat, but there are some steep gradients. The whole site covers an area of approximately 300 acres. Students with mobility difficulties are advised to use electric wheelchairs or scooters.
➡ The Map and Access Guide has now been updated.
➡ A support group for those people with unseen disabilities who wish to meet regularly and discuss relevant issues is facilitated by the Counselling Service.
➡ The support services are monitored and students are requested to offer feedback.

## The Disability Statement/Brochure:
Brief, dated document covering: Policy; admissions; accessibility; student guidance and welfare services; facilities and equipment; physical environment; future policy and action and further information.
Available on www.kent.ac.uk/guidance/studentdisabilitypolicy.htm

**Local disability public service providers:**
DIAL – Disabled Information Advice Line – 01227 771155.
Umbrella; Kent Association for the Blind.

---

### King Alfred's, Winchester
Winchester, Hants SO22 4NR

*General Enquiries:*
Tel: 01962 841515
Fax: 01962 842280
Website: www.wkac.ac.uk

**Welfare Adviser: Anne Baker**
**Tel: 01962 827439**
**Fax: 01962 827515**
**Email: A.Baker@wkac.ac.uk**

**Fields of study:**
American studies; archaeology; business; dance, drama and performing arts; education; English; film and media; history; horticulture; leisure, tourism and sport; social care studies, psychology and theology.

➡ Part-time study: **Yes.**
➡ Distance learning: **No.**

**About the college:**
The college was founded by the Church of England in 1840 to train schoolmasters for church elementary schools. The college now welcomes students of all races, religions and backgrounds. Winchester has a long history, having been the centre of King Alfred's Wessex and the 'capital' city of Saxon and Norman kings of England. There are many famous monuments including the Great Hall, which houses the Round Table of King Arthur, and the cathedral, where the college graduation ceremonies are held each year. Winchester is believed to have more pubs than any other comparable city – 47 at the last count!

Total number of students: 5,500    Number of disabled students: 220

**Learning support staff and services:**
Student Services Department
Welfare Adviser: Anne Baker.
Identify facilities needed and discuss courses, accommodation and accessibility; alternative examination and assessment arrangements; assistance in application for DSA; liaison with LEA; arrangement for students with dyslexia to have an initial screening session or a full educational psychologist's assessment.

Specialist dyslexia tutors run study skills courses and offer individual support for students with dyslexia.

It is possible to recruit notetakers and readers through the Job Shop run by Student Services.

### Home sweet home:

Newly designed and adapted hostel accommodation for disabled students who may require it. Accommodation with wheelchair access and for students who are D/deaf or hard of hearing with the requisite fire/smoke detectors fitted. Rooms available for PAs. Some rooms with additional power points and telephone sockets for Internet access.

Accommodation can be guaranteed for duration of student's course.

### Out and about:

College: The SU minibus is available for all students but does not have a wheelchair lift. Dedicated parking spaces near both accommodation and study areas.

Public transport: Some buses are wheelchair accessible.

### Taking it easy:

At college: All areas of SU are wheelchair accessible.

Locally: Winchester is hilly but accessible. Some city facilities are accessible. There is a Shopmobility scheme available in the city centre. The pavements are tactile. The local River Park Leisure Centre has a hoist for the swimming pool and a health suite. Restaurants and pubs have a mixture of very good and very bad access.

### And another thing ...

➡ The campus is situated on a steeply sloping, split-level site.

➡ King Alfred's was a member of the Southern Higher Education Consortium (SHEC), which was developing a regional collaborative approach to services and support. SHEC received funding from the HEFCE to help ensure that study is accessible to people with disabilities and learning difficulties. The members of the consortium were: Bournemouth University; University College, Chichester; King Alfred's, Winchester; Southampton Institute; University of Portsmouth; University of Southampton; and University of Surrey.

➡ There is Braille signage on the lift in the SU building, where signage is being improved throughout.

➡ The college has its own staff development programme and this includes sessions on general disability awareness training and dyslexia awareness.

➡ The college runs an Honours degree in Applied Social and Community Studies and an MSc in Disability Studies; academic staff, especially in that school, have particularly strong links with some local and national disability organisations.

➡ Small amount of funding is available to students who are ineligible for Hardship Funds or DSA.

➡ The college has close links with the Centre for Enabling Technologies at New College in Southampton, which assesses the study support needs of students with disabilities and runs various work experience schemes.

➡ The welfare adviser has a range of local and national links, including the RNID and RNIB, the latter of which conducted an institutional audit of the college.

## The Disability Statement/Brochure:
*Opportunities for Students with Disabilities*
Includes: Equal opportunities policy; examination and assessments; staff training; links; staff details; practical support available; welfare adviser; IT provision; library; Student Services; financial assistance; students with dyslexia; services; physical environment; local facilities; further information; monitoring and future development.

## Local disability public service provider:
Winchester Group for Disabled People.

---

### King's College London
Strand, London WC2R 2LS

*General Enquiries:*
Tel: 020 7836 5454
Email: enquiries@kcl.ac.uk
Website: www.kcl.ac.uk

**Disability Coordinator: Celia Cockburn**
**Tel: 020 7848 4026**
**Fax: 020 7848 1405**
**Email: welfare@kcl.ac.uk**
**Equal Opportunities Office:**
**020 7848 3398**

## Fields of study:
Biomedical sciences; dentistry; health and life science; humanities; law; medicine; nursing and midwifery; physical sciences and engineering; social science and public policy.

## About the college:
King's College (KCL) is one of the two oldest colleges of the University of London. When King George IV and the Duke of

Wellington founded King's in 1829 it was to create an education rooted in the religious principles of the Church of England. Today King's is for students of all faiths and beliefs. In 1998 King's and the United Medical and Dental Schools of Guy's and St Thomas's Hospitals merged. King's has five campuses, four by the River Thames in central London (Strand, Waterloo, Guy's and St Thomas's) and one in south London (King's Denmark Hill). Former King's graduates include the Archbishop of Cape Town Desmond Tutu, writer and film director Derek Jarman and writer Hanif Kureishi.

Total number of students: 16,500    Number of disabled students: 729

**Learning support staff and services:**
Student Services
One full-time disability coordinator in Equal Opportunities Office; and shortly one full-time disability assessor and support officer; disability coordinator in each school.
Departments may be able to provide the following: special seating; handouts and book lists in advance; rearranging timetables; long book loans; alternative examination arrangements; extra support from staff. KCL has links with the City Lit (see Directory), particularly notetaking and other services for students who are D/deaf or hard of hearing.

**Home sweet home:**
A limited number of rooms in the college's apartments are designed for students with disabilities – tel: 020 7848 2759; email: accomm@kcl.ac.uk. Accommodation can often be guaranteed for the duration of student's course.

**Out and about:**
College: There are dedicated parking spaces near both accommodation and study areas.
Public transport: All campuses are well served by public transport. Not all public transport in London, however, is fully accessible. Contact Access and Mobility (see Directory).

**Taking it easy:**
At college: No real facilities/services.
Locally: Artsline publishes a number of London access guides (see Directory).

**And another thing ...**
➡ Students with mobility difficulties may find some problems in attending some Strand-based departments.

➡ Financial assistance is available in certain circumstances from college-based and other sources for students with disabilities; further information from Student Loans and Awards Office – tel: 020 7848 2055 – or the Equal Opportunities Office.

## The Disability Statement/Brochure:
Disability Statement from the Web includes: Aims and objectives; admission; current students; management, information and evaluation and feedback.

| Kingston University |
|---|

Penrhyn Road, Kingston-upon-Thames, Surrey KT1 2EE

*General Enquiries:*
Tel: 020 8547 7053
Fax: 020 8547 7080
Email: admissions-info@kingston.ac.uk
Website: www.kingston.ac.uk/

**Disability Adviser/Dyslexia Coordinator: Mary Norowzian**
**Tel: 020 8547 8858**
**Fax: 020 8547 7019**
**Email: m.norowzian@ kingston.ac.uk**
**a.walsh@kingston.ac.uk**
**Text: 020 8547 8847**

## Fields of study:
Art, music and design; business; computing and information systems; engineering; healthcare sciences; human sciences; law; music; science; social work; surveying; teacher training.

➡ Part-time study: **Yes.**
➡ Distance learning: **No.**

## About the university:
Kingston was the only new university alongside four other institutions shortlisted for 'University of the Year' 2000 by the *Sunday Times*. The university has four main campuses – all within a 4-mile radius of and easily accessible from the busy shopping area of Kingston town centre. Kingston-upon-Thames is 25 minutes by train from central London and is set on the River Thames, surrounded by areas of parkland.

| Total number of students: 15,000+ Number of disabled students: 740 |
|---|

## Learning support staff and services:
Disability Support Service and Dyslexia Support Service

Disability Coordinator: Mary Norowzian; Disability Advisor: Alison Donald; Mental Health Advisor: Alex Jenkins; Dyslexia Coordinator: Anita Walsh.

Needs assessment; assistance with DSA applications; provision of auxiliary aids and services; advice and guidance; one-to-one/group tuition for students with dyslexia; alternative examination, assessment and study arrangements; support service for students with mental health issues; pre-application advice; liaise with relevant faculty and other university departments, LEAs and external agencies; arrangement of familiarisation training on the campus.

## Home sweet home:
A number of the university's halls of residence have rooms adapted for students with physical disabilities and for people who are visually impaired or who are D/deaf or hard of hearing, including vibrating pillows/flashing alarms. There is limited availability of rooms for PAs, so this should be discussed with the Disability Adviser. The university will adapt accommodation to meet individual needs. All halls are self-catering only; adapted rooms are not clustered together but integrated; all first-year students with disabilities will have priority for a place in halls. Please note, most halls are off campus.
Accommodation can be guaranteed for duration of student's course only if student could not otherwise attend the university.

## Out and about:
University: All four sites are connected by free university buses – with low-level access – to the local rail and bus stations as well as to most of the university halls of residence. Dedicated parking spaces near both accommodation and study areas.
Public transport: There are two mainline stations – Kingston and Surbiton, and numerous local bus routes. Some buses, trains, train stations and taxis are accessible to wheelchair users and people with visual impairments.

## Taking it easy:
At university: The Graduate (Postgraduates) Centre, which provides social space, is accessible by lift. There is a fitness and aerobics centre at Penrhyn Road with wheelchair access. Assistance in using the equipment can be given if required. There is a toilet and shower accessible to wheelchair users. The non-ball-playing gym at Kingston Hill is not wheelchair accessible. There is limited access at Tolworth Court Sports Ground. The accessibility of the SU facilities varies from site to site. For further information contact the Advice Centre.
Locally: Kingston town centre is flat, mainly pedestrianised, and has a

Shopmobility scheme. The town's facilities are accessible and the pavements are tactile.

## And another thing …

→ The university is based at four main sites with buildings of varying age, quality and accessibility.

→ The Kingston Hill Campus is hilly.

→ The SU has an elected disability officer to represent the interests of disabled students.

→ PC with a CCTV, screen reading and magnification software is being piloted in one of the learning resource centres. Other development plans are a disability access audit of the Kingston Hill site and redevelopment plans to include improved accessibility to Penrhyn Road and Knights Park sites.

→ Dyslexia software packages Read and Write and Inspirations available from September 2003.

→ Penrhyn Road: A mixture of old and modern buildings with lift access in all the main buildings. Although a large part of the campus is accessible, 'wheelchair routes' may involve going the long way round, with some heavy doors on the way.

→ Knights Park: Only one part of the campus is currently lift accessible, with limited lift access to the library (including computer facilities).

→ Kingston Hill: The steeply terraced site is unsuitable for students with considerable mobility difficulties and for wheelchair users, as access to most facilities is via numerous flights of steps, with steep pathways between buildings. Building works to improve access are planned for 2002/3.

→ Roehampton Vale: Modern campus – lift access to all floors.

→ Cooper House: Student Information and Advice Centre – automatic doors to the ground floor and lift access to all floors, although it is necessary to get assistance from the reception desk to use the lift.

→ Millennium House: Dyslexia Service is based on the third floor (with lift access).

→ All the above areas have toilet facilities for disabled people.

→ St George's Hospital Medical School: Accessibility of its establishments is varied and will be assessed as part of the admissions process.

→ Most teaching rooms do not have induction loops. Induction loops in Sopwith main lecture theatre and the main hall at Penrhyn Road and Lawley lecture theatre at Kingston Hill.

→ Wherever possible, lectures and seminar groups are timetabled in

ground-floor or lift-accessible venues for students with mobility disabilities.
➡ Provision of specialist software for students with dyslexia will be made available on central PC facilities during 2001/2.

## The Disability Statement/Brochure:
*Information for Students with Disabilities 2001/2002*
Includes: Applications; facilities and physical access; health and safety; study support; monitoring; checklist; contact and site maps.

### Local disability public service providers:
Kingston Social Services, The Physical Disability Services Team, Crescent Resource Centre, Cocks Crescent, Blagdon Road, New Malden, Surrey KT3 4TA; 020 8949 1955; text: 020 8949 0573.
Kingston Association of Disabled People, Siddeley House, 50 Canbury Park, Kingston-upon-Thames, Surrey KT2 6LY; 020 8255 2444 (voice and text).
Kingston Centre for Independent Living 020 8255 2444/2441.

---

| Laban Centre London |
| --- |

Creekside, London SE8 3DZ

*General Enquiries:*     **Disability Coordinator: Colin Bourne**
Tel: 020 8691 8600     **Tel: 020 8469 9426**
Fax: 020 8691 8400     **Fax: 020 8691 8400**
Email: info@laban.org     **Email: c.bourne@laban.org**
Website: www.laban.org

### Fields of study:
Choreography; community dance; dance science; dance theatre; dance history; European dance theatre practice; notation; performance; scenography (dance); teaching.

Part-time study: **Yes.**
Distance learning: **No.**

### About the centre:
Laban is named after Rudolf Laban, the Hungarian dance thinker, dancer, choreographer and teacher who was one of the founding figures of Central European modern dance. He believed in the importance of 'movement in life' and believed dance should be open and accessible to all. As one of the leading institutions for dance

artist training in Europe, Laban offers a teaching faculty with an unrivalled range of expertise and facilities. Laban is home to Transitions Dance Company and produces the *Dance Theatre Journal* and *Discourses in Dance*. In September 2002 Laban moved to a new state-of-the-art building at Deptford Creekside designed by Herzog and de Mouron, the Swiss architects behind Tate Modern. The building houses 11 dance studios, a 300-seat theatre, a library, dance health facilities and a public bar/café. Laban is 15 minutes from central London by train. The local area is home to a number of arts and performance organisations, e.g. Hales Gallery, one of the most contemporary arts spaces in London.

| Total number of students: 370 | Number of disabled students: 15 |
| --- | --- |

## Learning support staff and services:
There is no unit as such, but a named member of staff
Full-time staff: Learning and Teaching Coordinator: Colin Bourne; student advisor and personal tutor
Needs assessment; assistance with DSA applications; provision of auxiliary aids and services; advice and guidance; one-to-one/group tuition for students with dyslexia; alternative examination, assessment and study arrangements; support service for students with mental health issues and liaison with external organisations.

## Home sweet home:
There is no accommodation.

## Out and about:
Centre: There are dedicated parking spaces near to study areas.
Public transport: Contact Access and Mobility for information on London's public transport services (see Directory).

## Taking it easy:
At the Centre: There is an accessible café, theatre bar and theatre.
Locally: The town centre is fairly flat and some of the town's facilities are accessible. Artsline produces a number of guides regarding access in London (see Directory).

## And another thing ...
➡ The new Laban building is fully accessible.
➡ Laban has been first in the development of the interface between disabled people and dance.
➡ Laban was the home of CandoCo Dance Company for several years. CandoCo is an internationally renowned dance company

that integrates disabled and non-disabled dancers. With Laban, CandoCo developed the first training course available to a disabled dancer.

➡ Laban's Web-based 'Dance Resources on the Net' acts as a gateway to resources and information and extends the possibility of distance learning and research. Developments in technology will also allow people with disabilities to be involved in dance; for example choreographic software programmes will allow people with disabilities and limited communication skills to choreograph using computer software, and have dancers perform their work. The library has computers with Labanotation, LabanWriter and LifeForms specialist software.

➡ Laban aims to create a learning environment that places no physical or psychological obstructions in the way of participation, progress or achievement for all potential learners. Please contact Laban for further information.

➡ www.laban.org has detailed information about Laban's training opportunities, facilities and faculty, new building, latest news and forthcoming events. A text-only version of Laban's Website will be available in the near future.

**Local disability public service providers:**
Artsline (see Directory).
Access and Mobility (see Directory).

| Lancaster University |
|---|

Bailrigg, Lancaster LA1 4YW

*General Enquiries:*
Tel: 01524 65201
Fax: 01524 846243
Email: ugadmissions@lancaster.ac.uk
Website: www.lancs.ac.uk

**Student Adviser: Christine Quinn**
**Tel: 01524 592109**
**Fax: 01524 594868**
**Email: c.quinn@**
**lancaster.ac.uk**
**Text: 01524 592111**

**Fields of study:**
Arts and humanities; management; science and engineering; social sciences.

➡ Part-time study: **Yes.**
➡ Distance learning: **Yes, some courses.**

## About the university:

Lancaster University first opened its doors in 1964, when it was granted its Royal Charter. Lancaster is a campus university, set in 250 acres of parkland, located about 3 miles south of the historic city of Lancaster. Lancaster began as a Roman settlement on the banks of the River Lune and made its fortune in the eighteenth century as a port for the West India trade. Today the city has plenty to offer in the way of entertainment for students.

Total number of students: 10,000    Number of disabled students: 458

## Learning support staff and services:

Disabilities Service, Student Support Services
Full-time staff: Disabilities Student Adviser: Christine Quinn; technical adviser (assessment for study aids and strategies).
Part-time staff: Disabilities Service Manager: Rosemary Turner; secretary and PAs.
Advice and support on resources available: personal support; accommodation; student funding applications; assessment and support for dyslexia and technical needs; alternative examination and assessment arrangements; loan of small stock of equipment including some specialist computing equipment and assistance at graduation ceremonies; leaflets on a variety of issues available.
Disabilities Service works closely with the local social services mobility officers to provide mobility training. Communication support including sign language interpreters can be arranged through local organisations.

## Home sweet home:

Accommodation suitable for wheelchair users, with accessible kitchen and bathroom facilities, integrated with other student accommodation in four of the nine residential colleges. It may be possible to make adaptations to suit individual requirements, and rooms can be provided for PAs. Flashing light fire alarms and doorbells can be installed for D/deaf and hard of hearing students. Push button emergency call systems can also be fitted.
Accommodation can be guaranteed for duration of some students' courses.

## Out and about:

University: Dedicated parking spaces near accommodation.
Public transport: There are wheelchair accessible taxis. There is also an active local disability information and advice group. Some local bus services are accessible.

**Taking it easy:**

At university: The SU disabilities officer provides informal support to disabled students and sets up support groups according to demand. All facilities are accessible except the top floor of the Sport Centre Gallery. Campus facilities include a range of shops, cafés and bars. A wide range of films, plays and concerts are held in wheelchair accessible venues. The sports centre staff will assist you to find ways to use its facilities. The centre's swimming pool has changing facilities for disabled people with a hoist. There is a pool about 5 miles away with this facility.

Locally: Most of the city centre of Lancaster is pedestrianised and thus accessible and there is a Shopmobility scheme. The pavements are tactile. The *Disabilities Service Student Handbook* lists accessible venues and there is also a local area guide, *Access: Lancaster, Morecambe and District* produced by the Lancaster City Council and Lancaster District Access Group.

**And another thing ...**

➡ The Lancaster campus is compact, with traffic restricted mainly to the perimeter road. Almost all teaching and public buildings are accessible to people with mobility difficulties, though lifts in some buildings have narrow doors.

➡ There are some additional access difficulties for wheelchair users in the music and theatre studies departments.

➡ Easy-access toilet facilities are available in or near most buildings across campus.

➡ Access: the university aims to accommodate and, with sufficient notice, have accessible rooms at all sites.

➡ A map is available detailing wheelchair accessible routes and toilet facilities that are accessible.

➡ To simplify direction-finding the library building and contents are colour-coded. Students can be given one-to-one training and support within the library – libweb.lancs.ac.uk/g44.htm.

➡ The disabilities service technical assessor can provide assessments of study aids and strategies.

➡ Induction loop systems are available in several of the biggest lecture theatres and are gradually being fitted in others. Radio aids and portable induction loops can be loaned.

➡ High-quality printers and scanners and an optical character recognition system are available to all students. There is also a large screen monitor.

➡ The university library houses a PC with scanner and speech synthesiser, a Kurzweil Personal Reader and a CCTV enlarger.

➡ Sign language interpreters and lipspeaking services are arranged through an external agency. Telephone services for students are provided by an external agency.

➡ Students with disabilities and learning support needs receive a termly bulletin called *AbilityPlus*.

➡ The university's Student Learning Development Centre provides support for all students. Services include: regular study skills sessions; additional academic writing support; advice on study problems and strategies.

➡ Appropriate arrangements are made for students when they work/study on field trips/placements or study abroad.

➡ Developments include support systems for students with mental health difficulties and improved physical access.

## The Disability Statement/Brochure:

*Access at Lancaster*
Statement includes: Applications; general facilities; accessibility; personal assistance; accommodation; arrival; support; study support; examinations and assessments; field trips/placements/study abroad; financial support/monitoring and complaints; developments; students say; disability numbers; support organisations and access map.

## Local disability public service providers:

Deafway, Brockholes Brow, Preston PR2 5AL; 01772 796461; text: 01772 651524.
Lancaster Adult Dyslexics Group.
Morecambe Bay Area Health Authority (for mobility training, occupational therapy support).
DISC Disablement Information Support Centre, Trinity Community Centre, Middle Street, Lancaster LA1 1JZ; 01524 34411/32660.
Lancaster Adults Dyslexics Group.

| Leeds College of Music |
| --- |

3 Quarry Hill, Leeds, LS2 7PD

*General Enquiries:*
Tel: 0113 222 3400
Fax: 0113 243 8798
Email: enquiries@lcm.ac.uk
Web: www.lcm.ac.uk

**Student Adviser: Alison Meddings**
**Tel: 0113 222 3421**
**Fax: 0113 243 8798**
**Email: a.meddings@lcm.ac.uk**

## Fields of study:

DJ music technology; making and repairing musical instruments; music (classical, pop, jazz, Indian music).

➡ Part-time study: **Yes.**
➡ Distance learning: **Not currently, but may look into it in the future.**

## About the college:

The Leeds College of Music has a partnership with Leeds Metropolitan University, with which it offers joint degree courses in Music Technology. The college has close links with the Leeds Centre for Indian Music and Dance and runs the annual Leeds International Jazz Education Conference. The college occupies a new, specially designed building that is the most modern music college building in the country. Phase one, already built, includes rehearsal and recording studios, workshops, teaching rooms, library and learning resource centre, recital room and a bar. Phase two, a 350-seat concert hall, will be completed in autumn 2003. These new facilities are on Quarry Hill, in the centre of Leeds, beside the West Yorkshire Playhouse and the Yorkshire Dance Centre. The city of Leeds is the regional capital of northern England and has a lively social and cultural life. With two universities and ten colleges Leeds is one of the UK's major centres for higher education.

| Total number of students: 2,834 | Number of disabled students: 157 |
|---|---|

## Learning support staff and services:

Student Support Unit
Student Welfare and Disability Advisor: Alison Meddings; Head of Student Support/Senior Tutor: Peter Whitfield; Student Funding Advisor: Heather Holeham; Student Counsellors: Joanna Best and Kate Kent; Student Advisor (Welfare): Anne Best; Student Support Assistant: Wendy Parsisson.

Needs assessments; assistance with DSA applications and college's Learner Support Fund; provision of auxiliary aids and services; advice and guidance; one-to-one/group tuition for students with dyslexia; alternative examination, assessment and study issues; support service for students with mental health issues; apply for support provision from local education authority and social services where necessary; orientation sessions arranged; loan of specialist equipment; and liaison with external organisations.

There are four main sources of support at Leeds College of Music: the Group Tutorial System; the Student Support Unit; the Learning Support Centre; and the Library and Learning Resource Centre. Students have regular academic reviews with their group tutor, detailing goals, how they will be reached and the support needed to achieve them.

At the Student Support Unit students are assisted in seeking and managing support from external specialist agencies as appropriate and receive individual advice and support from the Student Advisor. The Learning Support Tutor can provide support with study skills; assessments that lead to an assessment by an educational psychologist. Learning Support is available overall for ten hours per week.

Extended loan periods on all borrowable items are available by arrangement with the Library and Learning Resource Centre.

### Home sweet home:

There is no student accommodation, but the Student Advisor for accommodation can offer advice on securing accommodation in Leeds. Contact Anne Best, Student Advisor: 0113 222 3514 or email: a.best@lcm.ac.uk

### Out and about:

College: Dedicated parking spaces near study areas.

Public transport: The local trains and train stations are wheelchair accessible and have recorded spoken announcements. Most local buses and some taxis are wheelchair accessible. There is an Access Bus which is accessible both to wheelchair users and to people with visual impairments. The train station and some buses, trains and taxis are accessible to people with visual impairments. Student advisors can provide details of local transport schemes for those with mobility disabilities.

### Taking it easy:

At college: There are some college enrichment activities and SU activities accessible to disabled students. The college bar is accessible. There is also a Disability Support Group for disabled students to meet and share experiences.

Locally: The city centre is flat and accessible. Its facilities are also accessible and there is a Shopmobility scheme. The pavements are tactile. Leeds City Council produces a *Leeds Access Guide for Disabled People*. There is also an *In Touch* newsletter for disabled people – ask the Student Advisor for further information.

### And another thing ...

➡ The main purpose-built teaching accommodation at Quarry Hill is accessible throughout to wheelchair users. The lift is equipped with Braille instructions and a voice announcement. There are accessible toilets dedicated for the use of disabled people on four levels. The internal walls are colour-coded.

- Paved areas around the college have high kerbs but are sloped at strategic intervals.
- The Shannon Street site, occupied by Music Instrument Technology and DJ courses, has all teaching facilities on the ground floor, ramped access to reception, and accessible toilets for disabled people on the ground floor.
- The college's Learning Support Fund may be available to disabled students depending upon circumstances.
- The college can fund needs assessments or assessments by an educational psychologist.
- The college does not provide support workers itself at present.
- Zoom text is available on one PC in the library, which also has a keyboard with enlarged symbols and can be adjusted on a sliding arm. All leaflets are available in raised text format for students with visual impairment.
- The Student Support Unit is a member of Skill.

## The Disability Statement/Brochure:
Includes: Choosing the right course; support available; finance; exams; time off; social life; access; should things go wrong …; staff and key staff list.

### Local disability public service providers:
Leeds City Council and Leeds Leisure Services: Equal Opportunities 0113 224 3589; text: 0113 224 3589; Website: www.leeds.gov.uk.
Leeds Tourist Information: 0113 242 5242.
Access Bus: 01274 304297.
Shopmobility: 0113 246 0125.
Leeds Access Centre: 0113 233 3927.
DIAL: Leeds Disability Helpline: 0113 214 3630.
Peer Support Service Leeds – a listening service run by disabled people for disabled people: 0113 214 3597.

| Leeds Metropolitan University |
| --- |

City Campus, Leeds LS1 3HE

*General Enquiries:*  **Disability Coordinator: Jackie Watson**
Tel: 0113 283 3113  **Tel: 0113 283 5948**
Fax: 0113 283 3114  **Fax: 0113 283 3063**
Email: course-enquiries@lmu.ac.uk  **Email: j.Watson@lmu.ac.uk**
Website: www.lmu.ac.uk  **Text: 0113 283 5971**

## Fields of study:
Accounting and finance; architecture and landscape; art and design; built environment; business; computing; cultural studies; film and TV (NFS); health and science; information management; languages; law; leisure and sport; management; nursing; planning and development studies; social sciences; teacher education and professional development; technology; tourism and hospitality management.

➡ Part-time study: **Yes.**
➡ Distance learning: **Yes.**

## About the university:
The origins of the university go back to the nineteenth century, when Leeds was seeking to meet the needs of its growing industries and the aspirations of its citizens for education and training. The university merged with Harrogate College in 1998 and now offers a range of diploma and degree courses in Harrogate. Rapidly growing in the Victorian era, Leeds transformed itself into a thriving industrial city built around clothing, textiles and engineering. Today it is one of Britain's most important financial centres outside London, and the home of major banks, insurance firms, consultants, solicitors and building societies.

> Total number of students: 23,000+
> Number of disabled students: approx. 600

## Learning support staff and services:
Student Services
Disability coordinator; disability services officer; dyslexia support staff; technical support staff.
Assistance with DSA applications; technical needs assessment; provision of notetakers and proofreaders; transcription of material on to tape; counselling; mobility support; study facilitator support; dyslexia tuition – study support and organisational skills.

## Home sweet home:
There is accommodation for wheelchair users and a deaf alerter system for students who are D/deaf or hard of hearing. Accommodation for disabled students can be guaranteed for duration of student's course.

## Out and about:
University: Accessible taxis are available for wheelchair users. Dedicated parking spaces near both accommodation and study areas.

Public transport: All of the new buses are wheelchair accessible, but some bus services are not.

**Taking it easy:**
At university: There is a wheelchair accessible swimming pool. The SU bar and services are accessible, but the gym is not. The canteen is accessible.
Locally: The local town has good accessibility.

**And another thing ...**
➡ The university operates a personal support scheme for students with disabilities requiring a range of support both in lectures and around campus.
➡ The university can provide the following facilities: portable induction loops, specialist software for students with dyslexia (including colour modification software) and visual impairment, enlarged PC screens, speech-synthesised text, readers and notetakers.
➡ Lecture theatres, teaching rooms and libraries are accessible for wheelchair users and fitted with induction loops.
➡ There is a designated accessible room for disabled students at both campuses with IT facilities, the necessary software and induction loops.
➡ The learning adviser has a microphone that can be fitted to one of the computers in the Learning Centre for the induction coil and at the issue desk.
➡ Sign language interpreters can be accessed from Deaf Start, a local organisation.

**QAA Report: Paragraphs 111 and 113, October 2001**
... The *Account* described recent enhancements to the staff support for the distribution of access funds, and services for disabled students, including learning support for dyslexia.
... A separate booklet, *Information for Applicants with Disabilities*, is provided for disabled students wishing to attend the University. The University has considered the section of the QAA *Code of practice* which addresses arrangements for students with disabilities, and was able to confirm to the audit team that its own arrangements are consistent with the advice offered by the *Code*.

**Local disability public service providers:**
Deaf Start.
LEA.

| University of Leeds |
| :---: |

Leeds LS2 9JT

*General Enquiries:*
Admissions Office
Tel: 0113 343 3999
Fax: 0113 343 3877
Email: admissions@leeds.ac.uk
Website: www.leeds.ac.uk

**Disability Coordinator: Judith Russell**
**Tel: 0113 343 3927**
**Fax: 0113 343 3944**
**Email: disability@leeds.ac.uk**
**Text: 0113 343 2616**

## Fields of study:
Arts; biological sciences; business; earth and environment; education; engineering; foundation routes in science and engineering; law; mathematics and physical sciences; medicine, dentistry, psychology and health; music, visual and performing arts; social sciences.

➡ Part-time study: **Yes.**
➡ Distance learning: **Yes.**

## About the university:
Leeds is one of the largest universities in the country and its campus is ten minutes' walk away from the city centre. In 2001 Bretton Hall College became part of the university, and its campus is situated 20 miles south of Leeds. The Bretton Hall campus is set in an eighteenth-century mansion surrounded by 500 acres of lakes and parkland.

| Total number of students: 28,000<br>Number of disabled students: 1,600 |
| :---: |

## Learning support staff and services:
Equality Unit
There are 13 full-time and two part-time staff in the Equality Unit. Judith Russell is the Disability Coordinator.
Needs assessments; assistance with DSA applications; advice and guidance; one-to-one/group tuition for students with dyslexia; alternative examination, assessment and study arrangements; support service for students with mental health issues; liaison with external organisations; transcription of material into Braille, large print and on to tape and disk; liaison with other departments and on-course/on-the-job support of qualified notetakers, readers, sign language interpreters and dyslexia strategy workshops.

**Home sweet home:**
There are adapted rooms including wheelchair accessible rooms with adapted kitchen/bathrooms and rooms available for PAs, rooms with flashing fire alarms/vibrating pillows. There are also rooms with extra shelving for Braille books and tapes. Accommodation can be guaranteed for duration of student's course.

**Out and about:**
University: The SU provides a small bus for women only that also carries disabled students on request. Dedicated parking spaces near accommodation area, but not near study areas.
Public transport: Trains, some train stations, buses and taxis are accessible to wheelchair users. Taxis and some buses and trains are accessible to people with visual impairments.

**Taking it easy:**
At university: SU activities are available to all students. The SU bar, theatre and sports centre are all accessible.
Locally: Leeds is wheelchair accessible, flat and has a Shopmobility scheme. The town's facilities are accessible and the pavements are tactile. Contact Leeds City Council for its access guide.

**And another thing ...**
➡ The University of Leeds was granted Access Centre status in 1999 and is a member of NFAC so that students can be offered a user-led assessment of their requirements for support. This is undertaken by a qualified assessor.
➡ With prior notice the university is able to provide orientation training for blind and visually impaired students.

## The Disability Statement/Brochure:
Due for review.
Statement includes: Admissions; support; disability services; further information; examinations; central academic services; residential and commercial services; Leeds University Union; student support network; campus access; monitoring and evaluation; confidentiality and disclosure; future developments and associate and franchise colleges and off-campus centres.

**Local disability public service provider:**
Leeds City Council.

## University of Leicester

University Road, Leicester LE1 7RH

*General Enquiries:*
Tel: 0116 252 5281
Fax: 0116 252 2447
Email: admissions@le.ac.uk
Website: www.le.ac.uk

**Head of AccessAbility Centre:**
**Dr Paula Dobrowolski**
**Tel: 0116 252 5002**
**Fax: 0116 252 5513**
**Email: accessable@leicester.ac.uk**
**Text: 0116 252 5002**
**Website: www.le.ac.uk/accessability/**

**Fields of study:**
Arts; law; medicine and biological science; science; social sciences.

➡ Part-time study: **Yes.**
➡ Distance learning: **Yes.**

**About the university:**
Founded in 1921 the University of Leicester is internationally renowned for discovering DNA genetic fingerprinting and houses one of the largest space science research groups in the EU. The university buildings sport various styles of architecture, with the first building dating back to 1837. The historic market town of Leicester, which is 700 years old, is, according to an independent retail survey, one of the top ten places to shop in the UK. It is an environmentally friendly city with plenty of cycleways including routes to the university.

Total number of students: 18,568 including distance learning
Number of disabled students: 569

**Learning support staff and services:**
The AccessAbility Centre, which is part of the Educational Development and Support Centre
Head of AccessAbility Centre: Paula Dobrowolski, working with all students but particularly students with mobility difficulties, long-term conditions, as well as applicants making pre-entry enquiries; Study Support Officer: Fiona White, working with students with dyslexia; Study Adviser: Liz Mason, working with students with dyslexia and those who are D/deaf or hard of hearing or blind or visually impaired; and Centre Secretary: Cathy Rae.
The provision of specialist facilities is based in an open-access user area that offers an initial informal assessment of needs; negotiated one-to-one support sessions with regular review; alternative

examination arrangements; demonstration of equipment and software; IT support; negotiated liaison – with the student's agreement – with the relevant department, university libraries, computer centre and the accommodation service; assistance with DSA applications and other sources of funding; study support sessions with a designated Study Adviser; regular review of learning support requirements; arrangements for an assessment by an educational psychologist for students with specific learning difficulties; loan of some equipment; assistance with Brailling essential information; assistance with the arrangement of personal support workers – readers are volunteers trained according to RNIB guidelines, and notetakers are trained according to CACDP guidelines; assistance with arranging campus orientation.

Each student will have a personal tutor (and a departmental tutor for those with specific learning disabilities) who acts as a point of contact between the department and the AccessAbility Centre and between the department and students with specific learning difficulties or disabilities if required.

The provision of overhead acetates used in lectures; provision of handouts in a range of formats; downloaded lecture or seminar material on the Campus Wide Information System (CWIS); extension of coursework deadlines; or appropriate arrangements to facilitate fieldwork or placements can be negotiated with the department concerned.

## Home sweet home:

There are a number of rooms with en-suite facilities and adapted bathrooms for wheelchair users. A number of these residences have roll-in showers and some residences have communal bathrooms with roll-in showers. There are also a number of rooms with a flashing light alarm system fitted to the ceiling of the room. In some buildings the basic Silent Alert system has been fitted which consists of: a transmitter, a clock and charger unit, a vibrating pager, a vibrating pillow pad.

Accommodation can be guaranteed for duration of student's course if required.

## Out and about:

University: There are a number of dedicated parking spaces for disabled drivers on the main campus and at least one at each of the outlying sites. There is ample parking near accommodation for all drivers. The SU has a wheelchair accessible minibus.

Public transport: Buses serve all of the accommodation at the various sites in the city and at Oadby. Accessible buses are not yet city-wide but are available on a growing number of routes. The railway station is close to the university – a 15- to 20-minute walk or 5 minutes by taxi.

## Taking it easy:

At university: Stair lifts have been fitted in the SU building and the Charles Wilson building where most catering outlets on the main site are situated. The SU has a part-time disability officer. The sports and recreation service runs a number of accessible indoor and outdoor games and facilities as well as two multi-gyms. The Richard Attenborough Centre for Disability and the Arts is an award-winning building and a unique facility. It runs courses for the whole community in art, dance, music, painting and sculpture and holds frequent professional evening and lunchtime concerts. The Harold Martin Botanical Garden at Oadby has wheelchair accessible paths, though some are gravelled, as well as dedicated parking areas.

Locally: The city centre is flat and accessible. Some of its facilities are accessible and there is a Shopmobility scheme. The pavements are tactile. The City of Leicester Consumer Services Centre provides the following guides free of charge: *Leisure in Leicester* and *Services for Disabled People*. These booklets are full of information about the city's many leisure, sports and cultural activities. The LeisurePass offers reductions on council sports and leisure activities for disabled people, and the LeisurePass Plus One entitles you to take along a friend at a discounted rate.

## And another thing ...

➡ Most departments are located on the main, compact campus. Most of its buildings are accessible with ramps outside to assist entry and exit, and stair lifts or lifts inside. The university will endeavour to adapt buildings where possible.

➡ The university location map gives guidance on the accessibility of the majority of its buildings – copies available from the AccessAbility Centre: www.le.ac.uk/maps/html

➡ Teaching is timetabled in accessible buildings.

➡ There is limited space for the storage of wheelchairs and equipment on campus.

➡ The AccessAbility Centre is also a quiet place to rest and leave books, for students who require this.

➡ *A Guide to University Library Services for Students with Disabilities and Specific Learning Difficulties* is available in a range of formats from the main library.

➡ Kursweil Reading Edge and colour and mono CCTVs are housed in the main library.

- Radio microphones for loan via audio visual services.
- Integral and portable loop induction systems.
- Wheelchair accessible toilet facilities are located in most university buildings.
- There are various catering outlets around the university; the main ones are accessible.
- The computer centre maintains a number of open-access user areas in various locations across campus.
- The Freeman's Common Health Centre is fully wheelchair accessible.
- Libraries are all accessible for wheelchair users.
- Information on funding and finance in general is provided in several publications – contact the AccessAbility Centre for details.

## The Disability Statement/Brochure:
*Information for Applicants with Specific Learning Difficulties and Disabilities*
Very comprehensive document; contents include: Applications; disclosure; facilities and services by disability; finance; access; accommodation; support; health and safety; examinations; campus facilities; Leicester city; case studies; monitoring and complaints; appendices.

## Local disability public service providers:
City of Leicester Consumer Services Centre, 0116 252 6480; text and voice: 0116 252 7362; Website: www.leicester.gov.uk. Contact AccessAbility Centre for details of other providers.

| University of Lincoln |
|---|

Brayford Pool, Lincoln LN6 7TS

*General Enquiries:*
Tel: 01522 882000
Fax: 01482 463052
Email: marketing@lincoln.ac.uk
Website: www.lincoln.ac.uk
Text: 01482 463571

**Senior Disability Adviser: Claire Wilson**
**Tel: 01522 886400**
**Fax: 01522 886489**
**Email: dart@lincoln.ac.uk**
**Text: 01482 463571**

## Fields of study:
Art and technology; business and management; social and life sciences.

- Part-time study: **Yes.**
- Distance learning: **Yes (limited).**

## About the university:
The University of Lincoln is split over two locations some 50 miles apart. The sites are very different in terms of architecture and subjects studied.

| Total number of students: 9,000 | Number of disabled students: 584 |
|---|---|

## Learning support staff and services:
Disability Access Resources and Technology (DART)
Head of DART and Access Centre Manager: Steve Metcalfe; Disability Adviser with responsibility for students with physical, hearing and visual impairments: Claire Wilson; Disability Adviser with responsibility for students with dyslexia and mental health difficulties: Gemma Bush; two Access Centre Assessor/Trainers: Mike Shortland and Lisa Creswell; Administrator: Elspeth Nicholson (Hull) and Julie Davenport (Lincoln).
Regional NFAC registered Access Centre; needs assessment from which will be produced a 'Report of Study Aids and Strategies'; alternative examination arrangements; confidential advice and information; a limited Braille embossing facility; assistance in finding appropriate support from external sources/agencies; dyslexia screening test and arrangements of formal diagnostic assessments; a pool of equipment for loan including PCs, scanners and some specialist software.

## Home sweet home:
There is accommodation in halls, which have been modified to accommodate wheelchair users, D/deaf or hard of hearing students and PAs. Every effort is made to accommodate individual needs. This integrated accommodation can be guaranteed for duration of student's course in the majority of cases, but it will need to be discussed with the student to ensure the service can be provided.

## Out and about:
University: Dedicated parking spaces near both accommodation and study areas.
Locally: There is no specific taxi scheme for disabled people, but companies are very reliable.

## Taking it easy:
At university: No specific facilities. Services are available to all students and made as accessible as possible. The campus at Lincoln has its own sports centre with wheelchair accessible toilet, changing and shower facilities. The SU has disability officers on both sites.

There are privately owned pubs on campus.
Locally: The city centre is both flat and hilly, but the main shopping area is accessible to wheelchair users. There is a Shopmobility scheme.

## And another thing ...

➡ The Lincoln campus is newly built, offering a high standard of accessibility. Certain parts of the site, however, are linked via bridges that are accessed by stairs or lifts. The recent developments of the School of Agriculture and the School of Art and Design in Lincoln are within historical buildings and may present access problems for students with mobility difficulties. The Hull campus consists of a mixture of buildings, some of which may present physical access problems. However, the university is moving its operations into Hull city centre, so such problems should be lessened.

➡ At the present time signage and aids to mobility for visually impaired people are poor on both campuses and in need of review.

➡ The university operates an NFAC-registered regional Access Centre, and so provides assistance and guidance to students who wish to access funds provided by DSA.

➡ Guide and hearing dogs are welcome on both campuses.

➡ Students with disabilities use the same computing and library facilities as all other students. Blind and visually impaired users can access any of the university's 2,000 computers using the screen reader or screen magnification software installed on the university network. Students with reading difficulties may use the text-to-speech scanning systems that are available in all learning resource centres.

➡ The university is investigating providing Braille output from any computer on its network. Certain diagrams are available in tactile format.

➡ The university has recently entered into a collaborative project with the University of Hull to develop group support sessions for students with dyslexia.

## The Disability Statement/Brochure:

*Support for Students with Learning Difficulties and Disabilities*
Includes: Applications; access on the campuses; accommodation; facilities and equipment; arrangements for teaching, learning and assessment; advice and information; financial support; how services are monitored; complaints and plans for the future.

| University of Liverpool |
|---|

150 Mount Pleasant, Liverpool L69 3GD

*General Enquiries:*
Tel: 0151 794 2000
Fax: 0151 708 6502
Email: adminsvc@liv.ac.uk
Website: www.liv.ac.uk

**Student Welfare and Disability Team: Beth Naylor**
**Tel: 0151 794 4714**
**Fax: 0151 794 4718**
**Email: p.v.campbell@liv.ac.uk/**
**sweenyd@liv.ac.uk**
**Text: 0151 794 4713**
**Website: www.liv.ac.uk/**
**studentservices/disst.htm**

**Fields of study:**
Arts; dentistry and law; engineering; medicine; science; social and environmental studies; veterinary science.

➡ Part-time study: **No.**
➡ Distance learning: **No.**

**About the university:**
Liverpool was one of the first universities in the country to offer a degree in e-business and the first to open departments of Architecture, Biochemistry and Civic Design. The university was also the first in Britain to appoint chairs in Dentistry, Orthopaedic Surgery, Social Anthropology and Spanish. The university precinct is a few minutes' walk or wheel turns from the city centre. The city of Liverpool is undergoing substantial regeneration, evidence of which can be seen in riverside developments such as the Albert Dock – which has retained all the character of Victorian wharf warehouses to become shops, restaurants, pubs and exhibition areas. Liverpool is home to the Walker Art Gallery, which has the largest collection of paintings outside London, and the countryside, beaches and seaside resorts are all close by.

| Total number of students: 23,000 |
|---|
| Number of disabled students: 1,000+ |

**Learning support staff and services:**
Welfare and Advisory Services
Student Welfare and Disability Adviser Team.
Advice on individual support requirements; use 'Student Support Documents' with student's consent to liaise with all academic departments, faculties and relevant university services to achieve

'person-centred support' for each individual; assistance in applying for DSA and other sources of funding; provision of guidance and support on educational psychological assessments and needs assessments; support in using the libraries and other academic support services; mobility training; help in organising non-medical helper support and advice on obtaining financial support for this; advice on technical support such as specialist computer software; liaison with other disability professionals to provide 'collective support' to achieve an accessible and independent living environment; meet regularly with a new service user group that has been formed by university's disability community to explore university issues. All work is confidential in nature.

## Home sweet home:
A number of rooms in the university residences have been adapted; these include rooms for wheelchair users, rooms with flashing fire alarms and doorbells. Guide dogs can be accommodated and, where reasonable notice is given, accommodation requests can normally be met. The self-catering residences are all within five minutes' walk or wheel turns of the university campus requirements. Contact accommodation adviser, tel: 0151 794 5872; email: L.Hobson@liv.ac.uk. Liverpool Student Homes (LSH) provides housing details for students looking for private sector accommodation. Staff at LSH will be able to give advice about properties that may be suitable for individuals.
Accommodation can be guaranteed for duration of student's course.

## Out and about:
University: Dedicated parking spaces near both accommodation and study areas. There is a regular bus service from the traditional halls of residence.
Public transport: See Liverpool John Moores entry.

## Taking it easy:
At university: Most of the building, including the bars and shops but excluding the basement, is wheelchair accessible. A recent disabilities audit of the guild has been completed and the guild will be looking at its provision when the results are known. The guild has a disabled students working party – contact guild welfare adviser, tel: 0151 794 4123.
Locally: See Liverpool John Moores entry.

## And another thing ...
➡ The university has been involved in a programme of modernisation and adaptation that includes the installation of lifts

and wheelchair accessible toilets in some buildings. However, some buildings are still difficult to access due to their old age. If the facilities are not suitable the university will look at reasonable adjustments.

➡ The university will make reasonable adjustments and offers a range of environments with accessible features, including induction loops, Texthelp on university computer software, Deaf Alerters and fire alarm pager systems. The university positively encourages students to discuss their support needs with members of the Welfare and Disability Team to arrange access and individual support. There are induction loops installed in some lecture theatres.

➡ Texthelp computer software for students with dyslexia will soon be available on the university network.

➡ Deaf Alerter, a fire alarm pager system, is available in the two main libraries.

➡ The university has a stairclimber for use by students. For more library information contact Carol Kay, tel: 0151 794 2685.

## The Disability Statement/Brochure:
*A Guide to Support and Services for Students with Disabilities*
Offers students information and guidance on university facilities and services including the Welfare and Disability Team.

### Local disability public service provider:
Visit www.merseyworld.com/community/charities.

---

| Liverpool Hope University College |
|---|

Hope Park, Liverpool L16 9JD

*General Enquiries:*
Tel: 0151 291 3000
Fax: 0151 291 3065
Website: www.hope.ac.uk

**Administrator for Students with Disabilities: Sheila Watts**
**Tel: 0151 291 3065**
**Fax: 0151 291 3770**
**Email: wattss@hope.ac.uk**
**Text: 0151 291 3065**

### Fields of study:
Business and information management; creative and performing arts; criminal studies; cultural studies; design; education; gender and women's studies; geography; human behavioural sciences; media studies; nursery management; science; science, health and physical

recreation; science sport studies; theology and religious studies; tourism and leisure.

➡ Part-time study: **Yes.**
➡ Distance learning: **Yes.**

## About the college:
Liverpool Hope is an accredited college of the University of Liverpool. Formed by the merger of three church colleges, Liverpool Hope takes faith seriously, being fully Anglican, fully Catholic, fully ecumenical and fully open to those of all faiths and beliefs. It has two main campuses. Hope Park is a 'mini-educational village' situated in Childwall, 4 miles from Liverpool city centre. Hope at Everton, opened in 1999, is within distance of the city centre. Liverpool Hope also has an outdoor education centre in Wales, set in 20 acres of secluded woodland in Snowdonia.

| Total number of students: 7,500 | Number of disabled students: 522 |
|---|---|

## Learning support staff and services:
Support Service for Students with Disabilities
Staff: Sheila Watts, Judith Fody, David Almer, Rob Hayward,
Administrator: Mary Tennant
Arrange needs assessments; assistance with DSA applications and other sources of funding; provision of auxiliary aids and services; advice and guidance; one-to-one/group tuition for students with dyslexia; alternative examination, assessment and study arrangements; support service for students with mental health issues; arrange for students with specific learning difficulties/dyslexia to be assessed by an educational psychologist; recruit non-medical support workers and liaison with external organisations.

## Home sweet home:
At Hope Park, Sherwin House is a male hall, which has a level-access shower room/wc. There are similar facilities in Angela House for female students. Both have larger kitchens to enable wheelchair user access, en-suite accessible rooms and automatic doors. Some rooms are adapted with flashing light door entry systems, flashing light smoke alarms; fridges provided free for students who have diabetes; extra sockets, shelving, etc. All accommodation at Hope Park is in catered halls.
Accommodation can be guaranteed for duration of student's course.

## Out and about:
University: Taxi fares are cleared through DSA. Dedicated parking spaces near both accommodation and study areas.
Public transport: See Liverpool John Moores entry.

## Taking it easy:
At university: The SU, student bar, gym and shop are accessible.
Locally: The city centre is flat and there is a Shopmobility scheme. The pavements are tactile. An Access Guide to Liverpool is available. Contact the Support Service for Students with Disabilities for further information.

## And another thing ...
➡ Business Bridge identifies suitable students to undertake projects for local organisations in the business and voluntary sector.
➡ Psychologist's assessments are paid for through Access to Learning Fund.
➡ All students who require support have a written Learning Support Plan which confirms the support agreed.

## The Disability Statement/Brochure:
Covers: Mission statement; policy; contacts; applications; accommodation; assessment and exams; student support and services; financial support; Sheppard Worlock library; estates information; unique Hope; information for students by disability; monitoring support services; proposals; external contacts; student experience; feedback form.

## Local disability public service providers:
Merseyside Society for Deaf People, Queens' Drive 0151 228 0888.
Liverpool Dyslexia Association: helpline 0151 724 5758.
Liverpool City Council.

---

### Liverpool Institute for Performing Arts (LIPA)
Mount Street, Liverpool L1 9HF

*General Enquiries:*
Tel: 0151 330 3000
Fax: 0151 330 3131
Email: reception@lipa.ac.uk
Website: www.lipa.ac.uk

**Disability Coordinator: Rob Hughes**
**Tel: 0151 330 3013**
**Fax: 0151 330 3055**
**Email: r.hughes@lipa.ac.uk**
**Text: 0151 330 3055**

## Fields of study:
Acting; community arts; dance; management; music; performance design; performing arts; popular music and sound technology; sound technology; theatre and performance technology.

➡ Part-time study: **No.**
➡ Distance learning: **No.**

## About the institute:
LIPA, which is based in former Beatle Paul McCartney's old school, opened in 1996, being a unique vocational higher education institute designed to meet the needs of the arts and entertainment economy. LIPA was created with the help of leaders from across the professions, with Sir Paul McCartney as lead patron. Liverpool has a very strong investment in its heritage, from the grandeur of its buildings and art collection to the life of its people, and there are eight museums and galleries across Merseyside.

| Total number of students: 800 | Number of disabled students: 100 |
|---|---|

## Learning support staff and services:
Deaf and Disabled Student Support Service
One part-time member of staff.
Advice and information; coordination of support; assistance with accommodation; benefits assistance and accessing local area.
LIPA students can also access the disability unit at Liverpool John Moores University free of charge (see contact details below and JMU entry).

## Home sweet home:
The institute does not have its own accommodation, but has good relationships with local private companies who provide high-quality accessible accommodation. The institute has a contract with a local housing company and is also in the planning stages of new buildings where possible. Accommodation can be guaranteed for duration of student's course.

## Out and about:
Institute: Dedicated parking spaces near both accommodation and study areas.
Public transport: Some of the local buses, trains, train stations and taxis are accessible to wheelchair users and people with a visual impairment. Students are provided with information regarding transport during their first week of college.

## Taking it easy:

At institute: Students are encouraged to use the SU where there are various forms of social support. LIPA also has a fully wheelchair accessible garden and bar, which hosts events most weeks.

Locally: Liverpool is both flat and hilly but good on access; however, there are still restrictions. The city centre is accessible, as are its facilities. There is a Shopmobility scheme. Pavements are *not* tactile. Local information available from Mersey Tourist Information.

## And another thing ...

➡ LIPA's main building on Mount Street is wheelchair accessible to all areas except for the upper circle in the Paul McCartney Auditorium. LIPA's Hope Street Building is due to be refurbished, but a number of adaptations have been made to ensure all teaching areas are fully accessible for wheelchair users. The RNIB has completed a disability audit for both buildings.

➡ LIPA graduates are awarded JMU degrees, and LIPA students have access to the JMU learning resource centres, Student Services and SU.

➡ Financial assistance may be offered to students with disabilities. This is considered on an individual basis.

## The Disability Statement/Brochure:

*LIPA Information for Students with Disabilities*

Contents include: LIPA's commitment; before you come; after you arrive; monitoring; services for disabled students; physical access and staff contact.

## Local disability public service providers:

Liverpool Association of Disabled People.

JMU Welfare Office, Rodney House, 70 Mount Pleasant, Liverpool L3 5UX; 0151 231 3564.

North West Disability Arts Forum (NWDAF).

Liverpool Voluntary Society for the Blind 0151 221 0888.

Liverpool Disabled Living Centre 0151 298 2055.

---

| **Liverpool John Moores University** |
|---|

Roscoe Court, 4 Rodney Street, Liverpool L1 2TZ

*General Enquiries:*
Tel: 0151 231 2121
Fax: 0151 231 3194

**Disability Coordinator:**
**Claire Corrigan/Surya Shaffi**
**Tel: 0151 231 3315**

Email: disability@livjm.ac.uk  **Fax: 0151 231 3791**
Website: www.livjm.ac.uk  **Email: disability@livjm.ac.uk**

## Fields of study:
Art and design; biological and earth sciences; bio-molecular sciences; built environment; business; community and social sciences; computing and mathematical sciences; critical and creative arts; education; engineering; health and human sciences; international school; law and applied social studies; media; pharmacy and chemistry.

➡ Part-time study: **Yes.**
➡ Distance learning: **Yes (currently being developed).**

## About the university:
JMU is a multisited university. It has three main geographical sites, two based in the city centre – the Northern campus – and one based in nearby Aigburth – IM Marsh campus. The academic schools are structured into two divisions. Liverpool's origins go back almost 800 years, from a tiny fishing village on the banks of the River Mersey to a thriving, bustling city with two cathedrals, two football clubs and home to the most famous group in the world – The Beatles. There has been massive investment in Liverpool over the last 16 years.

| Total number of students: 22,000 |
| :-- |
| Number of disabled students: 1,000 |

## Learning support staff and services:
Disability Team within Student Welfare Services
Full-time staff: Claire Corrigan and Surya Shaffi, and admin support. Organisation and setting-up of needs assessments; assistance in DSA applications; equipment training; use of Equipment Resource Centre; group tuition for students with dyslexia; dyslexia assessments; liaison with academic staff; recommendations for policy work; general awareness raising; pool of NMHs (non-medical helper).

## Home sweet home:
JMU has a range of self-catering halls of residence near all campus sites. All are based on a flats system and shared between four or five students. Many of these residences include adaptations for mobility and D/deaf or hard of hearing students, including wheelchair access, adapted bathrooms, kitchens, etc. An additional room can be used within the flat for PAs. The majority of accommodation is in private-sector halls based within Liverpool, and is well adapted. There is an

accommodation guide available; contact the Accommodation Office, tel: 0151 231 4165, fax: 0151 231 5598.
Accommodation can be guaranteed for duration of student's course in certain circumstances.

## Out and about:

University: There is a free shuttle bus for all students that is wheelchair accessible. Dedicated parking spaces near both accommodation and study areas.
Public transport: Mersey Travel is the main local operator of local trains and buses within Merseyside. Smart Buses are accessible to people with all disabilities. They have low entrances, ramps and electronic information display boards and talking bus stops. Mersey Link provides a free door-to-door service. To use this service you will need to meet eligibility criteria, and book in advance. Mersey Travel also provides free annual passes for disabled people subject to their meeting certain criteria. Liverpool has a number of taxis accessible to wheelchair users. There is also an extensive Mersey rail service available within the Merseyside region. Not all stations are accessible to wheelchair users.

## Taking it easy:

At university: SU provides some accessible leisure facilities and clubs and societies.
Locally: Liverpool is a vibrant multiracial city with a lively social scene. The city centre is flat and is moderately accessible. A local area disability access guide is available called *The Liverpool City Centre Access Guide*. Much of the city has been regenerated and includes major tourist attractions such as the Albert Dock, Mersey Ferries and The Beatles Story. It also has major sporting attractions. Many of these services/facilities are accessible to disabled people. Greenbank Project has a brand-new, fully equipped sports centre for disabled people. A Shopmobility scheme is in operation. Pavements are becoming increasingly tactile.

## And another thing …

➡ JMU is committed, wherever possible, to improving access for all people and is currently increasing the provision of facilities and services to disabled students. At present some of the services are available when required by individual students and therefore not contained within the university.
➡ A leaflet detailing access to JMU buildings for students with physical and sensory disabilities is available from the welfare adviser.

- Northern City Campus: there is a mix of fully accessible buildings and partially accessible buildings, i.e. all buildings are accessible, though not all are user friendly.
- IM Marsh Campus: most of the buildings are accessible to all disabled students, some are old Grade II listed buildings which pose difficulties for wheelchair users.
- In some areas there are lecture theatres with fixed seating, heavy doors, doors with transparent panels (magic eyes), laboratory benches at fixed heights.
- Signs throughout the university are blue/black on grey, situated at various levels and in upper and lower case letters. Numbers/signs on doors are generally smaller, and visually impaired students may encounter difficulties in reading some of these.
- Guide dogs are permitted in all JMU teaching buildings.
- Students following study programmes across different schools should be aware that they will need to travel between sites.
- All students are able to apply for normal funds and loans and there is also the JMU Hillsborough Trust Fund.
- The University does not directly employ specialist support workers/communication support workers or interpreters.
- Each campus site has a learning resource centre that provides services for students with disabilities.
- Avril Robarts Learning Resource Centre on the city centre campus has full access including lifts to all floors, induction loop systems and toilet facilities accessible to disabled students.

## The Disability Statement/Brochure:
*A Guide for Students with Disabilities*
Includes: Applications; DSA; services available for disabled students; access; accommodation; travel; SU; local groups and organisations.

### Local disability public service providers:
Merseyside Society for Deaf People, Queen's Drive, West Derby, Liverpool L13 0DJ; 0151 228 0888 (voice/text); email: jayne_mooney@hotmail.com.
Liverpool Association of Disabled People, Lime Court Centre, Upper Baker Street, Liverpool L6 1NB; 0151 263 8366; text: 0151 260 3178; email: ladisabled@aol.com.
Mersey Travel, 24 Hatton Gardens, Liverpool L3 2AN; 0151 227 5181 or 0151 236 7676; (voice/text): transport access officer 0151 330 1291.
The Greenbank Project, Greenbank Lane, Liverpool L17 1AG; 0151 733 7255; email: Eking@greenbank.demon.co.uk; Website: www.greenbank.demon.co.uk.

| University of London |
| --- |

Information Centre, Senate House, Malet Street, London WC1E 7HU

*General Enquiries:*
Tel: 020 7862 8000
Fax: 020 7862 8358
Email: enquiries@external.lon.ac.uk
Website: www.lon.ac.uk

**Fields of study:**
Arts; economics; education; engineering; humanities; law; medicine; music; philosophy; science; theology.

**About the university:**
The University of London is one of the oldest and largest universities in the UK. It is a federal university, comprising institutions of varying size and academic profile in which teaching and research are carried out. Each of the 17 colleges is separately incorporated, self-governing and directly funded, together with a range of central academic activities. (These latter activities are called the central University of London Institutes and Activities.) Some are large multifaculty colleges; others are small specialised institutes. Students belong both to the college or institute at which they study and to the university, which awards the degree. The colleges of the University of London are: Birkbeck, British Institute in Paris, Courtauld Institute of Art, Goldsmiths College, Heythrop College, Imperial College of Science, Technology and Medicine, Institute of Education, King's College London, London Business School, London School of Economics and Political Science, London School of Hygiene and Tropical Medicine, Queen Mary, Royal Academy of Music, Royal Holloway, Royal Veterinary College, St George's Hospital Medical School, School of Advanced Study, School of Oriental and African Studies, School of Pharmacy and University College London.

| Total number of students: 120,000 |
| --- |

**Learning support staff and services:**
For further information, refer to individual college entries, where available.

## London Academy of Music and Dramatic Art (LAMDA)

155 Talgarth Road, Barons Court, London W14 9DP

*General Enquiries:*
Tel: 020 8834 0500
Fax: 020 8834 0501
Email: enquiries@lamda.org.uk
Web: www.lamda.org.uk

**Fields of study:**
Drama and dance; music.

➡ Part-time study: **No.**
➡ Distance learning: **No.**

**About the academy:**
LAMDA is an academy specialising in the performing arts. It has recently moved premises to Talgarth Road in west London. As part of the development of this established site, provision will be made for access to all areas and facilities. Students considering auditioning and attending LAMDA should contact LAMDA direct.

Total number of students: 230
Number of disabled students: approx. 30

**Learning support staff and services:**
Enquiries and advice regarding courses, support and access are dealt with on an individual level by course leaders and the registrar. Needs assessments; assistance with obtaining financial support from the Student Support Fund; advice and guidance; one-to-one/group tuition for students with dyslexia and alternative examination, assessment and study arrangements.
LAMDA uses the Dyslexia Centre at the Maria Assumpta Convent for dyslexia support. LAMDA will organise an initial assessment. A further Needs Assessment may be required and will be paid for by LAMDA. (LAMDA offers Dance and Drama Awards, and any student who is accepted may, at the time they have completed an initial assessment, apply to the Student Support Fund for monies to pay for any assistance that is recommended in the needs assessment.)
Students who are visually impaired or D/deaf or hard of hearing will be provided for individually; however, LAMDA does not employ specialist support staff. Students who are D/deaf or hard of hearing tend to use the services of the City Lit (see Directory) and pay

directly. Where a written exam or sight reading is required, alternative arrangements can be made.

## Home sweet home:
There is no student accommodation. Students organise their own accommodation. Accommodation *cannot* be guaranteed for duration of student's course.

## Out and about:
Academy: There are no dedicated parking spaces near study areas. Public transport: The local tube station, Barons Court, is not accessible. Local buses are accessible for wheelchair users. Some trains and taxis are accessible to wheelchair users and people with visual impairments. The London Taxi Card Scheme operates in this area (see below). London Underground provide lists of accessible stations. Contact Access and Mobility for information about London's public transport services (see Directory).

## Taking it easy:
At the academy: There are no dedicated leisure facilities, but the student common room is accessible.
Locally: The city centre is mainly flat and accessible. Its facilities are accessible and the pavements are tactile. There is a local area disability access guide available from the Council. Artsline publishes a number of access guides about the city of London (see Directory).

## And another thing ...
➡ Funding from the DSA is not available as LAMDA is not a higher education institution. The Student Support Fund (see above) is the alternative source of finance.
➡ LAMDA can provide only limited support for students who are not eligible for a payment from the Student Support Fund. This is reviewed on an individual basis and students should discuss their situation with the Registrar.
➡ LAMDA will pay for additional classes in Alexander Technique, speech therapy and undertake voice assessments for students who need additional support in realising the work, following an assessment by specialist staff.
➡ LAMDA gives consideration to access when hiring external spaces for teaching purposes.
➡ LAMDA is able to provide Braille texts and welcomes guide dogs.
➡ The large majority of assessment is undertaken through practice.

## The Disability Statement/Brochure:
The statement covers: Admissions; student support; dyslexia; students with visual impairment and those who are D/deaf or hard of hearing; health and safety; assessments; financial assistance; building and facilities; examinations and monitoring.

## Local disability public service provider:
Social Services Department, Hammersmith and Fulham Council; 020 8748 3020; website: www.rbhf.gov.uk.
London Taxi Card Scheme 020 7484 2929

---

| London Bible College |
|:---:|

Green Lane, Northwood, Middlesex HA6 2UW

*General Enquiries:*
Tel: 01923 456000
Fax: 01923 456001
Email: mailbox@londonbiblecollege.ac.uk
Website: www.londonbiblecollege.ac.uk

**Disability Coordinator:**
**Tel: 01923 456103**
**Fax: 01923 456101**
**Email: jenny.aston@**
**londonbiblecollege.ac.uk**

## Fields of study:
Christian life and ministry; theology; theology and counselling; theology, music and worship.

➡ Part-time study: **Yes.**
➡ Distance learning: **Yes.**

## About the college:
The London Bible College (LBC) has the largest full-time theology faculty in Britain, with training and preparation for a range of jobs in the ministry, in mission or in the marketplace. Rural Hertfordshire and Buckinghamshire are within easy reach. Central London and its bustling West End are 30 minutes by tube from Northwood station.

| Total number of students: 330 | Number of disabled students: 8 |
|---|---|

## Learning support staff and services:
There is not a Learning Support Unit for students with disabilities, but the following support can be obtained.
Assistance with DSA applications; advice and guidance; alternative examination, assessment and study arrangements and liaison with external organisations.

## Home sweet home:
One adapted room and shower/toilet facilities for wheelchair users. Room can be made available as required for PA. Further adaptations can be made if necessary. Accommodation can be guaranteed for duration of student's course.

## Out and about:
College: Dedicated parking spaces near both accommodation and study areas.
Public transport: Some buses and taxis are accessible to wheelchair users. Contact Access and Mobility for information on London's public transport services (see Directory).

## Taking it easy:
At college: The college is currently obtaining planning permission for a lift to the Student Centre lounge, which is the main social area for students.
Locally: The town centre is hilly and accessible as are some of the town's facilities. The pavements are tactile. There is a Shopmobility scheme in Watford, which is close by. A variety of access guides on the city of London are available from Artsline (see Directory).

## And another thing ...
➡ LBC has been steadily improving access for disabled students. There are ramped entrances to the ground floor of the main building (Laing Hall), the Guthrie Centre (research and Islamic studies) and the female students' residence, Mitchell Hall. A platform lift has been installed to the first floor of Laing Hall, where the dining-room and main lecture rooms are housed. Contact the college administrator for further details.
➡ There are general bursary funds for students in financial need.

## Local disability public service provider:
DASH Hillingdon.

---

| **London College of Fashion** |
| --- |

20 John Princes Street, London W1M 0BJ

*General Enquiries:*
Tel: 020 7514 7400
Fax: 020 7514 7672
Email: enquiries@lcf.linst.ac.uk
Website: www.lcf.linst.ac.uk

**Disability Representative: Susan Orr**
**Tel: 020 7514 7400**
**Fax: 020 7514 7456**
**Email: s.orr@lcf.linst.ac.uk**

## Fields of study:
Cosmetic science; costume and make-up for the performing arts; design technology; fashion management/promotion; fashion studies.

➡ Part-time study: **Yes.**
➡ Distance learning: **No.**

## About the college:
London College of Fashion, which is part of the London Institute, provides a unique environment for specialist fashion-related studies. It benefits from a long-established reputation and liaison with the fashion and media industries, and staff have wide research, consultancy and professional experience within the specialist areas. The London Institute is Europe's largest centre for education in art, design and communication. It brings together five of the world's most distinguished art and design colleges: Camberwell College of Arts, Central St Martins College of Art and Design, Chelsea College of Art and Design, London College of Fashion and London College of Printing.

| Total number of students: 3,150 | Number of disabled students: 54 |
| --- | --- |

## Study support staff and services:
College Disability Representative: Susan Orr; Dyslexia Coordinator: to be confirmed.
See London Institute entry for further information and contact details of the Disability Team who are responsible for setting up support arrangements.

## London College of Music and Media (LCM2)

Thames Valley University, St Mary's Road, Ealing, London W5 5RF

*General Enquiries:*
Tel: 020 8231 2304
Fax: 020 8231 2546
Email: enquiries.lcm2@tvu.ac.uk

## Fields of study:
Media and creative technologies; music.

➡ Part-time study: **Yes.**
➡ Distance learning: **No.**

## About the college:

The London College of Music and Media has its origins in the nineteenth century. In 1991, the London College of Music moved to form the music department of Thames Valley University (TVU) and in 1997 it expanded its curriculum to offer ground-breaking courses in both media and music. The Music Department benefits from being a contemporary conservatoire within a forward-looking university. There are wide-ranging performance opportunities for the college's students. Specialist facilities include Ealing Film Studios.

---

Total number of students: approx. 2,300

---

## Disability staff and services:

Kris Evans, the Special Needs Coordinator at TVU, provides support for all students at LCM2. Please refer to TVU's entry for further details.

---

## London College of Printing

Elephant and Castle, London SE1 6SB

*General Enquiries:*
Information Centre
Tel: 020 7514 6500
Fax: 020 7514 6535
Email: info@lcp.linst.ac.uk
Website: www.lcp.linst.ac.uk

**Disability Representative: Celia Bishop**
**Tel: 020 7514 6607**
**Fax: 020 7514 8068**
**Email: c.bishop@lcp.linst.ac.uk**

## Fields of study:

Business communication and management; film and video; graphic and media design; journalism; journalism and digital media production; marketing and advertising; media and cultural studies; photography; print media; print media management; printing/retail design management; publishing; sound and music design technologies; visual merchandising.

➡ Part-time study: **Yes.**
➡ Distance learning: **No.**

## About the college:

Since 2001 the London College of Printing (LCP) has become the first of the London Institute colleges to operate from a single campus location. The college has significant links with the communications industries. A recent survey revealed that 81 per cent of the college's students find work in the highly competitive worlds of television, media, advertising and publishing. LCP is centrally located in a major media centre. The London Institute is Europe's largest centre for education in art, design and communication. It brings together five of the world's most distinguished art and design colleges: Camberwell College of Arts, Central St Martins College of Art and Design, Chelsea College of Art and Design, London College of Fashion and London College of Printing.

| Total number of students: 9,000 | Number of disabled students: 300 |

## Learning support staff and services:
College Disability Representative: Celia Bishop; Dyslexia Coordinators: Celia Bishop, Heather Symmonds, Steve Simmons.
See London Institute for further information and contact details of the Disability Team who are responsible for setting up support arrangements.

## London Contemporary Dance School (LCDS)

The Place, 12 Duke's Road, London WC1H 9PY

*General Enquiries:*
Tel: 020 7387 0152
Fax: 020 7383 3976
Text: 020 7387 7246
Email: lcds@theplace.org.uk
Website: www.theplace.org.uk

**Head of Student Support:**
**Shane Fitzgerald**
**Email: shane.fitzgerald@**
**theplace.org.uk**
**Text: 020 7387 7246**

### Fields of study:
Choreography; contemporary dance; dance for the screen; dance training and education and research; performance.

➡ Part-time: **Yes, postgraduate only.**
➡ Distance learning: **No.**

### About the school:
The London Contemporary Dance School, which is based at The Place in central London, offers vocational training for dancers, choreographers and dance artists. In 1982, the school was the first in Europe to be awarded a practical dance degree. LCDS is part of the Conservatoire for Dance and Drama, a HE institution with courses at certificate, degree and postgraduate level.

London Contemporary Dance School (LCDS)

| Total number of students: 190 | Number of disabled students: 16 |

## Learning support staff and services:
As part of the Conservatoire for Dance and Drama, LCDS has received funding to employ a Disability Officer. Recruitment for this post will commence from January 2003.

Auditions are open to all who apply, and there are students currently at LCDS who have dyslexia, epilepsy, physical disabilities, visual impairment and students who are D/deaf or hard of hearing.

## Home sweet home:
There is no on-campus accommodation for any students. The School does provide advice, support and assistance on finding somewhere to live in London.

## Out and about:
School: There is dedicated on-street parking near the area of study.
Public transport: Bus services 18, 30, SL1 and SL2 are accessible to wheelchair users. The nearest accessible tube station is Caledonian Road (Piccadilly line). For further information contact Access and Mobility (see Directory).

## Taking it easy:
At school: The canteen is accessible.
Locally: Central London is flat and most town facilities are accessible. Artsline publish a number of guides on access in London (see below).

## And another thing ...
➡ The Place makes every effort to be accessible to everyone.
➡ There is level access to the foyer at both the Duke's Road and Flaxman Terrace entrances and a lift to all floors.
➡ All studios, backstage area, body conditioning studio, showers and changing rooms are accesible for wheelchair users.
➡ The school theatre has full wheelchair access with four spaces for wheelchair users in the auditorium.
➡ The Place has building projects in the pipeline to modernise further, with lottery funding.
➡ The auditorium, box office and bar are equipped with an induction loop.
➡ Guide dogs and hearing dogs are welcome.

## Local disability public service provider:
Artsline (see Directory).

| The London Institute |
|---|

65 Davies Street, London W1Y 2DA

*General Enquiries:*
Tel: 020 7514 6000
Fax: 020 7514 6131
Email: studentservices@linst.ac.uk
Website: www.linst.ac.uk
Text: 020 7629 6371

**Disability Coordinator: Judy Fink**
**Tel: 020 7514 6157**
**Fax: 020 7514 6219**
**Email: j.fink@linst.ac.uk**
**disability@linst.ac.uk**
**Text: 020 7493 4524**

**Fields of study:**
Art, design and communications.

➡ Part-time study: **Yes.**
➡ Distance learning: **No.**

**About the institute:**
The London Institute brings together in a single federated structure five of the world's leading colleges of art, design and communications: Camberwell College of Arts, Central St Martins College of Art and Design, Chelsea College of Art and Design, London College of Fashion and London College of Printing. The size of the London Institute means students are able to benefit from access to a wide range of learning resources and specialist facilities. The various college libraries, for example, hold many unique collections and archives.

| Number of disabled students: 1,031 |
|---|

**Learning support staff and services:**
Disability Team in Student Services
Full-time staff: Disability Coordinator: Judy Fink; Disability Advisors: Suzanne Russell (020 7514 8139) and Adriana Sutters (020 7514 6156).
Part-time staff: College Dyslexia Coordinators: Claire Lofting and Elaine Wallace (Central St Martins); Pauline Courtenay and Gareth Mason (Chelsea College of Art and Design); Heather Symonds (London College of Printing); and one at London College of Fashion; College Disability and Dyslexia Coordinator: Eve Graves (Camberwell College of Arts); Disability Representatives: Margarita Moscoso (Central St Martins); Phillip Courtenay (Chelsea College of Art and Design); Susan Orr (London College of Fashion); and Celia Bishop (London College of Printing).
Needs assessments; assistance with DSA applications and Hardship Fund; access to Funderfinder, a database of charities that give small

grants; provision of auxiliary aids and services; advice and guidance; one-to-one/group tuition for students with dyslexia; support for students with dyslexia including: screening, a tutor's report, referral to an educational psychologist for a diagnostic assessment; alternative examination, assessment and study arrangements; support service for students with mental health issues via the Counselling Team; and liaison with external organisations.

Students who are D/deaf or hard of hearing will normally be supported by the City Lit Centre (see Directory), which provides support facilities to assist studies. Support services include communicators or notetakers.

As students prepare to come to the London Institute, Student Services offers information and advice on rented accommodation, childcare, disability, funding, your rights and immigration. Once enrolled, students have access to the Careers and Counselling Service. For more information visit the Student Services Website at www.linst.ac.uk/student.

## Home sweet home:

The Housing Services Department can offer information on halls of residence and other managed accommodation at the London Institute. There is some accessible accommodation, and this can be guaranteed for the duration of the student's course. For further information contact Housing Services – 020 7514 6240.

Housing Services also offers information and advice on finding and living in privately rented houses and flats. For more information, contact tel: 020 7514 6240 or email: accommodation@linst.ac.uk.

## Out and about:

Colleges: There are dedicated parking spaces near the accommodation and study areas. Students can use the London Taxi Card scheme.

Public transport: Most London buses, trains and taxis are accessible. Contact Access and Mobility (see Directory).

## Taking it easy:

At colleges: The colleges can use the London Institute SU facilities.

Locally: The Shopmobility scheme operates in some areas, and most pavements are tactile. Artsline publishes a number of access guides to the city of London (see Directory).

## And another thing ...

➡ The institute admits that wheelchair access to its buildings can be difficult, but it is determined to improve access and aims to adapt each site to meet the needs of disabled students. For further information about access to a particular college please contact the disability representative at the relevant college.

➡ The institute is now exploring innovative solutions to learning within studio settings.

➡ The institute is committed to developing alternative teaching methods aimed at the needs of disabled students.

➡ Following on from the work of the institute's externally funded project, 'Enhancing the Course Offer', a Deaf Student Forum has been set up. There is also a Deaf Students' Society supported by the London Institute's SU.

➡ Each college's computing centre has an open-access policy.

## The Disability Statement/Brochure:

*Breaking the Barriers: A handbook for disabled students at the London Institute*
Includes: Policy; developments; admission procedures; academic life; health and safety; access; finance; checklist for prospective students; useful contacts internally and externally; glossary and forms.

### Local disability public service providers:

London Borough Councils include: Southwark, Lambeth, Camden and Kensington and Chelsea.
Southwark Disablement Association, 020 7701 1391; text: 020 7703 6901; email: scla@dircon.co.uk.
Greater London Action on Disability (GLAD), 336 Brixton Road, London SW9 7AA; tel: 020 7346 5800; email: info@glad.org.uk.
Disability in Camden.
Southwark Disablement Association, tel: 020 7701 1391.

---

| London Metropolitan University |
|---|

London E1 7QA

Central University:
Tel: 020 7320 1203/3462
Fax: 020 7320 3462
Email: admiss@lgu.ac.uk
Website: www.lgu.ac.uk

**City Campus**
**Deputy Service Manager**
**Disabilities: Tarlochan Ghale**
**Deputy Manager Dyslexia:**
**Carol Jones**
**Tel: (Disability) 020 7320 1137**
**Tel: (Dyslexia) 020 7320 1094**
**Fax: 020 7320 1237**
**Email: disabilities.city@londonmet.ac.uk**
**dyslexia.city@londonmet.ac.uk**

**North Campus:**
**Disabilities and Dyslexia Service**
**Manager: Geraldine Tohan**
**Tel: (Disability and Dyslexia)**
**020 7133 2188**
**Fax: 020 7133 2322**
**Email: disability.north@**
**londonmet.ac.uk**
**dyslexia.north@londonmet.ac.uk**

**Fields of study:**
North London campus: business; computing; engineering;
environment; humanities and education; science; social studies.
London City campus: accountancy and financial business; art; civil
aviation studies; computing; design and technology; economics;
educational development; information systems and mathematics;
language studies; law; management and professional development;
politics and modern history; psychology; sociology and applied social
studies.

➡ Part-time studies: **Yes.**
➡ Distance learning: **No.**

**About the university:**
London Metropolitan University was formed on 1 August 2002
following the merger of the University of North London and the
London Guildhall University.

| |
|---|
| Total number of students: 28,000<br>Number of disabled students 600+ |

**Learning support staff and services:**
City Campus:
Deputy Manager Disabilities: Tarlochan Ghale; Deputy Manager
Dyslexia: Carol Jones
North Campus: Independent Learning Unit
Disabilities and Dyslexia Manager: Geraldine Tohan; Disability Officer:
David White
Needs assessments (currently only for students with dyslexia);
assistance with DSA applications and applications for other sources
of funding; provision of auxiliary aids and services; advice and
guidance; one-to-one/group tuition for students with dyslexia;
alternative examination, assessment and study arrangements; support

service for students with mental health issues and liaison with external organisations.

## Home sweet home:
There is accessible accommodation on the North Campus only. Accommodation can be guaranteed for duration of student's course.

## Out and about:
University: There are limited dedicated parking spaces near study areas.
Public transport: Some buses, train stations and taxis are accessible to people who are wheelchair users. Contact Access and Mobility for information about London's public transport services (see Directory).

## Taking it easy:
Locally: London varies in its accessibility. Most town facilities are accessible and some pavements are tactile. City Campus is based around the City and east Londo,n and North Campus is mostly based on the Holloway Road. Artsline publishes a variety of access guides on the city of London and its facilities (see Directory).

## And another thing ...
➡ The university runs a course in design for disability.

## Local disability public service providers:
London Borough of Tower Hamlets.

---

| London School of Economics and Political Science |
|---|

Houghton Street, London WC2A 2AE

*General Enquiries:*
Tel: 020 7955 7124
Fax: 020 7955 6001
Email: vg-admissions@lse.ac.uk
Website: www.lse.ac.uk

**Disability Coordinator: Jean Jameson**
**Tel: 020 7955 6034**
**Fax: 020 7955 6625**
**Email: jm.jameson@lse.ac.uk**

## Fields of study:
Accountancy and finance; anthropology; economic history; economics; geography and the environment; government; industrial relations; information systems; international history; international relations; law; logic and scientific method; mathematics; operational research; philosophy; social policy; social psychology; sociology and statistics.

London School of Economics and Political Science

➡ Part-time study: **Yes (postgraduate courses).**
➡ Distance learning: **Yes, partial.**

## About the school:

The London School of Economics and Political Science (LSE) was founded in 1895 by Beatrice and Sidney Webb. It is one of the largest colleges within the University of London and concentrates on the full range of social, political and economic sciences. It is based in central London with a wide host of amenities.

| Total number of students: 7,000 | Number of disabled students: 300 |
| --- | --- |

## Learning support staff and services:

Disability Office
Full-time adviser to students with disabilities/dyslexia and full-time administrator.
Assistance with DSA applications; provision of auxiliary aids and services; advice and guidance; one-to-one/group tuition for students with dyslexia; alternative examination, assessment and study arrangements; support service for students with mental health issues; drop-in service and appointments and liaison with external organisations.

## Home sweet home:

Two halls of residence have adapted bedrooms. One has parking space. Rooms can be made available for PAs, and accommodation can be guaranteed for the duration of the student's course.

## Out and about:

School: There are two dedicated parking spaces at the main site and spaces are provided at some residences.
Public transport: London buses are accessible, as are some of the tube stations, trains, train stations and taxis. All are accessible to people with visual impairments. Contact Access and Mobility for information on London's public transport services (see Directory).

## Taking it easy:

At the school: There is a wheelchair accessible student bar and canteen. Sports facilities are not accessible. There is a SU Society for Students with Disabilities and a Dyslexia Support Group.
Locally: Central London is a mix of accessible and non-accessible areas. The city centre is flat and some of its facilities are accessible. Some boroughs operate a Shopmobility scheme. The pavements are tactile in some areas. Artsline publishes several access guides about London (see Directory).

**And another thing ...**
➡ Disabled Students Fund from the SU for non-UK students.

**Local disability public service providers:**
Westminster City Council.
RNIB, RNID and DEAFWORKS – London.

---

| **London School of Hygiene and Tropical Medicine** |
|:---:|

Keppel Street, London WC1E 7HT

*General Enquiries:*
Tel: 020 7636 8636
Fax: 020 7436 5389
Email: registry@lshtm.ac.uk
Web: www.lshtm.ac.uk

**Student Disability Coordinator:**
**Deborah Gibberd**
**Tel: 020 7612 7833**
**Fax: 020 7636 7679**
**Email: Deborah.gibberd@lshtm.ac.uk**

**Fields of study:**
Epidemiology and population health; infectious and tropical diseases; public health and policy.

Part-time study: **Yes.**
Distance learning: **Yes.**

**About the school:**
The mission of the London School of Hygiene and Tropical Medicine is to contribute to the improvement of health worldwide through the pursuit of excellence in research, postgraduate teaching, advanced training and consultancy in international public health and tropical medicine.

| Total number of students: 1,728 | Number of disabled students: 30 |
|---|---|

**Staff and services:**
Part-time staff: Student Disability Support Coordinator: Deborah Gibberd
Assistance with DSA applications; advice and guidance; alternative examination, assessment and study arrangements; support service for students with mental health issues; liaison with external organisations.

**Home sweet home:**
Accommodation will be adapted to suit needs.
Accommodation can be guaranteed for duration of student's course.

## Out and about:
Public transport: Some buses, trains, train stations and taxis are accessible to people who are wheelchair users and/or who have visual impairments. There is a taxi scheme for disabled people operating in the area. Contact Access and Mobility (see below) for further information.

## Taking it easy:
Locally: The city centre is flat and mostly accessible. Some of the town's facilities are accessible, but there is not a Shopmobility scheme. Most of the pavements are tactile. Artsline (see below) publish a number of access guides for London.

## Local disability public service providers:
Artsline (see Directory).
Access and Mobility (see Directory).

---

### London South Bank University
103 Borough Road, London SE1 0AA

*General Enquiries:*
Tel: 020 7928 8989
Fax: 020 7815 8155
Email: registry@lsbu.ac.uk
Website: www.lsbu.ac.uk

**Learning Support Manager: Alison Egan**
**Tel: 020 7815 6405/6400**
**Fax: 020 7815 6464**
**Email: eganas@lsbu.ac.uk**

## Fields of study:
Course provision at LSBU is divided into the following faculties: Arts and Human Sciences; Business, Computing and Information Management; Combined Honours; Engineering, Science and the Built Environment; Health and Social Care.

➡ Part-time study: **Yes.**
➡ Distance learning: **Yes.**

## About the university:
Culturally, the university occupies a prime position, being so close to the South Bank Arts Centre. The Royal Festival Hall, Hayward Gallery, Royal National Theatre, National Film Theatre and Tate Modern are all nearby.

---

Total number of students: 17,000    Number of disabled students: 890

**Learning support staff and services:**
The Learning Support Team
Full-time staff: Learning Support Manager; two Learning Support Officers; Office Manager and an Administrator.
Part-time staff: Two Learning Support Officers and a Technical Support Officer.
Support needs assessment; assistance in DSA applications; liaison with course tutors and cross-university staff to ensure appropriate support; support in acquiring a non-medical assistant for study-related assistance; alternative examination and assessment arrangements; appropriate diagnostic assessment; find a trained dyslexia tutor for one-to-one support and provision of group sessions to develop effective study methods for students with dyslexia. The service also offers focus group sessions for students with disabilities that provide feedback on the effectiveness of the provision. Issues raised at those sessions are passed on to the Disabilities Steering Group.

**Home sweet home:**
Most university halls of residence include a small number of rooms designed for students with mobility difficulties. On campus there are purpose-built and adapted flats fitted with emergency flashing lights to supplement alarm bells. Three halls of residence are purpose-built. An accommodation guide is available from the Accommodation Office; see www.lsbu.ac.uk/housing.
Depending on the individual disability needs of a student, accommodation may possibly be guaranteed for duration of student's course, but each case must be looked at individually.

**Out and about:**
University: The university contributes towards accessible transport in some cases. Dedicated parking spaces near both accommodation and study areas.
Public transport: About 75% of buses are low floor. Some underground stations and some national rail stations are accessible. Timetables are available in large print. There is a taxi scheme for disabled people operating in the area: Taxi Card 020 7484 2929. Mobility buses have routes across London (020 7582 5505). South East London Dial-a-Ride (01689 896333). Contact Access and Mobility for further information regarding access to London's public transport services (see Directory).

## Taking it easy:

At university: There are support groups for students with disabilities. Locally: The local area is flat and accessible. The local leisure centre has a disabled area and many of the London area attractions, including museums and art galleries, are accessible including Surrey Quays Cinema, Elephant and Castle Leisure Centre, Imperial War Museum and IMAX 3-D Cinema. Some pavements are tactile. *Southwark Directory for Disabled People* gives information on local access and is available from Southwark Council. Artsline publishes a number of guides about access in London (see Directory).

## And another thing ...

➡ An induction session for students with disabilities is hosted by members of the Learning Support Team.

➡ The Learning and Development Centre works closely with other departments and faculties in the university. It offers a range of academic and personal services throughout the student's course and sometimes beyond.

➡ A handbook for students with disabilities/dyslexia, entitled *Enabling You*, is available from Caxton House. The Learning and Development Centre publishes a separate flyer on the equipment available for students with disabilities/dyslexia, available on the website: www.lsbu.ac.uk/caxton.

➡ The university has had success in its consistent ability to secure HEFCE funding for special initiatives projects on disabilities, which include a CD-ROM for dyslexic students.

➡ The university is a member of Skill.

## Local disability public service providers:

London Borough of Southwark, Disabilities Service, 151 Walworth Road, London SE17 1RY; 020 7525 2149; fax: 020 7525 2317. Southwark Disablement Association, 2 Bradenham Court, London SE17 2QB.

---

| **Loughborough University** |
| :---: |

Loughborough, Leicester LE11 3TU

*General Enquiries:*
Tel: 01509 222498/9
Fax: 01509 223905
Email: admissions@lboro.ac.uk
Website: www.lboro.ac.uk

**Disability Coordinator: David Jackson**
**Tel: 01509 222769**
**Fax: 01509 223933**
**Email: d.jackson@lboro.ac.uk**
**Text: 01509 222770**

**Fields of study:**
Art and design; engineering; science; social sciences and humanities.

➡ Part-time study: **Yes, depends on course.**
➡ Distance learning: **No.**

**About the university:**
The university is housed on a large campus on the edge of Loughborough, with easy access into the town centre. A survey in the *Financial Times* published in 2000 placed Loughborough and Cambridge first equal for teaching quality. Loughborough is a friendly English market town that also supports major research-based industries. The English countryside is on the doorstep: Charnwood Forest next door, the Peak District nearby. The cities of Leicester, Nottingham and Derby are close neighbours.

Total number of students: 12,000    Number of disabled students: 350

**Learning support staff and services:**
Disabilities and Additional Needs Service (DANS)
Full-time staff: Disability Coordinator: David Jackson; head of service; secretary.
Part-time staff: Student Adviser: Christopher Hopkins; Mental Health Support Advisor: Dan Doran; Administrator.
Needs assessments; advice and guidance; assistance with DSA applications, Hardship Funds and grants; provision of auxiliary aids and services; provision of support workers for students; provision of one-to-one disability-specific counselling; provision of CSVs to act as PAs; pre-admission advice and information to prospective students all the way through to full applicant; a forum for students to give their views via the DANS Sub-committee; alternative assessment and examination arrangements; liaison with departments: one-to-one/group tuition for students with dyslexia; support service for students with mental health problems and liaison with external organisations.

**Home sweet home:**
Every hall of residence has some adapted accommodation to meet all needs, which is integrated so students 'don't find themselves in a "disability ghetto"'. Rooms can be adapted as needed. Wheelchair users, people with visual impairment and those who are D/deaf or hard of hearing are catered for. Rooms for carers/personal assistants are provided.
Accommodation can be guaranteed for duration of student's course.

## Out and about:
University: Dedicated parking spaces near both accommodation and study areas.
Public transport: The train station is accessible. Some buses, trains and taxis are accessible to wheelchair users. Some buses, trains and taxis are accessible to people with visual impairments.

## Taking it easy:
At university: Disabled students can use all the facilities on campus, although there is nothing specifically for disabled people.
Locally: The town is flat with a few slight hills and is mainly accessible. Some of its facilities are accessible for wheelchair users. There is a Shopmobility scheme. The pavements are tactile. Charnwood Disability Group meets in Loughborough regularly and there is also a swimming club with disabled members. A disability guide is available from the Town Hall.

## And another thing ...
➡ The 220-acre campus is fairly accessible to students who are wheelchair users or who have mobility disabilities.
➡ Most of the buildings on campus are wheelchair accessible, with one or two exceptions. The university has carried out a comprehensive survey of all its buildings and has drawn up a plan, based on the survey, of how to improve access, which includes signage around campus.
➡ The delivery of dyslexia-specific one-to-one support is provided by the ELSU (English Language Study Unit) in conjunction with DANS.
➡ DANS has recently been successful in bidding for funding from the HEFCE for the assessment and provision of support specific to the needs of students with mental health difficulties.
➡ Links with RNIB, NAS (National Autistic Society), Derby College for Deaf People and local LEA support services.

## The Disability Statement/Brochure:
Covers: Applications; facilities and services; access; personal support; advice and support; examinations and assessments; financial support; Student Services Committee and DANS staff. A4, nine pages.

## Local disability public service providers:
MOSAK (formerly Leicestershire Guild of Disabled People).
Leicester DIAL.
The Equalities Officer, Charnwood Borough Council, Loughborough, Leicestershire.

## University of Luton
Park Square, Luton LU1 3JU

*General Enquiries:*
Tel: 01582 734111
Fax: 01582 743400
Website: www.luton.ac.uk

**Disabilities Adviser: Gillian Malins**
**Tel: 01582 489342**
**Fax: 01582 489349**
**Email: gillian.malins@luton.ac.uk**
**Text: 01582 743422**

### Fields of study:
Acute and clinical care; applied social studies; business; computing and information systems; design; education; finance systems and operations; health and social organisation; human resource management; language; law; marketing; media arts; psychology; public health and primary care; sport exercise and biomedical sciences; tourism and leisure.

➡ Part-time study: **Yes.**
➡ Distance learning: **Yes.**

### About the university:
At the heart of Luton lies the modern university, which has been described as the country's second 'most improved' university, according to the *Daily Telegraph*'s Good Universities league table 2000. The university has consistently appeared within the top ten among all universities for getting graduates into employment (according to the Higher Education Statistics Agency). Luton is a lively town, only half an hour away from London but surrounded by countryside. Luton's roots lie in the industrial and manufacturing areas. During recent years several multimillion-pound projects have enhanced the town's physical appearance and facilities including a new focus on arts, culture and leisure.

Total number of students: 1,200     Number of disabled students: 500

### Learning support staff and services:
Additional Resource Unit
One full-time and one part-time Disability Adviser; one dyslexia support tutor.
Needs assessment; examination support; dyslexia tuition; personal support; provision of notetakers, sign language interpreters, etc.

## Home sweet home:
Adapted accommodation for wheelchair users on ground floor, visual alarms in rooms for D/deaf or hard of hearing students.
Accommodation can be guaranteed for duration of student's course.

## Out and about:
University: Dedicated parking spaces near both accommodation and study areas.
Public transport: Some buses have wheelchair access on local routes, as do hackney carriages.

## Taking it easy:
At university: Sports facilities are shared with Vauxhall Motors but are not very accessible for wheelchair users.
Locally: The city centre is flat, pedestrianised and accessible. Accessible town facilities, including cinema complex and main library, and there is a Shopmobility scheme. The pavements are tactile. No current disability guide.

## QAA Report: Paragraphs 68 and 69, May 2002
The University's commitment to supporting disabled students is demonstrated, for example, by the importance it attaches to supporting students with special needs through its Special Needs Unit and Student Advisor (Disabilities) within the Student Centre. The University's clear and comprehensive Disability Statement articulates its commitment 'to ensuring that disabled candidates are able to demonstrate their ability in an examination setting while ensuring that they are not put at a disadvantage compared with other candidates'. These constitute an important aspiration within the University's support arrangements.
… University's examinations auditor undertakes a regular and thorough audit of examination processes and practices. This addresses the operation of the system, but also comments on the general experience and behaviour of students and staff in the examinations location. The audit team particularly noted concerns that had been expressed relating to the level of consideration given to disabled students in examination settings. The University will wish to consider the particular importance of ensuring that equal opportunities and disability issues are scrutinised rigorously and taken forward through appropriate committee and management channels, as well as through formal staff development and training linked to the work of the University's special needs agencies.

**Local disability public service provider:**
The Disability Resource Centre, Paynters Road, Dunstable,
Bedfordshire.

| University of Manchester |
| --- |

Oxford Road, Manchester M13 9PL

*General Enquiries:*
Tel: 0161 275 2000
Fax: 0161 275 5697
Email: ug.admissions@man.ac.uk
Website: www.man.ac.uk

**Coordinator of Disability
Developments: Elaine Shillcock
Tel: 0161 275 2051
Fax: 0161 275 2407
Email: elaine.shillcock@man.ac.uk
disability@man.ac.uk
Text: 0161 275 2794**

**Fields of study:**
Arts; biological sciences; education; science and engineering; social
sciences and law.

➡ Part-time study: **Yes.**

**About the university:**
Founded in 1851, the University of Manchester was the first of
England's great civic universities. No fewer than 20 former staff or
students have gone on to become Nobel Prizewinners. The University
of Manchester campus, which is mainly on a single site, is relatively
flat and well served by public transport. The campus covers an area
of about 40 hectares, 1 mile south of Manchester city centre.

| Number of disabled students: 801 |
| --- |

**Learning support staff and services:**
Disability Support Office
University Coordinator of Disability Developments: Elaine Shillcock;
Disability Support Officer (to be appointed); Administrator: Jan
Lancaster; Secretary: Audrey Williams.
Advice and information; assistance with DSA applications; full
assessment of study support requirements; liaison with other
members of staff in academic departments and central services;
advice on suitable technology/equipment; alternative examination
and assessment arrangements; assistance with PAs and support
workers; advice on external sources of financial support and

assistance with the application of such funds; preparation and distribution of specific disability-related information and delivery of appropriate staff/student training.

The Disability Support Office can help you organise PAs and support workers. Through Social Services and Henshaws Society for the Blind a programme of mobility training is available for blind and visually impaired students.

From the student's assessment of needs a personal support and learning plan (PSLP) is produced. The PSLP details the agreed support from the university and indicates the responsibilities of the student for the implementation of that support.

Most departments and central service areas have a designated disability contact.

**Home sweet home:**
A variety of accommodation is available for students with disabilities, including adaptations made for students who use wheelchairs and flashing alarms for those who are D/deaf or hard of hearing. It is usually possible for a room to be available for PAs either next to the student or close by if necessary. Special items, such as a fridge to store insulin, can usually be provided with prior notice. Wherever feasible, the university will try to organise more adaptations. Some residences are self-catering and some kitchens have been adapted for wheelchair users; some halls of residence are catered with bed and breakfast provided. Many bedrooms, in both self-catering and catered residences, have private bathrooms (most with showers, some with baths) and telephone and Internet points.

**Out and about:**
University: Dedicated parking spaces near both accommodation and study areas.
Public transport: The City Council issues travel permits for those who are eligible. There is a frequent bus service, a metro link service, a national coach service and three mainline railway stations in the city centre (Greater Manchester Transport Association, tel: 0161 228 7811 – voice and text).

**Taking it easy:**
At university: The university, jointly with the City Council, UMIST and Manchester Metropolitan University, was involved in the building of the Commonwealth Games Swimming Pool on Oxford Road adjacent to the main campus. The complex has several fully accessible pools. The Armitage Sports Centre is wheelchair accessible to both levels, and some parts of the McDougall Sports Centre currently have

restricted access. Contact Sports Directorate, tel: 0161 275 6991. The SU buildings are fully accessible, providing social facilities such as bars, cafés and clubs. A new society, Enable, for anybody interested in disability issues has recently been set up.
Locally: There is a Shopmobility scheme in operation in the city-centre Arndale Shopping Centre (tel: 0161 839 4060; fax: 0161 839 5110) and in the nearby Trafford Centre (tel: 0161 749 1728).

**And another thing ...**
➡ The Estates Office is in the process of conducting an access audit of the campus.
➡ Nearly all of the 30 or more buildings on the main campus have at least one wheelchair accessible entrance, though there is not always wheelchair access to every floor. In addition, many buildings have adapted toilet facilities.
➡ Wherever possible, scheduled classes are moved to accessible rooms when access is needed.
➡ Induction loops have been fitted in some rooms in the university. Where this facility is not available, portable loops and/or conferencing microphones will be provided for students who require them.
➡ Wheelchair accessible entrances and toilet facilities are indicated on the university maps and are also signposted around campus. A map and details of the campus and buildings, including sports facilities, are set out in the Disability Statement appendices. A tactile map, prepared by RNIB, is available from the Disability Support Office.
➡ As a member of Access Summit the university has access to a register of personal support workers undertaking a range of roles.
➡ Disability training is offered to students through the SU's Certificate in Personal Development Scheme, to ensure all union societies are aware of specific needs and to provide advice on making sure all events are accessible to all students.

**QAA Report: Paragraphs 61 and 67, November 2000**
The account stated that 'all students receive university-wide induction information before arrival from both the university and the union'. Students also receive departmental induction information before arrival, and programme handbooks during registration week. These matters were confirmed by the audit team in discussion with students representing a cross-section of the faculties. An important part of the student induction process was the advance information presented to them, including the information made available on the university's Web pages. This appeared to the team to be very comprehensive,

covering such matters as examination processes, appeal, grievance procedures, residence and accommodation, and also policies pertaining to students with disabilities. The team concluded that the information provided to, and communication with, students during the induction process were appropriate and accurate. The induction process itself involved a wide range of individuals drawn from across the university, with the SU playing an active and important part. The major central services for student support include the Central Academic Advisory Service, which offers confidential advice on matters relating to academic progress, the Counselling Service, the Student Health Centre and the Disability Support Office ... The team heard from the staff and students alike about the general satisfaction with the central services, and noted the evident enthusiasm with which the services performed their supporting role. The team gained the impression that the monitoring of these services contributed to the maintenance of high standards in these areas, and ensured that the university was aware of the standards of the services so provided. The team concluded that the work of the central support services enabled students and staff to perform at a level that helped to maintain the quality and standards of the university. The university has a Charter for Learning, which states that 'students may expect to receive an education of high quality with high standards of teaching resources and support services'. The team had confidence that this statement was being upheld.

In points for commendation par 96 point iii the audit team commends 'the initiatives directed towards student support'.

## The Disability Statement/Brochure:

*Opportunities for Students with Additional Support Needs*
Includes: The Disability Support Office; general information before you apply; information for undergraduate and postgraduate applicants; facilities; PAs; numbers of students with disabilities; future activity and policy development and appendices.

### Local disability public service providers:

Access Summit, St Peter's House Precinct Centre, Oxford Road, Manchester M13 9GH; 0161 272 7847; text: 0161 273 7307; fax: 0161 272 7001; email: access.summit@umist.ac.uk.
Coalition of Disabled People (Manchester), Carisbrook, Wenlock Way, Gorton M12 5LF; 0161 273 5154; fax: 0161 273 4164.

## Manchester Metropolitan University

All Saints, Manchester M15 6BH

*General Enquiries:*
Tel: 0161 247 2000
Fax: 0161 247 6390
Email: enquiries@mmu.ac.uk
Website: www.prospectusmmu.ac.uk

**Learning Support Coordinator:**
**Emma Flynn**
**Tel: 0161 247 3491**
**Fax: 0161 247 3491**
**Email: l.support@mmu.ac.uk**
**Text: 0161 247 3492**

### Fields of study:
Art and design; business; community studies, law and education; humanities and social science; science and engineering.

➡ Part-time study: **Yes.**
➡ Distance learning: **In some instances.**

### About the university:
Manchester Metropolitan University is located in over 80 buildings, across seven major sites, five in the Manchester area and two at Alsager and Crewe in Cheshire. Most of the buildings were constructed in the 1960s, but some date back to the eighteenth and nineteenth centuries. Manchester city has an ambitious construction programme to provide some of the best sporting and cultural facilities in the country.

Total number of students: 32,000 Number of disabled students: 1,384

### Learning support staff and services:
Learning Support Unit
Full-time staff: Disability Coordinator: Emma Flynn; Learning Support Advisors: Trish Richards, Vikki Plant, Nicki Ho.
Part-time staff: Learning Support Advisors: Linda Horbury, Rob Hayward, Ian Webb and Kiri Thomas.
Needs assessment; assistance with DSA applications, Hardship Funds and financial support from various charities; provision of auxiliary aids and services; advice and guidance; one-to-one/group tuition for students with dyslexia (arranged through the Access Centre); initial screening for dyslexia; alternative examination, assessment and study arrangements; support service for students with mental health issues; access to specialist equipment such as computer and appropriate software and liaison with external organisations.
There are seven faculties, each with a senior member of administration to coordinate support to students with disabilities.

**Home sweet home:**
The new Cambridge Halls of Residence on the All Saints site include adapted study bedrooms with en-suite shower and toilet facilities for 11 residents, with kitchens designed to be accessible. There are also flashing lights and vibrating alarm systems in study bedrooms for visually impaired and D/deaf or hard of hearing residents. There are additional rooms for PAs in the privately owned halls. Information about accessible private accommodation (rented houses, flats and privately owned halls) is available on the Manchester Student Homes Web page: www.msh.man.ac.uk. Accommodation can be guaranteed for duration of student's course.

**Out and about:**
University: Dedicated parking spaces near both accommodation and study areas on most campuses.
Public transport: Train stations, taxis and some buses and trains are accessible to people who are wheelchair users. Buses, trains, train stations and some taxis are accessible to people with visual impairments.

**Taking it easy:**
At university: The SU has set up a new group called capABLE intended to be a social and supportive group for students with disabilities and their friends. The SU has new, high-quality and accessible facilities at both Manchester and Alsager.
Locally: The city centre is flat and accessible. The facilites are accessible and there is a Shopmobility scheme. The pavements are tactile. The SU has a disabilities officer and an equal opportunities officer who can advise you about access in Manchester.

**And another thing ...**
➡ CALIM (the Consortium of Academic Libraries in Manchester) has published a booklet outlining the facilities of all the university libraries in Manchester, available from any site library or the Learning Support Team.
➡ The Careers Service has organised a number of joint initiatives including Interact, a mentoring scheme for students with disabilities.
➡ Various publications available. Contact the Learning Support Team or visit www.mmu.ac.uk/lsu.

**QAA Report: Paragraph 116, January 2001**
SSU (Student Support Unit) provides institution-wide professionally staffed services including counselling; careers advice; health;

accommodation; sport and learning support, with special arrangements for disabled overseas students.

## The Disability Statement/Brochure:
Covers: First steps; contacts; applications; who to approach; what happens next; support available; course requirements; examinations and assessments; resources and facilities; building access; accommodation; future provision; what happens if needs change; other support available; social and recreational opportunities; other sources of information; disclosure and relevant publications.

**Local disability public service provider:**
Manchester Disability Access Group: email: admin@mdpag.org.uk.

| Middlesex University |
| --- |

White Hart Lane, London N17 8HR

*General Enquiries:*
Admission Enquiries
Tel: 020 8411 5898
Fax: 020 8411 5649
Email: admissions@mdx.ac.uk
Website: www.mdx.ac.uk

**Coordinator: Bryan Jones**
**Tel: 020 8411 5366**
**Fax: 020 8411 6237**
**Email: disability@mdx.ac.uk**
**Text: 020 8411 5639**

## Fields of study:
Art and design, and electronic arts; biological sciences and the environment; business; computing and information technology; dance, drama, music and performing arts; education; health; humanities, languages and cultural studies; product design and engineering; social sciences and work-based learning studies.

➡ Part-time study: **Yes.**
➡ Distance learning: **Yes.**

## About the university:
Middlesex is a modern, multi-campus university based in north London. Ranging in style from modern centres to historic buildings, the university's campuses include a mansion house and country park estate, purpose-built sites and bases at four leading teaching hospitals. Beyond the campus grounds north London's many local attractions have much to offer. Central London is only a short distance away.

> Total number of students: 23,000
> Number of disabled students: 1,085

## Learning support staff and services:

Disability Support Service, based at the Enfield campus
Manager: Brian Jones; two disability support officers (dyslexia); administrative team; support assistants; specialist IT trainers; health adviser; mental health coordinator; and student counsellors.
Needs assessment; provision of auxiliary aids and services; advice and guidance; one-to-one/group tuition for students with dyslexia; support service for students with mental health issues; instruction in use of specialist equipment; help establish support groups and offer professional support; alternative assessment and examination arrangements; assistance with DSA applications; where students are not eligible for DSA, assistance from the university's existing resources or other agencies; scheduling classes in rooms that are appropriate to the student's needs; alerting tutors to individual needs in terms of teaching and learning method; and liaison with external organisations.
The Centre offers a well-equipped resource room with a wide range of assistive and supportive software and hardware.
The Dyslexia Support Service provides: a full psychological assessment; an assessment of needs; a 'bridging course' in academic skills prior to enrolment; flexible examination arrangements; one-to-one tutorial support; recommendations for hardware and software; technical skills training; assistance with DSA applications; staff development and training.

## Home sweet home:

The University has 2,400 single study bedrooms spread over 13 separate halls of residence. Some halls are traditional in style, with shared bathroom and kitchen facilities; others are flats with a number of study bedrooms grouped around a kitchen/dining area. In some flats the study bedrooms have en-suite shower rooms and toilet. In other rooms there are shared bathrooms. Several of the halls of residence have rooms adapted for students with mobility difficulties.
Accommodation can be guaranteed for the duration of the student's course.

## Out and about:

At university: There are dedicated parking spaces for disabled drivers near the accommodation and study areas. A Taxicard scheme operates in the area.

Public transport: Some buses, trains, train stations and taxis are accessible to people who are wheelchair users, and/or have visual impairments. Contact Access and Mobility for information on public transport services in London (see Directory).

**Taking it easy:**
Locally: Artsline publishes a number of guides about access in London (see Directory).

**And another thing ...**
➡ All new buildings are based on universal architectural good practice. Consequently 80 per cent of buildings are accessible to wheelchair users. However, since the university operates on a number of campuses, accessibility varies; there are particular difficulties in parts of the Trent Park campus, where 'heritage' buildings are subject to special planning constraints. The university is committed to improving accessibility, and priorities include: new lifts and chairlifts, upgrading lifts; more access ramps and alteration of door thresholds; more toilet facilities accessible to disabled people.
➡ A small bank of equipment is held for lending on a short-term basis. Training is also provided so students can become confident in equipment use and care.
➡ The university extends advice and support on disabilities to a number of its associate colleges including Oakhill Theological College and the Royal Veterinary College.
➡ Barnet College has a self-financing Sign Language Bureau, which provides BSL interpreters for the deaf community in Greater London and beyond.
➡ Other facilities include: Braille translation; sign language interpreters, lipspeaking; induction loops in most major lecture theatres; local area loops systems at library issue and student office counters; notetakers and communication support.
➡ Specialist software for students with dyslexia/visual impairment.

## The Disability Statement/Brochure:
Covers: Partnership for enablement; administrative statistics; special facilities and support; development strategies and policy and specialist staff.

| Myerscough College |
|---|

Bilsborrow, Preston, Lancashire PR3 0RY

*General Enquiries:*
Tel: 01995 642222
Fax: 01995 642333
Email: mailbox@myerscough.ac.uk
Website: www.myerscough.ac.uk

**Learning Support Centre Manager:**
**Val Senior**
**Tel: 01995 642222**
**Fax: 01995 642333**
**Email: vsenior@**
**myerscough.ac.uk**

## Fields of study:
Agriculture; animal studies; arboriculture; business and management; countryside studies; creative design; equine studies; golf studies; horticulture; landscape studies; mechanisation and motor sports; sport and leisure; veterinary nursing.

Part-time study: **Yes.**
Distance learning: **Yes.**

## About the college:
The campus and adjoining estate of Myerscough College extend to about 600 hectares. Although set in beautiful Lancashire countryside, the college is close to the town of Preston. It is situated 1 mile from the main A6 Preston to Lancaster Road, 6 miles north of Preston. The college provides FE and HE and has links with the University of Central Lancashire, which validates its degrees and with which it jointly operates the land-based faculty together with two universities in the United States. The college has a new purpose-built sports centre.

| Total number of students: 850 | Number of disabled students: 40 |
|---|---|

## Learning support staff and services:
Learning Support Centre
Full-time staff: Dyslexia Coordinator: Denise Jarvis; Learning Support Coordinator: Noreen Goonan; BSL Sign Language Interpreter: Mark Gavin; Administrator/Notetaker: Alison Ferguson.
Part-time staff: 30 learning support assistants.
Needs assessment; assistance with DSA applications, Access Fund and bursaries; provision of auxiliary aids and services; advice and guidance; one-to-one/group tuition for students with dyslexia; alternative examination, assessment and study arrangements; support service for students with mental health issues; specialist expertise;

information on appropriate materials and equipment; loan of equipment; and liaison with external agencies.

### Home sweet home:
Six rooms currently accessible for people who are wheelchair users, which are self-catering. From September 2004 there will be two further rooms accessible to wheelchair users.
Accommodation *cannot* be guranteed for duration of the student's course.

### Out and about:
College: Dedicated parking spaces near both accommodation and study areas.
Public transport: Some taxis are accessible to wheelchair users and people with visual impairments. Buses, trains and train stations are not accessible.

### Taking it easy:
At college: REACT is a local group for disabled and non-disabled people. ASD is the Autistic Spectrum Disorder support group.
Locally: Preston has a pedestrianised city centre which is flat and accessible. There is a Shopmobility scheme and the pavements are *not* tactile.

### And another thing ...
➡ The library is housed on the ground floor of the £3 million learning resource centre.
➡ HE students are able to use the facilities at the University of Central Lancashire.
➡ The college has a range of centres throughout the north west, where courses are offered in land-based subjects. These are currently predominantly FE courses except at Croxteth Park, Liverpool. The college is hoping to extend HE courses to other centres in the region.

### Local disability public service provider:
Lancashire County Council 01772 261743.

| **Napier University** |
| :---: |

10 Colinton Road, Edinburgh EH10 5DT

*General Enquiries:*
Tel: 0131 444 2266
Fax: 0131 455 6333
Email: info@napier.ac.uk
Website: www.napier.ac.uk

**Special Needs Coordinator:**
**Jacky Robinson**
**Tel: 0131 455 5111**
**Fax: 0131 455 5113**
**Email: j.robinson@napier.ac.uk**
**Text: 0131 455 5133**

**Fields of study:**
Alternative medicine and complementary therapies; built environment and civil engineering; business management; communication and creative industries; computing and information technology; e-business and information management; engineering; financial services and accounting; life sciences; nursing and midwifery; social sciences; tourism and hospitality.

➡ Part-time study: **Yes.**
➡ Distance learning: **Yes.**

**About the university:**
Napier was established in 1964 and is a multi-site institution with many old and listed buildings on different campuses. Edinburgh is one of the most student-friendly cities in the UK, with students making up a large percentage of Edinburgh's population. On one side there is the medieval charm of the historic Old Town and on the other the grandeur of the classically laid out New Town with its fine Georgian architecture. Every year Edinburgh hosts the biggest arts festival in the world – the Edinburgh International Festival and its Fringe.

| Total number of students: approx 12,500 |
| :---: |
| Number of disabled students: 900 |

**Learning support staff and services:**
Special Needs and Disabilities Team
One full-time and two part-time staff including: Special Needs Coordinator: Jacky Robinson; Dyslexia Adviser: Monica Gribben; Technology Adviser/Trainer: Bruce Darby; one special needs assistant.
In addition, each academic school (department) has one or more named disability contacts to assist students with disabilities and

special needs in matters relating to their academic programme and examination allowances.

Support students' needs in terms of access to: teaching facilities, including computer and other laboratories; learning information services; social areas and general student facilities; arrangement of diagnostic assessment for students with specific learning difficulties; alternative examination and assessment arrangements; advice on DSA applications.

## Home sweet home:

The university provides some accommodation that has been adapted for a student who is D/deaf or hard of hearing. Facilities include a vibrating paging system for the fire alarm, doorbell and personal alarm. There is also adapted accommodation for wheelchair users and people with mobility difficulties. Facilities include widened doorways and halls, kitchens and bathrooms with easy access and 'drive-in' showers. All are on the ground floor. Access to upper floors is by stairs only. It is possible to negotiate accommodation for a PA. Accommodation can sometimes be guaranteed for duration of student's course depending on circumstances.

## Out and about:

University: Dedicated parking spaces both near accommodation and at some campuses for Blue Badge holders.

Public transport: Details of bus routes to all sites are available from the university, but private transport can be an advantage in accessing certain buildings. Campuses are linked by Lothian buses. Some routes, but not all, have wheelchair accessible buses. All local taxis are wheelchair accessible.

## Taking it easy:

At university: Most student-run facilities are accessible.

Locally: The city centre is both flat and hilly and accessible. The local facilities are accessible including social facilities, which are close to the student accommodation. Many of the pavements are tactile.

## And another thing ...

➡ Wheelchairs are available for use at most sites.

➡ Craighouse Campus is difficult for students with a mobility impairment to negotiate, so advice should be sought about teaching locations.

➡ Study material can be provided in appropriate format. More and more material is being made available on the Web and in electronic format.

➡ The university employs a consultant educational psychologist (part-time) for assessments for students with specific learning difficulties.

➡ Each campus has its own library; some have dedicated resource rooms for students with disabilities.

➡ There is a Special Needs and Disabilities Committee.

➡ A variety of equipment is available for short-term loan within the university.

## The Disability Statement/Brochure:
*Information for Students with Disabilities and Special Needs*
Includes: Key staff; university policy; pre-entry guidance; accommodation; facilities; academic support; equipment and technology; Student Support Services; financial matters; future activity and policy development and university contacts.
Available on website:
www.napier.ac.uk/depts/sss/SpecialNeeds/default.html or from the Special Needs Team.

### Local disability public service provider:
Lothian Coalition of Disabled People, Norton Park Centre, 57 Albion Road, Edinburgh EH7 5QY; 0131 475 2300.

---

| National Film and Television School (NFTS) |
|---|

Beaconsfield Studios, Station Road, Beaconsfield, Bucks HP9 1LG

*General Enquiries:*
Tel: 01494 731425
Fax: 01494 674042
Email: admin@nftsfilm-tv.ac.uk
Web: www.nftsfilm-tv.ac.uk

### Fields of study:
Animation; cinematography; documentary; editing; fiction direction; producing; screen design; screen music for film and television; screenwriting; sound design; sound production recording for film and television.

Part-time study: **No.**
Distance learning: **No.**

**About the school:**
The National Film and Television School (NFTS) is a centre for professional training in film, television and related media industries. It is unusual amongst film schools in being able to offer students the experience of training in professional-standard film and television studios and post-production facilities. The NFTS is funded by the government via the Department for Culture, Media and Sport and by the British film and television industry.

| | |
|---|---|
| Total number of students: 140 | Number of disabled students: 3 |

**Learning support staff and services:**
Student Welfare
Full-time staff: Student Welfare Officer: Judith McDonnell
Needs assessment; assistance with DSA applications; provision of auxiliary aids and services; advice and guidance; one-to-one/group tuition for students with dyslexia; alternative examination, assessment and study arrangements; support service for students with mental health issues; provision of special accommodation, equipment or adaptation needs and liaison with external organisations.

**Home sweet home:**
There is no student accommodation, but the NFTS will discuss your accommodation needs with you and try to find a solution.

**Out and about:**
School: Dedicated parking spaces near study areas.
Public transport: Trains, train stations and some buses and taxis are accessible to wheelchair users. Buses, trains, train stations and taxis are accessible to people with visual impairments. Dial-a-Ride operates in the area.

**Taking it easy:**
At school: There are no leisure facilities at the school, but the SU is accessible.
Locally: The town centre is flat and accessible. The pavements are tactile.

**And another thing …**
➡ Advances in new technology have already made several areas of filmmaking less physically demanding, and most equipment can be adapted to meet individual needs.
➡ The NFTS has two lifts that are accessible to wheelchair users to enable access to the upper floors of the main building. The Tutor

block, which also gives access to Head Tutor offices and the Curriculum unit, is accessible via a ramp.

➡ The ground floor toilet is accessible to wheelchair users.

➡ Not all the school's buildings are easily accessible to people with mobility problems, but the NFTS can usually make temporary access arrangements to awkward spaces that students might want to visit, or arrange alternatives where possible. Work continues to improve access where it is currently limited.

➡ Not all courses are equally accessible. Some courses may present particular difficulties for people who have certain types of disability. Contact the Registry for advice.

**Local disability public service provider:**
South Buckinghamshire District Council.

---

| Newcastle College |
|---|

Rye Hill Campus, Scotswood Road, Newcastle upon Tyne NE4 5BR

*General Enquiries:*
Tel: 0191 200 4399
Fax: 0191 200 4399
Email: aborg@ncl-coll.ac.uk
Website: www.ncl-coll.ac.uk
Text: 0191 272 3304

**Additional Support Manager:**
**Alison Borg**
**Tel: 0191 226 3143**
**Fax: 0191 200 4399**
**Email: aborg@ncl-coll.ac.uk**
**Text: 0191 272 3304**

**Fields of study:**
Art and design; beauty and related therapies; business; computing; early childhood studies and public services; health care; hospitality; IT and engineering; leisure; music and performing arts; sport; tourism; travel.

➡ Part-time study: **Yes.**
➡ Distance learning: **Yes.**

**About the college:**
Newcastle College has invested millions of pounds to create a study environment to reflect the college's commitment to student-centred learning. Newcastle College is located in Newcastle upon Tyne, close to major shopping and leisure facilities and convenient for all public transport links. The city is the regional capital – the major industrial, commercial, cultural and communications centre of the north east.

Total number of students: 22,000
Number of disabled students: 1,600

## Learning support staff and services:
Additional Support Services
Full-time staff: Coordinator for Students with Emotional/Behavioural
Difficulties: Rachel Smith; Coordinator for Students with Physical and
Learning Difficulties: Sarah Hamblin; Coordinator for Students with
Dyslexia: Brenda Ellidge; Coordinator for Deaf Tutors and Courses:
Val Molyneux; Specialist Courses for Students with Learning
Disabilities: Jackie Brown.
Needs assessment; individual support programme agreed; learning
support – notetakers, etc – and special equipment; personal welfare;
additional tutorials and alternative examination and assessment
arrangements; technical support. A taster experience is arranged pre-
application stage, to give students with disabilities the opportunity to
spend time at the college to see what it would be like to study there.
Support is reviewed every term.

## Home sweet home:
Accommodation is accessible to students with sensory and learning
disabilities. There are currently no specifically adapted flats for
students with mobility difficulties or for wheelchair users. Please
contact Alison Borg for more information about accessibility at the
college.

## Out and about:
College: There is a regular, free bus service linking the main
campuses and residential accommodation. There is also an
accessible minibus for students taking specialist programmes; taxis
are also used when appropriate. Dedicated parking spaces near both
accommodation and study areas.
Public transport: Quite a few of the local buses are accessible. The
nearest metro station is Central Street, Newcastle. The station and
metros are accessible, but this does depend on the accessibility of
the station you get off at or come from.

## Taking it easy:
At college: Catering is available in many college buildings, and all
facilities are accessible via lifts and/or ramps.
Locally: Newcastle has an indoor shopping centre with good
accessibility. There is a Shopmobility scheme. For more information
check www.ncle.gov.uk.

## And another thing ...

➡ The Rye Hill campus is on a steep gradient. Additional Support Services can arrange assistance for wheelchair users who require it. All buildings on the Rye Hill campus are accessible except the concert hall on the first floor of the Armstrong building and the dance/drama studios in the Centre for Performing Arts.

➡ Physical access information is available from Learning Support Service along with other information.

➡ Newcastle College employs teachers for D/deaf or hard of hearing students and qualified dyslexia support tutors. The college also has established links with RNIB, Community for Autistic People and various specialist colleges.

➡ Learning support staff have appropriate professional and specialist qualifications.

➡ For details on workshops, individual tutorials or group sessions in English, maths and IT contact the Skills for Life (basic skills) manager.

➡ Counselling and career services are open to all students but it is possible to arrange specialist careers guidance and counselling from staff who have experience of working with students with individual needs.

➡ Software for students with dyslexia.

➡ Notetakers/readers and communication support workers can be provided.

➡ CCTVs and software for blind computer users as well as a Braille embosser.

## The Disability Statement/Brochure:

Includes: Additional Support Services; assessment of needs; support available; other facilities and services; access; complaints and contacts.

## Local disability public service providers:

Please check www.ncle.gov.uk.

| University of Newcastle upon Tyne |
|---|

Newcastle upon Tyne NE1 7RU

*General Enquiries:*
Tel: 0191 222 6000
Fax: 0191 222 5594
Email: sro.enquiries@ncl.ac.uk

**Disability Officer: Sandra Chilton**
**Tel: 0191 222 7610**
**Fax: 0191 222 5539**
**Email: disability.unit@ncl.ac.uk**

Website: www.ncl.ac.uk

**sandra.chilton@ncl.ac.uk**
**Text: 0191 222 5545**

**Fields of study:**
Arts; biological and agricultural sciences; engineering; law and business; medical and biomedical sciences; physical sciences; social science.

➡ Part-time study: **There is only one part-time degree programme.**
➡ Distance learning: **No.**

**About the university:**
The University of Newcastle upon Tyne was founded in 1834 and is a single-site, 45-acre campus located in the heart of the city. The university is consistently in the top ten UK universities for its expenditure per student on libraries, computing facilities, language learning facilities and other academic services. The city's surrounding countryside has many designated areas of outstanding beauty. In addition to the relics of the Roman occupation, including Hadrian's Wall, there are many castles in the region.

Total number of students: 15,000 full-time students
Number of disabled students: 700

**Learning support staff and services:**
Disability Support Services
Full-time staff: Head of Service: Sandra Chilton; dyslexia adviser; disability coordinator (learning and teaching); sensory support adviser; project officer.
Part-time staff: technical adviser and two disability advisers (dyslexia).
Needs assessments; assistance with DSA applications; provision of auxiliary aids and services; advice and guidance; one-to-one/group tuition for students with dyslexia; screening programme; alternative examination, assessment and study arrangements; technical support – resources and tuition; support worker service; support service for students with mental health issues; involved with university policy regarding disability issues and raising disability awareness amongst staff and liaison with external organisations. Dyslexia assessments are paid for.

**Home sweet home:**
Some adapted accommodation for wheelchair users including wheel-in showers, adapted kitchen and accessible toilets.
Accommodation guaranteed for duration of student's course.

## Out and about:
University: There are some dedicated parking spaces near both accommodation and study areas.

Public transport: Train stations and some buses, trains and taxis are accessible to people who are wheelchair users. Some buses, trains, train stations and taxis are accessible to people with a visual impairment. A taxi scheme for disabled people operates in the area.

## Taking it easy:
At university: Sports facilities are only partially wheelchair accessible. The SU has a disability officer to facilitate social arrangements.

Locally: The city is flat and accessible. Some of the town's facilities are accessible and pavements are tactile.

## And another thing ...
➡ Financial assistance is given for psychologist assessments and screening.

## Local disability public service providers:
Disability North – 0191 284 6480.
RNIB Darlington.

---

### NEWI: North East Wales Institute of Higher Education

Plas Coch, Wrexham LL11 2AW

*General Enquiries:*
Tel: 01978 290666
Fax: 01978 290008
Email: k.mitchell@newi.ac.uk
Website: www.newi.ac.uk

**Disability Coordinator: Geoff Jenkins**
**Tel: 01978 293056**
**Fax: 01978 293254**
**Email: g.jenkins@newi.ac.uk**

## Fields of study:
Art and design; business; education and humanities; engineering; health and community studies; science and computing.

➡ Part-time study: **Yes.**
➡ Distance learning: **No.**

## About the institute:
North East Wales Institute of Higher Education (NEWI) is an associate college of the University of Wales and has two main campuses, Plas Coch and Regent Street, near to the centre of Wrexham, and is easily

accessible by road and rail. Wrexham is the largest town in north Wales, lying on the borders between England and Wales. Wrexham has recently had a considerable face-lift with new shopping centres opening in the centre and outskirts of town. Wrexham is placed between town and country, with Liverpool, Manchester and Snowdonia an hour's journey away.

| Total number of students: 5,800 | Number of disabled students: 450 |
|---|---|

## Learning support staff and services:
Learning Support
Each of NEWI's academic areas has a disability coordinator, in addition to the institute's Disability Coordinator, Geoff Jenkins and admin support, based in Information and Student Services.
Needs assessment; assistance of DSA applications and other funding including Access, Assembly Learning Grants and educational trusts; provision of auxiliary aids and services; advice and guidance; one-to-one/group tuition for students with dyslexia; alternative examination, assessment and study arrangements; support service for students with mental health issues; liaison with external organisations and IT support.

## Home sweet home:
Student Village is on the main campus, which is a flat terrain. Each hostel block has ground-floor fully adapted suites with wheelchair access and adapted kitchens.
Accommodation *cannot* be guaranteed for duration of student's course.

## Out and about:
Institute: Dedicated parking spaces near both accommodation and study areas. There is a minibus with lift available.
Public transport: The train stations, some buses, trains and taxis are accessible to wheelchair users. Some buses, trains, train stations and taxis are accessible to people with visual impairment.

## Taking it easy:
At institute: A new sports complex opened in 1999 that has full access and integrated facilities. The SU's disability, welfare and leisure officers organise accessible social events. There is a student disability officer and Students' Forum (Disabilities) self-help group.
Locally: The town centre is flat and accessible and readily reached from the main campus. Most town facilities are accessible. There is a Shopmobility scheme and the pavements are tactile. Contact the Wrexham Access Group.

## And another thing ...

➡ A Disability Working Group meets regularly to promote understanding and awareness across the institute of disability and learning difficulties.

➡ Room F is part of the library facility – it houses PCs, scanners, printer, CCTV, large monitors, specialist software, orthopaedic chairs, adjustable tables and adapted lighting. A 'buddy' system operates in the library.

➡ The library 'buddy' scheme consists of teaming up volunteer Information and Student Services staff members with individual students with disabilities, to help make full use of the library and IT facilities.

## The Disability Statement/Brochure:

Brief document covering: Policies; examinations and assessments; complaints and appeals; quality assurance and monitoring; staff development policy; existing provision; Disability Working Group; assessment; location and accommodation; Information and Student Services; future development and further information.

## Local disability public service provider:

Wrexham Access Group.

---

| Newman College of Higher Education |
|---|

Genners Lane, Bartley Green, Birmingham B32 3NT

*General Enquiries:*
Tel: 0121 476 1181
Fax: 0121 476 1196
Email: registry@newman.ac.uk
Website: www.newman.ac.uk

**Disability Officer: Lesley Plant**
**Tel: 0121 476 1181 ext: 2421**
**Fax: 0121 476 1196**
**Email: L.Plant@newman.ac.uk**

## Fields of study:

Art; biology; drama; early years studies; English; geography; history; information and communications technology; initial teacher training (primary and secondary); mathematics; PE and sports studies; PGCE; science.

➡ Part-time study: **Yes.**
➡ Distance learning: **Yes.**

## About the college:

A small college on the outskirts of one of the UK's major cities, Newman was founded in 1968 by the Catholic Education Council, to specialise in teacher training. Newman College consistently has one of the best employment rates for its students of any college or university in the UK.

The college is situated in a quiet, residential suburb in south-west Birmingham, right next to the city's green belt and opposite the reservoir and sailing club. The centre of Birmingham is a short drive away. The M5 motorway can also be reached in minutes. Birmingham and the Black Country are steeped in industrial history, and many of the glassware, jewellery, chocolate and leathermaking centres now have museums and visitor centres.

| Total number of students: 2,000+ | Number of disabled students: 77 |
|---|---|

## Learning support staff and services:

Student Support Services

Full-time staff: Student Support Services Manager: R. Gutteridge

Part-time staff: Disability Officer: Lesley Plant; Literacy Support Tutor (Basic Skills): Sarah Allsop; Careers and Placements Advisor: Rae Karimjee; Specialist Dyslexia Support Tutor: Lorraine Loveland-Armour; three other specialist dyslexia support tutors.

Needs assessment; assistance with DSA applications; provision of auxiliary aids and services; advice and guidance; one-to-one/group tuition for students with dyslexia; alternative examination, assessment and study arrangements; support service for students with mental health issues; provision of information about support services; staff training and development; extended library loans; arrangements for additional needs support from lecturers, tutors and relevant support staff; work placement advice and help and liaison with external organisations.

Student Support Services is housed on the second floor of the new library block, is easily accessible by lift for wheelchair users and has accessible toilets.

## Home sweet home:

A limited number of ground floor rooms available in the halls of residence for students with physical disabilities: by September 2005 there will be dedicated accommodation available.

## Out and about:

College: There are dedicated parking spaces for disabled drivers near both accommodation and study areas.

Public transport: Train stations and some buses, trains and taxis are accessible to people who are wheelchair users. All buses, trains, train stations and taxis are accessible to people with visual impairments.

**Taking it easy:**
At college: The catering and bar facilities are accessible as are the toilet facilities, sports hall and gym.
Locally: The city centre is hilly in places but mostly flat and accessible. The town facilities are accessible.

**And another thing …**

➡ The college has been working towards improving its buildings and physical space, inside and out, for students with disabilities. Ramps have been installed internally and externally, along with dropped kerbs externally, and yellow markings on all steps and handrails. Parking spaces are available for people with physical disabilities. Three lifts are planned along with additional internal ramps to improve accessibility. However, due to the physical aspects of the college site (built into the side of a hill), students with limited mobility may still experience some problems with access to some buildings on the campus. It is therefore advisable to contact the Disability Officer as early as possible to visit the site before accepting an offer.

➡ Specific support available in lectures may include the use of radio aids, special seating and table arrangements, enlarged print and overhead transparencies and handouts on appropriately coloured paper. Arrangements can be made for lectures to be taped and copies of lecture notes made available in advance or at the start of lectures. The college library's disability provision includes extended loan periods, different coloured paper for photocopying and text enlargement. Books can be ordered in large print, tape or Braille, if a course reading list is handed in to the librarian at the start of academic year, term 1. There is a well-resourced IT centre with network access to all students.

➡ The college has a portable hearing loop system available for students with a hearing impairment, plus Ezee loops and a Hearing Helper radio microphone pack. Specialist software is available for the use of students with dyslexia, and Dictaphones and other equipment are also available on loan from the Disabilities Officer.

➡ Students are strongly advised to disclose any disabilities they have that may affect their ability to study in any way, their performance, and/or their attendance on their application forms or to the Disability Officer before the start of term 1.

## The Disability Statement/Brochure:
Includes: Current policy; current provision – staff, specific support, IT provision; college facilities; student numbers and future development.

### Local disability public service providers:
Birmingham City Council 0121 303 9944.
RNIB 0845 702 3153.
Autism West Midlands 0121 450 7575.
Birmingham Association for Mental Health 0121 554 7123.
Birmingham Institute for the Deaf 0121 246 6100.
Birmingham Mencap 0121 427 5703.

---

| **Northern School of Contemporary Dance** |
| --- |

98 Chapeltown Road, Leeds LS7 4BH

*General Enquiries:*
Tel: 0113 219 3000
Fax: 0113 219 3030
Email: ann.miller@nscd.ac.uk
Website: www.nscd.ac.uk

**Learner Support Coordinator:**
**Pauline Fitzmaurice**
**Tel: 0113 219 3012**
**Fax: 0113 219 3030**
**Email: Pauline.fitzmaurice**
**@nscd.ac.uk**

### Field of study:
Contemporary dance.

➡ Part-time study: **No.**
➡ Distance learning: **No.**

### About the school:
The Northern School of Contenporary Dance (NSCD) offers a select group of students the opportunity to train in a conservatoire environment. NSCD was the first specialist dance school in the higher education sector and has recently spent £3.2 million developing new state-of-the-art dance training facilities that include six large studios and a theatre. The school is affiliated to the University of Leeds. The city of Leeds is the third largest metropolitan district in England and is easily accessible via the M1. With the cultural and social regeneration of Leeds, 2001 saw Nelson Mandela officially open Millennium Square.

| Total number of students: 134 |
| --- |
| Number of disabled students: 14% of student population |

## Learning support staff and services:

Learner Support Coordinator: Pauline Fitzmaurice. All staff are trained in basic methods of supporting students, particularly those with dyslexia, who make up the majority of students with individual needs at the school.

Arrangements for diagnostic testing for dyslexia with educational psychologist; one-to-one assistance; coaching session and drop-in session on Friday afternoons for general support needs; assistance with DSA applications; arrangement of support workers such as sign language interpreters.

Students work very closely with their personal tutors.

## Home sweet home:

The school provides no accommodation for any of its students. Over the summer holiday two days are spent working in conjunction with Unipoll house-hunting for students to find appropriate accommodation.

## Out and about:

School: There are no dedicated parking spaces.
Public transport: Local transport offers bus services with low-floor access for wheelchair users.

## Taking it easy:

At the school: There are no leisure facilities.
Locally: Leeds offers plenty of accessible sports, leisure centres and cinemas and has a compact and largely pedestrianised centre.

## And another thing ...

➡ The building is fully accessible for people with mobility disabilities and partially adapted for people with visual impairment. Three working areas are equipped with hearing loops for D/deaf and hard-of-hearing students.

➡ One studio and one seminar room are fitted with an induction loop.

➡ There is full wheelchair access throughout the building. The school houses a public theatre, which is also used by the students.

➡ There are accessible toilet and shower facilities.

➡ The school has the following facilities: specialist software for dyslexic students. Sign language interpreters, readers and notetakers can be arranged.

➡ All applicants are auditioned and the school operates an admission policy based on merit and the ability to benefit from, and be successful in, the programme of study. Students are in school from 9.30 to 5.30 Mondays to Fridays and sometimes at weekends as well. The courses are 75 per cent practical.

➡ Many of the school's students are from non-traditional HE backgrounds. They are offered places on the basis of their dance ability and the ability to benefit from the course of study, not on their academic ability.

➡ With the majority of students who are identified as having dyslexia the school works on the assumption that what is good for a dyslexic student will be good for all students, so, e.g., there is software suitable for students with dyslexia on all computers.

➡ All first-year students identified as having learning support needs are entitled to an automatic one-week extension, without penalty, to deadlines for written work. Additionally, the academic courses in year-one and two are tutored on a one-to-one basis. There are no exams. Second-year students with identified learning support needs can apply for an authorised extension to deadlines.

➡ All teaching staff are trained in basic strategies for enabling students with dyslexia and other learning difficulties to fully participate in the programme of study, and there is interest among staff in finding ways of minimising difficulties in order to enable students to succeed.

➡ See Laban Centre London entry.

## The Disability Statement/Brochure:
*Widening Participation Strategy 2001–2004*
Pages 8–11: Support and guidance for students enrolled on courses; course description and assignments; individual support; suitable support mechanisms for students with additional learning needs; supplementary studies; student review board; personal tutor; assessment handbook; profiles; careers; financial support and student feedback.

## Local disability public service providers:
Deaf Start is part of the Leeds Education Special Services: 0113 242 9111.
Leeds City Council: www.leeds.gov.uk.

## University of Northumbria at Newcastle

Newcastle City Campus, Ellison Place,
Newcastle upon Tyne NE1 8ST

*General Enquiries:*
Tel: 0191 232 6002
Fax: 0191 227 4017
Website: www.northumbria.ac.uk

**Senior Disabilities Adviser:**
**Karen Newton**
**Tel: 0191 227 3385**
**Fax: 0191 227 4553**
**Email: Karen.Newton@**
**northumbria.ac.uk**
**Text: 0191 222 1051**

**Fields of study:**
Arts; business and e-commerce; education; engineering, science and technology; English literature; health, social work and education; history; history and environmental studies; psychology; social sciences; sociology; tourism.

➡ Part-time study: **Yes.**
➡ Distance learning: **Yes.**

**About the university:**
The University of Northumbria only came into existence in 1992, but its roots stretch back to Newcastle's illustrious nineteenth-century past. Three years after its creation, Northumbria merged with two more local colleges, consolidating its position as one of the largest universities in the country. League tables in the *Sunday Times* and the *Daily Telegraph* in 2000 made Northumbria the leading new university. Northumbria stretches over the two counties of Northumberland and Durham where Hadrian's Wall, Lindisfarne and more castles and forts than in any other English county can be found. And yet in the middle of all this antiquity lies a city that has been voted among the top ten in the world for entertainment.

Total number of students: 21,000
Number of disabled students registered with Disabilities Service: approx. 750

**Learning support staff and services:**
Disabilities Services
Full-time staff: Senior Disabilities Adviser: Karen Newton; Disabilities Adviser (Mental Health); Associate Disabilities Adviser (Sensory Support); Associate Disabilities Adviser (Dyslexia); Dyslexia Support

Tutor and Support Worker Service Coordinator: Jayne Hey.
Part-time staff: 15 support workers.
Needs assessment; assistance with DSA applications and Hardship Fund; provision of auxiliary aids and services; advice and guidance; one-to-one/group tuition for students with dyslexia; alternative examination, assessment and study arrangements; support service for students with mental health issues; assisting with appropriate placement arrangements; support worker service (with University of Newcastle) and liaison with external organisations.

### Home sweet home:
The university has some accommodation adapted for wheelchair users, which is subject to availability and located in several of the halls of residence. Extra rooms for PAs are available. There are some adaptations for D/deaf or hard of hearing students. Further adaptations may be made.
Accommodation can be guaranteed for duration of student's course.

### Out and about:
University: Dedicated parking spaces near both accommodation and study areas.
Public transport: Trains, train stations, taxis, metro and some buses are accessible to people who are wheelchair users. All modes of public transport are accessible for people with visual impairments. WAV, Gateshead, taxi scheme for disabled people, operates in the area.

### Taking it easy:
At university: Sports centres and most bars are accessible. Some problems for electric wheelchair access to higher floors of SU although these should be addressed as a new lift is soon to be installed.
Locally: The city of Newcastle is committed to improving access within the city and is currently undertaking a programme to achieve this. The city centre is flat and accessible. Its facilities are mainly accessible and there is a Shopmobility scheme. The pavements are tactile.

### And another thing ...
➡ The Study Skills Centre is a learning resource established to aid students' study and learning and is able to give specialist help to students with dyslexia.
➡ There are four libraries – the City campus library has ramped access and a lift to all floors. The other libraries are also accessible.

➡ Specialist equipment: inducted loop system (in some lecture theatres); special headphones in the language labs; minicoms in each faculty office; minicom with associate disabilities adviser (sensory support); Braille notetakers; portable loop system; CCTV (Magni-Link Viewers) available for those with a visual impairment.

➡ JAWS and Supernova currently being networked throughout university, accessible via password.

➡ TextHELP and Inspirations are available in the Study Skills Centre.

➡ The leaflet 'Information Services for Library Users with Disabilities' outlines the support and facilities available in all the libraries and is available from the Disability Support Team in large print, Braille and audio copy form.

➡ The university has undertaken an access audit. Some buildings are accessible but the university intends to adapt other buildings in the future.

➡ Most rooms are wheelchair accessible. Prospective students who are wheelchair users are strongly recommended to visit prior to application to see if all areas they would need to access meet their needs.

➡ All buildings have wheelchair accessible toilets.

➡ Students showing a need for an educational psychologist's report on their dyslexia can apply to the Hardship Fund via a fast-track system.

➡ Member of Regional Transcription Consortium to provide fast and efficient transcription of materials.

## The Disability Statement/Brochure:

Statement includes: The university's current policy; examinations and assessments; quality assessment; external links; current provision; physical access; accommodation; specialist equipment; medical facilities; future development and contacts.

### Local disability public service provider:

There are a number of local disability/deaf services that can provide advice and practical support to disabled/deaf people, including Disability North, Castle Farm Road, Gosforth, Newcastle. The disabilities advisers can provide details.

| Norwich School of Art and Design |
| --- |

St George Street, Norwich, Norfolk NR3 1BB

*General Enquiries:*
Tel: 01603 610561
Fax: 01603 615728
Email: info@nsad.ac.uk
Website: www.nsad.ac.uk

**Learning Support Adviser: Jane Key**
**Tel: 01603 610561 ext 3083**
**Fax: 01603 615728**
**Email: j.key@nsad.ac.uk**

**Fields of study:**
Animation; art; craft; creative writing and cultural studies; design; design for publishing; graphic design; illustration; painting; photography; printmaking and photomedia; sculpture; textiles.

➡ Part-time study: **Yes.**
➡ Distance learning: **No.**

**About the school:**
Norwich School of Art and Design originated in 1845 and is an independent higher education institution in the university sector with a reputation for excellence. In the 2003 QAA's national Subject Review of art and design, the school achieved the highest award of 'broad confidence'. Located in the centre of Norwich, the school is housed in a number of buildings, some of historical interest. The city is less than two hours from London by train and is surrounded by beautiful countryside and miles of sandy beaches.

| Total number of students: 980 | Number of disabled students: 180 |
| --- | --- |

**Learning support staff and services:**
Learning Support Centre
Full-time staff: Learning Support Adviser: Jane Key.
Needs assessment arrangements; assistance with DSA applications; provision of auxiliary aids and services; advice and guidance; one-to-one tuition for students with dyslexia; screening for dyslexia; arrangement of assessments by an educational psychologist; personal learning plans; liaison with academic staff and liaison with external organisations.
Students with dyslexia may also be able to have additional tutorials from critical studies tutors.

**Home sweet home:**
The school has a house in the city centre that has been adapted to accommodate disabled students. It has wheelchair access and an

adapted kitchen and shower room; one room is equipped for a student who is D/deaf or hard of hearing. In addition the school has an allocation of rooms in the halls of residence belonging to City College Norwich, some of which have been adapted for use by disabled students.

Accommodation cannot be guaranteed for duration of student's course.

## Out and about:
School: There are no parking facilities for any students.
Public transport: Train stations, some buses, trains and taxis are accessible to wheelchair users.

## Taking it easy:
At the school: There are currently no facilities or services for the social support of disabled students. The SU and bar are on the top floor, which is not accessible to wheelchair users.
Locally: The city centre is hilly but mainly accessible. Most venues in Norwich are new and accessible. The Forum Central Library and Norwich Shopping Mall are accessible. Details of accessibility are given in the Norwich Access Group's *Guide to the City*. The pavements are tactile at pedestrian crossings.

## And another thing …
➡ Norwich School of Art and Design is housed in a range of buildings which date from the medieval period to the 1950s. The inaccessibility of some buildings may cause difficulties for wheelchair users or those with mobility difficulties. However, students with a variety of disabilities and special requirements have successfully studied at the school.
➡ The library is accessible to wheelchair users only on the ground floor.
➡ The lecture theatre is easily accessible to wheelchair users and it has a loop system for D/deaf students.
➡ The main reception and library desk have a loop induction system.
➡ The school is fully committed to continuing its policy of improving and extending access where practicable and to increasing awareness of the requirements of people with disabilities.

## Local disability public service providers:
Norfolk County Council, County Hall, Martineau Lane, Norwich NR1 2SQ, website: www.getphysical.socs@norfolk.gov.uk.
BBC Disability Norfolk Webpages:
www.bbc.co.uk/norfolk/you/access/disability/index.shtml.

| University of Nottingham |
|---|

University Park, Nottingham NG7 2RD

*General Enquiries:*
Tel: 0115 951 5151
Fax: 0115 951 3666
Website: www.nottingham.ac.uk

**Officer for Disability Issues:**
**Ellen Sanders**
**Tel: 0115 951 5766**
**Fax: 0115 951 4376**
**Email: studentsupport@**
**nottingham.ac.uk**
**Text: 0115 951 4378**

**Fields of study:**
Arts; education; engineering; law and social sciences; medicine and health studies; science.

➡ Part-time study: **Yes.**
➡ Distance learning: **Yes.**

**About the university:**
Nottingham was granted its Royal Charter in 1948, but the university originally started life in 1798, moving to its current site after the First World War. This large estate, 3 miles west of the city, was provided by Sir Jesse Boot, founder of the Boots Company. It has gradually expanded into today's 330-acre University Park campus. There are also campuses at Sutton Bonington and Jubilee. The Jubilee campus, which cost £50 million to build, opened in 1999. Nottingham is a cosmopolitan city and its central location offers good transport links to other major cities.

| Total number of students: 27,887 Number of disabled students: 1,294 |
|---|

**Learning support staff and services:**
There are currently two units:
The Office for Disability Issues, which deals with policy; queries from prospective students; accommodation and transport.
The Study Support Centre is an Access Centre.
Needs assessments; assistance with DSA applications and other sources of funding – British Council, research bodies, NHS; provision of auxiliary aids and services; advice and guidance; one-to-one/group tuition for students with dyslexia; alternative examination, assessment and study arrangements; timetabling arrangements; support service for students with mental health issues; liaison with external organisations.

## Home sweet home:

About 24 rooms available in halls and self-catering flats are adapted for wheelchair users, some with en-suite facilities. Rooms are provided for personal assistants where required. There are also rooms with flashing and vibrating fire alarms. Students with disabilities can expect the same level of support from hall wardens, tutors, managers and other staff. All rooms now have telephone points. Accommodation can be guaranteed for duration of student's course.

## Out and about:

University: Because of the hilly nature of the University Park campus the university has a designated minibus (which can accommodate three wheelchair users) to transport students with mobility difficulties around the campus. The minibus also runs between the University Park Jubilee and Sutton Bonington campuses. The bus is provided free of charge to eligible students. Free bus service for all students running between the three campuses. Dedicated parking spaces near both accommodation and study areas.

Public transport: Some buses, trains, train stations and taxis are accessible to wheelchair users and people with visual impairments. There are various taxi companies which provide training in a range of disability areas.

## Taking it easy:

At university: The same as for all other students, and discussion groups for D/deaf and dyslexic students. The SU runs a large number of clubs as well as a small theatre. There is also a nationally acclaimed art gallery and concert hall. The university has excellent and accessible sports facilities. There is also a swimming pool at the University Park campus with facilities for users who have a disability and a hoist for those who require it.

Locally: The city centre is hilly, though some parts are accessible. There is a Shopmobility scheme and some city faciliites are accessible. Some of the pavements are tactile. There is a local area disability guide.

## And another thing ...

➡ University Park campus covers a large, hilly, parkland site, which can be challenging for students with certain kinds of mobility impairments. Although most of the buildings date from the 1960s most teaching and residential buildings are now accessible to students who have a disability.

➡ Disability Action, in the SU, is a voluntary, student-run group that works to ensure fair and comprehensive provision for all students who have a disability, as well as raising awareness of disability issues among the student population.

➡ Each school has appointed a disability liaison officer who has specific responsibility for disability matters.

➡ Funding is available to improve generic services, e.g. equipment and capital works.

➡ The University is committed to implementing a programme of continuous improvement to all aspects of its provision.

## QAA Report: Paragraph 59, July 2001

The account explained that a new student administration system is being implemented that makes use of the recently developed Student Administration System for the University of Nottingham (SATURN). The account also set out the range of specialist support services for students covering: finances; counselling; study support; accommodation; health and child care; careers advice; disability support; and support for international students. There are close links between the university in the provision of this support and services offered by the students union. The account drew attention to the university's commitment to 'the need for equity of treatment for all students as paramount' and at the same time pointed to the university's vehicle for monitoring the operation of these services, which is through the annual collection of student opinion in the annual Omnibus Survey. The account explained that it had initiated a Student Omnibus Survey, which is organised by the university's survey unit, to collect general feedback from a random sample of students about the operation of its central services. After analysis the results are published and given wide circulation. The data is used to improve the performance of central services and also provides a benchmark against which to measure performance on an ongoing basis. During the visit the audit team came to understand that this was a powerful tool, which had potential for monitoring and enhancing quality. The university is therefore to be commended in general for the activities of its survey unit; and in particular for the implementation of the Student Omnibus Survey from which data can be used in the setting of benchmarks for the institution as a whole and that can monitor on a regular basis the quality and standards of the student experience. In points for commendation para 88 point v the audit team commends the university for the quality of student support services.

## The Disability Statement/Brochure:

Contents include: applications; campuses; services to support including learning experience; monitoring, current and future developments and statistics.

**Local disability public service providers:**
City of Nottingham Social Services.
Nottingham Leisure Services.

---

| **Nottingham Trent University** |
| --- |

Burton Street, Nottingham NG1 4BU

*General Enquiries:*
Tel: 0115 941 8418
Email: marketing@ntu.ac.uk
Website: www.ntu.ac.uk

**Service Coordinator: Chris Baxter**
**Tel: 0115 848 6163**
**Fax: 0115 848 6014/4371**
**Email: chris.baxter@ntu.ac.uk**
**Text: 0115 848 6163**

**Fields of study:**
Art and design; business; construction and the environment; economics and social sciences; education; engineering and computing; humanities; law; science and maths.

➡ Part-time study: **Yes.**
➡ Distance learning: **Yes.**

**About the university:**
The university comprises 26 academic departments, grouped into nine faculties. The City site, largest of the university's campuses, is conveniently situated in the heart of Nottingham. In total, over 70 per cent of the university's activities take place at the City site, which forms a self-contained quarter of Nottingham, intersected by a number of public highways. The Brackenhurst campus is 12 miles from the city centre. The Clifton campus is 4 miles from the city centre with easy access to the M1.

| Total number of students: 23,000 | Number of disabled students: 915 |
| --- | --- |

**Learning support staff and services:**
Student Support Services; Disability Support Services
Service Coordinator: Chris Baxter; Disability Officer: Phil Stephenson; dyslexia support specialists.
Aims to coordinate support and access arrangements across the university for students with disabilities and specific learning difficulties. A small resource base of equipment is available for people who are not able to access DSA; needs assessments carried out as a NFAC; advice and screening for students with dyslexia and referral, where

appropriate, to a chartered educational psychologist; individual support, usually one hour a week for students with specific learning difficulties; management of a Disability Support Workers Scheme, which supports workers for disabled students in HE by way of recruitment, training, monitoring and payment of support workers on behalf of individual students. Support workers include PAs, readers, notetakers, communication support workers, interpreters and mentors.

## Home sweet home:
There are seven wheelchair accessible bedspaces located on the City site or within easy driving distance of the city, and eight bedspaces that have been adapted for students who are D/deaf or hard of hearing (including flashing light doorbell and fire alarm alerts). Private sector accommodation, managed by the university under the Head Leasing Scheme, offers a further two wheelchair user accessible study bedrooms. Clifton campus offers one wheelchair accessible en-suite study bedroom. A further three bedspaces have been adapted for D/deaf or hard of hearing students. Accommodation facilities can also be made available for PAs. Accommodation is guaranteed for duration of the student's course.

## Out and about:
University: At present there are no arrangements for students with disabilities as regards university transport. Dedicated parking spaces near both accommodation and study areas.
Public transport: The City and Clifton campuses are served by regular bus services (some of which are wheelchair accessible) and wheelchair accessible taxi services.

## Taking it easy:
At university: All SU buildings are accessible to wheelchair users, with the exception of the Clifton executive office. The union encourages the involvement of disabled students and will make every effort to provide further additional assistance if required.
Locally: The city centre is variable in terms of its terrain, but is mostly accessible. There is a Shopmobility scheme. Pavements are tactile. Some of the city facilities are accessible. A local access guide is available from Nottingham City Council.

## And another thing ...
➡ Access for people with mobility disabilities is good along the pedestrian routes and fair to poor at the periphery of the City site due to hills and the number of kerbs. Some buildings on this site are inaccessible for wheelchair users.

➡ Work on a new Nottingham tramway through the City site (with a campus stop) will be complete in early 2004.

➡ The Clifton campus is based on flat land and benefits from a good network of wheelchair accessible roads and paths.

➡ Current building developments at the Clifton site include a new education block and a new 300-seat lecture theatre, designed to ensure accessibility. A lift was commissioned in 2003 for the Clifton campus, making it fully accessible.

➡ 73 per cent of general teaching rooms are now wheelchair accessible.

➡ Induction loops are now fitted to 18 lecture theatres and large conference rooms throughout both sites.

➡ Timetabling of rooms with specialised equipment, resources and access is in operation at the university.

➡ Software for students with visual impairment/dyslexia is not yet widely available.

➡ Full details of access are available from Student Support Services.

➡ A Pathways Programme is provided at Brackenhurst for students with learning difficulties or disabilities who wish to benefit from a programme that develops aspects of rural life and raises self-confidence.

➡ Communication and IT services offer technical solutions for, and provide support to, disabled students. C&IT intends to provide appropriate adaptive technology; access to the university's academic network; provision of learning support materials in large print or Braille; and individual technology needs assessments.

➡ C&IT and the libraries are accessible to wheelchair users.

## The Disability Statement/Brochure:
*Information for Applicants with Disabilities*
Contents include: Student profiles; services to support the learning experience; the university environment and monitoring and development.

## Local disability public service provider:
Nottingham City/County Council Social Services.

---

### Oak Hill Theological College
Chase Side, Southgate, London N14 4PS

*General Enquiries:*
Tel: 020 8449 0467
Fax: 020 8441 5996
Email: mailbox@oakhill.ac.uk
Website: www.oakhill.ac.uk

**Field of study:**
Theology.

➡ Part-time study: **Yes.**
➡ Distance learning: **Yes.**

| Total number of students: 150 | Number of disabled students: 6 |
| --- | --- |

**Learning support staff and services:**
There are no specific staff or services for students with disabilities.

**Home sweet home:**
Adapted en-suite bedroom with adapted shower and emergency assistance alarm. An extra room for a PA is available opposite this room. Accommodation may be guaranteed for duration of student's course, depending on the course undertaken.

**Out and about:**
College: Dedicated parking spaces near both accommodation and study areas.
Public transport: Some buses are accessible. Contact Access and Mobility for information on London's public transport services (see Directory).

**Taking it easy:**
At college: There is no SU or bar facilities.
Locally: Artsline publishes a range of guides on access in London (see Directory).

**And another thing ...**
➡ Arrangements for specialist facilities are made on an individual basis.
➡ Alternative assessment and examination arrangements can be made for students with dyslexia.

**Local disability public service provider:**
Chicken Shed Theatre: www.chickenshed.org.uk; info@chickenshed.demon.co.uk; tel: 020 8292 6161; text: 020 8350 0676, Chase Side, Southgate, London N 14 4PE.

## Open University

Head Quarters, Walton Hall, Milton Keynes MK7 6AA

Tel: 01908 653231
Fax: 01908 655072
Email: general-enquiries@open.ac.uk
Website: www.open.ac.uk

**Fields of study:**
Arts; business; education and language; educational technology; health and social welfare; knowledge of media; law; maths and computing; science; social sciences; technology.

➡ Part-time study: **Yes.**
➡ Distance learning: **Yes.**

**About the university:**
The Open University is Britain's largest university, designed to meet the needs of students wishing to study in their own homes or workplaces, in their own time, throughout the UK, Ireland and beyond. The courses use a range of teaching media: specially produced textbooks, TV and radio programmes, audio and video tapes, computer software and home experiment kits. Locally based tutors, a network of regional study centres in the UK and overseas and annual residential schools provide personal support for the students. Undergraduate courses are open to all regardless of qualifications. More than 150 OU courses use IT to enhance learning, which include virtual tutorials and discussion groups, electronic submission (and marking) of assignments, multimedia teaching materials and computer-mediated conferencing. Fourteen OU courses are delivered via the Internet. OU researchers have developed new applications of IT for learning: the 'virtual field trip' for level 1 science students, and an Internet stadium capable of hosting mass audience events with up to 100,000 participants.

Total number of students: 200,000+
Number of disabled students: 7,696

**Learning support staff and services:**
Each region has a Specialist Needs Team.
Information and advice; coordinating local services; provision of services to meet individual needs; alternative examination arrangements including home-based examinations.

The Study Support or Disability and Additional Requirements Team in the local regional centres can deal with queries. There is an evening out-of-hours advice line: 0870 333 1444.

## Residential courses:
Some courses have a compulsory residential school that can last up to a week. These are held at sites belonging to other institutions, so access and facilities vary. In order to meet the needs of disabled students the OU provides: assistants for mobility support and other purposes*; communication support facilities; a range of equipment, e.g. wheelchairs, cassette recorders and bed boards. It is important to discuss needs with the Regional Centre before making a course decision. Further information can also be found at: www.open.ac.uk/residential-schools.

## And another thing ...
➡ The OU has close links with the RNIB.
➡ There is a free residential study skills weekend held in Milton Keynes. The programme includes advice and preparation for studies with the student's particular needs in mind. There is an opportunity to try specialist equipment, talk to other students and tutors and to attend guest lectures as well as socialise.
➡ The OU may provide equipment, e.g. assistive hardware and software or human resources such as notetakers. Alternative formats, e.g. subtitled TV programmes, transcripts and audio cassettes, are available in some cases.
➡ For practical work the OU may provide a PA or academic assistant or other facilities for residential schools, but normally students will make their own arrangements for home-based practical work.
➡ A fact sheet is available on home learning.

## The Disability Statement/Brochure:
*Meeting Your Needs*
Information on how the OU can support students, by disability.

---

* Students may take a friend or relation familiar with the student's needs or the OU will provide a volunteer. Either way, the OU will bear the costs of the PA's meals and accommodation.

| University of Oxford |
|---|

University Offices, Wellington Square, Oxford OX1 2JD

*General Enquiries:*
Tel: 01865 270000
Fax: 01865 270708
Email: undergraduate.admissions
@ox.ac.uk
Website: www.ox.ac.uk

**Disability Adviser: Alex Larg**
**Tel: 01865 280562**
**Fax: 01865 280300**
**Email: Alex.Larg@**
**admin.ox.ac.uk**

## Fields of study:
Arts; biological sciences; classics; clinical medicine; mathematical sciences; medieval and modern languages and literatures; music; oriental studies; philosophy; physical sciences; physiological sciences; Portuguese; psychological studies; social studies; theology.

## About the university:
Oxford is Britain's oldest university and has been growing organically with its host city for over 800 years. University buildings are therefore located throughout the city and there is no campus or university precinct, although there are significant concentrations of university and college buildings in the city centre. Oxford has a collegiate system of 41 colleges.

| Total number of students: 16,400 |
|---|
| Number of disabled students: approx. 600 |

## Learning support staff and services:
Disability Coordinator: Deborah Popham; Disability Adviser: Alex Larg. Advice is available to students, departments and colleges. Needs assessment is in conjunction with colleges and departments; assistance and advice with application for DSA and other sources of funding; liaison with the learning resource centre coordinator for the university's computing services, to improve links between the two services. A series of fact sheets is available.

## Home sweet home:
Accommodation can be guaranteed for duration of student's course but this would need to be negotiated with the student's college.

## Out and about:
University: Help can be provided to arrange transport. Oxford is not a campus university, so parking can be difficult, but colleges and

university departments may be able to provide designated spaces for drivers with disabilities in addition to those areas provided by the local authorities.

Public transport: Some buses are wheelchair accessible. The railway station has level access to both platforms.

## Taking it easy:
At university: The University Sports Centre is not accessible to wheelchair users and neither is the SU. First-year students are allocated two second-year students to look after them.

Locally: There is a range of accessible facilities including shops, banks, doctors' surgeries and places of worship, although in many cases, because the city is so old, access is not ideal. Contact Oxford City Council for a guide.

## And another thing ...
➡ An advisory panel on disability aims to increase the accessibility of Oxford University.
➡ An access guide, detailing information on university and college facilities, is obtainable from the Admissions Office or disability staff.
➡ The university's libraries have a recording service to put books on to tape.
➡ Oxford has designated funds to assist disabled students, although these can be oversubscribed. One of these funds is for the support of students with disabilities who need equipment or other support. The university also has a Dyslexia Fund, which provides grants for assessments or specialist tutors.

## The Disability Statement/Brochure:
Brief statement, which does not cover leisure. The statement includes: Current policy; current provision; future activity and policy development. A4, seven pages.

## Local disability public service providers:
Deborah Whelen, Access Officer, Oxford County Council, 01865 815688.
Oxford Coalition of Disabled People.

## Oxford Brookes University

Oxford OX3 0BP

*General Enquiries:*
Student Recruitment
Tel: 01865 484848
Fax: 01865 483073
Email: query@brookes.ac.uk
Website: www.brookes.ac.uk

**Head of Student Disability
Service: Madeleine Collin**
**Tel: 01865 484658**
**Fax: 01865 484656**
**Email: mpcollin@brookes.ac.uk**

### Fields of study:
Architecture; art, publishing and music; biological and molecular sciences; business; computing and mathematical sciences; education; engineering; health care; hotel and restaurant management; humanities; languages; planning; social sciences and law.

➡ Part-time study: **Yes.**
➡ Distance learning: **Yes.**

### About the university:
Oxford Brookes University is based on three main campuses, with additional smaller sites at the John Radcliffe Hospital and Dorset House. Oxford Brookes has been rated top UK university five years in succession (*The Times Good University Guide*). Oxford Brookes pioneered modular degrees in the UK more than a quarter of a century ago.

Total number of students: 17,500   Number of disabled students: 1,200

### Learning support staff and services:
Student Disability Service; Student Services.
Head of Service: Madeleine Collin; Disabled Students' Adviser: Nicola Colao; Support Worker Scheme Manager: Beryl Henshaw; Dyslexia Support Tutor: Ginny Stacey; Dyslexia Adviser: Ros Stevenson. Providing assistance and advice from the pre-application stage onwards. Admission arrangements; personal and learning support; funding issues; advice on equipment purchase and alternative exam arrangements.
Ginny Stacey assists dyslexic students to develop their innate, non-language intelligences and explore how to use them as study skills.

### Home sweet home:
Self-catering accommodation suitable for independent wheelchair users is available in Warneford Hall, Paul Kent Hall and Morrell Hall in

Cheney Student Village. There is a high demand for these places. Accommodation can be guaranteed for duration of student's course.

## Out and about:
University: Dedicated parking spaces near both accommodation and study areas.
Public transport: There are low-level buses on university's inter-campus services and on local city services.

## Taking it easy:
At university: The SU and bar and all sports and recreational facilities are accessible.
Locally: Headington is a suburb of Oxford and is not pedestrianised. Oxford has a Shopmobility scheme and one area that is totally pedestrianised.

## And another thing ...
Students may use the Support Worker Scheme, which provides notetaking, domestic and personal assistance on a flexible basis, so that the amount and type of care can be negotiated by individuals according to their requirements – also the provision of specialist staff for D/deaf or hard of hearing students.

## QAA Report: Paragraph 62, March 2002
... Central services provide appropriate support for groups with particular needs such as students with disabilities, mature students, and international students. The audit team reviewed a range of publications aimed at such groups, and would commend the University on the clarity, coherence and accessibility of these publications.

## Local disability public service providers:
Access Office, Oxford County Council, 01865 815 688.
Oxford Coalition of Disabled People.

---

### University of Paisley

High Street, Paisley, Renfrewshire, Scotland PA1 2BE

*General Enquiries:*
Tel: 0141 848 3000
Fax: 0141 848 3333
Email: uni-direct@paisley.ac.uk
Website: www.paisley.ac.uk

**Disability Coordinator:**
**Tel: 0141 848 3518**
**Fax: 0141 848 3804**
**Email: specialneeds@**
**paisley.ac.uk**

## Fields of study:
Biological sciences; business management; chemical sciences; civil engineering; education; environmental sciences; health and social sciences; information and communication technologies; law; mathematical and physical sciences; mechanical engineering; media; psychology; real estate; science; science and technology; tourism.

➡ Part-time study: **Yes.**
➡ Distance learning: **Yes.**

## About the university:
The University of Paisley, founded in 1897, gained university status in 1992 and has three campuses. The Paisley campus is at the heart of the town (Scotland's largest town) and extends over 20 acres. The campuses at Ayr and Crichton are set in large areas of parkland.

| Total number of students: 8,000 | Number of disabled students: 600 |
|---|---|

## Learning support staff and services:
Full-time staff: special needs development adviser. Part-time staff: special needs coordinator; special needs secretarial assistant and a dyslexia support officer.
Advice and information; assistance with disability assessments; specialist dyslexia support; DSA application assistance; liaising with academic staff; raising staff awareness; alternative exam arrangements; help with accommodation, physical access problems and liaising with outside organisations; keeping university management informed of legislation relating to disabilities.

## Home sweet home:
Two adapted flats at Paisley campus with a second room for a PA. It is policy to try and accommodate the student for the duration of their course but this *cannot* be guaranteed.

## Out and about:
University: Specialist transport can be arranged for disabled students. Dedicated parking spaces near both accommodation and study areas. Public transport: Generally good access. Paisley Gilmour Street station has a lift from street level to station platform.

## Taking it easy:
At university: Sports centre accessible for wheelchair users. The SA is currently not accessible to wheelchair users, but a new SA with access is planned.

Locally: Access is generally good but there is no guide available.

### And another thing ...
➡ Arrangements can be made for overnight parking and battery charging of motorised wheelchairs.
➡ The university is represented on the working group of the SHEFC SUCCEEDS project, whose aim is to provide work experience for disabled people.
➡ Plans include the creation of a disability Website for use by both students and staff.
➡ Each school has a named member of staff responsible for liaising with specific needs students to ensure their needs are met.

### The Disability Statement/Brochure:
Includes: policy, pre-entry guidance; admission; facilities; student support services; academic support; sports and recreation; finance; future activity and policy development; special needs contact. Available on disk.

### Local disability public service provider:
Renfrewshire Disability Resource Centre, 0141 848 1123.

---

| University of Plymouth |
|---|

Drake Circus, Plymouth PL4 8AA

*General Enquiries:*
Tel: 01752 600600
Fax: 01752 232141
Email: admission@plymouth.ac.uk
Website: www.plymouth.ac.uk

**Disability Coordinator: Sarah Warn**
**Tel: 01752 232289**
**Fax: 01752 232279**
**Email: s.warn@**
**plymouth.ac.uk**
**Text: 01752 232278**

### Fields of study:
Arts and education; business; human sciences; land, food and leisure; medicine; science; technology.

➡ Part-time study: **Yes.**
➡ Distance learning: **No.**

### About the university:
The University of Plymouth, with an educational history dating back to 1825, is in partnership with many local colleges including Bicton, City

of Bristol, Cornwall, Duchy, East Devon, Exeter, Highlands, North Devon, Penwith, Plymouth College of Art and Design, Schumacher, Somerset College of Arts and Technology, South Devon, St Austell, Truro and Weymouth. The university has been chosen by the British government to run the first new undergraduate medical school to be established in the country for 30 years – the Peninsula Medical School – a joint collaboration with the University of Exeter. Plymouth is the largest city on the south coast and is the industrial, economic and cultural hub of the south-west peninsula.

**Learning support staff and services:**
Disability ASSIST Services (DAS)
Eleven full-time and eight part-time members of staff.
Provide support for students with disabilities and/or dyslexia.

**Home sweet home:**
Accessible accommodation for students is available.
Accommodation *cannot* be guaranteed for duration of student's course.

**Out and about:**
University: Dedicated parking spaces near both accommodation and study areas.
Public transport: There are low-floor buses with extra-wide seats and seatbelts.

---

### University of Portsmouth

University House, Winston Churchill Avenue, Portsmouth PO1 2UP

*General Enquiries:*
Tel: 023 9284 8484
Fax: 023 9284 3082
Email: info.centre@port.ac.uk
Website: www.port.ac.uk

**Disability Coordinator: Gail Hine**
**Tel: 023 9284 3462**
**Fax: 023 9284 3460**
**Email: disability@port.ac.uk**
**Text: 023 9284 3462**

**Fields of study:**
Business; environment; humanities and social sciences; science and technology.

➡ Part-time study: **Yes.**
➡ Distance learning: **Yes.**

**About the university:**
The University of Portsmouth was inaugurated in 1992 and is now at the forefront of a rapidly changing and thriving city. Portsmouth offers a modern and diverse campus and is situated at the heart of the city and adjacent to over 4 miles of coastline. The university has invested close to £1 million on access improvements to its estate during 2003 and is embarking on the expenditure of a further £1.5 million on premises and equipment over the next two years.

---

Total number of students: 18,568
Number of disabled students: 1,066

---

**Learning support staff and services:**
Disabilities Advice Centre
Full-time staff: Manager: Bob Belcher; Disability Coordinators: Gail Hine and Pauline Hunter; Administrative Assistant: Sarah Harkmett; Study Skills Tutors: Martyn Stahl (IT) and Hillary Corr.
Part-time staff: Study Skills Tutor: Kathy Mather; Administrator: Kay Bennett.
Services include: Needs assessments; assistance with DSA applications, Access, Hardship funds and charitable trusts; provision of auxiliary aids and services; advice and guidance; one-to-one/group tuition for students with dyslexia; support service for students with mental health issues; advice on university or premises; IT provision; policies; regulators; reasonable adjustments of all types in all contexts and liaison with external organisations.
The university is committed to providing equal opportunities for all its students, and aims to ensure disabled students attain their full potential. The Disability Advice Centre can offer advice and referral on every aspect of student life, including; psychological assessment, computer familiarisation, hearing loops and specialist tutors. There is a dedicated private room where individual needs can be discussed and facilities arranged. Friendly and supportive staff are available to assist you with any questions or anxieties that may arise throughout your student career.

**Home sweet home:**
Opened in September 2003, the brand-new James Watson Hall is located in the heart of Portsmouth's vibrant urban campus. Student en-suite study rooms accessible to people who are wheelchair users are provided across the campus in both catered and self-catered halls. All of these rooms have adapted en-suite shower and toilet facilities, and height-adjusted basins and worktops.
Accommodation can be guaranteed for all students.

## Out and about:

University: Dedicated parking spaces allocated on the majority of sites, including near accommodation and study areas. There is also an intersite bus that is wheelchair accessible.

Public transport: All buses, trains, train stations and taxis are accessible to people who are wheelchair users and/or who have visual impairments. The local bus company is First Provincial, which has accessible transport on some routes. The local train company is South West Trains. There are two train stations, Portsmouth & Southsea (providing access to the main shopping area) and Portsmouth Harbour (providing access to the Gosport Ferry and Isle of Wight Ferry). Aqua Cars and Streamline are taxi schemes for disabled people operating in the area.

## Taking it easy:

At university: The university's new purpose-built Student Centre is a top venue for nightlife and music on the south coast. All refectories and coffee shops are wheelchair accessible, with non-slip floor surfaces and vending machines with practical coin mechanism and selection buttons. The main university library, situated in the beautiful Ravelin Park, was refurbished in 2003 and provides all students with the perfect environment to relax and study.

Locally: The main shopping area is pedestrianised and Portsmouth is fairly flat. The train station is only minutes away. Promenades have been created around the harbour and the Gunwharf Quays. There is a wide selection of restaurants, pubs and clubs to suit all tastes, with excellent resources for people with disabilities. Portsmouth's Historic Dockyard and many other attractions provide high levels of access and additional support so that people can make the most of their visit. In addition, there is a local area access guide that can be obtained from the Tourist Information Centre, and Portsmouth City Council's Leisure Service has also produced a guide for people with disabilities covering leisure facilities in the city.

## And another thing ...

➡ The Student Finance Centre team can give advice on benefit entitlement and DSA. Help can be provided with the cost of a dyslexia assessment through the Access to Learning Fund. The Centre also holds information on trusts and charities that accept applications from disabled students. The Student Finance Team is available to assist and advise students before, during and after their course. Further information and application forms are available from the Disability Adviser in Student Advice Services.

➡ In 2003, Portsmouth University unveiled an additional sports hall, following a £1 million refurbishment to provide state-of-the-art sports and gym facilities. The gym equipment is approved by the 'inclusive fitness initiative' and includes both cardiovascular and strength equipment. The staff are specially qualified to advise on specific needs, including loss of limb, quadriplegia, obesity, epilepsy and for people who are D/deaf or hard of hearing and/or visually impaired. The inclusive gym equipment provides a fitness programme that can be tailor-made to individual requirements.

## The Disability Statement/Brochure:
*Information for Students with Disabilities*
Includes: Applications; facilities and equipment; access; support; study, assessments and exams; financial support; monitoring; future developments; contacts.

## Local disability public service providers:
The Dove Centre in Portsmouth.
Portsmouth City Council has a Disability Forum.

## Queen Margaret University College
Corstorphine Campus, Edinburgh EH12 8TS

*General Enquiries:* Admissions
Tel: 0131 317 3000
Fax: 0131 317 3248
Email: admissions@qmuc.ac.uk
Website: www.qmuc.ac.uk

**Access and Community Development Officer:**
**Jacqui Skelton**
**Tel: 0131 317 3163**
**Fax: 0131 317 3185**
**Email: mwilkinson@qmuc.ac.uk**

## Fields of study:
Business and management; communication and information; health; social science; theatre arts.

➡ Part-time study: **Yes.**
➡ Distance learning: **No.**

## About the college:
Queen Margaret University College is located on three campuses. The main campus at Corstorphine is about 4 miles west of Edinburgh; the second campus is at Leith. The third campus is a new state-of-the-art International Drama Centre at the Gateway Theatre, which is a

mere stone's throw from Edinburgh's city centre. Edinburgh is an exciting city with easy access to all parts of Scotland and its spectacular scenery.

| Total number of students: 3,500 | Number of disabled students: 210 |
| --- | --- |

## Learning support staff and services:
Department of Educational Needs
Each department has a special needs coordinator who acts as the first point of contact for students on disability issues, which include: assessment of needs; DSA applications and liaison with admissions and other staff in the relevant department.
Part-time Access and Community Development Officer who has administrative support.
Advise; liaise with external bodies on current disability issues; liaise and coordinate with departmental special needs coordinators and arrange meetings and training events.

## Home sweet home:
Two rooms at the Corstorphine campus, which are wheelchair accessible and on the ground floor. Facilities include widened doorways, adapted kitchens with easy-access sinks and cupboards and a 'wheel-in' shower. An extra room may be available for a personal assistant. Security staff at the Corstorphine campus are trained to deal with emergencies. They will provide assistance in the event of an emergency. It is aimed to address further adaptations to accommodate individual needs, e.g. clearer signage, removing obstructions, flashing light linked to the fire alarm, vibrator pad alarm or flashing light for personal doorbell.
Accommodation can be guaranteed for duration of student's course.

## Out and about:
University: University college staff are happy to help sort out any difficulties regarding travelling between campuses.
Dedicated parking spaces near both accommodation and study areas.
Public transport: Most of the buses are accessible for wheelchair users. Details of bus routes to all campuses are available from Queen Margaret University College reception.

## Taking it easy:
At university: There is a dyslexic students' support group. The swimming pool at the Corstorphine campus is not accessible to students with mobility difficulties.

Locally: Edinburgh is accessible and there is a guide available.
Contact the Access and Community Development Officer for further
details.

## And another thing ...
➡ Significant improvements to access were made during the year
   1995/6, which are continually reassessed.
➡ The University is a member of EASTDC (East of Scotland Disability
   Coordinators Consortium).
➡ There are special needs coordinators at both libraries.
➡ Future developments include producing general leaflets for all
   visitors to each campus, including a map, information about
   parking, public transport and access for disabled visitors.
➡ The University College Fund can be accessed to provide financial
   assistance to those students who are not eligible for DSA.

## The Disability Statement/Brochure:
Contains: Staff; campus accessibility; admissions; accommodation;
academic support; complaints and appeals; staff development; library
and information technology centre support provision; student support
services; DSA; future developments and contacts.

## Local disability public service providers:
Lothian Accessibility.
Lothian Community Transport Services.
Grapevine.

| Queen Mary, University of London |
| --- |

Mile End Road, London E1 4NS

*General Enquiries:*                    **Disability Coordinator: Val Morgan**
Tel: 020 7882 5000                             **Tel: 020 7822 3132**
Fax: 020 7882 3617                             **Fax: 020 7882 3617**
Email: welfare@qmul.ac.uk          **Email: v.a.morgan@qmul.ac.uk**
Website: www.qmul.ac.uk

## Fields of study:
Biological sciences; business studies; chemistry; computer science;
e-commerce and computing; economics; electrical engineering;
engineering; English and drama; film studies; geography; history; law;
materials; mathematical sciences; medical-related subjects; medicine
and dentistry; modern languages; physics; politics.

Queen Mary, University of London

➡ Part-time study: **Some.**
➡ Distance learning: **No, not for undergraduates.**

## About the college:
Part of the University of London, Queen Mary is one of the largest
colleges and one of only a few campus universities in central London.
Queen Mary's campus is only a few hundred yards from the bustle of
Mile End. Although some college buildings date back to the 1880s
the campus has benefited from substantial investment and expansion
in recent years.

| Total number of students: approx. 10,000 |
| --- |

## Learning support staff and services:
Full-time staff: Disability Coordinator: Val Morgan, based in the Advice
and Counselling Service.
Part-time staff: dyslexia coordinator, administrator and several
dyslexia tutors based in the Learning Support Service, part of the
Learning Development Unit (LDU).
Provision of support via dyslexia tutors, notetakers, campus support
workers, readers, etc.; advice and support on a range of issues
including alternative exam and study arrangements; specialist
equipment or assistance; possible funding sources.
The range of Queen Mary's disability and dyslexia resources is
detailed on the college Website.

## Home sweet home:
Catering is offered in some accommodation and there are wheelchair
accessible rooms. PAs can be accommodated in adjacent rooms, and
some kitchens and bathrooms are adapted. There is Internet
access/phone lines. Accommodation guaranteed for duration of
student's course.

## Out and about:
At college: There are dedicated parking areas near both the
accommodation and study areas.
Public transport: There are some local low-floor buses. No lifts at
local tube stations, Stepney Green/Mile End. *Access to the
Underground – Tube Access* is a guide map available from
underground stations or telephone 020 7222 1234. Contact Access
and Mobility for further information on London's public transport
services (see Directory). Taxicard and Freedom Card operate a taxi
scheme for disabled people in the area.

**Taking it easy:**
At college: Bars, sports facilities as for student population as a whole. Locally: The city centre is flat and some facilities are accessible. Pavements are tactile. For more information contact the Access officer (see below); also Artsline publishes a number of access guides to London (see Directory).

## QAA Report: Paragraphs 37, 74 and 75, March 2001
Admission to taught programmes … The college has recently approved an internal code of practice for the admission of students with a declared disability to enable such applications to be handled fairly.

The college has put particular effort into support for students with disabilities including dyslexia and other special needs, and the college's recently agreed Statement on Disability is consistent with the precepts of the QAA Code of Practice on students with disabilities, which came into force in December 2000. A disability coordinator based in Advice and Counselling Service was appointed in 1999. Advice and support for students begins at the applications and admissions stage to ensure that each individual student's needs are met and that academic departments are supported in meeting these needs.

The account described the support LDU offers students with special learning needs, including specialist tutorial support for students with dyslexia and other learning difficulties; notetakers; readers; transcription facilities and so on; for students with visual and hearing impairment and assistance for students with mobility difficulties. The college is commended for its thorough approach to reviewing its arrangements for supporting students with disabilities and special learning needs for consistency with the precepts of the QAA Code of Practice on students with disabilities.

Points for commendation (no iii). Its thorough approach to reviewing its arrangements for supporting students with disabilities and special learning needs in the light of the precepts of the QAA Code of Practice (paragraph 75).

## Local disability public service provider:
Contact the Access officer, 020 7332 1995, for information on accessibility of area.

## Queen's University Belfast

Belfast BT7 1NN, Northern Ireland

*General Enquiries:*
Tel: 028 9033 5081
Fax: 028 9024 7895
Email: admissions@qub.ac.uk
Website: www.qub.ac.uk

**Disability Services Coordinator:**
**Linda Maguire**
**Tel: 028 9027 3225**
**Fax: 028 9033 5375**
**Email: disability.office@qub.ac.uk**

### Fields of study:
Agriculture and food science; education; engineering; humanities and social sciences; law; medicine and health sciences; sciences.

➡ Part-time study: **Yes.**
➡ Distance learning: **Yes.**

### About the university:
The university's charter of 1908 guaranteed women equal eligibility to hold any office and enjoy any advantage at Queen's – 12 years before women were admitted to Oxford and a full decade before they were given the vote. The Belfast Festival at Queen's is the showcase of the performing and visual arts that, over the past 40 years, has grown larger in scope and size than any other British or Irish festival with the exception of the Edinburgh Festival. Near to Queen's is the Ulster Museum and Art Gallery, set in the Botanic Gardens.

Total number of students: 23,000   Number of disabled students: 535

### Learning support staff and services:
Disability Services
Disability Services Coordinator: Linda Maguire; disability officer; research assistant; one part-time clerical officer; one full-time clerical officer.
Arrangement of support workers; assistance with application for DSA; liaising with faculty staff to ensure they are aware of the individual's requirements.

### Home sweet home:
The university has a number of rooms designed to meet the accommodation needs of students with a wide range of disabilities. Accommodation includes wheelchair accessible, lowered-level kitchen units and rooms for D/deaf or hard of hearing students with flashing fire alarms, etc. It should be noted that students are advised

to contact Disability Services prior to entry to ensure their accommodation needs can be met.
Accommodation can be guaranteed for duration of student's course.

## Out and about:
University: Disability Services will apply for funding for wheelchair accessible taxis through DSA. Dedicated parking spaces near both accommodation and study areas. Parking permits can be arranged through Disability Services.
Public transport: It is the opinion of Disability Services that much work needs to be done to make the transport system fully accessible.

## Taking it easy:
At university: Students are encouraged to participate in over 150 clubs and societies. The university is also in a prime location with a wide range of social venues nearby.
Locally: Many of the main facilities within the city are accessible. Disability Services strongly advise that contact be made with them in advance for specific details.

## And another thing ...
➡ The age and design of some of the buildings could cause difficulty with physical access. It is the policy of the university that students should contact the Disability Services to discuss their requirements before entry. The university will try to meet individual needs by moving classes to accessible venues.
➡ Disability Services will try to arrange sign language interpreters when required by students, depending on availability.

---

## Ravensbourne College of Design and Communication
Walden Road, Chislehurst, Kent BR7 5SN

*General Enquiries:*
Tel: 020 8289 4900
Fax: 020 8325 8320
Email: info@rave.ac.uk
Web: www.rave.ac.uk

**Student Welfare Officer**: Sue Cowan
**Tel: 020 8289 4982**
**Email: s.cowan@rave.ac.uk**

## Fields of study:
Broadcasting; CAVE (constructed and virtual environments); fashion; moving image design; visual information design and interactive digital media.

**About the college:**
Ravensbourne is a relatively small, specialist university sector college, located on a single-site campus in south-east London. Ravensbourne College has been purpose-built as a design and broadcasting college. The buildings are light and spacious and the open-plan studios are large and airy. The college is affiliated to the University of Sussex, which validates all its undergraduate and postgraduate programmes. The mission of the college is to 'creatively apply digital technology to design and communication'.

---

Total number of students: over 1,000
Number of disabled students: 15%

---

**Staff and services:**
Student Services
Full-time staff: Student Welfare Officer: Sue Cowan.
Needs assessments; assistance with DSA applications, Access and Hardship Funds; advice and guidance; one-to-one group tuition for students with dyslexia; alternative examination, assessment and study arrangements; support service for students with mental health problems; organise a personal learning needs plan; provision of necessary equipment where possible; arrange diagnostic assessment through an educational psychologist for students who might have dyslexia (and meet cost where possible); conduct or arrange Study Aids and Study Strategies Assessments (SASSA) with advice on support, equipment and training; organise support workers and liaison with external organisations.

**Home sweet home:**
There are 24 houses and a bungalow. One of these houses is fully equipped for students with disabilities. Contact the Accommodation Officer to reserve a place.

**Out and about:**
College: Dedicated parking spaces near study areas.

**Taking it easy:**
At college: The student refectory and bar are both fully accessible.

**And another thing ...**
➡ The buildings on campus are mainly accessible to people with mobility difficulties. Adjustments will be made where reasonable.
➡ The college has recently improved physical access to its buildings, with the introduction of a ramp to facilitate access to all ground-

floor rooms and a passenger lift to provide access to the upper floor. Arrangements for access to workshop facilities for those with mobility difficulties will need to be assessed on an individual basis.

➡ Ravensbourne College recognises that a coordinated approach is required to achieve successful provision for students with disabilities. Attention is given to a range of aspects of the college's work, including curriculum design, assessment strategies, strategies for improvements to the physical environment and staff development.

➡ The college will endeavour to consider alternative modes of delivery where a student may not be able to participate fully in some components of their programme.

➡ The student counsellor is available to support students in developing strategies for overcoming a range of difficulties. The student counsellor can also offer initial assessment of needs for any student seeking to establish whether or not they are experiencing symptoms of dyslexia.

➡ The college has an ongoing programme of staff development in the area of dyslexia to ensure all staff are equipped with the skills and knowledge to offer support and advice to dyslexic students. Students with dyslexia will therefore receive support from their course tutors.

➡ The college will arrange for formal assessments to take place and will assist students with the cost.

➡ The college is a member of a Consortium of Arts and Design Institutions in the South East (CADISE). Ravensbourne is committed to making full use of the potential to develop its provision that is presented by this collaborative relationship and will explore areas of enhancement related to provision for disabled students.

## The Disability Statement/Brochure:

The information covered includes: Access; facilities and equipment; student support; assessment and examinations; financial information; enhancing provision; future plans and contact details. Available on: www.rave.ac.uk/about/disability.html.

| University of Reading |
|---|

Whiteknights, PO Box 217, Reading RG6 6AH

*General Enquiries:*                    **Special Needs Coordinator:**
Tel: 0118 987 5123                           **Tel: 0118 931 8115**
Fax: 0118 931 4404                          **Fax: 0118 987 4722**
Website: www.reading.ac.uk   **Email: k.h.dickinson@reading.ac.uk**

## Fields of study:
Education and community studies; letters and social sciences; life sciences; science; urban and regional studies.

➡ Part-time study: **Yes.**
➡ Distance learning: **No.**

## About the university:
Founded in the nineteenth century, the University of Reading has two campuses, one in the middle of England's 'silicon valley' – a competitive business centre – and the other set in the Thames Valley region between London and Oxford. The university boasts 4,600 study bedrooms.

| Total number of students: 12,000    Number of disabled students: 400 |
|---|

## Learning support staff and services:
Full-time special needs coordinator; full-time and part-time study adviser.
Arrangements for academic support provision; assistance with DSA applications, etc.; assessment and ongoing support for dyslexia.
Each department has its own disability representative.

## Home sweet home:
Several of the halls of residence have study bedrooms adapted for wheelchair users (with en-suite adapted shower rooms) and for D/deaf or hard of hearing students (Deaf Alerter fire alarm). Minor adaptations can be made where necessary and a room can be provided nearby for a personal assistant – who will be charged at the student rate.
Accommodation guaranteed for duration of student's course.

## Out and about:
University: Dedicated parking spaces near both accommodation and study areas. The SU operates a regular minibus service between the

Whiteknights and Bulmershe Court campuses. The current minibus can be accessed by students with mobility difficulties.
Public transport: Readibus 'Dial-a-Ride' service. Bookings must be made on previous day.

**Taking it easy:**
At university: Most facilities open to all students are accessible to those with disabilities.
Locally: Good access. Access guide available from Reading Borough Council.

**And another thing ...**
➡ Information leaflet available for students with mobility difficulties regarding access to buildings and facilities on campus.
➡ Regular surveys on the university's disability provision are carried out among students with disabilities. Their responses help to prioritise the university's programme of improvements in accessibility and support systems.
➡ Students with disabilities who are not eligible for DSA may be able to get a small grant from the John Hayes Memorial Fund.
➡ A limited number of items of equipment are available for loan from the special needs coordinator, including laptop computers, tape recorders and radio and conference microphones.
➡ ReadiAccess is an occasional newsletter that gives students news of developments relating to disability provision within and outside the university.
➡ Plans include improving the range of IT equipment and extending disability awareness training.

## The Disability Statement/Brochure:
Concise document, does not include information about leisure or the local area. Contents: Policy; application; arrival at Reading; physical environment; facilities and equipment; health, welfare and advice; your future; funding; monitoring provision; proposed developments; contact details.

**Local disability public service provider:**
Reading Borough Council, Civic Centre, Reading RG1 7TD; 0118 939 0900; Text: 0118 939 0700.

## Robert Gordon University
School Hill, Aberdeen AB10 1FR

*General Enquiries:*
Tel: 01224 262000
Fax: 01224 263000
Email: admissions@rgu.ac.uk
Web: www.rgu.ac.uk

**Disability Advisers: Annette
Davidson and Lorraine Grant
Tel: 01224 262142/262102
Fax: 01224 262029
Email: disability@rgu.ac.uk**

**Fields of study:**
Business and management; design and technology; health and social
care.

Part-time study: **Yes.**
Distance learning: **Yes.**

**About the university:**
The university was named after Robert Gordon, the noted
cartographer who put Scotland on the map in Blaeu's Atlas in 1654.
The university is a leader in the field of e-learning via the Virtual
Campus and award-winning Faculty Intranets. The Aberdeen Business
School is part of the Robert Gordon University (RGU). The location of
the university in the oil capital of Europe is reflected in a range of
commercial activities and in the Offshore Management, which is
partly industry funded.

Total number of students: 10,000   Number of disabled students: 506

**Disability staff and services:**
Disability Advisory Service based in the Study Support Centre, St
Andrew's Street.
Full-time staff: Disability Adviser: Annette Davidson; Assistant
Disability Adviser: Lorraine Grant; Dyslexia/Writing Skills Tutor:
Catherine Samiei; Study Support Centre Manager: Chetna Patel;
Maths and IT Tutor: John Little.
There is also a disability contact in each school.
Provision of auxiliary aids and services; advice and guidance; one-to-
one/group tuition for students with dyslexia; alternative examination,
assessment and study arrangements; negotiate with academic and
support staff to meet students' needs; arrange for copies of lecture
notes and permission to tape lectures if appropriate; arrange for the
loan of specialist equipment; dyslexia pre-screening and advice about
obtaining an assessment report from an educational psychologist;

support offered in IT, maths and statistics as well as in use of enabling technology; support service for students with mental health issues and liaison with external organisations.

Enabling technology (such as magnification, mind mapping and proofreading) is available in the Study Support Centre, each of the site's libraries and at various locations at the Garthdee site.

## Home sweet home:
There is student accommodation at RGU that is accessible to students who are wheelchair users (including wheel-in showers and adapted kitchens), visually impaired or D/deaf or hard of hearing. Individual adaptations can be made when necessary, e.g. moving sockets, raising bed heights, vibrating fire alarms, lighting etc. Accommodation can be guaranteed for the duration of the student's course.

## Out and about:
University: Dedicated parking spaces near both accommodation and study areas.

Public transport: Train stations and some trains, buses and taxis are accessible to people who are wheelchair users. Some buses, trains, train stations and taxis are accessible to people with visual impairments. Aberdeen City Council Taxicard Scheme operates in the area.

## Taking it easy:
At university: There are no accessible sports facilities and the SU bar is on the first floor. A lift is being built for the SU which is due to be completed by autumn 2004. New construction of the sports facilities began in autumn 2003.

Locally: The city-centre sites are in a flat area, but the Garthdee site is on a river bank and much steeper. The majority of the buildings at this site are new and therefore have ramps, etc. and there is a walkway between each of the buildings. There are tactile pavements all around the city-centre site and a Shopmobility scheme.

## QAA Report: Paragraph 58, January 2002
At the time of the visit, the University had in excess of 350 students with recognised special needs. The University has appointed an Adviser to Students with Disabilities and written guidance has also been made available on the intranet. The institution's *Account* stressed the University's commitment to improving support for students with disabilities and noted that it was participating in two SHEFC funded projects. While considerable effort has been invested

in making buildings safe and accessible, in raising staff and management awareness of disability issues, and in mapping 'compliance' against QAA's *Code of practice* on students with disabilities, the University recognised in its *Account* that 'further developments across all areas of the University' will be necessary in order to satisfy the QAA *Code*. It has accordingly established a Disabilities Working Party to formulate an appropriate action plan. From the evidence available to it, the audit team was satisfied that the University was giving appropriate recognition to the needs of students with special needs and was making appropriate progress in providing for disabilities issues.

**Local disability public service providers:**
Aberdeen Action on Disability.
Aberdeen and North East Deaf Society.
Grampian Society for the Blind

---

## Roehampton, University of Surrey

Roehampton Lane, London SW15 5SJ

*General Enquiries:*
Tel: 020 8392 3000
Fax: 020 8392 3470
Email: enquiries@roehampton.ac.uk
Website: www.roehampton.ac.uk

**Disability Officer/
Dyslexia Coordinator:
Tel: 020 8392 3113/
020 8392 3403
Fax: 020 8392 3431/
020 8392 3735
Email: disabilities@
roehampton.ac.uk
RED@roehampton.ac.uk**

**Fields of study:**
Anthropology; art for public space and art history; biological studies; business; childhood and society; classical civilisation; cultural studies and politics; ecology and conservation; education; English; environmental studies/science; film and TV studies; French and Spanish; geography and history; health; human resource management; humanities; marketing; modern languages; natural resource studies; painting and printmaking; performing arts studies; philosophy; psychology; retail management; sociology; sport science; TESOL (teaching English to speakers of other languages); theology and religious studies; women's studies; zoology.

➡ Part-time study: **Yes.**
➡ Distance learning: **Yes.**

## About the university:
Located 6 miles from the heart of London, but set in beautiful parkland, Roehampton, University of Surrey is located on two campuses with four colleges.

> Total number of students: 7,000
> Number of disabled students: approx. 500

## Learning support staff and services:
Learning Support Service
Full-time staff: disabilities officer; dyslexia coordinator; dyslexia tutor; three administrators.
Part-time staff: a number of dyslexia tutors.
The Learning Support Service coordinates support for students with disabilities, dyslexia and specific learning disabilities across the university.
Assistance with DSA applications; coordination of alternative arrangements in teaching, learning, library resources as well as examinations; specialist training on IT software; one-to-one tuition; diagnostic tests and individual assessment of needs; Learning Support Assistants scheme and study skills and numeracy support available to all students.

## Home sweet home:
Accommodation is limited and priority is given to applicants who accept RUS as their first choice; it is allocated on a first come, first served basis although students with disabilities requiring accommodation will be given particular consideration. Residential accommodation is provided in each of the four colleges and allocation of places is administered by college staff. Rooms designed for use by students with individual access requirements are provided in Digby Stuart College, Southland's College and Whiteland's. Special vibrating pillow alarms and door beacons can be provided for D/deaf or hard of hearing students in all halls of residence. Refrigerators for storing medication can be supplied. All security officers are qualified first aiders and trained in disability awareness. If a student with specific needs wishes to be on campus for the duration of the course this can be arranged.

## Out and about:
University: A free bus service runs between the campuses. There are dedicated parking spaces near both accommodation and study areas.

Public transport: Contact Access and Mobility for information about London's public transport services (see Directory).

**Taking it easy:**
At university: The Student Union building is fully accessible to all students.
Locally: See *Access in London*, published by Disability Net 1998. Artsline also publish several access guides to London (see Directory).

**And another thing ...**
➡ There is an SU officer for students with disabilities.

## The Disability Statement/Brochure:
Brief document detailing support offered to students with specific disabilities. Includes: Disclosure; Disabilities Office; financial assistance; academic support; information on accessibility and support by disability; facilities; services; SU; other sources of information; checklist; monitoring; confidentiality; disclaimer.

**Local disability public service providers:**
Wandsworth Borough Council.
Wandsworth Sensory and Physical Disability Team, Lyon House, 102–104 Wandsworth High Street, London SW18 4LA; 020 8871 8487.

---

| Rose Bruford College |
|---|

Lamorbey Park, Sidcup, Kent DA15 9DF

*General Enquiries:*
Tel: 020 8300 3024
Fax: 020 8308 0542
Email: admiss@bruford.ac.uk
Website: www.bruford.ac.uk

**Student Adviser/Counsellor:**
**Gail Moore**
**Tel: 020 8308 2638**
**Fax: as above**
**Email: gail@bruford.ac.uk**

**Fields of study:**
Acting USA/UK; actor musicianship; American and European theatre arts; costume production; directing; dramatic writing; lighting design; music technology; opera studies; performing and visual arts; research; scenic arts; sound and image design; stage management; theatre and performance studies; theatre design; theatre practices; theatre studies.

➡ Part-time study: **No.**
➡ Distance learning: **Yes.**

## About the college:
Rose Bruford College is located on two campuses – Greenwich and Lamorbey Park. Rose Bruford founded the college so that actors could be trained in preparation for their chosen career. The last 20 years have seen Rose Bruford College identify and develop a holistic approach to theatre training and education, creating a learning environment that properly reflects the collaborative and interactive process in theatre making, music and digital technologies. The college is divided into two faculties and six departments. Faculty staff are supported by a network of tutors drawn from theatre, film, television and the music industry.

| Total number of students: 600 | Number of disabled students: 50 |
|---|---|

## Learning support staff and services:
Student Adviser/Counsellor: Gail Moore; Simon Hopper: Dyslexia Tutor.

## Home sweet home:
The college does not have its own accommodation, but does its utmost to find local accommodation.

## Out and about:
College: There is no dedicated parking.
Public transport: Local transport is not accessible.

## Taking it easy:
At college: There are currently no leisure facilities.
Locally: Sidcup is a suburban high street with few facilities for disabled people. The other local town is Greenwich.

## And another thing ...
➡ The college has had a large extension built which gives access for students with disabilities.

## Local disability public service provider:
BADP (Bexley Association of Disabled People), 20 Whitehall Lane, Slade Green, Kent DA8 2DH; 01322 350988, fax: 01322 351430. Open Tuesday, Wednesday, Thursday 10am–4pm.

## Royal Academy of Music

Marylebone Road, London NW1 5HT

*General Enquiries:*
Tel: 020 7873 7372
Fax: 020 7873 7374
Email: registry@ram.ac.uk
Website: www.ram.ac.uk

**Disability Officer:**
**Tel: 020 7873 7372**
**Fax: 020 7873 7374**
**Email: p.white@ram.ac.uk**

**Field of study:**
Music.

➡ Part-time study: **No.**
➡ Distance learning: **No.**

**About the academy:**
The Royal Academy of Music, which was founded in 1822, consists of three buildings dating from 1825, 1911 and 1926 that have been joined together over the years. Arthur Sullivan was a student here before joining up with Gilbert. The academy is five minutes' walk from Baker Street and Regent's Park tube stations and ten minutes from Euston rail station.

| Total number of students: 700 | Number of disabled students: 60+ |
| --- | --- |

**Learning support staff and services:**
Welfare and Disability Working Group
The Welfare and Disability Working Group is attended by five members of staff, who all have part-time responsibilities for students with disabilities.
Needs assessment; assistance with DSA applications and RAM disability funds and bursaries; provision of auxiliary aids and services; advice and guidance; one-to-one/group tuition for students with dyslexia; alternative examination, assessment and study arrangements; support service for students with mental health issues and liaison with external organisations.
Practical study support for students with disabilities is considered on an individual basis in conjunction with relevant teachers and tutors.

**Home sweet home:**
There is no academy residential accommodation at present but students are helped to find appropriate accommodation in student hostels or the private sector. The estates officer assists students with

individual residential needs to find suitable accommodation, tel: 020 7873 7387; email: estates@ram.ac.uk.

## Out and about:
Academy: The academy has no general car park. The very limited parking is only available for essential purposes and with the permission of the principal. Parking cannot be made available to disabled students on a regular basis. There is parking on meters nearby in Regent's Park and in a car park at Regent's College ten minutes' walk away.

Public transport: Some buses, trains, train stations and taxis are accessible to people who are wheelchair users and/or have visual impairments. Contact Access and Mobility for information about public transport in London (see Directory).

## Taking it easy:
At academy: There is a common room, bar and canteen that can be accessed via a ramp at York Gate, but it is rather a long way round. Locally: London is mainly flat in the centre with many facilities accessible and the pavements are tactile. Artsline publishes a number of guides on access in London (see Directory).

## And another thing ...
➡ Within the academy there are many changes of level. A portable ramp is available for the entrance steps, but is not suitable for wheelchair users without assistance. Most of the front section of the building is accessible by lift. This includes the concert hall, restaurant, student common room, bar and toilets and some teaching and practice rooms. However, the remainder of the building is only accessible via corridors linked by steps and staircases, some narrow and steep. A portable ramp giving access to the library from the street is available on request. There are two first aid/rest rooms, one of which is near the entrance hall. With students' agreement, academy first aiders and security staff are informed of any students with disabilities who may need assistance. There are no accessible toilet facilities.
➡ Most performances are not amplified and most teaching takes place in small classes, not large lectures. There is no induction loop system.
➡ The academy is actively seeking to increase its accommodation for teaching and practice and to provide its own hostel accommodation. Expansion in these areas will include provision for students with disabilities wherever practicable.

➡ The academy has no medical services on the premises, apart from named and trained first aiders.

## The Disability Statement/Brochure:
Includes: Access and admissions; examination and assessments; staff development; financial assistance; student services; premises; accommodation; health care; locality and future activity and development.

## Local disability public service providers:
RNIB.
Westminster Council.

---

## Royal Agricultural College
Cirencester, GL7 6JS

*General Enquiries:*                    **Disability Officer: Dr John Conway**
Tel: 01285 652531                       **Tel: 01285 889934**
Fax: 01285 650219
Email: admissions@royagcol.ac.uk
Website: www.royagcol.ac.uk

## Fields of study:
Agriculture; business; equine management; rural land and property management.

➡ Part-time study: **Yes.**
➡ Distance learning: **No.**

## About the college:
The Royal Agricultural College is an independent college that was founded in 1842 for the education and training of young people who wished to follow careers in agriculture. The Royal Charter was awarded in 1845 and since this time the college has been contributing to the development of the land and business associated with agriculture. The college is situated on the outskirts of Cirencester and is easily accessible by road and rail.

| Total number of students: 580 | Number of disabled students: 90+ |
| --- | --- |

## Disability staff and services:
Part-time staff: Disability Officer (also a specialist in dyslexia): Dr John Conway; disability tutor.

Discussion of how to adapt the course curriculum and the teaching and learning methods employed to deliver it to suit individual needs; assistance with DSA applications; provision of auxiliary aids and services; advice and guidance; one-to-one/group tuition for students with dyslexia; alternative examination, assessment and study arrangements and liaison with external organisations.

**Home sweet home:**
There are five study bedrooms that are accessible to wheelchair users. The college will try to address any problems concerning accommodation.
Accommodation can be guaranteed for the duration of the student's course.

**Out and about:**
College: Dedicated parking spaces near study areas.

**Taking it easy:**
At college: The SU building/bar and sports facilities are all accessible.
Locally: The city centre is flat.

**And another thing ...**
➡ The college is small and easy to get around. It is all on one site and all at ground level.
➡ A programme of work has just been completed to ensure all key buildings have level or ramped access.
➡ The main teaching block and administration/refectory buildings have accessible toilet facilities.
➡ Dedicated parking places for disabled drivers are located close to the teaching block, the library and the administration/refectory buildings.

---

**Royal Free and University College Medical School**
Rowland Hill Street, Hampstead, London NW3 2PF

*General Enquiries:*
Tel: 020 7679 2000
Fax: 020 7679 7801
Email: degree-info@ucl.ac.uk
Website: www.ucl.ac.uk

**Disability Coordinator:**
**Alistair Appleby**
**Tel: 020 7679 1343**
**Fax: 020 7916 8530**
**Email: Alistair-Appleby@ucl.ac.uk**

Royal Holloway, University of London

**Fields of study:**
Clinical sciences; health informatics and multiprofessional education (CHIME); life sciences; primary care and population science.

**About the school:**
In August 1998 the new Royal Free and University College Medical School (RF&UCMS) was created when two separate medical schools merged to meet the demanding academic needs of the new century. The medical school also includes a number of famous institutions including the Institute of Child Health (Great Ormond Street), the Institute of Neurology (the National Hospital for Neurology and Neurosurgery), the Institute of Laryngology and Otology and the Institute of Ophthalmology (Moorfields Eye Hospital). In April 2000 a major new development, the Wolfson Institute for Biomedical Research, was opened. The RF&UCMS is located on three campuses in Bloomsbury, Hampstead and Highgate.

| Total number of students: 260 |
| --- |

**Learning support staff and services:**
Services for students with disabilities are administered through University College London. Please see this entry for further information.

| **Royal Holloway, University of London** |
| --- |

Egham, Surrey TW20 0EX

*General Enquiries:*
Tel: 01784 434455
Fax: 01784 437520
Website: www.rhul.ac.uk

**Disability Coordinator:**
**Educational Support Office**
**Tel: 01784 414289**
**Fax: 01784 436359**
**Email: Educational_Support**
**@rhul.ac.uk**
**Text: 01784 414357/6/7**

**Fields of study:**
Classics; computer sciences; economics; English; European studies; French, German and Italian; geography; geology; Hispanic and Japanese studies; management; mathematics; media arts; performing arts; psychology; science and the media; sciences; social and political science.

➡ Part-time study: **Yes, some.**
➡ Distance learning: **No.**

## About the college:

The college stands in 183 acres of mainly green-belt land just outside the 'M25 ring' at Egham in Surrey. The college also maintains a Georgian terraced house at Bedford Square in London, which currently accommodates some inter-collegiate teaching undergraduates and postgraduates (mainly history), and a research group. At the main site in Egham academic buildings are situated on both sides of the A30. There are also academic buildings at the Royal Holloway Institute for Environmental Research about 1 mile away from the main site.

| Total number of students: 5,798 | Number of disabled students: 270 |
|---|---|

## Learning support staff and services:

Full-time educational support officer and part-time assistant educational support officer.

Offer confidential advice on study support, equipment and funding on an individual basis. Liaise on students' behalf with academic departments and central services and represent students' needs on college committees and external bodies. Raise disability awareness among college staff.

## Home sweet home:

Provision includes rooms that have been adapted to make them accessible to wheelchair users and rooms fitted with flashing lights and pillow vibrators for use by students who are D/deaf or hard of hearing. Full-time personal assistants/carers can be housed in adjacent rooms. Normal residence fees will be charged for the personal assistant's/carer's room. There is catered and self-catering accommodation available.

Accommodation can be guaranteed for the duration of the student's course.

## Out and about:

College: There are dedicated parking spaces near both accommodation and study areas.

Public transport: Some local buses are accessible to wheelchair users.

## Taking it easy:

At college: The college boasts a new sports hall, opened in 1999, which offers a wide programme of activities and therapies, details of which can be found in the *Sports Handbook* available from the SU. Access to the sports centre is by a path that has a steep gradient but there is a car park next to the sports centre. For more information please refer to the college access guide. The SU and bar are accessible to wheelchair users.

Locally: There is a disability guide available from DAIR (see below) but it is mostly aimed at elderly people.

**And another thing ...**
➡ The main building is built on a slope. The geography of the campus and the large number of older buildings can make access difficult for those with mobility difficulties. Some students regard electric wheelchairs or scooters as essential equipment.
➡ Essential information regarding college accessibility can be found on the Educational Support Office Web page. It will allow you, for example, to request digital images of the campus. The access guide is particularly useful to wheelchair users and includes an index of the accessibility of the college buildings. The college has a Disability Working Group that reviews the level of provision for disabled persons at the college and makes recommendations for change and improvements to the college's Equal Opportunities Committee, which itself reports to Council.

## The Disability Statement/Brochure:
*The Handbook for Students with Special Needs*
Includes: Support (current policy and provision); admissions policy; Educational Support Office and what it does; about the campus; academic support; welfare support; financial assistance; complaints procedures; future activities and policy development; other useful documents and contact information.

**Local disability service provider:**
DAIR: Disability Advice and Information for Runnymede, 01932 566622.

---

**Royal Military College of Science, Cranfield University**
Shrivenham, Swindon SN6 8LA

*General Enquiries:* Admissions
Tel: 01793 785400
Fax: 01793 785768
Email:j.laxon@rmcs.cranfield.ac.uk
Website: www.rmcs.cranfield.ac.uk

**Student Support Coordinator:**
**Caroline McKenna**
**Tel: 01793 785396**
**Fax: 01793 785141**
**Email: c.mckenna@**
**rmcs.cranfield.ac.uk**

**Fields of study:**
Aerospace, powers and sensors; defence management and security
analysis; engineering systems; environmental and ordnance systems;
informatics and simulation; materials and medical sciences.

➡ Part-time study: **Yes.**
➡ Distance learning: **Some courses in the pipeline.**

**About the university:**
Cranfield is the top UK university for industrially sponsored research
in its own fields and Europe's largest university centre for applied
research. Swindon is the nearest town, under 10 miles, and the
villages of Shrivenham and Watchfield adjoin the campus.

**Learning support staff and services:**
Student Support Coordinator: Caroline McKenna.
Help with assessments; provision of one-to-one help, group work or
appropriate self-study resources, i.e. computer-based packages and
books. Support can be accessed through Student Services.

**Out and about:**
University: There are dedicated parking spaces for disabled drivers.

**Taking it easy:**
Locally: The centre of Swindon is pedestrianised.

**QAA Report: Paragraph 56, July 2001**
According to the account some 2.5% of students declare a disability
– dyslexia accounts for about one-third of this – and the university
has a variety of policies and practices in disability issues including a
dedicated working group. Since the number of students with a
disability is small, the team concurred with the university's view that
most of these people are helped individually, for example by moving
classes to ground-floor rooms for anyone with restricted mobility.

| **Royal Northern College of Music** |
|---|

124 Oxford Road, Manchester M13 9RD

*General Enquiries:*
Tel: 0161 907 5000
Fax: 0161 273 7611
Email: info@rncm.ac.uk
Website: www.rncm.ac.uk

**Deputy Academic Registrar:**
**Jane Hallam**
**Tel: 0161 907 5361**
**Fax: 0161 273 7611**
**Email: jane.hallam@rncm.ac.uk**

## Fields of study:
Composition and contemporary music; keyboard studies; strings; vocal and opera studies; wind and percussion.

➡ Part-time study: **Yes.**
➡ Distance learning: **No.**

## About the college:
In the late nineteenth century Sir Charles Hallé, the founder of the renowned Hallé Orchestra, established the Royal Manchester College of Music. In 1973 the Northern School of Music amalgamated with Hallé's college to become the present-day RNCM. As a conservatoire, students are prepared for performance and composition. The college also serves as an arts centre, hosting a wide variety of events including music, dance, TV and theatrical productions.

| | |
|---|---|
| Total number of students: 610 | Number of disabled students: 57 |

## Learning support staff and services:
Welfare Team
Full-time staff: Head of Academic Administration: Jane Hallam; senior assistant (registrations/welfare).
Part-time staff: Learning Support Tutor: Cheryll McCandlish; Counsellor: Bryan Fox.
Assistance with DSA applications: provision of auxiliary aids and services; advice and guidance; one-to-one tuition for students with dyslexia; alternative examination, assessment and study arrangements; support service for students with mental health issues; keeping up to date with disability legislation; and liaison with external organisations.

## Home sweet home:
The college has a modern, well-equipped hall of residence adjacent to the main college, offering en-suite facilities to all students. Access has been provided to accommodate the needs of disabled students. Accommodation *cannot* be guaranteed for duration of the student's course.

## Out and about:
College: Dedicated parking spaces near both accommodation and study areas.
Public transport: Taxis, low-floor buses and metro system are easily accessible for wheelchair users. Trains, train stations and taxis are

accessible to people with visual impairments. Mantax taxis are a scheme for disabled users in the area.

## Taking it easy:
At college: No specific services are available for the social support of disabled students. The university shopping precinct, which has wheelchair access and includes banking and post office facilities, is situated within a hundred yards of the College.
Locally: The city centre is flat and accessible. Local town facilities (including theatres, cinemas and concert halls) are accessible and pavements are tactile. There is a Shopmobility scheme.

## And another thing ...
➡ All teaching and learning facilities are housed in two adjacent buildings on a single site. There is unaided access for people who are wheelchair users to all levels, except the Upper and Lower Concourse and Opera Theatre auditorium (where assistance is needed). Plans currently under discussion provide for improved disability access to the Opera Theatre auditorium and the upgrading of an audio loop system in the main auditoria for those people who are D/deaf or hard of hearing.
➡ Assessment procedures may be modified to take account of the special needs of students with disabilities. In the schools of keyboard studies, strings, vocal and operatic studies and wind and percussion, however, all students are required to pass end-of-year recital examinations and participate in the internal recital scheme and reach a satisfactory standard in the final recital examination.
➡ The College has a student counselling service with professionally qualified counsellors.
➡ The New Library which opened in 1997 provides assisted wheelchair access to all borrowing, listening and reference materials. Trained staff are available to assist users with disabilities.

## The Disability Statement/Brochure:
Includes: Policy and provision.

## Local disability public service providers:
Manchester City Council.
Shopmobility Manchester Unit 129, Upper Mall, Market Way, Arndale Centre 0161 839 4060.

| **Royal Scottish Academy of Music and Drama** |
| :---: |

100 Renfrew Street, Glasgow G2 3DB

*General Enquiries:*
Tel: 0141 332 4101
Fax: 0141 332 8901
Email: registry@rsamd.ac.uk
Website: rsamd.ac.uk

**Academy Counsellor:**
**Jane Balmforth**
**Tel: 0141 270 8282**
**Fax: 0141 332 8901**
**Email: j.balmforth@rsamd.ac.uk**

**Fields of study:**
Music and drama.

➡ Part-time study: **Yes, postgraduates only.**
➡ Distance learning: **No.**

**About the academy:**
The Royal Scottish Academy of Music and Drama is located in the heart of Glasgow close to the Theatre Royal and the Glasgow Royal Concert Hall. As well as being a centre for music and drama students the academy is also a public building and provides access for audiences who attend the many plays, operas and concerts performed by students and guest performers. Glasgow is a historic city, built on several hills, with a population of about 600,000.

| Total number of students: 625 | Number of disabled students: 82 |
| :--- | :--- |

**Learning support staff and services:**
There is no specific unit covered by a disability coordinator.
Full-time staff: Academy Counsellor/Disability Adviser: Jane Balmforth.
Needs assessment; assistance with DSA applications and Hardship Funds; provision of auxiliary aids and services; advice and guidance; one-to-one/group tuition for students with dyslexia; arrange dyslexia assessments; alternative examination, assessment and study arrangements; support service for students with mental health issues; set up learning agreements with academic staff; organising lunchtime meetings with dyslexic students; personal counselling for students and staff; welfare information and advice and liaison with external organisations.

**Home sweet home:**
Currently accommodation is provided by Glasgow University halls, which have dedicated facilities with access for people who are wheelchair users, and adapted kitchen and bathrooms. From 2004 it

is planned that accommodation will be offered in private halls. This accommodation will not be on the academy site, but in leased blocks in a hall of residence and will be accessible to students who are wheelchair users or who have visual impairments. In addition, the academy is able to offer advice to students seeking accommodation in the private sector.

Accommodation can be guaranteed for duration of student's course.

### Out and about:

Academy: Dedicated parking spaces near both accommodation and study areas.

Public transport: Trains, train stations, some buses and taxis are accessible for people who are wheelchair users. Buses, trains, train stations and some taxis are accessible to people with visual impairments. Local taxi schemes for disabled people operate in the area: Quality West of Scotland Travel and Disabled Transport (Q West).

### Taking it easy:

At academy: The bars/cafés are all fully wheelchair accessible, as are all auditoria (concert halls and theatre). A Disability Awareness Committee has been established where disabled students can bring up issues about provision in the academy.

Locally: The city centre is flat, pedestrianised and accessible, but it is hilly nearby. The facilities are accessible and there is a Shopmobility scheme. The pavements are tactile. Consult *The Ultimate Guide to Disability, Access and Transport within Glasgow* for more information on the town's accessibility. The *Guide* is available from the Greater Glasgow and Clyde Valley Tourist Board (see below).

### And another thing ...

➡ The Fyfe Lecture Theatre and all auditoria are fitted with induction loops. Wheelchair spaces are provided in the academy's two concert halls and two theatres, and staff will assist if necessary.

➡ Gordon Hunt, Head of Information Services, can give advice and information about access to the library.

## The Disability Statement/Brochure:

*RSAMD Information for Students with Disabilities*

Includes: Existing policy; local environment; physical environment; applications and admissions; counselling service; academic registrar and staff tutors; examinations and assessments; equipment provision; library; accommodation; financial support; SA; careers advice; medical services; future development and contacts.

**Local disability public service providers:**
Greater Glasgow and Clyde Valley Tourist Board, 0141 204 4400.
Glasgow City Council, 0141 287 2000.

| **Royal Veterinary College, University of London** |
|---|

Royal College Street, London NW1 0TU

*General Enquiries:*
Tel: 020 7468 5000
Fax: 020 7388 2342
Email: registry@rvc.ac.uk
Website: www.rvc.ac.uk

**Disability Coordinator: Anne Tynan**
**Tel: 020 7468 5056**
**Fax: 020 7468 1177**
**Email: atynan@rcv.ac.uk**

**Field of study:**
Veterinary sciences.

➡ Part-time study: **Yes.**
➡ Distance learning: **Yes.**

**About the college:**
The Royal Veterinary College is the UK's first and largest veterinary school and a constituent college of the University of London. The college is based on two main campuses, the Camden campus in London and the Hawkshead campus in Hertfordshire.

| Total number of students: 1,000 | Number of disabled students: 25 |
|---|---|

**Learning support staff and services:**
Part-time staff: Student Disability Officer: Anne Tynan.

**Home sweet home:**
There are college halls on both campuses.
Accommodation cannot be guaranteed.

**Out and about:**
College: Dedicated parking spaces near both accommodation and study areas.
Public transport: Contact Access and Mobility for information regarding access to public transport in London (see Directory).

**Taking it easy:**
At college: Accessible leisure facilities are provided by the University of London SU. The RVC is in the process of assessing its SU facilities,

Royal Welsh College of Music and Drama – Coleg Cerdd a Drama Cymru

but it does not currently offer full accessibility.
Locally: Artsline publish a number of access guides to London (see directory).

## The Disability Statement/Brochure:
Available on Website or from Student Disability Officer.

---

### Royal Welsh College of Music and Drama – Coleg Cerdd a Drama Cymru

Castle Grounds, Cathays Park, Cardiff CF10 3ER

*General Enquiries:*
Tel: 029 2034 2854
Fax: 029 2039 1304
Email: info@rwcmd.ac.uk
Website: www.rwcmd.ac.uk
Text: BT service utilised

**Assistant Director, Academic Support: Kym Roberts**
**Tel: 029 2034 2854**
**Fax: 029 2039 1303**
**Email: robertsKT@rwcmd.ac.uk**

### Fields of study:
Acting; arts management; music; music therapy; performance studies; popular music; stage management; theatre design.

➡ Part-time study: **Part-time mode available for music postgraduate programmes and arts management courses.**
➡ Distance learning: **No, but more technology courses are being developed.**

### About the college:
The Royal Welsh College of Music and Drama (RWCMD) is the national conservatoire for Wales. It was founded in 1949 when it was housed in Cardiff Castle, and in 1979 moved to its purpose-built premises in the Castle Grounds just a few hundred yards from the city centre. Former students are to be found working in major symphony and chamber orchestras in the UK and abroad. Cardiff is a growing European capital city with much to offer in the way of arts, culture, sport, green open spaces and social life.

| Total number of students: 550 | Number of disabled students: 48 |

### Learning support staff and services:
Part-time staff: Coordinator for Students with Disabilities: Kym Roberts, coordinates provision throughout the college; the assistant

principal has overall responsibility for students with disabilities; course leaders (music) and heads of programme (drama).

For music students the course leader (for the course on which the student is enrolled) is responsible for specific arrangements for students with disabilities. The course leader is assisted by the student's pastoral tutor of the student's chosen study area.

For drama students the head of programmes is responsible for specific arrangements for students with disabilities for the programme on which the student is enrolled. The head of programme is supported by the student's year tutor.

Needs assessments; assistance with DSA applications and financial guidance offered; provision of auxiliary aids and services; advice and guidance; one-to-one/group tuition for students with dyslexia; study skills tutorials; alternative examination and assessment arrangements; support service for students with mental health issues; IT assistance; encourage the social inclusion, personal growth and independence of the individual student; and liaison with external organisations.

**Home sweet home:**
The college does not have its own accommodation, but is able to access halls of residence with accessible accommodation. Students are assisted in finding accommodation (including accommodation that is accessible to wheelchair users) through the Find a Friend Scheme, organised by the SU. The accommodation is shared student houses within the city centre, i.e. private. There is access to purpose-built student accommodation (for first-year students, overseas students and disabled students, depending on what their preference is), which is shared with Cardiff University.

Accommodation can be guaranteed for duration of student's course, as Cardiff is well provided for in terms of student accommodation.

**Out and about:**
College: Although parking is very limited at the college, and student parking is generally not possible, the college does make provision for registered mobility-impaired students. There are dedicated parking spaces for disabled drivers near to study areas. As a centre of training and education for the music and drama professions, there are times when students attend rehearsals or performance outside the main college buildings. Assistance will be offered for students with transport needs. There are some dedicated parking spaces near to accommodation.

Public transport: Buses, trains, train stations and taxis are accessible to both wheelchair users and people with visual impairments. Many local taxi companies offer a service for disabled passengers.

Royal Welsh College of Music and Drama – Coleg Cerdd a Drama Cymru

## Taking it easy:

At college: The SU, student bar and catering facilities are accessible to wheelchair users. There are no sporting facilities. The college is based in the city centre and access to the surrounding facilities is mostly level access.

Locally: Cardiff is well served by transport, leisure and shopping facilities and park areas. The city centre is pedestrianised, flat and accessible. The facilities are accessible and there is a Shopmobility scheme. Pavements are tactile and there is a local area access guide published by Cardiff County Council.

## And another thing …

➡ The college's Raymond Edwards building and the Anthony Hopkins Centre are accessible to students with specific access requirements, though some assistance may be necessary with the lift operation in the former. There are accessible toilet facilities on the ground and second floors of the Raymond Edwards building and the ground floor of the Anthony Hopkins Centre.

➡ The Anthony Hopkins Centre adaptations include clear signage and colour-contrasting interiors and mirrored lifts to assist students, staff and visitors.

➡ The college library is situated on the first floor of the Raymond Edwards building and is accessible to students with mobility impairments.

➡ Computer facilities are accessible to wheelchair users and can be adapted to provide large font format for students with visual impairments. All computers are equipped with specialist software to aid study skills support for students with dyslexia.

➡ The college has a portable induction loop suitable for smaller performance spaces and the smaller teaching areas. Induction loop facilities are available in the larger performance spaces in the Raymond Edwards building and the Anthony Hopkins Centre.

➡ The college intends to review access to courses as part of its Disability Plan, and an exploration of the curriculum with a view to increasing participation for students with disabilities is also on the agenda.

➡ The college has developed links with Cardiff University's Dyslexia Resource Centre and Support Services.

➡ RWCMD will pay 75% of costs for diagnostic reports as long as certain criteria are met.

## The Disability Statement/Brochure:

Available through the college Website: www.rwcmd.ac.uk.
Includes: Current policy; registration and induction; examination and

assessments; complaints and appeals; current provision; future development.

**Local disability public service providers:**
Cardiff County Council.
Disability Wales.
Arts Disability Wales.
RNID.
RNIB.

---

| **University of St Andrews** |
| --- |

79 North Street, St Andrews, Fife KY16 9AJ

*General Enquiries:*
Tel: 01334 476161
Email: registry@st-andrews.ac.uk
Website: www.st-andrews.ac.uk

**Disabilities Team**
**Tel: 01334 462038**
**Fax: 01334 462246**
**Email: disabilities@
st-andrews.ac.uk**

**Fields of study:**
Arts; divinity; science (including medical science).

➡ Part-time study: **Yes.**
➡ Distance learning: **No.**

**About the university:**
Founded in 1410, the University of St Andrews is the oldest university in Scotland and the third oldest in the UK. The university is not a campus university, but closely integrated with the town. The most popular form of transport is the bicycle, as a car is not needed. The antiquity of St Andrews is visible in its monuments, buildings, city walls and medieval street plan. There are relatively few inclines to be considered; however, cobblestones are a feature of some of the main streets.

| Total number of students: approx. 7,000 Number of disabled students: 900 |
| --- |

**Learning support staff and services:**
The Disability Team is based in Student Support Services
Full-time staff: disabilities adviser; secretary.
Part-time staff: dyslexia adviser.

Providing support, information and advice to students on any problem that directly or indirectly affects their academic performance; referral to specialist services such as RNIB, RNID, HE Access Centre; loan of specialised equipment; ensure individual needs of students are met; mediate if problems occur; assistance in DSA applications; arrange functional needs assessments where necessary; arrangements for any personal support workers.

Disability coordinators have been appointed in each school or group of academic teaching and research units. The coordinators help the disability team to monitor provision for students with disabilities in each school of study.

The assistant director of Student Support Services (academic) deals with academic aspects of welfare or individual needs problems. The assistant director of Student Support Services (finance) gives advice on funding and administers these funds.

**Home sweet home:**
Some of the residences could prove difficult for wheelchair users. However the more modern residences (e.g. New Hall) were designed with mobility difficulties in mind, as were those residences that have been refurbished. The accommodation on offer caters for students with many different needs, whether it is independent living with self-catering; meal programmes including some special diets; wheelchair access; or telephone and computer access. Wherever feasible; adaptations have been made to suit specific needs. A number of showers, bathrooms and toilets have been redesigned or adapted. All residences have a telephone along with the provision of computer suites, and there are computer sockets in each bedroom.

In certain circumstances accommodation may be guaranteed for duration of student's course.

**Out and about:**
University: Car parking places are available in the town and university for registered disabled drivers near both accommodation and study areas.

Public transport: The main buildings of the university are all within half a mile of the bus station. Local station (approx. 7 miles away) is accessible to wheelchair users. The name of the taxi scheme operating in the area is Town and Country Taxis.

**Taking it easy:**
At university: The SA building recently completed a refurbishment that included the installation of a lift allowing wheelchair access to all floors where, previously, there had been very limited access. With the

opening of the new outdoor floodlit sports facilities has come provision of new changing and showering facilities for physically disabled athletes. Two separate single shower/changing room/toilet facilities are provided for outdoor and indoor sports. The sports centre is situated on a flat site amidst the playing fields, so there is access to all ground-level facilities. There is one upper-floor activity, which is not served by a lift.

Locally: The local town is not pedestrianised but is accessible. Town facilities are accessible and the pavements are tactile.

### And another thing ...

➡ Although some buildings may cause access problems a lot can be and has been done, by means of ramps or by finding alternative venues. There is an ongoing programme incorporated in the university's estates strategy for improving access to older buildings.

➡ Access can be a problem for some teaching and administration buildings.

➡ Accessible toilets are being installed in most of the teaching and administration buildings, and construction work on the maths and physics buildings is incorporating access improvement.

➡ Members of a volunteer team of 25 students called the SupNet, who are trained in welfare and counselling issues, give assistance in helping someone settle into the student community. The SupNet also runs a number of self-help groups, such as a dyslexia support group, and networks for, amongst others, those who have ME or depression, students with eating disorders and ethnic minority students.

➡ The main university library is a modern four-storey building in North Street, which is accessible via ramp to the main entrance. There is a lift to all floors.

➡ An officer has been appointed in the main library with responsibility for students with disabilities.

➡ In addition to the several open-access computer rooms, there is a room attached to the main library for exclusive use by students with a disability.

➡ The University of St Andrews has joined with three other HE institutions in Tayside to found the Tayside and Fife HE Access Centre based in Dundee. The Centre offers assessment, advice and training services to enable students with disabilities to study independently and is a member of NFAC.

### The Disability Statement/Brochure:

*Information for Students with Disabilities and Learning Difficulties*
Includes: Applications/admissions; support offered; examination

arrangements; accessibility; accommodation; continuing support; student support service; other support; other agencies; financial support; policy monitoring and review and future developments.

**Local disability public service provider:**
Access for the Disabled Group.

---

| **St George's Hospital Medical School** |
|---|

Cranmer Terrace, London SW 17 0RE

*General Enquiries:*
Tel: 020 8725 5201
Fax: 020 8725 0841
Email: adm-med@sghms.ac.uk
Website: www.sghms.ac.uk

**Disability Coordinator:**
**Caroline Persaud**
**Tel: 020 8725 5201**
**Fax: 020 8725 0841**
**Email: cpersaud@sghms.ac.uk**

**Fields of study:**
Biomedical sciences; health care sciences; medicine; nursing and midwifery and social work.

➡ Part-time study: **No.**
➡ Distance learning: **No.**

**About the school:**
St George's Hospital was founded in 1733 at Hyde Park Corner in London, and has trained medical students since then. It was decided shortly after the Second World War that St George's should be relocated to Tooting. In 1995 the Joint Faculty of Health Care Sciences was established with Kingston University. Despite being the centre of British politics, business and finance, London has a vast number of peaceful parks, walks beside the River Thames and the canals of the city, and some of the most historic buildings in the world. The new London Transport Student Photocard has reduced the cost of travelling in the capital by 30 per cent.

| Total number of students: 1,100 | Number of disabled students: 9 |
|---|---|

**Learning support staff and services:**
There is no disability unit as the institution is so small. There is an Occupational Health Department for the use of students, as well as two full-time counsellors who can give advice and arrange additional facilities and support.

## Home sweet home:
There is no accessible accommodation at present, but the accommodation is to be modified in summer 2003 and will include rooms for students with a disability.
Accommodation *cannot* be guaranteed for duration of student's course.

## Out and about:
School: Dedicated parking spaces near both accommodation and study areas.
Public transport: Local buses all have a lower platform for accessibility. Contact Access and Mobility for information about London's public transport services (see Directory).

## Taking it easy:
At school: All student social areas are accessible. Local sports facilities only have partial access.
Locally: The area is accessible and there is a local disability guide. Artsline publishes a number of access guides to London (see Directory).

---

| College of St Mark and St John |
| --- |

Derriford Road, Plymouth PL6 8BH

*General Enquiries:*
Tel: 01752 636700
Email: admissions@marjon.ac.uk
Website: www.marjon.ac.uk

**Disability Officer: Heather Morris**
**Tel: 01752 636700 ext 8674**
**Email: hmorris@marjon.ac.uk**
**disability@marjon.ac.uk**

## Fields of study:
Art and design; community studies; design and technology; drama studies; English language studies; English literary studies; geography; history; information technology; leisure and tourism studies; management studies; media studies; outdoor adventure education; public relations; sociology; sports and recreation studies; sports science and coaching; theology; theology and philosophy.

➡ Part-time study: **Yes.**
➡ Distance learning: **No.**

## About the college:
The College of St Mark and St John, or Marjon as it is often known, has been providing higher education since 1840. Marjon is a Church

of England voluntary college and until 1973 was based in London – where its constituent colleges, St John's and St Mark's, are located – before moving to Plymouth. The historic Barbican area in Plymouth from which the Pilgrim Fathers sailed to America is a focal point for visitors. Based on a single campus, the college is situated relatively near to the Cornish and Devonshire coastlines.

Total number of students: 5,000    Number of disabled students: 287

## Learning support staff and services:
Student Learning Centre
Full-time staff: Disability Coordinator: Heather Morris; Study Skills Coordinator (Generic Service): Dawn Edwards.
Part-time staff: Specific Learning Difficulty Specialist Tutor: Judy Roughton.
Needs assessments arranged through an accredited Access Centre, or with other professionals; assistance with DSA applications; provision of auxiliary aids and services; advice and guidance; one-to-one/group tuition for students with dyslexia; alternative examination, assessment and study arrangements; support service for students with mental health issues; student mentoring; PAs; support services including technical support; liaises with LEA as necessary; referral to appropriate academic or support staff or outside professionals as appropriate; treats students with courtesy and respect; guarantees confidentiality; offers opportunity for feedback on all aspects of the service provided; and liaison with external organisations.

## Home sweet home:
There are two self-catering houses in village including wheelchair accessible study bedrooms, bathrooms and an adapted ground-floor kitchen shared with fellow students, and four self-contained study bedrooms, en-suite in catered halls, suitable for wheelchair users, with automatic access.
Accommodation can be guaranteed for duration of student's course, subject to availability.

## Out and about:
College: Dedicated parking spaces near both accommodation and study areas.
Public transport: Contact Plymouth City Council with public transport enquiries.

**Taking it easy:**
At college: The students organise an annual sports day for students with disabilities at the sports centre.
Locally: The local town is very wheelchair user friendly. Kerbs are lowered and the actual city centre has full access. There is a disability shop that provides wheelchairs for people who require them.

**And another thing ...**
➡ Access to college locations varies. Most areas are now accessible. A summary of access limitations is available from the Disability Advice and Support Service (DASS) staff.
➡ The Centre for Information Technology in Education (CITE) has an IT-trained tutor who can confirm requirements for specialist equipment.
➡ Advice and guidance is available in person, by telephone or by email on request from the DASS or admissions staff.
➡ The college is a member of Skill and works closely with accredited Access Centres, such as the South West Regional Access Centre at the University of Plymouth.

## The Disability Statement/Brochure:
Includes: Current policy; current provision and future strategy and provision.

## Local disability public service provider:
South West Regional Access Centre at the University of Plymouth.

| St Martin's College |
|---|

Lancaster Campus, Bowerham Road, Lancaster LA1 3JC

*General Enquiries:* Admissions
Tel: 01524 384200
Fax: 01524 384385
Email: admission@ucsm.ac.uk
Website: www.ucsm.ac.uk

**Disability Officer: Joanna Smith**
**Tel: 01524 384680**
**Fax: 01524 384459**
**Email: j.smith@ucsm.ac.uk**

**Fields of study:**
Arts; education; health; humanities and social sciences.

➡ Part-time study: **Yes, some.**
➡ Distance learning: **Yes, some.**

**About the college:**
St Martin's College is located on three campuses – Lancaster, Ambleside and Carlisle. The first St Martin's campus opened in Lancaster in 1963, the same year as Lancaster University, which validates all courses. Each campus has a mix of old and new buildings.

| Total number of students: 10,000 Number of disabled students: 292 |
| --- |

**Learning support staff and services:**
Disability Office (based at Lancaster Campus)
Disability Officer: Joanna Smith; Disability Learning Support Assistant: Anne Tanner; Learning Support Coordinator: Bob Dewhirst.
Advice and guidance; provision of support to staff in supporting students; assistance with DSA applications; provision of auxiliary aids and services; one-to-one/group tuition for students with dyslexia; support service for students with mental health issues; advice on all disability-related issues except benefits; provision of supportive technology; alternative examination arrangements; links with external agencies that can offer support, e.g. sign language interpreters; college-based educational support workers and liaison with external agencies.
Students with specific learning difficulties such as dyslexia can benefit from the college's learning support service available at all three campuses.

**Home sweet home:**
The college has a refurbishment programme to provide adapted accommodation at all sites by 2004. Carlisle campus has a newly built hall with accessible rooms for wheelchair users and D/deaf and hard of hearing users.
Accommodation can be guaranteed for duration of the student's course.

**Out and about:**
College: There are dedicated parking spaces near both accommodation and study areas.
Public transport: Taxis, some trains and train stations are accessible to wheelchair users. Some buses, trains, train stations and taxis are accessible to people with visual impairments. The accessibility of the local transport services varies depending on the site you are studying at. Contact the Disability Office for further information. There is a taxi scheme for disabled people operating in the area.

## Taking it easy:

At college: All facilities provided for leisure pursuits are accessible. Locally: Carlisle is flat and Lancaster is hilly. Ambleside is on a very steep hill. Access guides are available for Lancaster and Carlisle. Contact the Disability Office for further information.

## And another thing ...

➡ The college is multi-sited and geographically dispersed. Some courses are available at all sites. Each campus offers a unique atmosphere. Ambleside, set in the Lake District, is hilly. Lancaster campus, the largest site, is set on a hilltop overlooking Lancaster and Morecambe Bay. Carlisle campus, by contrast, is an urban campus, which is relatively small and flat and is undergoing extensive refurbishment.

➡ College publications can be obtained in alternative formats.

## Local disability public service providers:

DISC (Disablement Information Support Centre), Trinity Community Centre, Middle Street, Lancaster LA1 1JZ, 01524 34411.
PDSI (Physical and Disability Sensory Impairment Forum), St Leonard's House, Leonard Gate, Lancaster LA1 1NN, 01524 382764, text: 01524 383461.
DACE, (Disability Association Carlisle & Eden), California Road, Carlisle CA3 0BX.
Contact the Disability Officer for further information.

---

### St Mary's College

Waldegrave Road, Strawberry Hill, Twickenham TW1 4SX

*General Enquiries:*
Tel: 020 8240 4000
Fax: 020 8240 4255
Website: www.smuc.ac.uk

**Disability Coordinator: Pat Culshaw**
**Tel: 020 8240 4353**
**Fax: 020 8240 4255**
**Email: culshawp@smuc.ac.uk**

## Fields of study:

Cultural studies; drama; education and employment; English; geography; health and human biology; health, nutrition and lifestyle; history; Irish studies; management studies; media arts; physical education; PGCE primary and secondary; professional and creative writing; psychology; sociology; sport rehabilitation; sport science; teaching; theology and religious studies.

➡ Part-time study: **Yes.**
➡ Distance learning: **No.**

## About the college:
St Mary's is a college of the University of Surrey. Founded in 1850, it is the oldest Catholic college. It is located on a single self-contained campus in a pleasant suburb on the edge of London and within easy reach of the West End.

| Total number of students: 2,750 | Number of disabled students: 200 |
| --- | --- |

## Learning support staff and services:
Special Needs/Student Services
Full-time staff: Special Needs Officer: Patricia Culshaw.
Part-time staff: dyslexia tutors (number varies according to demand) and tutor for hearing impaired students.
Assistance with DSA applications; provision of auxiliary aids and services; advice and guidance; one-to-one/group tuition for students with dyslexia; alternative examination, assessment and study arrangements; support service for students with mental health issues and liaison with external organisations.

## Home sweet home:
A limited number of rooms are adapted with, for example, wider access, rails and en-suite facilities. The college can make adjustments as per requirements, e.g. provision of a dog pen/run for guide dogs. New work is in progress to include fully adapted rooms. Students with disabilities can remain on campus for the duration of their course. Accommodation can be guaranteed for the duration of the student's course, dependent on nature of disability.

## Out and about:
College: There are dedicated parking spaces near both the accommodation and study areas.
Public transport: Some buses, trains, train station and taxis are accessible to people who are wheelchair users and/or who have visual impairments.
Contact Access and Mobility for information about London's public transport services (see Directory).

## Taking it easy:
At college: The Students Union is accessible and has a lift to the post room and offices, and the bar and gym are accessible.
Locally: The city centre is flat and accessible. Some of the town's

facilities are accessible and there is a Shopmobility scheme. Most pavements are now tactile. Artsline publishes a number of access guides to London (see Directory).

## And another thing ...

➡ St Mary's campus consists of many buildings; several are listed and not very accessible to wheelchair users. An accessibility audit has been conducted and the results are directing the college to make adjustments where possible.

## The Disability Statement/Brochure:

All policy statements are reviewed and updated to include disability issues. Leaflets on individual needs and dyslexia are available on request and sent out to students who indicate a disability on their UCAS forms.

---

| University of Salford |
|---|

Salford, Greater Manchester M5 4WT

*General Enquiries:*
Tel: 0161 295 5000
Fax: 0161 295 5999
Email: course-enquiries@salford.ac.uk
Website: www.salford.ac.uk

**Disability Adviser: Denise Anthony**
**Tel: 0161 295 2833**
**Fax: 0161 295 2018**
**Email: d.m.anthony@**
**salford.ac.uk**

## Fields of study:

Art and design; business; engineering; environment; food and hospitality management; humanities; information technology; management; nursing, health care; politics; social sciences; sports and tourism.

➡ Part-time study: **Yes.**
➡ Distance learning: **Yes.**

## About the university:

The University of Salford is just a mile and a half from the main city centre next to the River Irwell, at the starting point of the Irwell Valley nature trail. Manchester, the UK's second largest city, is a 24-hour city where you can always find something to do. It is surrounded by national parks, and the Lake District, the Peak District, Snowdonia and the Lancashire coast are all within easy travelling distance.

| Total number of students: 21,690 |
|---|
| Number of disabled students: 1,736 |

**Learning support staff and services:**
Equality and Diversity Office
Full-time staff: Assistant Registrar: Andy Lie; Ethnicity: Gar-Ming Hui; Assistant Disability Adviser: Louise Thompson; Administrator: Caroline Coupland; Clerical Assistant: Jean Philips.
Part-time staff: Disability Advisers: Denise Anthony and Pauline Lamb.
Needs assessments; assistance with DSA applications and Hardship Funds; provision of auxiliary aids and services; support, information and advice to both staff and students; equipment loan scheme; initial screening for dyslexia assessments; one-to-one/group tuition for students with dyslexia; alternative examination, assessment and study arrangements; information on specialist equipment; support service for students with mental health issues; a peer support scheme for students with mental health difficulties and liaison with external organisations such as RNIB, RNID, Dyslexia Association, Skill and Workable.
The Equality and Diversity Office works alongside Access Summit – a Joint Universities Disability Resource Centre – which can provide further support.

**Home sweet home:**
John Lester and Eddie Colman Courts, Castle Irwell and Constantine Court all provide accommodation that is accessible for people who are wheelchair users. John Lester Court has a Deaf Alerter system. Accommodation can be guaranteed for duration of student's course.

**Out and about:**
University: There are dedicated parking spaces near both accommodation and study areas.
Public transport: Some buses, trains and taxis (including black cabs) are accessible to people who are wheelchair users. The campus train station has steps. Buses, trains, train stations and taxis are all accessible to people with visual impairments.

**Taking it easy:**
At university: The SU, student bar and sports centre are accessible and there is a lift into the swimming pool.
Locally: The city centre is flat and accessible. There is a Shopmobility scheme and some pavements are tactile, but only on the main routes.

**And another thing ...**
➡ Examples of specialist equipment available within the university include induction loops and infrared loop systems in major lecture theatres.
➡ The majority of the university's 30+ buildings (across four major campuses) are accessible.

➡ Wheelchair users should normally be able to take any route across the campus. All buildings have ramped access.

➡ An Opening Doors audit is available for information on access to specific sites, procedures, facilities and services for students with disabilities.

➡ AIS (Academic Information Services) have established a Disability/Access Team with a view to improving its services to students with disabilities – email: advisor@ais.salford.ac.uk or telephone Joanna Wilson on 0161 295 2440.

## The Disability Statement/Brochure:
Covers: Services offered; contacts; declaration of disability; financial assistance; examinations; equipment and software provision; physical access and library and computing.

### Local disability public service providers:
Greater Manchester Coalition of Disabled People.
Salford Dyslexia Association.
Salford Mental Health Forum.

---

| School of Advanced Study |
|---|

Senate House, Malet Street, London WC1E 7HU

*General Enquiries:*
Tel: 020 7862 8000
Fax: 020 7862 8080
Email: susan.small@lon.ac.uk
Web: www.lon.ac.uk

### Fields of study:
Advanced legal studies; classical studies; Commonwealth studies; English studies; Germanic studies; historical research; interdisciplinary studies; Latin American studies; philosophy; romance studies; United States studies.

Part-time study: **Yes.**
Distance learning: **No.**

### About the school:
The School of Advanced Study (SAS) has ten member institutes, some of which are based in Senate House and others in Bloomsbury.
The Warburg Institute is dedicated to the interdisciplinary study of the

classical tradition: to exploring the abiding influence of the ancient world on every aspect of European culture, and in particular on art, thought, literature, religion and social customs.

| |
|---|
| Total number of students: 270<br>Number of disabled students: Not known |

**Staff and services:**
There are no specific staff or services for students with disabilities.

**Out and about:**
School: There are dedicated parking spaces near both accommodation and study areas.
Public transport: Taxis and some buses, trains and train stations are accessible to people who are wheelchair users. Some buses, trains, train stations and taxis are accessible to people with visual impairments. Contact Access and Mobility for further information (see Directory).

**Taking it easy:**
At school: The school uses the facilities of the University of London Union.
Locally: the city centre is flat and some facilities are accessible. The pavements are tactile. Artsline publish a number of access guides to London (see Directory).

| |
|---|
| **School of Oriental and African Studies** |

University of London, Thornhaugh Street, Russell Square,
London WC1H 0XG

*General Enquiries:*
Tel: 020 7637 2388
Fax: 020 7436 4211
Email: study@soas.ac.uk
Website: www.soas.ac.uk

**Student Disability Officer:**
**Zoe Davies**
**Tel: 020 7074 5018**
**Fax: 020 7074 5039**
**Email: zd@soas.ac.uk**

**Fields of study:**
Anthropology and sociology; art and archaeology; development studies; economics; geography; history; languages and cultures of Africa, East Asia, Near and Middle East, South Asia, South East Asia; law; linguistics; music; political studies; religions.

School of Oriental and African Studies

➡ Part-time study: **Yes.**
➡ Distance learning: **Yes.**

## About the school:
The School of Oriental and African Studies (SOAS) is the only higher education institution in the UK specialising in the study of Asia and Africa and is now the world's largest institution of its kind. Established in 1916, SOAS is part of the federal University of London and is situated in Bloomsbury. Most teaching takes place in the main building or in the adjacent Brunei Gallery. The British Museum, Oxford Street, Covent Garden and the West End are all close by.

| Total number of students: 3,000 | Number of disabled students: 160 |
|---|---|

## Learning support staff and services:
Student Disability Officer: Zoe Davies.
Liaison with staff and external agencies; alternative examination arrangements.

## Home sweet home:
SOAS makes use of two student residences available for the sole use of its students – Dinwiddy House and Paul Robeson House. Both have purpose-built bedrooms and parking bays for use by disabled residents. Both are approximately 20 minutes from the school. Accommodation *cannot* be guaranteed for duration of student's course but staff will make every effort to assist students where necessary.

## Out and about:
School: There are some dedicated parking spaces near both accommodation and study areas, although these are not under the control of the school.
Public transport: Contact Access and Mobility regarding information on London's public transport services (see Directory).

## Taking it easy:
School: Accessible leisure facilities, e.g. SU, bar, sports and clubs are provided by the University of London SU. SOAS SU also aims to make venues accessible.
Locally: Artsline publishes a number of guides about access in London (see Directory).

## And another thing ...
➡ The recommendations of an access audit carried out at the Russell Square buildings are being implemented on an ongoing basis. In general, SOAS buildings are accessible for wheelchair users, with accessible toilet facilities, lifts and Braille and tactile signage.

## The Disability Statement/Brochure:
Available on Website or from Disability Officer.

---

### School of Pharmacy, University of London
29–39 Brunswick Square, London WC1 1AX

*General Enquiries:*
Tel: 020 7753 5831
Fax: 020 7753 5829
Email: registry@ulsop.ac.uk
Website: www.ulsop.ac.uk

**Registrar: Margaret Stone**
**Tel: 020 7753 5831**
**Fax: 020 7753 5829**
**Email: Margaret.stone@**
**ulsop.ac.uk**

### Fields of study:
Pharmacy; pharmaceutical science.

➡ Part-time study: **Yes, for postgraduates only**
➡ Distance learning: **No.**

### About the school:
Founded in 1842 by the (now Royal) Pharmaceutical Society, the school is an independent specialist one within the University of London. Its collaboration with teaching hospitals such as the Royal London and St Bartholomew's allows for clinical training. The School has many links with the hospital service, with community pharmacy and with industry. It is located on the University of London's central campus in Bloomsbury, with its famous university library, the University of London Union and six of the intercollegiate halls of residence only minutes away.

| Total number of students: 1,100 | Number of disabled students: 38 |
|---|---|

### Learning support staff and services:
Registrar: Margaret Stone.
General advice and information on funding. The registrar responds to individual needs as they arise.

## Home sweet home:
The school can guarantee a place in one of the University of London intercollegiate halls for students whose disability makes it necessary to live close to the school.

## Out and about:
School: There are no dedicated parking spaces.
Public transport: Bus services are accessible in the main. Contact Access and Mobility for further information on London's public transport services (see Directory).

## Taking it easy:
At school: The SU bar is wheelchair accessible. Students use the leisure facilities provided by the University of London.
Locally: Access guides are available from Artsline (see Directory).

## And another thing ...
➡ As part of the School's Pastoral Care Scheme all students are assigned to a personal tutor or supervisor. The Registrar serves as the School's Welfare Officer.
➡ Toilet facilities are not wheelchair accessible.
➡ There is no specialist software, Brailling facilities, video phones, but there is an enlarged PC screen.
➡ Support workers such as sign language interpreters, readers and notetakers and facilities, e.g. induction loops, would be provided if required.

---

### Scottish Agricultural College

National College for Food, Land and Environmental Studies, SAC Ayr,
Auchincruive Estate, Ayr KA6 5HW

*General Enquiries:*
Tel: 0800 269453
Fax: 01292 525349
Email: ETSU@au.sac.ac.uk
Website: www.sac.ac.uk

**Senior Tutor: Alison Murray**
**Tel: 01292 525157**
**Fax: 01292 525349**
**Email: a.murray@au.sac.ac.uk**

## Fields of study:
Agriculture; business management; countryside and tourism management; environmental resource management; horticulture and landscape; leisure management; science and technology.

➡ Part-time study: **Yes.**
➡ Distance learning: **Yes.**

## About the college:

The Scottish Agricultural College's (SAC) mission is to 'enhance the sustainability of rural areas and communities and viability of the industries on which they depend'. In addition to its role in education SAC has a research and development programme and runs an international advisory and consultancy service. SAC has three campuses – Aberdeen, Ayr and Edinburgh – and seven farms distributed around Scotland, with a comprehensive range of farming activities represented.

> Total number of students: 1,000
> Number of disabled students: approx. 10%

## Learning support staff and services:

Senior Tutors: Dr Alison Murray (Ayr); Dr Collette Cole (Aberdeen); Dr Mark Hocart (Edinburgh).
Dyslexic assessments; individual support needs and provision of teaching tools; liaison with student's year tutor, who feeds information to teaching staff; alternative examination arrangements; assessment support; provision of scribes; information on DSA and provision of forms; put into place support mechanisms as need arises.

## Home sweet home:

At Aberdeen and Ayr there are halls of residence. At Ayr there are dedicated rooms for disabled students on the ground floor with private bathrooms. Accommodation can be guaranteed for duration of student's course. In Edinburgh SAC has no accommodation under its own direct control, but rooms are available for SAC students in one of the University of Edinburgh's halls. Resident wardens in the halls will be aware of students with disabilities and take appropriate action.
There are wheelchair accessible rooms with accessible toilets and bathrooms at Aberdeen, and arrangements can be made at Ayr, e.g., students with mobility impairments at Ayr have been allocated rooms on the ground floor with their own private bathrooms. It is possible to have an extra room for a PA. Fridges for medication or diets are available at both sites, as are helpful staff. The halls of residence at Aberdeen have datapoint connections for computer use.
Accommodation can be guaranteed for duration of student's course. The University of Edinburgh has suitable accommodation for students with physical disabilities, including wheelchair access.

Accommodation in the University of Edinburgh halls of residence is available for first-year students only.

## Out and about:
College: There are plenty of parking places, and disabled students are allocated parking permits that allow them to park where they want. At Ayr and Aberdeen there are dedicated parking spaces near accommodation and study areas.
Public transport: The local bus, which stops outside the Ayr campus, is not accessible.
Aberdeen is a rural campus. The bus stops approximately 1 mile from the main teaching facilities. Some buses have disabled access.
Some of the buses in Edinburgh, including those that travel near King's Buildings, are accessible. There are no specific parking bays at Edinburgh, but permits would be given to ensure a space near the SAC building.

## Taking it easy:
Locally: Ayr is flat and accessible with tactile pavements. In the main Ayr shopping centre, pavements have been widened and the only through traffic allowed is buses, taxis and vehicles having disabled drivers, who are allowed to park in the main area. Many of the shopping facilities are accessible.
Aberdeen is flat and local facilities are accessible. It is a thriving town centre with a number of shopping centres and precincts, including reserved parking for disabled people, toilet facilities, talking pelican crossings. Taxis and public transport cater for wheelchairs.
Edinburgh is both flat and hilly in areas and has many shopping centres and leisure centres that are accessible. These include a number of designated parking spaces in the city centre, Shopmobility schemes, talking pelican crossings, taxis and public transport catering for wheelchair users, etc. Some pavements are tactile.

## And another thing …
➡ Most of the teaching facilities at Aberdeen are in a new, purpose-built building, which has good access for those with mobility impairments, and a lift to all floors. Ayr and Edinburgh have predominantly older buildings with more limited access; the libraries and many of the teaching rooms and laboratories are accessible only by stairs.
➡ The nature of some of SAC's courses requires manual dexterity and mobility and may present problems for students with certain physical disabilities.
➡ SAC is committed to offering courses by flexible learning. This means that increasingly students will be able to study part time or

at times that suit them best, or to study from home interactively as courses become available on the Internet.

➡ Study skills are dealt with in most SAC courses, none specifically directed at students with disabilities.

➡ SAC has no professional counsellors on its staff.

➡ SAC's degree courses are validated by Aberdeen, Edinburgh and Glasgow universities, with which SAC is formally associated. This 'associate' status allows access in many cases to services provided by the universities.

➡ A blind member of the board of the British Computer Association of the Blind and a member of the IT support and development staff will provide advice and assistance.

➡ Computer hardware and software are available to help students with dyslexia or visual impairment. Voice recognition software can be made available at all campuses.

➡ A Braille embosser is available.

➡ There is an induction loop driver with microphone at Ayr and access to the use of radio microphone equipment at Aberdeen and Edinburgh.

➡ There are accessible toilet facilities at Aberdeen and Ayr, but not at Edinburgh.

➡ Stairs at all sites have white-line edges.

➡ Student Services maintains a wide range of literature relating to disability and individual needs.

➡ SAC is a member of Skill, and has links with RNIB, RNID and with LEAD (for students with physical disabilities, visual impairments and who are D/deaf or hard of hearing).

## The Disability Statement/Brochure:

Includes: facilities and equipment; sources of support; access; accommodation; study/assessment/examinations; finance; monitoring.

### Local disability public service provider:

Shopmobility scheme.

| University of Sheffield |
| --- |

14 Favell Road, Sheffield S3 7QX

*General Enquiries:*
Tel: 0114 222 2000
Fax: 0114 273 9826
Email: ug.admissions@sheffield.ac.uk
Website: www.shef.ac.uk

**Student Adviser: Lynne Healy**
**Tel: 0114 222 1322**
**Fax: 0114 222 1304**
**Email: l.healy@**
**shef.ac.uk**

University of Sheffield

## Fields of study:
Architectural studies; arts; engineering; law; medicine; pure science; social sciences.

- ➡ Part-time study: **Yes.**
- ➡ Distance learning: **Yes.**

## About the university:
The University of Sheffield was granted a Royal Charter in May 1905 and has developed into one of the UK's leading research institutions. Four Nobel Prizes have been won by graduates and staff of the University of Sheffield, two of which were awarded in the 1990s. Recent government crime statistics show that Sheffield – the fifth largest city in Europe – is the safest city in England.

| Total number of students: 23,000+ |
| Number of disabled students: 1,300 |

## Learning support staff and services:
Learner Support

Full-time staff: Learner Support Coordinator: Lynn Healey; disability support coordinator; disability officer.

Part-time staff: two disability officers; Brailler; IT tutor; and clerical support. Assistance with DSA applications and other sources of funding including liaising with financial bodies; provision of auxiliary aids and services; advice and guidance; one-to-one/group tuition for students with dyslexia; alternative examination, assessment and study arrangements; support service for students with mental health issues; meeting prospective students; information on support available; organising needs assessments; purchasing equipment; technical support; transcribing academic material into Braille or large print on site; personal support; recruiting non-medical helpers; organising loan equipment; organising library concessions; liaising with departments and external organisations.

Support is available to D/deaf and hard of hearing students via a contract with the Sheffield College Hearing Impaired Service. This includes an assessment of specialist equipment and study strategies that can be undertaken at a specialist assessment centre.

Dyslexic students who are in receipt of DSA can have a full assessment undertaken in an Access Centre. Students who have a visual impairment may have mobility training.

Staff offer support, advice and information, and there is frequent liaison with other services such as Housing and Careers and also with academic departments.

**Home sweet home:**
Some rooms within the halls of residence and university self-catering flats have been specifically adapted for students who are wheelchair users or students who are D/deaf or who have hearing impairments. Disabled students are given special consideration in allocation of places. Accommodation is guaranteed for duration of student's course.

**Out and about:**
University: Dedicated parking spaces near both accommodation and study areas, but spaces are often limited at the residential sites. Public transport: All buses, trains, train stations, taxis and trams are accessible to people who are wheelchair users and/or who have a visual impairment. Students who have a disability or impairment and live in South Yorkshire may be entitled to a mobility pass. This pass enables travel on buses, trams and local trains at the current concessionary fare, or free of charge in some cases. The Sheffield Supertram network opened in 1994 and connects the university to the city centre and various other landmarks. Supertram stops and trams are all accessible for people with mobility impairments and wheelchair users. A map showing local bus routes is available from the Student Services Information Desk. Sheffield Community Transport provides a door-to-door service for people to whom public transport is not accessible. There is a small charge for this service.

**Taking it easy:**
At university: The newly refurbished university sports centre has had many modifications, including wheelchair access, designated changing rooms and access to the pool via a hoist. The Union of Students building, one of the largest in the country, is almost fully accessible to students with mobility difficulties.
Locally: The city centre is very hilly and partly accessible (Meadow Hall is fully accessible). Town facilities are accessible. Some of the pavements are tactile. The Body and Soul Fitness Studio at Sheffield YMCA has adapted sports facilities for disabled users, a talking notice board and adapted lighting for visually impaired people. The Hillsborough Leisure Centre is wheelchair accessible and has a swimming pool designed to be accessible.

**And another thing ...**
➡ Wheelchair users and students with mobility difficulties should be aware that some departments and services of the university are not fully accessible.
➡ Library services are available from nine sites across the university. Accessibility varies between branches, e.g. St George's Library is

accessible for wheelchair users, whilst parts of the main library are not.

➡ Financial support from university-administered funds is sometimes available but cannot be guaranteed.

➡ Students with medical conditions such as epilepsy, asthma or ME will be offered the same level of service as other students with individual needs.

➡ Disabled and dyslexic students are eligible for extended loans and other alternative library services.

➡ The SU has a Students with Disabilities Committee.

## The Disability Statement/Brochure:
*Information for Disabled Students, Dyslexic Students 2003/04*
Includes: Accommodation; support; admissions; support by disability; DSA and financial support; services; examinations and contacts.

### Local disability public service provider:
Forum of People with Disabilities, 116 The Wicker, Sheffield S3 8JD; 0114 275 5679.

---

### Sheffield Hallam University
City Campus, Howard Street, Sheffield S1 1WB

*General Enquiries:*
Tel: 0114 225 5555
Fax: 0114 225 3398
Website: www.shu.ac.uk
Text: 0114 225 3816

**Disability Coordinator:**
**Tel: 0114 225 3964 Text**
**Fax: 0114 225 2161**
**Email: guidance@shu.ac.uk**

### Fields of study:
Art and design; built and natural environment; business, finance and management; computing; education and teacher training; engineering and technology; English and humanities/critical studies; environment; health and social care; law; leisure, food, recreation and hospitality; mathematics; media; science; social sciences; sport.

➡ Part-time study: **Yes.**
➡ Distance learning: **Yes (limited number of courses available).**

### About the university:
Sheffield Hallam University boasts the second largest computer network of any UK university. Based on three campuses, one of which

is located in Sheffield city centre, the university is situated in England's safest city according to Home Office crime figures (January 2001).

Total number of students: 23,692
Number of disabled students: 746 registered

### Learning support staff and services:
The Disabled Student Support Team consists of 19 core members of staff, seven of whom are involved in assessing students and handling the associated paperwork. There are also four full-time sign language interpreters, dyslexia support tutors, technicians, in addition to approximately 50 support staff working for the university in various roles – notetakers, PAs, etc.
Needs assessments; assistance with DSA applications and Access Funds; provision of auxiliary aids and services; advice and guidance; one-to-one individual/group tuition for students with dyslexia; alternative examination, assessment and study arrangements; support service for students with mental health problems; screening for dyslexia; guidance to teaching and non-academic staff; provision of specific induction sessions; learner support tutorials and workshops; disability awareness throughout the university and liaison with external organisations.

### Home sweet home:
Pillow vibrators, flashing door and fire alarms are available in some of the university's accommodation. Deaf Alerter system installed with vibrating alerters available. There are also rooms accessible to wheelchair users with wheel-in showers and lowered work surfaces. Rooms to accommodate a person with a guide dog are available and there is generally a 'spending pen' nearby.
Accommodation can be guaranteed for duration of student's course.

### Out and about:
University: Specialist transport is provided where necessary. There are dedicated parking spaces near both accommodation and study areas.
Public transport: Low-level access buses.

### Taking it easy:
At university: Student Services Centre is a base for meeting, through induction and social events.
Locally: Very accessible.

**And another thing …**

➡ Occasional financial assistance to students from the university's budget.

➡ The university operates as part of the Sheffield Regional Acess Centre (jointly with Sheffield College), and is a member of the NFAC.

➡ To ensure that disabled students always have a point of contact, a disability coordinator is appointed in every school and department and in the Learning Centre.

**QAA Report: Paragraph 46, May 2001**

At central level, a wide range of organised student support and guidance is available and has been the subject of praise in JEFCE/QAA subject review reports. Most non-academic support is organised through SSC, a federal structure that brings together a range of services. The audit team noted that a very good range of support was provided and the staff involved were enthusiastic and committed. The team noted in particular, in the light of QAA's Code of Practice on students with disabilities, the work of SSC's Disabled Student Support Unit and the way in which it operated in tandem with designated disability coordinators in schools to provide support for the university's students with disabilities, numbering around 1000. This arrangement provided an example of the university's awareness of the importance of both providing a central service and ensuring that academic and other operation units took specialist needs into account in their own provision.

## The Disability Statement/Brochure:

At the time of writing, the disability statement was being updated. Up-to-date information can be found at www.shu.ac.uk/services/ssc/uk.

**Local disability public service provider:**

Family Community Services, Redvere House, Union Street, Sheffield.

---

| Slade School of Fine Art |
|:---:|

University College London, Gower Street, London WC1E 6BT

*General Enquiries:*
Tel: 020 7679 2313
Fax: 020 7679 7801
Email: enquiries@ucl.ac.uk
Website: www.ucl.ac.uk/slade

**Disability Coordinator:**
**Alistair Appleby**
**Tel: 020 7679 1343**
**Fax: 020 7916 8530**
**Email: Alistair.Appleby@ ucl.ac.uk**

**Fields of study:**
Art history and theoretical studies; fine art – painting, sculpture; fine art media – electronic media, film and video, photography, printmaking; theatre design and research.

➡ Part-time study: **No.**
➡ Distance learning: **No.**

**About the school:**
The Slade School of Fine Art is a department of University College London, which was founded in 1871. Since 1994 the Slade has had students on the MPhil/PhD programme who form an active research community within the school. The school's location in the centre of London, close to many galleries, museums and theatres, provides excellent opportunities for students to access a wide range of learning resources and research opportunities.

| Total number of students: 260 | Number of disabled students: 10 |
|---|---|

**Learning support staff and services:**
All administration for students with disabilities and individual needs is handled by University College London. Please refer to this entry for further information.

| **Somerset College of Arts and Technology** |
|---|

Wellington Road, Taunton, Somerset TA1 5AX

*General Enquiries:*
Information Centre:
Tel: 01823 366331
Fax: 01823 366418
Email: enquiries@somerset.ac.uk
Website: www.somerset.ac.uk

**Support Tutor: Pat Griffin**
**Tel: 01823 366525**
**Fax: 01823 366418**
**Email: ptg@somerset.ac.uk**
**Text: 01823 366362**

**Fields of study:**
Antiques; archaeology; beauty and theatrical media make-up; business and management; combined arts; communication arts; construction; engineering; fashion; fine art; health and social care; interior decoration; IT; product design; psychology; science; sports; teaching and training; textiles; tourism.

➡ Part-time study: **Yes.**
➡ Distance learning: **Limited, please enquire.**

## About the college:
The Somerset College of Arts and Technology is the Somerset centre of the University of Plymouth, with whom the college is in partnership. Taunton is the county town of Somerset in south-west England in the heart of the countryside. The outlying villages and towns offer cultural diversity and the college is near to the north Devon beaches.

Total number of disabled students: 800 (HE and FE)

## Learning support staff and services:
Support Tutor: Pat Griffin; Learning Support Team: learning facilitators.
Individual examination arrangements; assistance with DSA applications; arrangement of personal support requirements; assistance with mobility; support students in class or workshop; support students on work placements if required; students assisted in the learning centres on projects or assignments; computer and other equipment assistance. The learning support team is experienced and well qualified to support students with dyslexia/specific learning difficulties, visual impairment, students who are D/deaf or hard of hearing and those with mental health issues, behavioural difficulties, learning disabilities and physical disabilities.

## Home sweet home:
Accommodation Officer (01823 366486) will assist with all aspects of accommodation.
The hall of residence is situated on the edge of Taunton and there are four rooms adapted for students with disabilities.
Accommodation is usually available for duration of student's course.

## Out and about:
College: Dedicated parking spaces near both accommodation and study areas.
Public transport: Some local buses, train stations are wheelchair accessible and accessible to visually impaired people.

## Taking it easy:
At college: Sports centres, SU and bar are not accessible to wheelchair users.
Locally: The town centre is part-pedestrianised. The local access guide is available at the Tourist Information Centre. Taunton has a Shopmobility scheme.

## And another thing ...

➡ The main college campus is fairly level, with a gentle incline to the sports hall and G block. There are path ramps that enable access across campus. A support assistant can help students learn their way round and meet students from their bus or car at the beginning of term.

➡ Access to upper floors is limited for wheelchair users. An audit of access to the college has been undertaken. Improvements for access are planned through an entirely new building. Visual fire alarms have been fitted.

➡ There are accessible toilets in blocks A, E and G with a shower in E block. The Bishops Hull centre has an accessible toilet.

➡ There is a portable loop system and fixed wiring for the loop at various points. There are radio aids.

➡ The college has a range of specialist support that may be available to students on FE courses following assessment. However, the college stresses that students with disabilities on HE courses will unfortunately only have access to additional support if they are in receipt of DSA.

➡ Additional resources include: Portable loop system and fixed wiring for the loop at various points. Radio aids are available, also CCTV, computers and switches, spellcheckers and copy cards, Intellikeys, ergonomic keyboards, specialist mice, etc. Individual programmes may be available. Please enquire.

## The Disability Statement/Brochure:

Includes: Admission; support staff; resources and equipment; examination arrangements; other services; disability statement; documents and policies; equal opportunities statement; feedback.

## Local disability public service provider:

Disability Advocate – Richard Pitman 01823 327453.

| Southampton Institute |
|---|

East Park Terrace, Southampton SO 14 0RU

| *General Enquiries:* | **Disability Coordinator: Sara Luxford** |
|---|---|
| Tel: 023 8031 9000 | **Tel: 023 8031 9665** |
| Fax: 023 8022 2259 | **Fax: 023 8031 9904** |
| Email: enquiries@solent.ac.uk | **Email: sara.luxford@** |
| Website: www.solent.ac.uk | **solent.ac.uk** |
| Text: 023 8031 9912 | **Text: 023 8031 9912** |

## Fields of study:

Art and design (including fine arts valuation); business and finance (including accountancy, marketing, personnel); computing, construction and engineering; environment; human and social science; law; leisure, sport and tourism; maritime; media, film and journalism.

➡ Part-time study: **Yes, but not for all courses.**
➡ Distance learning: **Yes, but not all courses.**

## About the institute:

Southampton Institute is on the south coast of England just over an hour from London and within easy reach of Bournemouth, Portsmouth and Winchester. The institute is committed to reducing its impact on the environment and so its buildings are primarily heated by geothermal energy on a district ring main. The institute's new buildings are designed to be energy efficient and it is investing in energy-saving control systems. Situated in the heart of the city, the campus enjoys proximity to spacious parks as well as easy access to the shops, nightlife and halls of residence.

> Total number of students: approx. 15,100
> Number of disabled students: approx. 900

## Learning support staff and services:

Disability and Learning Support are part of the Study Assistance Unit
Full-time staff: Disability Coordinator: Sara Luxford; Senior Study Assistance Tutor: Polly Osbourne.
Part-time staff: Dyslexia Tutor: Karen Rowberry; Study Assistance Tutor (IT): Lorna Campbell.
Liaise and work closely with local Access Centre; informal assessments of provision provided; assistance with DSA applications; provision of auxiliary aids and services; advice and guidance; one-to-one/group tuition for students with dyslexia; alternative examination, assessment and study arrangements; support service for students with mental health issues; mobility training; arrangements for library support; screening for dyslexia and the arrangement of an assessment with an educational psychologist and liaison with external organisations.

## Home sweet home:

The Accommodation Office tries to meet the needs of disabled students where possible. There are some purpose-built study rooms with low-level controls and en-suite facilities suitable for wheelchair users. Some rooms have been adapted for students with sensory impairment. Larger rooms are available for students who require extra space for specialist equipment. Accommodation is available for PAs. The Accommodation Office is always happy to discuss specific adaptations students need on an individual basis. Students with disabilities are given priority when applying for rooms in halls of residence.

Accommodation can be guaranteed for duration of student's course.

## Out and about:
Institute: Dedicated parking spaces near both accommodation and study areas.

Public transport: Some buses, trains, train stations and taxis are accessible to people who are wheelchair users.

## Taking it easy:
At institute: There is full access to the SU building via a lift. There are no accessible toilets in the sports centre. The institute refectories are accessible to wheelchair users.

Locally: The city centre is flat and very close to the institute. Some of the pavements are tactile and there is a Shopmobility scheme.

## And another thing ...
→ There is wheelchair access to most teaching areas; however, a small number of areas remain inaccessible. Classes can be rescheduled into accessible venues.

→ Students at Warsash Maritime Centre and Marchwood site are required to meet the employers' criteria for fitness in the maritime industry. These sites are not at present suitable for people with mobility difficulties or visual impairments.

→ An important long-term objective is to ensure that all teaching and resource areas are accessible to wheelchair users and that all signage is appropriate for visually impaired people.

→ The institute seeks to increase its representation of students with disabilities.

→ A map detailing the most accessible routes for those with mobility difficulties is available.

→ Academic Information Service (AIS) provides support facilities for disabled students in using the institute library and IT facilities. A Blue Card enables students with disabilities to obtain extra assistance and services.

→ The institute is a member of Skill and has links with Hampshire Association for the Deaf and the Southampton Centre for Independent Living (SCIL).

## The Disability Statement/Brochure:
*Information for Students with Disabilities*
Includes: Current policy; disability statement; access and admissions; examination and assessments; financial support; external links; support services; physical environment; laboratories; studios; car parking; SU; accommodation; student profiles; future policy and further information.

## Local disability public service providers:
Hampshire Association for the Deaf.
Southampton Centre for Independent Living, run and controlled by disabled people; 023 8033 0982; text: 023 8063 5167.

---

### University of Southampton
Highfield, Southampton SO17 1BJ

*General Enquiries:*
Tel: 023 8059 5000
Fax: 023 8059 3939
Email: webmaster@soton.ac.uk
Website: www.soton.ac.uk

**Disability Coordinator: Deb Viney**
**Tel: 023 8059 5644**
**Fax: 023 8059 6815**
**Email: enable@soton.ac.uk**
**Dyslexia Services/Learning Differences Centre**
**Coordinator of Dyslexia Services: Janet Skinner**
**Tel: 023 8059 2759**
**Fax: 023 8059 5565**
**Email: dyslexia@soton.ac.uk**
**Website: www.dyslexia.soton.ac.uk**

➡ Part-time study: **on some courses**.
➡ Distance learning: **on some courses**.

## About the university:
The University of Southampton is located on several campuses, including Highfield, Avenue, New College, Southampton Oceanography Centre and Winchester School of Art. Most of the campuses and facilities are accessible to wheelchair users, but there are some specific areas of difficulty.

---

Total number of students: approx. 20,000
Number of disabled students: approx. 1,800

---

## Disability Staff and Services:

Disability Coordinator: Deb Viney; Disability Officer: Pauline Mills; Coordinator, Mentor Service: Sue Meads; Mentor: Carol Greene.
The university encourages all disabled applicants to make a prospective visit to the campus to meet the academic staff and disability team.
Services include: assistance offered in identifying needs; facilitate practical support by providing information, referral to LEA and Access centres as necessary; facilitate support worker and specialist tutor arrangements through local staff banks; liaison with Schools to negotiate alternative examination arrangements, or support students who wish to negotiate independently; assist the university in developing policy and procedure based on best practice and offer support and training to other members of staff.

## Dyslexia Services:

Coordinator of Dyslexia Services: Janet Skinner; Dyslexia Tutor – Highfield and Winchester School of Art: Allene Tuck; Dyslexia Tutor – Highfield and New College campuses: Fanny Surtees; Dyslexia Tutor – Highfield campus: Jane Lapraik; Dyslexia Tutor – Highfield campus: Gail Alexander.
Dyslexia Services/the Learning Differences Centre provide dyslexia support for all university students. All students must register with the Centre in order to ensure that appropriate support is provided.
Dyslexia Support is provided at New College and at Winchester School of Art Campuses as well as at Highfield Campus.
Services include: recommendations for alternative examination arrangements; academic study skill tutorials provided individually or in small groups; assistance with all aspects of study skills such as notetaking, reading techniques, essay planning, proofreading skills; arrange dyslexia screening and educational psychologist assessments; arrangements made for educational psychologist assessments and assistance with DSA applications.
The support offered is tailored to individual need.
The Centre for Enabling and Learning Technologies (CELT) (NFAC Assessment Centre) is at the New College Campus, 023 9059 7233; email: CELT@soton.ac.uk.

## Home sweet home:

Several of the residences have accessible rooms with various facilities including en-suite shower rooms with level access, accessible kitchen facilities, visible alarms, though the student common rooms are not wheelchair accessible in some halls. There are telephones with voicemail facilities in every room and the halls are being networked for Intranet and WWW access too. Most halls also have 'public' IT suites. Prospective visits to review the hall facilities are strongly recommended; contact Carole Phillips (023 8059 7726). Preview days are held in late June; contact Admissions Office or Disability Service for details, or private visits can be arranged. The accommodation is in several locations within the city, and there is some close to most campuses. Personal or domestic care (up to 24 hours) can be arranged if required and this should be discussed with the Disability Coordinator during a prospective visit. Students with disabilities are given priority in the allocation of rooms; in some cases accommodation can be offered for the duration of the student's course.

### Out and about:
University: Vehicle parking can be arranged close to campus/residence. There is an accessible minibus with tail lift provided during office hours that is free of charge for academic activities. Outside office hours local taxi services are used to provide transport: more information is available on request.
Public transport: Unilink buses are available, serving the university campuses, the residential blocks and the wider city, airport, coach and train stations. They have low floors and good access with two wheelchair spaces per bus in most cases.

### Taking it easy:
At university: Banks, shops, some bars and SU are all accessible to wheelchair users.
Locally: The city centre is fairly flat and most of the facilities are accessible. There is a Shopmobility scheme and some pavements are tactile.

### And another thing ...
➡ The university's buildings vary in their accessibility because they vary in age and design. An early visit gives the Estates and Buildings Department time to try and arrange any changes to physical access that might be required to accommodate the student's needs.
➡ At the university the main library, banks, shops, SU and other services all offer good wheelchair access. The branch libraries on other campuses may have more restricted access to upper floors due to older building stock but staff will collect items from those floors on request.
➡ Most teaching rooms do not have induction loops built in, but portable systems that work with your telecoil (T switch) are

available for loan, and most larger lecture theatres have public address systems.

➡ Accessible IT facilities: specialist equipment is available in the Assistive Technology Centre and also in some small workstation areas on the other campuses. The equipment available includes: Braille embosser, scanners and CCTV, voice activated software, tactile diagram machine. Some assistive technology software is available on the university Intranet.

➡ An Assistive Technology Centre in the Hartley Library has recently been opened with staff to support students who have a learning difficulty or disability – ext. 27620 at the Hartley Library; email: ats@soton.ac.uk

➡ Improving physical access for students who have mobility or other disabilities is one of the key features of the university's strategic plan. The university aims to improve access to and within buildings, both as part of the rolling programme of refurbishment and on an 'as and when required' basis. Access audits have highlighted the changes that need to be made on each of the sites, and the programme of improvements for existing buildings is kept under review. All new buildings are designed with the needs of disabled people in mind.

➡ Orientation sessions of the campus are available as are tactile maps of the campus, on request.

➡ The university is a member of the Southern Higher Education Consortium (SHEC) along with six other HE institutions in the region including King Alfred's, Winchester – please see King Alfred's entry for further details.

➡ The university is a member of Skill.

➡ Future developments include investing in developing the university's sports facilities, within which more sporting facilities will be made available for students with disabilities.

## The Disability Statement/Brochure:
www.soton.ac.uk/~acreg/dis/disintro.html or select *Information for Students with Disabilities and Dyslexia* via the Professional Services/Student Services section on the home page (www.soton.ac.uk).
Includes: Introduction; information for those with a specific learning difficulty; information for students with disabilities; physical access; accommodation; Disability Support Service; DSA; links and future plans.

### Local disability public service provider:
Southampton Centre for Independent Living, Archer's Road, Southampton.

## Spurgeon's College: University of Wales
South Norwood Hill, London SE25 6DJ

*General Enquiries:*
Tel: 020 8653 0850
Fax: 020 8771 0959
Email: enquiries@spurgeons.ac.uk
Website: www.spurgeons.ac.uk

### Fields of study:
Baptist and Anabaptist studies; Biblical studies; Christian doctrine; church planting and evangelism or pastoral studies; Divinity; preaching; theology; urban ministry and research.

➡ Part-time study: **Yes.**
➡ Distance learning: **Yes.**

### About the college:
Spurgeon's College prepares Christians for mission and ministry. Charles Haddon Spurgeon founded the college in 1856. He maintained a world perspective, and the maxim 'from the heart of London into all the world' remains as true today as it was then. Today's college is set on the second highest hill in south London, a strategic location only 8 miles from the centre of the capital and just a mile north of Croydon. The college is home to one of the best theological resources centres in the south of England.

| Total number of students: 270 | Number of disabled students: 8 |
|---|---|

### Learning support staff and services:
No specific staff and services.

### Home sweet home:
No specific accommodation for people with disabilities yet, but a project has been agreed to provide wheelchair access and lifts to all floors. The project is scheduled to finish by September 2003. Accommodation can be guaranteed for duration of student's course.

### Out and about:
College: Dedicated parking spaces near both accommodation and study areas.
Public transport: Some buses and taxis are accessible to wheelchair users and people with visual impairments. Contact Access and

Mobility for information about London's public transport services (see below).

**Taking it easy:**
At college: The personal tutors offer social support to students with disabilities.
Locally: The city centre is flat and is accessible as are the town's facilities. There is a Shopmobility scheme and the pavements are tactile. A local area disability guide is available from London Borough of Croydon Council. Artsline publishes a number of guides regarding access in London (see Directory).

**Local disability public service providers:**
Access and Mobility (see Directory).
LB Croydon, Taberner House, Croydon CR9 3BT.

---

| **Staffordshire University** |
| --- |

Stoke Campus, College Road, Stoke-on-Trent ST4 2DE

*General Enquiries:*
Tel: 01782 292753
Fax: 01782 292740
Email: admissions@staffs.ac.uk
Website: www.staffs.ac.uk

**Head of Disability Services:**
**Alexandra Evans**
**Tel: 01782 295822**
**Fax: 01782 292786**
**Email: l.lewis@staffs.ac.uk**
**Text: 01782 294564**

**Fields of study:**
Art and design; biology; business and management; community and citizenship; computing and IT; criminology; design technology; drama and theatre arts; economics; engineering; English; environment; forensic science; geography; geology; health, midwifery and nursing; history; languages; law; media and entertainment technology; new media; philosophy; psychology; social studies and social work; sport and leisure.

➡ Part-time study: **Yes.**
➡ Distance learning: **No.**

**About the university:**
The university is based on two main campuses in the Staffordshire area – Stoke and Stafford. The campuses are 17 miles apart: the Stoke campus is in the centre of the city of Stoke-on-Trent; the

Staffordshire University

Stafford campus 1¹/₂ miles from Stafford town. Staffordshire is ideally located – at the centre of England – for road and rail networks and it is a short ride away from Liverpool, Manchester, Birmingham and Nottingham and an hour and a half away from London and the seaside.

Total number of students: 16,272   Number of disabled students: 476

**Learning support staff and services:**
Disability Services
Full-time staff: Manager: Liz Lewis; Disability Advisor: Jenny Stephens; Clerical Assistant: Jean Amison.
Part-time staff: disability advisor.
Needs assessments (Staffordshire Regional Access Centre); assistance with DSA applications and Hardship Funds; advice and guidance; one-to-one/group tuition for students with dyslexia; alternative examination, assessment and study arrangements; support service for students with mental health problems via the Counselling Service; provision of support as well as a managed network of part-time support workers; mobility training around campus; specialist communication support for D/deaf and hard of hearing students; diagnostic testing for dyslexia; liaison with teaching and other service staff; coordination of assessed support within a framework of shared confidences; a Disability Statement in a range of formats and liaison with external organisations.

**Home sweet home:**
A range of wheelchair accessible accommodation is available on both main campuses at Stoke-on-Trent and Stafford – some with en-suite bathroom facilities with a high level of access features. There are a number of rooms integrated into halls of residence with access to adapted bath, shower and toilet facilities, low-level kitchens and wheelchair charging space. Rooms for PAs are available, with telephone or intercom link to the student's room. Some rooms have flashing/vibrating fire alarms for D/deaf or hard of hearing students. There are guide dog 'spending' compounds on both main campuses. Accommodation can be guaranteed for duration of student's course.

**Out and about:**
University: An accessible people carrier vehicle is available to hire for students via Disability Services. It is suitable for five passengers including one wheelchair user. The university insurance policy is extended to support worker drivers aged 21 and over. Dedicated parking spaces near both accommodation and study areas.

Public transport: Some buses, trains, train stations and taxis are accessible to people who are wheelchair users and/or who have visual impairments. Disability Services have a list of recommended taxi services including Roseville and Blue Cabs.

**Taking it easy:**
At university: SU venues are all wheelchair accessible. Student support workers are allowed free entry to social events. There is a wheelchair accessible vehicle that students can borrow.
Locally: The city centre is mostly flat and the pedestrian area and main shopping centre are accessible. There is a Shopmobility scheme and the pavements are tactile. The local cinemas and theatres are accessible. There is an accessible swimming pool close to the university in Stoke-on-Trent. *Contacts* is the name of the local area disability guide.

**And another thing ...**
➡ The university provides enabling technology in its libraries and learning centres for access to e-learning.
➡ There is a limited number of 17" TFT monitors and a limited number of licences for ZoomText screen magnification software.
➡ There is no specific colour modification software, but the university does have limited licences for Texthelp Read and Write, which allows background and text colours to be altered.
➡ There is some JAWS screen reading software for blind/visually impaired users.
➡ The university is also hoping to get a site licence for MindGenius 'mind mapping' software.
➡ The careers service offers a mentoring scheme for disabled students.
➡ The SU has a students with disabilities officer for further information and advice.
➡ The university has invested considerable resources into a rolling programme of improvements to physical access; for example talking lifts with low-level Braille controls and accessible toilet facilities serve main buildings, and dropped kerbs and controlled pedestrian crossings make sure each site is user friendly.

## The Disability Statement/Brochure:
Includes: Introduction; admissions procedures; Disability Services; personal support; continuing support; academic life; assessment and examinations; specialist equipment and information technology; finance; accommodation; access to the university; useful contacts and appendices.

## Local disability public service providers:
Disability Solutions, 01782 683100; text: 01782 683111; fax: 01782 683120.
Deaflinks: 01782 219161.

---

| **University of Stirling** |
| :---: |

Stirling FK9 4LA

*General Enquiries:*         **Disability Adviser: Catriona Mowat**
Tel: 01786 473171             **Tel: 01786 467080**
Fax: 01786 466800           **Fax: 01786 466806**
Email: admissions@stir.ac.uk     **Email: catriona.mowat@**
Website: www.stir.ac.uk            **stir.ac.uk**

## Fields of study:
Arts; human sciences; management; natural sciences.

➡ Part-time study: **Yes.**
➡ Distance learning: **No.**

## About the university:
The University of Stirling was opened in 1967 on a brand-new campus built on the estate of the eighteenth-century Airthrey Castle. The university is responsible for the teaching of nurses and midwives in the Forth Valley, Highlands and Western Isles; consequently there are other university campuses in both Inverness and Stornoway. The main university campus lies on the outskirts of the town of Stirling, an ancient town that has played a pivotal role in Scotland's history. The town is dominated by the famous Stirling Castle, the ancient seat of the Scottish crown. Today, however, Stirling is a modern manufacturing, administrative, shopping and tourist centre that offers easy access to the Highlands of Scotland as well as Glasgow and Edinburgh.

| Total number of students: approx. 8000 |
| :---: |
| Number of disabled students: 300+ |

## Learning support staff and services:
Student Information and Support Service (SISS)
Full-time staff: Disability Adviser: Catriona Mowat; assistant disability adviser: Elspeth McGregor; three counsellors; three additional advisers; administrative/reception staff.

Needs assessments; assistance with DSA applications; provision of auxiliary aids and services; advice and guidance; one-to-one/group tuition for students with dyslexia; alternative examination, assessment and study arrangements; support service for students with mental health issues; equipment applications; informing students of the outcome of their applications; briefing staff with responsibility for implementing agreed arrangements; offering familiarisation programme on the use of university-supported IT equipment and software; library support; information on university facilities or local area; assistance with any student needs; provision of information leaflets; providing a forum for discussion of issues for the SA; assistance arranging PAs and liaison with external organisations. There is also a support worker and access to counselling service at the Highland campus in Inverness.

**Home sweet home:**
There are no lifts in the residences and so access is limited to the ground floor. Some accommodation has adapted facilities, which may be suitable for some students. In some cases adaptations can be made according to need. Accommodation can be guaranteed for duration of student's course.

**Out and about:**
University: Dedicated parking spaces near both accommodation and study areas.
Public transport: Trains, train stations and some buses and taxis are accessible to people who are wheelchair users. All buses, trains, train stations and taxis are accessible to people who have visual impairments. Dial-a-Journey is the local taxi scheme for disabled people.

**Taking it easy:**
At university: The university sports centre welcomes all participants and makes provision for users with disabilities. Access to the building is by level entry on two levels. Some designated parking spaces are provided, and toilet facilities are available on both levels. There are adapted changing and showering facilities, the pool water temperature is high, and all playing and circulation areas are well illuminated. The tennis centre has level access, with adapted changing and toilet facilities. The design features for people with disabilities received an award. Where appropriate, staff have gained qualifications in the teaching and coaching of people with disabilities. The Scottish National Swimming Academy, located on campus, is fully accessible; the SU and MacRobert Arts Centre are also accessible.

Locally: The city centre is hilly and mostly accessible. Some of the facilities are accessible, some of the pavements are tactile and there is a Shopmobility scheme. An access guide, *Access All Areas*, is available from Student Information and Support Service.

## And another thing ...

- ➡ Most footpaths have gentle gradients, though some are steeper or have steps. Although access is not ideal most areas are accessible by wheelchair users, except Airthrey Castle and the residences. All other buildings have level access.
- ➡ Most main lecture theatres have been recently refurbished with modern audio/visual and other support systems installed. Lectures can be taped by students who need to do this.
- ➡ Accessible toilet facilities are provided within all main buildings.
- ➡ Teaching and central area buildings are equipped with passenger lifts and most classrooms are accessible for wheelchair users.
- ➡ The library is accessible via a lift to all levels.
- ➡ An ongoing building refurbishment programme includes further improvements to facilities for disabled people.
- ➡ External steps are white edged. Internal stairs are mostly fitted with contrasting edge nosings. Lighting levels can sometimes be altered on request within specific working areas.
- ➡ Some doors on campus may be difficult to use but are necessary for fire safety. Some of these are currently being replaced in the main teaching buildings.
- ➡ Campuses at Inverness and Stornoway are both located within hospital trust buildings. Stornoway has good access but at present wheelchair access is not possible at Inverness.
- ➡ For academic work there is a range of equipment and IT, including a dedicated computing facility located within the residence area of campus.
- ➡ There is an IT assessment service for students using enabling technologies.
- ➡ The library can provide course material in alternative formats, e.g. audiotape or Braille.
- ➡ The Special Academic Arrangements Panel (SAAP)) deals with applications from students with disabilities who feel they would benefit from additional academic arrangements to help them with their studies.
- ➡ The SA has a disabilities officer.
- ➡ The university has links with RNIB, RNID and is a member of Skill.

## The Disability Statement/Brochure:
*Information for Students with Disabilities*

Includes: Access; accommodation; local facilities; applications; advice and welfare; studying, coursework and exams; SUCCEEDS; safety; Disability Advisory Group; staff awareness and other sources of information.

**Local disability public service provider:**
Shopmobility 01786 449606.

| University of Strathclyde |
|---|

Glasgow G1 1XQ

*General Enquiries:*
Tel: 0141 552 4400
Fax: 0141 552 0775
Email: scls@mis.strath.ac.uk
Website: www.strath.ac.uk

**Head of Special Needs Service: Anne Simpson**
**Tel: 0141 548 3402**
**Fax: 0141 548 2414**
**Email: a.simpson@mis.strath.ac.uk**
**Text: 0141 548 4739**

**Fields of study:**
Arts and social sciences; business; education; engineering and science.

➡ Part-time study: **Yes.**
➡ Distance learning: **No.**

**About the university:**
The University of Strathclyde, which was founded in 1796 and became a university in 1964, is located on two campuses in Scotland's largest city, Glasgow. Glasgow is situated on the banks of the River Clyde and is also host to some very exciting arts and cultural activities. The city is identified with innovative architecture, art and design.

| Total number of students: 16,000   Number of disabled students: 800 |
|---|

**Learning support staff and services:**
Special Needs Service
Five full-time and two part-time staff including special needs advisers and assistive technology advisers.
Identify services, assessments, equipment or grants for equipment to support the individual needs of the student; identify and acquire appropriate equipment and train students in its use.

## Home sweet home:
Limited adapted accommodation.
Accommodation can be guaranteed for duration of student's course.

## Out and about:
University: Dedicated parking spaces near both accommodation and study areas.
Public transport: The local transport is mainly accessible. The local authority provides a taxi scheme for disabled people in the area.

## Taking it easy:
At university: All student services are available to disabled students. (For SU accessibility, please see below.)
Locally: The city centre is both flat and hilly. The roads and pavements have recently been relaid and the area is accessible. The facilities are accessible and a Shopmobility scheme operates in some areas. The pavements are tactile in some areas. There is an access guide called *Tourist Guide to Glasgow*.

## And another thing ...
➡ The city centre campus is on a very steep hill and is intersected by two main roads. Whilst access to buildings is continuously being improved not all rooms are as yet accessible to all possible users. However, wheelchair users are successfully studying at Strathclyde, and most classes can be timetabled in rooms that are accessible.
➡ The SU building is wheelchair accessible for the most part. Levels 7, 9 and 10 cannot be reached by lift so access cannot be gained to the student development zone, commercial services department or admin. The university is currently progressing plans to enhance physical access.

## The Disability Statement/Brochure:
The university no longer produces a disability statement, but the Special Needs Service will provide any information requested on the university's provision for disabled students.

## Local disability public service provider:
Glasgow District Council, George Square, Glasgow.

| University of Sunderland |
| --- |

Edinburgh Building, Chester Road, Sunderland SR1 3SD

*General Enquiries:*
Tel: 0191 515 3000
Fax: 0191 515 3805
Email: student-helpline@
sunderland.ac.uk
Website: www.sunderland.ac.uk

**Disability Services Manager:**
**Marge Surtees**
**Tel: 0191 515 2001**
**Fax: 0191 515 2107**
**Email: disability.support@**
**sunderland.ac.uk**
**Text: 0191 515 2107**

**Fields of study:**
Arts, design and media; business; computing; education; engineering and technology; humanities and social sciences; sciences.

➡ Part-time study: **Yes, some.**
➡ Distance learning: **Yes, some.**

**About the university:**
The University of Sunderland is located in the heart of the city on two main sites, with some satellite bases. All are within the equivalent of 15–20 minutes' walk of one another. The university buildings date from Victorian times to the present day, with the most recent development being the new award-winning campus at St Peters. Sunderland is home to 300,000 people and offers all the facilities you expect in a modern city, yet is only an hour away from Weardale or the North York Moors. A few minutes more and you can be in the heart of the Lake District.

| |
| --- |
| Total number of students: 11,231<br>Number of disabled students: approx. 750 |

**Learning support staff and services:**
Disability Support Team
Full-time staff: Disability Services Manager: Sue Cain; Disability Support Adviser: Marge Surtees; Disability Support Administrator: Marsha Wilkinson; SpLD Tutor (four days a week): Sue Severs. Part-time staff: Administrators: Joan Hartley and Judith Richardson. Needs assessments; assistance with DSA applications and other sources of funding via the University Student Office; advice and referral of auxiliary aids and services; advice and guidance; one-to-one/group tuition for students with dyslexia; alternative examination, assessment and study arrangements; limited support service for students with mental health issues; assessments for dyslexia; brain

gym for students with dyspraxia; advice on assistive technology, equipment, mobility and access to buildings; equipment needs; learning support and strategies; arrangements for personal support workers; registering student volunteers; information leaflets and liaison with external organisations.

All Disability Support Team staff have British Sign Language level 1. Two experienced and qualified dyslexia tutors run a regular support group, which is open to all students with specific learning difficulties. Students can develop multi-sensory learning skills and study techniques that have been developed for people with dyslexia, or book a short one-to-one session for individual advice and guidance. Each school has a disability support tutor.

### Home sweet home:

Disabled students are given priority in the allocation of rooms and great emphasis is placed on helping students find somewhere that suits their needs and lifestyle. The main wheelchair user accessible locations are The Forge, Clanny House and Scotia Quay, some of which include en-suite bathrooms; all are close to accessible shower rooms, toilets and lounges. Kitchens have been fitted with wheelchair users' needs in mind and incorporate low-level work surfaces, sinks and cooking facilities. The Housekeeper's Lodge and laundry facilities are also wheelchair user accessible. Other rooms have visual alarms and doorbells fitted or have points for a phone and textphone. The signage and layout of The Forge makes particularly good use of tactile surfaces. The majority of halls are self-catering and provide good kitchen facilities. From Monday to Friday breakfast and evening meals are provided for residents and non-residents at Wearmouth Hall – the refectory is accessible to wheelchair users. The university operates a head tenancy scheme whereby local landlords agree to sub-let exclusively to students. The most accessible university house is All Saints, near St Peter's campus. All halls and All Saints have a senior resident tutor to help students adjust and talk about any problems they may have.

Accommodation can be guaranteed for duration of student's course.

### Out and about:

University: The university operates a free bus service, linking the campuses and the student halls of residence. The main buses are currently not accessible to wheelchair users but the Estates Department does have wheelchair accessible alternatives. The SU owns several minibuses, including some that are wheelchair accessible and disabled students may be able to get assistance from their union – tel: 0191 515 2024. Any student who wishes to use a taxi on a regular basis can contact the Disability Support Team for a list of local companies, some of which have wheelchair accessible vehicles. Dedicated parking spaces near both accommodation and study areas.

Public transport: Some buses, trains, train stations, taxis and local transport groups are accessible to wheelchair users. Wearside Mobility provides wheelchair accessible transport – tel: 0191 514 3706.

**Taking it easy:**
At university: The Sport and Leisure Service provides a range of activities. As well as the sports centre, the Service has extensive access to city facilities including the Crowtree Leisure Centre and Silksworth Sports Complex. Students with mobility difficulties should check physical access with Sports Service staff – tel: 0191 515 2937. The university intends to investigate the feasibility of building a new sports and recreation centre that will have full access.

Locally: The city centre is flat and accessible. The town's facilities are accessible and there is a Shopmobility scheme. The pavements are tactile. Please refer to www.sunderland.gov.uk to begin search for further information.

**And another thing …**
➡ The campus is generally quite accessible, although wheelchair users will have difficulty in some locations and some buildings. The award-winning St Peter's campus has good general access but some of the older buildings are regrettably not so user friendly for those with restricted mobility. However these are being systematically upgraded and include adaptations such as ramps and automatic doors, induction loops and tactile surfaces. As far as possible, lectures are scheduled in accessible locations to accommodate disabled students' needs, or alternative measures are explored. Information on campus access can be obtained from the Disability Support Team and found in the *Resource Guide for Disabled Students and Students with Specific Learning Difficulties*; Website: www.sunderland.ac.uk/disability-support/.
➡ Chester Road and St Peter's libraries have good provision for wheelchair users. Access to Ashburne House and Hutton libraries is not so good. However, a system has been developed to enable students to have books sent to their nearest accessible library.
➡ The university is home to the North East Regional Access Centre (NERAC). NERAC can provide students with an assessment of their study needs.

University of Sunderland

➡ A 20-credit module about dyslexia called 'Get Sussed' is open to students via Specific Learning Difficulties.
➡ The university is planning to build a new school of arts, design and media at St Peter's campus, opening up more opportunities to those with mobility difficulties.
➡ The university has external links with a number of organisations including RNIB, RNID, the Dyslexia Institute, and the Employers' Forum on Disability.

### QAA Report: Paragraph 53, June 2001

At central level, the university's Student and Academic Services provide support for students in a range of areas, including disabilities, careers, counselling and health and welfare. Specific support for international students is provided by the Centre for International Education. Additional learning support is available from Learning Development Services (LDS), which offers, for example, help with study skills and mathematics, whilst the university's mainstream curriculum incorporates modules designed to develop skills in specific areas: examples include a suite of introductory IT modules available in the undergraduate curriculum, and 'Get Sussed', a module aimed specifically at providing information about dyslexia. The account acknowledged the difficulties encountered by the university in ensuring that 'equivalent' standards of student support were sustained for part-time students, and reported on steps taken to address their particular needs, including the extension of academic advice sessions into the evenings.

The university monitors student views on support services through the biennial survey, the findings of which have suggested a high level of satisfaction with the standard of provision. The audit team had access to a wide range of written material relating to student support. It was satisfied that the university was responding to student needs, and had taken steps to review its provision against relevant section of QAA's Code. The team noted in particular the existence of a disabilities support network, centring on a dedicated Disabilities Support Team within Student and Academic Services, and disability support tutors in all schools; senior staff informed the team that personal tutors were linked to disability support tutors to ensure early diagnosis of special needs. The team noted that the Disability Support Team's work on adherence to QAA's Code relating to students with disabilities had resulted in revisions to the university's disability statement.

### The Disability Statement/Brochure:
*Information for Students with Disabilities or Specific Learning Difficulties*

Includes: Applications; access; accommodation; Disability Support Team; assessing needs; facilities and equipment; academic support; support for students with specific learning difficulties; financial support; disability working party; volunteer programme; other sources of student support; monitoring; future developments; appendices.

**Local disability public service providers:**
Sunderland Council for the Disabled – leisure, transport and social services – 100 Norfolk Street, Sunderland; 0191 514 3346.
Wearside Disablement Trust, 4/5 Mary Street, Sunderland; 0191 567 4955.
Disability Action North East, 0191 230 4111.
Disability North, 0191 284 0480.
Accessibility Ltd, 0191 281 5656.

---

## Surrey Institute of Art and Design

Falkner Road, Farnham, Surrey GU9 7DS

*General Enquiries:*
Tel: 01252 722441
Fax: 01252 892616
Email: registry@surrart.ac.uk
Website: www.surrart.ac.uk

**Special Needs Coordinator:**
**James Kirby/Lorraine Byers (Epsom)**
**Tel: 01252 892738/01372 202431**
**Fax: 01252 892623**
**Email: jkirby@surrart.ac.uk**
**lbyers@surrart.ac.uk**

**Fields of study:**
Animation; arts and media; ceramics, glass, metalwork and jewellery; design management; fashion; fashion journalism; fashion promotion and illustration; film and video; fine art; graphic design, new media and visual communication; interior design; journalism; packaging design; photography; product design sustainable futures; textiles; three-dimensional design; time-based new media and TV drama.

➡ Part-time study: **Yes, fine art degree/foundation FE and Access.**
➡ Distance learning: **No.**

**About the institute:**
The Surrey Institute of Art and Design aims to be the specialist university college with an international reputation for education and research in the creative industries. The Surrey Institute is unusual in that it runs more than 30 different programmes in the specialist areas of art, design, media and communication. The students at the institute

work in the beautiful environment of a market town, on modern campuses. Students at both Epsom and Farnham are close enough to London to benefit from all the capital offers.

| Total number of students: 3,000 Number of disabled students: 600 |
| --- |

## Learning support staff and services:
Open Learning Support Drop-in Service and Dyslexia Tutor Service
Full and part-time staff: Special Needs Coordinator: James Kirby; Special Needs Assistant: Lorraine Byers; nine study skills support tutors; specialist learning mentor; four learning support assistants (coordinated through Special Needs); learning and teaching coordinators.
Needs assessments; assistance with DSA applications and other sources of funding; provision of auxiliary aids and services; advice and guidance; one-to-one/group tutition for students with dyslexia; alternative examination, assessment and study arrangements; support service for students with mental health issues; provision of a screening service for students who think they may be dyslexic; very comprehensive support for dyslexic students; liaison with the Surrey Physical and Sensory Support Service for visually impaired and D/deaf or hard of hearing students and liaison with external services.

## Home sweet home:
Some accommodation is available for students who are D/deaf or hard of hearing and for students with physical disabilities who need little or no personal assistance. There are wider doors on both the Farnham and Epsom campuses, but Farnham campus is on a slope and not easily accessible by wheelchair users.
Accommodation can be guaranteed for duration of student's course under certain criteria, but it must be reapplied for each year.

## Out and about:
Institute: There are dedicated parking spaces near to accommodation and study areas.
Public transport: Taxis and some trains and train stations are accessible to people who are wheelchair users. Some buses, trains, train stations and taxis are accessible to people with visual impairments.

## Taking it easy:
At institute: There are currently no facilities or services for the social support of disabled students.
Locally: The local town is flat and reasonably accessible, as are some of its facilities. The pavements are tactile, though some are in need of repair.

## And another thing ...

➡ The campus is not at present accessible for students with mobility disabilities, but renovations are currently being examined following an access audit.

➡ Students needing updated or new educational psychologist's assessments may apply for financial assistance to meet the cost.

## The Disability Statement/Brochure:

*The Surrey Institute of Art and Design, University College Support for Students with Disabilities and Dyslexia*
Contains: Advice before you arrive; applications; information for students with specific types of disability; access; support; examination and assessments; monitoring procedures and future developments.

## Local disability public service provider:

Surrey CC Physical and Sensory Support Service, 020 8393 2872.

---

| **University of Surrey, Guildford** |
|:---:|

Guildford, Surrey GU2 7XH

*General Enquiries:*
Tel: 01483 300800
Fax: 01483 300803
Email: information@surrey.ac.uk
Website: www.surrey.ac.uk

**Disability Coordinator: John Beaumont**
**Tel: 01483 689766**
**Fax: 01483 689500**
**Email: j.beaumont@**
**surrey.ac.uk**

## Fields of study:

Aerospace; biomedical and life sciences; business management; chemical engineering; chiropractic; civil engineering; computing; dance and music; economics; international hospitality and tourism management; language and international studies; law; mathematics and statistics; mechanical and materials engineering; midwifery and nursing; psychology and sociology; retail management; science; sound recording.

➡ Part-time study: **Yes.**
➡ Distance learning: **Yes.**

## About the university:

The University of Surrey (UniS) is built on a hillside leading up to Guildford Cathedral on a single campus site. It is surrounded by playing fields, gardens and a lake. The Nicholas Grimshaw-designed Duke of Kent building was opened in 2000 and the Advanced Technology Institute and business school are currently under construction. UniS has topped *The Times'* employment league tables for the past four years. At UniS over 80 per cent of graduates have spent a year on professional placement, and around 20 per cent of those have been abroad. A student can typically expect to earn £12,000 to £14,000 during the professional training year. The historic town of Guildford, with its cobbled high street and its medieval buildings, is the equivalent of ten minutes' walk away. The Surrey countryside is a designated area of outstanding natural beauty.

---

Total number of students: 15,005 Number of disabled students: 2,531

---

## Learning support staff and services:
Student Advice and Information Service
John Beaumont, Disability Coordinator; Bridget Middlemas, Learning Support Tutor; Janet Swirski, Learning Support Tutor and Dyslexia Assessor.
Alternative examination arrangements; loan of equipment; dyslexia assessments; one-to-one learning support; assistance with DSA applications.

## Home sweet home:
Four fully adapted rooms for students with mobility difficulties, eight rooms adapted for students who are D/deaf or hard of hearing. Accommodation can be guaranteed for the first year in campus accommodation; after that students must make an application to the Accommodation Office.

## Out and about:
Some local buses have low floors. The railway station has level access from Walnut Tree Close. The ticket office and information desk have level access. Access is level to platforms one and two and a Radar National Key Scheme toilet is available. Access to all other platforms is via poorly lit steep ramps on which handrails are not provided.

## Taking it easy:
At university: The SU and sports facilities have very limited access. Locally: Some areas within Guildford shopping area are pedestrianised. There is a Shopmobility scheme. Guildford Borough Council have produced an *Access Guide* (see below).

## And another thing ...
➡ UniS is built on a hill and as a result the campus as a whole has limited access for people with mobility difficulties, although many parts can be reached by wheelchair.

➡ January 2000 saw the opening of the Assistive Technology Centre on the ground floor of the library. This houses workstations with specific needs technology, such as Inspirations (mind mapping programmes) and Text Help (advanced spellchecks). There is screen magnification and text-to-speech software and a Braille embosser. Staff are always available to assist and train students.

## QAA Report: Paragraphs 101 and 104, November 2001

In the university's papers in the base room and from its discussions with members of the services involved in student support and guidance and students, the audit team found ample evidence of responsive and professional service provision backed up by genuine concern for the welfare of individual students. Students who met the team commented appreciatively on the assistance provided by the university with induction; special needs; language support for international students; dyslexia testing and assistance; and careers guidance. This testimony to service effectiveness is supported by the positive outcomes of HEFCE and QAA subject review evaluations of student support and guidance across the university.

As noted in paragraph 62, the university's recent review of the needs of part-time students points to one aspect of its more general self-critical awareness of the need to adapt student services to the specific needs of sub-sections of the student body. The university's arrangements for international students (currently 21% of the student body) coordinated by the dean of international students are indicative of this targeted care and concern. Similarly, there is appropriate and developing provision for students with special needs and for mature students. The commitment to the implementation of the recommendations of the report of the Working Group of Part-time Students, together with consideration of recent strategic papers on Widening Participation and Modularisation, indicate that the university is alive to the support needs of a more diverse student body. The strategic thinking gives further ground for confidence that the university's student guidance and support service provides both general and specific responses to student needs, and is subject to continuous review and development.

## Local disability public service providers:

Access Officer, Access Guildford, Guildford Borough Council, Millmead House, Millmead, Guildford GU2 4BB; 01483 444914.
Disability Information Service Surrey (DISS) – 01306 875156; fax: 01306 741740; text: 01306 742128.
Surrey Voluntary Association for the Blind, 01372 377701.
Surrey Physical and Sensory Support Service, 01483 419368.

## University of Sussex
Falmer, Brighton BN1 9QH

*General Enquiries:*
Tel: 01273 606755
Fax: 01273 678545
Email: UG.Admissions@sussex.ac.uk
Website: www.susx.ac.uk

**Student Support Unit:**
**Tel: 01273 877466**
**Fax: 01273 877475**
**Email: studentsupport@**
**sussex.ac.uk**

### Fields of study:
Arts and humanities; biological sciences; chemical, physical and environmental sciences; computing and information technology; engineering; languages; mathematical sciences and social sciences.

➡ Part-time study: **Yes.**
➡ Distance learning: **No.**

### About the university:
Sussex University is situated in a designated area of outstanding natural beauty on the south coast of England. The university was recently awarded £10 million from the Joint Infrastructure Fund for two new science buildings on campus. Brighton has a vibrant nightlife, the seaside and the largest arts festival in England.

Total number of students: 9,515     Number of disabled students: 603

### Learning support staff and services:
Student Support Unit
Two disability coordinators; learning support coordinator; two dyslexia advisers; mental health coordinator; administrator and receptionist (jobshare).
Offers advice and assistance in securing support to both prospective and new students and throughout a student's time at the university. Specific arrangements for examinations can be catered for. The disability coordinator can assist in: arranging PA provision; liaising with academic and other staff about support needs; arranging notetakers, etc.; advice about physical access and site facilities; information about funding and support. The learning support team can support students with their studies, screening and assessments for dyslexia learning and learning support group or individual sessions.
Learning support is also provided within the Centre for Continuing Education.

**Home sweet home:**
Kulukundis House has recently been refurbished and has four study bedrooms fully adapted for wheelchair users and people with mobility disabilities. Kitchen, bathrooms and bedrooms are fully adapted. There are rooms for PAs. There are also other halls of residence with some adaptations and adjustments are made where possible. Accommodation can be guaranteed for duration of student's course.

**Out and about:**
University: Dedicated parking spaces near both accommodation and study areas.
Public transport: There are a small but increasing number of buses that are wheelchair accessible. Brighton station is wheelchair accessible but smaller stations can be a problem.

**Taking it easy:**
The ground floor of Falmer House is accessible to wheelchair users. This includes the main reception of the SU's Falmer Bar and the Hothouse nightclub. However, the rest of Falmer House is not accessible. Sports facilities are located on two sites on the campus. The sport centre's ground floor is accessible, where one of the main halls, the Lifestyles Studio and Sports Injuries Clinic and changing facilities are located. The Falmer Sports Complex fitness room is on two floors and the ground floor is accessible, including the bar and catering facilities. However, there is a steep gradient approaching this complex from the residences. Staff are happy to provide assistance wherever possible. The Gardner Arts Centre has wheelchair access at ground level, but there are only stairs to the auditorium and gallery. Locally: The local area disability guide is available from Brighton and Hove Disability Advice Centre. Local area is hilly.

**And another thing ...**
➡ Sussex Regional ACCESS Centre, based in Lancaster House, is a member of NFAC. The Centre offers training and assessment of needs for students applying for DSA and Hardship Funds and those who require further assistance as their course progresses.
➡ The Student Advice Centre is not accessible to wheelchair users.
➡ The university has carried out an audit of access and facilities to draw up a schedule of improvements as part of its commitment to improve access.
➡ A guide, *Access to Campus*, is available on the university website.

**The Disability Statement/Brochure:**
Available on the university website.

**Local disability public service provider:**
Brighton and Hove Disability Advice Centre, 6 Hove Manor, Hove Street, Hove BN3 2DF; 01273 203016.

| Swansea Institute of Higher Education |
| --- |

Mount Pleasant, Swansea SA1 6ED

*General Enquiries:*
Tel: 01792 481000
Fax: 01792 481085
Email: enquiry@sihe.ac.uk
Website: www.sihe.ac.uk
Text: 01792 481191

**Student Counsellor: Jill Nicholls**
**Tel: 01792 481193**
**Fax: 01792 481206**
**Email: j.nicholls@sihe.ac.uk**
**Text: 01792 481191**

**Fields of study:**
Accounting and finance; art and design; automotive portfolio; built and natural environment; business and management; computing; digital media portfolio; engineering; health studies; humanities portfolio; industrial design portfolio; law; leisure, tourism and sports and recreation management; teacher education; transport.

➡ Part-time study: **Yes.**
➡ Distance learning: **No.**

**About the institute:**
Swansea Institute of Higher Education achieved its status as an independent Higher Education Corporation in 1992, but its roots go back over 100 years. The institute is firmly rooted in the community it serves, and maintains close links with industry, commerce and the public services. The institute is an associate college of the University of Wales. Swansea is the second city of Wales, and the bay upon which it stands provides the city with a picturesque and hilly setting.

| Total number of students: 5,000 | Number of disabled students: 300 |
| --- | --- |

**Learning support staff and services:**
Student Services
Student Counsellor: Jill Nicholls; Student Services Secretary: Julie Hutchinson.
Provision of advice to disabled students, including assistance with DSA applications; liaising with academic staff; monitoring provision; alternative examination arrangements; arrangement of support

workers, e.g. sign language interpreters or lipspeakers. There is also a dyslexic support tutor who offers tuition to all dyslexic students. A pool of equipment can be loaned to students. Notetakers or speed text operators are also available.

## Home sweet home:
Townhill and Mount Pleasant campuses both have halls of residence. Three rooms in Townhill have been upgraded for students with disabilities. They have extra space for wheelchair users, improved lighting, additional power points and alarm systems. One has a multi-positional bed. Adapted showers and toilets are located opposite, and PAs can be accommodated in adjacent rooms. Further adaptations to these or other rooms can be made according to need. Accommodation can be guaranteed for duration of the student's course but special request has to be made on the grounds of a disability or health problem.

## Out and about:
Institute: There are dedicated parking spaces near both the accommodation and study areas. During term-time a bus travels between Townhill and Mount Pleasant every half-hour.
Public transport: Many local buses and trains are accessible for wheelchair users.

## Taking it easy:
At institute: A disabled group meets regularly. Townhill has a multi-gym fitness centre and the institute also funds free access to some facilities at Swansea Leisure Centre, which has a swimming pool and a new gym equipped for people with disabilities.
Locally: The city centre is hilly but accessible. The cinema, theatre, most pubs and leisure centres are accessible for disabled users and there is a Shopmobility scheme. Some of the pavements are tactile. The City and County of Swansea has taken very useful steps to improve accessibility in the city. For more information about this, contact Student Services. A local area access guide is available.

## And another thing ...
➡ Many of Swansea Institute's buildings are old and situated on steep hills. Some parts of the campus are not accessible to wheelchair users, which the Institute is striving to improve. A full access audit of the institute's sites has been undertaken and its recommendations are included in the estate's strategy.
➡ Lifts and chairlifts have been installed to provide access to many parts of the older buildings. All refurbished buildings are designed

to be accessible wherever possible. A stairclimber wheelchair is available for use in some areas where there is no lift access. Ramps and handrails can be installed according to need wherever practicable. More toilets designed for disabled users have been added.

➡ Course books can be provided on audio tape, and lecture notes can be made available in large print. Adjustments to lighting can be made where necessary.

➡ Guide dogs are welcome.

➡ Swansea has an active Access Group that would welcome involvement from students with disabilities, tel: 01792 649126.

➡ The institute has a store of equipment such as computers and chairs that it can loan to students who need them urgently, e.g. whilst waiting for DSA funding.

➡ Vibrating alarms can be loaned to students.

➡ Two members of reception staff are trained in BSL.

➡ Planned developments include continued improvements to buildings and exploring the use of new technology and distance learning techniques to cover those areas where it is not feasible to alter buildings.

➡ The institute aims to continue the developments in provision for dyslexic students, establish a volunteer system to support students with disabilities, strengthen links with disability groups and increase recruitment of students with disabilities.

## The Disability Statement/Brochure:

Covers: Admissions procedures; funding; support for students by disability; IT provision; exams; personal support, health and safety; refectories; careers service; financial advice; students union; accommodation; getting around; sport and entertainment; academic quality, complaints and appeals; staff development; monitoring; the future.

## Local disability public service provider:

City and County of Swansea, County Hall, Oystermouth Road, Swansea SA1 3SN.

## Teesside University

Borough Road, Middlesbrough TS1 3BA

*General Enquiries:*
Tel: 01642 218121
Fax: 01642 342067
Website: www.tees.ac.uk

**Unit Manager: Jill Berry**
**Tel: 01642 342269**
**Fax: 01642 342289**
**Email: j.berry@tees.ac.uk**

### Fields of study:
Accounting; art and design; business and economics; computing and multimedia; criminology; engineering; English studies; forensic investigation; health and social care; history; law; leisure and tourism; life science; marketing and public relations; media; psychology; science; sociology and youth studies; sport and exercise and higher national diplomas.

➡ Part-time study: **Yes.**
➡ Distance learning: **Yes.**

### About the university:
The university is based around one main city-centre campus made up of a variety of old and new buildings, including the prestigious Learning Resource Centre and the School of Health building. The close proximity to Middlesbrough city centre means that the university has all the usual shops and services nearby.

Total number of students: 18,000
Number of disabled students: approx. 750

### Learning support staff and services:
Student Support Unit
Full-time staff: Disability Advisers: Gill Bell, Fiona Hyslop and Jo Fenwick; Manager of Unit: Jill Berry.
Needs assessments; assistance with DSA applications and Hardship Fund; advice and guidance; one-to-one/group tuition for students with dyslexia; alternative examination, assessment and study arrangements; ongoing support and monitoring assessment of need; liaison with academic staff and LEAs, etc. to secure resources; dyslexia screening; tutor support and diagnostic assessment arranged; support service for students with mental health problems and liaison with external organisations.

## Home sweet home:

There are four halls of residence, all of which offer accommodation on a self-catering basis. There are seven wheelchair accessible rooms in Woodlands Halls, with en-suite bathroom/shower room – shared kitchen and living area. At Parkside houses and flats 12 rooms have been designed to accommodate wheelchair users. Two bedrooms within the Woodland complex are equipped with a doorbell warning light system and adapted for students who are D/deaf or hard of hearing. Small adaptations, e.g. extra shelving, vibration fire alarm, can be made after discussion with the Accommodation Department. Accommodation can be guaranteed for the duration of student's course.

## Out and about:

University: The institution does not provide specialist transport for its disabled students, but this can be arranged for individual students if necessary. Dedicated parking spaces near both the accommodation and study areas – access is with the appropriate pass.

Public transport: Some buses, trains, train stations and taxis are accessible to people who are wheelchair users, and some taxis are accessible to people with visual impairments. There is a taxi scheme for disabled people operating in the area – contact the Student Support Unit for further information.

## Taking it easy:

At university: The University of Teesside students union (UTU) mission is to enhance the student experience by ensuring that all students matter equally and have the same rights to educational, social, cultural, recreational and welfare opportunities. The UTU building is accessible to disabled students. The union has a part-time officer elected to represent disabled students. The Activities and Skills Centre coordinates and supports UTU's existing activities, ensuring they are accessible to all members.

The Sport and Recreation Unit of the Department of Student Services operates a number of sports facilities on campus, as well as coordinating access to a number of local external facilities. Sport and recreation staff are available to deal with any enquiries regarding accessibility.

Locally: The city centre is flat and accessible as are the town's facilities. There is a Shopmobility scheme and the pavements are tactile. Middlesbrough County Council produces information for the public about access. There are many new buildings being developed, but the city remains a mix of buildings.

## And another thing ...
➡ There is a pen for guide dogs outside Woodlands Halls.
➡ The university has a variety of accessible catering facilities, from 'coffee stops' to cafés, including 'Cameo' in the Student Centre, and a refectory.

## The Disability Statement/Brochure:
Contents: Current policy and practice; applying to the university; accommodation; staff and services; students union; physical environment; access to the curriculum; equipment provision; finance; quality; university plans; summary of sources of information and assistance.

## Local disability public service providers:
North East Sensory Partnership.
Middlesbrough County Council.

| Thames Valley University |
|---|

18–22 Bond Street, Ealing, London W5 5AA

*General Enquiries:*
Learning Advice Centre
Tel: 020 8579 5000
Fax: 020 8566 1353
Email: learning.advice@tvu.ac.uk
Website: www.tvu.ac.uk

**Special Needs Coordinator:**
**Kris Evans**
**Tel: 020 8231 2058/2654**
**Fax: 020 8231 2587**
**Email: kris.evans@tvu.ac.uk**

## Fields of study:
Business, management and law; health and human sciences; music, media and creative technologies; tourism, hospitality and leisure.

➡ Part-time study: **Yes.**
➡ Distance learning: **Yes.**

## About the university:
Although Thames Valley University (TVU) only became a university in 1992, it has over 130 years' experience in technical and vocational education. There are now two campuses at TVU, one in Ealing, one of London's greener boroughs, and the other at Slough, a relatively new community, near to Windsor Castle. TVU's main arterial route, the M4 motorway, links many new and growing industries, especially high-technology firms, in the region, which has been dubbed the UK's 'Silicon Valley'.

| Total number of students: 26,739   Number of disabled students: 943 |

## Learning support staff and services:
Special Needs Unit, Student Services
Special Needs Coordinator, full-time: Kris Evans.
Provision of confidential support and information for students with disabilities and specific needs; liaising with LEA: DSA application assistance; disclosure of faculties; setting up individual learning plans; developing assistive technology throughout the university; staff training; production of disability statistics; provision of promotional literature – Disability Statement, Disability Booklet, policies and procedures; reports to HEFCE and internal Disability Committee. Continually updating facilities to improve access and support differing demands: alternative examination arrangements; provision of notetakers or special equipment; provision of assistance with assessments for students with dyslexia; individual support sessions; group workshops; matching learning styles and brain gym.
The team works closely with tutors and the Learning Support Team and has connections with local and national organisations that provide long-term support for people with disabilities.

## Home sweet home:
The university does not have its own halls of residence. Rooms can be accessed in the adjacent YMCA. Contact the University Accommodation Team for further information, tel: 020 8231 2511; email: uas@tvu.ac.uk.

## Out and about:
University: Dedicated parking spaces near both accommodation and study areas.
Public transport: The tube is not accessible. Accessibility on bus routes varies. There are some buses that lower their height for wheelchair access. Contact Access and Mobility for information about London's public transport services (see Directory).

## Taking it easy:
At university: Disabled students are encouraged to join in the social activities of the university. At least twice a year disabled students are invited to attend a social event organised by the Special Needs Unit. The education and representation officer or the education and research coordinator will be able to answer any questions relating to the kind of support and/or guidance that can be offered by the SU, tel: 020 8231 2319.

Locally: Ealing has an accessible pedestrianised shopping mall. Artsline publishes a number of guides about access in London (see Directory).

## And another thing ...

➡ The majority of students who attend TVU do so at one of the three main sites: Slough, St Mary's Road or Westel House. In addition to these sites there are also a number of smaller buildings that house teaching and learning activities. About 95 per cent of the campuses are wheelchair accessible.

➡ Facilities (Campus Services) is responsible for ensuring accessibility to sites on a day-to-day basis, as well as on special occasions, e.g. award ceremonies – tel: 020 8231 2099; email: facilities@tvu.ac.uk.

➡ The university has learning resource centres at St Mary's Road and Slough that include assistive technology suites containing specialist software and hardware.

## The Disability Statement/Brochure:
Includes: Current policies; current provision; accommodation; facilities; Ealing and Slough; admissions; examination and assessments; students with a disability at TVU; future developments.

## Local disability public service provider:
Ealing Council.

---

### Trinity and All Saints College (University of Leeds)
Brownberrie Lane, Horsforth, Leeds LS18 5HD

*General Enquiries:* Admissions
Tel: 0113 283 7100
Fax: 0113 283 7200
Email: e_brier@tasc.ac.uk
Website: www.tasc.ac.uk

**Disability Coordinator:**
**Deborah Altman**
**Tel: 0113 283 7138**
**Fax: 0113 283 7200**
**Email: d_altman@tasc.ac.uk**

## Fields of study:
Communication and cultural studies; English; exercise and nutrition; history; management; marketing; media; primary education; psychology; sociology; sport, health, leisure and nutrition; theology.

➡ Part-time study: **Yes.**
➡ Distance learning: **No.**

## About the college:
The college is a single-campus institution in an attractive suburb of Leeds. The college is said to be warm and friendly, offering a naturally supportive environment in which all students, including those with disabilities, can thrive.

| Total number of students: 2,100 | Number of disabled students: 138 |
|---|---|

## Learning support staff and services:
Disability Services
Part-time staff: Disability Coordinator: Deborah Altman; Administrative Assistant: Patricia Bannister; two part-time dyslexia tutors; ten part-time student support assistants.
Needs assessments; assistance with DSA applications; provision of auxiliary aids and services; advice and guidance; one-to-one/group tuition for students with dyslexia; dyslexia assessment of needs; alternative examination, assessment and study arrangements; provision of support assistants; dyslexia initial screening; drop-in service; support service for students with mental health issues and liaison with external organisations. Other providers for: Braille transcription; other assessments; psychological assessment; hearing impairment support.

## Home sweet home:
There are four fully catered, purpose-built, wheelchair-accessible study bedrooms on the ground floor of Kirkstall Hall. Facilities include emergency call, kitchenette, room for PA, en-suite washbowl and toilet, accessible bath and shower.
Accommodation can be guaranteed for the duration of student's course.

## Out and about:
College: Dedicated parking spaces near both the accommodation and study areas.
Public transport: Some buses, trains, train stations and taxis are accessible to people who are wheelchair users. Leeds Access Bus is the name of the taxi scheme for disabled people operating in the area.

## Taking it easy:
At college: The SU building and bar are accessible, as are the sports facilities with adapted changing rooms. Chaplaincy offers a lively social scene.
Locally: The city centre is reasonably flat and accessible, with many of the town facilities being accessible. There is a Shopmobility scheme

and the pavements are tactile. Full details in the *Leeds Disability Directory*, available from DIAL (see below).

## And another thing ...

➡ Although the site is not level, a number of adaptations have been made to make most parts of the campus accessible to students with mobility impairments. Sometimes the alternative routes go outside. However, the campus is relatively compact, so this does not usually cause too many problems.

➡ Specially designed accessible facilities include: induction loops in most teaching rooms and the college chapel; ground-floor study bedrooms with wheelchair accessible bathroom facilities; access to sports facilities and accessible changing rooms; a new, fully accessible learning centre including library and IT facilities.

➡ Some areas of the college are not yet accessible to students with mobility impairments. If necessary, alternative timetabling arrangements are made.

➡ Over the next few years the campus is to be redesigned to improve access and welcome for everyone. This will include increasing the number and quality of level routes between buildings. Facilities for learning and teaching will continue to improve, with the introduction of further accessible technology. Staff at Trinity and All Saints participate in regular staff development sessions with the aim of continually improving the quality of learning and teaching activities offered – part of their commitment to an inclusive learning environment.

➡ The college has a comprehensive programme of staff development and workshops for students to raise disability awareness across campus.

➡ As part of their induction, disabled students will be invited to meet existing students for mutual support and information sharing.

➡ All students new to the college will be invited to participate in an initial screening process to identify possible literacy difficulties.

➡ Students with disabilities are required to undertake two six-week periods of practical experience, on the same basis as all college students. The Disability Coordinator liaises with the students, tutors and the College–Employer Partnership Service to identify and set up appropriate attachments.

➡ The college purchases items of equipment or carries out essential building adaptations not otherwise covered.

## The Disability Statement/Brochure:

*Trinity and All Saints College Disability Statement: A Guide for Students with Disabilities*

Covers: Current policy; current provision including student support services and people to contact; future activity and policy development.

**Local disability public service provider:**
Disablement Information and Advice Line (DIAL), Armley Resource Centre, Armley, Leeds 0113 214 3630; text: 0113 268 2689; email: d..i..a..l.ss@leeds.gov.uk; website: www.leeds.gov.uk/leedscom/advice/dial.html.

---

## Trinity College Carmarthen – Coleg y Drindodd Caerfyrddin

The University Sector College of West Wales, Carmarthen SA31 3EP

*General Enquiries:*
Tel: 01267 676767
Fax: 01267 676766
Email: registry@trinity-cm.ac.uk
Web: www.trinity-cm.ac.uk

**Disability Adviser: Tom Evans**
**Tel: 01267 676677**
**Fax: 01267 676766**
**Email: t.e.evans@**
**trinity-cm.ac.uk**

**Fields of study:**
Creative, performing and cultural arts; education and training; environment.

➡ Part-time study: **Yes.**
➡ Distance learning: **Yes, under review.**

**About the college:**
Trinity College Carmarthen is the second oldest HE institution in Wales. The college was founded in the eighteenth century to train teachers for church schools. The college has close links with the Central University of Iowa, USA with which exchange visits are arranged. The English and Welsh languages are given equal respect. South-west Wales features prominently in Welsh history and culture, and its busy town life, beautiful countryside and sandy beaches make it a major tourist attraction. Carmarthen is a busy market town served by major road and rail networks and within easy reach of ferry services to and from Ireland.

| Total number of students: 4,600 | Number of disabled students: 320 |
|---|---|

**Disability staff and services:**
Student Support

Part-time staff: Tutors: Gre.g. Stevenson and Bernice Brewer.
Needs assessments provided from external sources; assistance with DSA applications; advice and guidance; one-to-one/group tuition for students with dyslexia; alternative examination, assessment and study arrangements; support service for students with mental health problems and liaison with external organisations.
The Study Support Unit is situated near Student Services with accessibility for wheelchair users. The college has recently invested in new software designed for the support of students with specific learning difficulties, such as dyslexia. There is a free screening service to diagnose dyslexia and offer individual tutorial support.

**Home sweet home:**
Old traditional buildings place constraints on access. The two newest halls have rooms specially designed for students with disabilities. Wherever possible, older buildings have been adapted to improve access. Accommodation can be guaranteed for duration of student's course, depending on circumstances.

**Out and about:**
College: Dedicated parking spaces near study areas.
Public transport: Some trains, train stations and taxis are accessible to people who are wheelchair users.

**Taking it easy:**
At college: The SU is accessible.
Locally: The city centre is fairly level and accessible. Town facilities are accessible and a large portion of Carmarthen town is pedestrianised.

**And another thing ...**
➡ All new buildings, including the library, have been built with consideration for those with disabilities.
➡ The college takes into account the guidelines for best practice provided by Skill, the British Dyslexia Association, RNIB, RNID and the Wales Council for the Deaf.
➡ There are loop systems for students who are D/deaf or hard of hearing.
➡ There is a free counselling service for all students.
➡ Future developments include: widening tutorial support for those with specific learning difficulties; improving access across the campus for those with mobility problems, e.g. stair trolleys, extra ramps; and extending availability of specialist technologies, e.g. hearing loops, software for specific learning difficulties.

## The Disability Statement/Brochure:
*Special Needs: Opportunities for students with disabilities or special needs*
Includes: Existing policy; admissions; existing provision.

## Local disability public service providers:
Carmarthen County Council, 3 Spilman Street, Carmarthen.
Gateway Club.

| Trinity College of Music |
| --- |

King Charles Court, Old Royal Naval College, Greenwich, London
SE10 9LF

*General Enquiries:*
Tel: 020 8305 3880
Fax: 020 8305 3881
Email: info@tcm.ac.uk
Website: www.tcm.ac.uk

**Disability Project Officer:**
**James Hitchins**
**Tel: 020 8305 4418**
**Fax: 020 8305 9418**
**Email: jhitchins@tcm.ac.uk**

## Fields of study:
Performance; string, keyboard, composition, vocal, conducting, wind, brass and percussion, jazz and early music; teaching studies.

➡ Part-time study: **Yes.**
➡ Distance learning: **No.**

## About the college:
With a musical inheritance stretching back to the Tudor Court of Henry VIII and the Golden Age of Elizabeth I, Trinity's move to the historic World Heritage site at Greenwich also looks ahead, and across the River Thames, to a dynamic future characterised in the world business centre that is Docklands. The college is fostering collaboration across the performing arts and education world – with a distinct role in the south-east 'quadrant' of London and the UK, but also farther afield in the USA, in Japan and with many partnerships in the European Union.

| Total number of students: 570 | Number of disabled students: 29 |
| --- | --- |

## Learning support staff and services:
Student Services Department
Full-time staff: Disability Project Officer: James Hitchins; Warden:

Roger Pope (020 8305 5515; email: rpope@tcm.ac.uk);
Administrator: Linda Gisby.
Part-time staff: Dyslexia Support Tutor: Claire McDonald; External
Specialist IT Consultant: Jason Arthur.
Needs assessments; assistance with DSA applications and advice on
scholarships and bursaries; provision of auxiliary aids and services;
advice and guidance; one-to-one/group tuition for students with
dyslexia; alternative examination, assessment and study
arrangements; support service for students with mental health issues;
assistance with finding local accommodation and liaison with external
organisations.
Trinity works with RNIB to accommodate visually impaired students to
ensure full integration. Visually impaired students are given a
thorough training in the use of IT applications through Musicians in
Focus.

**Home sweet home:**
Reserved ground-floor accommodation for visually impaired students
– shared 'bungalow' flat for three. Ground-floor accommodation is
also reserved for disabled students as required. Unite Trust
accommodation is used for students, but is some distance from the
college. University accommodation close to the college can be
negotiated for students with disabilities. Adaptation for disabled
students to be built into redevelopment over the next three years.
Accommodation can be guaranteed for duration of student's course.

**Out and about:**
College: Dedicated parking spaces near study areas.
Public transport: Trains, train stations, taxis, river boats and some
buses are accessible to people who are wheelchair users. All modes
of transport are accessible to people with visual impairments. The bus
travels from college gate to halls of residence. Contact Access and
Mobility for information about London's public transport services (see
Directory).

**Taking it easy:**
At college: No specific facilities/services for the social support of
disabled students. Students can access all college performances.
Locally: Greenwich city centre is flat and accessible and the facilities
are accessible. There is a Shopmobility scheme in Lewisham and the
pavements are tactile. Disability guides available through local
authority and/or University of Greenwich. Artsline also publishes a
number of guides about access in London (see Directory).

## And another thing ...

➡ Personal timetabling can be organised for students to avoid access problems.

➡ The college works closely with its sister organisation, Trinity College London, whose music staff includes an officer who recently spent four years with RNIB as a Braille music specialist.

➡ The library offers specialist facilities for visually impaired students. IT facilities include scanning, screen reading and optical character recognition software, and Brailling facilities for text and music.

➡ Specialist computer facilities are provided for dyslexic students, including screen reading, voice recognition, mind mapping, screen enlargement software, colour modification and specialist grammar and spelling checker.

➡ Standards required nowadays to achieve success in a performing career are unyieldingly high and the pressures to sustain them are merciless. Response to such tensions naturally varies. Apart from dealing with individual instances as they arise, Trinity's response has been to develop, through various curricular initiatives (notably individual and group tuition in Alexander Technique) the physical and mental approaches that discourage stress-related illnesses. As a result there has been a significant decline in the incidence of such problems.

➡ The college has its own experienced counselling staff.

➡ All college documents are available in Braille and digital formats.

**Local disability public service provider:**
Greenwich, London Borough Council.

---

| **University of Ulster** |
| --- |

Cromore Road, Coleraine, County Londonderry BT52 1SA

*General Enquiries:*
Tel: 028 7004 0700
Fax: 028 7032 3005
Email: online@ulst.ac.uk
Website: www.ulst.ac.uk

**Disability Awareness Officer:**
**Jennifer Smyth**
**Tel: 028 9036 6336**
**Fax: 028 9036 6896**
**Email: ja.smyth@ulster.ac.uk**

**Fields of study:**
Arts; business and management; engineering and built environment; informatics; life and health sciences; social sciences.

➡ Part-time study: **Yes.**
➡ Distance learning: **Yes.**

## About the university:

Ulster University's roots date from 1845 when a local philanthropist founded the Magee College in Londonderry. The New University of Ulster was born in the late 1960s, and merged with Ulster Polytechnic in the mid-1980s. The university is spread over five different sites in Northern Ireland, making it the biggest university in Ireland.

> Total number of students: 21,000+
> Number of disabled students: approx. 7%

## Learning support staff and services:

Department of Student Support
Disability Advisers: Norma Conn and Liz Donaghy; Disability Awareness Officer: Jennifer Smyth; Chartered Psychologist: Dr Joan McQuoid. Practical support to students with disabilities; disseminates information on disability to staff; works with Physical Resources Department and suggests improvements to physical access within the university.
The faculties' representatives liaise with the Counselling and Guidance Service and the university psychologist in order to address needs in the most practicable manner possible for each particular student. The faculties work closely with Student Support and the disability awareness officer.

## Home sweet home:

Future developments include purpose-built flats for students with disabilities, which will be part of a larger scheme of building new accommodation for students on the Coleraine and Magee College campuses, to supplement existing adapted accommodation. Vivian Chestnutt: Accommodation Manager, tel: 028 9036 6942; email: accommodation@ulst.ac.uk.

## Taking it easy:

At university: There are sports centres on the Magee, Coleraine and Jordanstown campuses that are accessible to wheelchair users. There is also a 25m, eight-laned swimming pool, diving pool and hydrotherapy pool with a hoist. The SU has disability awareness officers. SU, tel: 028 7032 4373 (Coleraine), 020 9036 6050 (Jordanstown), 028 7137 5226 (Magee).

## And another thing ...

➡ There are major new accessible learning resource centres at Jordanstown and Magee.

➡ The Customer Support Librarian has cross-campus responsibility for services to library users with disabilities – contact Ciaran Cregan, 028 7137 5256 or email cr.cregan@ulster.ac.uk. At the Jordanstown and Coleraine central libraries a study carrel has been reserved for specialist equipment. Wheelchair accessible PCs are available in each of the libraries.

➡ University facilities include: texthelp software; portable induction loop; CCTV for text enlargement.

➡ There is specialist software for students with dyslexia and specific learning difficulties.

➡ Several of the IT labs are accessible to wheelchair users.

## QAA Report: Paragraph 59, September 2002

Student Affairs has also played an important role in formulating the University's response to needs arising from the growing diversity of the student population. Examples of its work include the production and promulgation of a policy on Managing Diversity and a Code of Practice for Teachers of Students with Disabilities; monitoring of both is undertaken by SSC and QAEC. The audit team noted that, by having in place established policies and procedures, the University had been able to respond positively to developments in the external environment. It had used the section of QAA's *Code* relating to students with disabilities to audit its own provision, making adjustments as appropriate and, through QAEC, was addressing the requirements of the Disability Discrimination Act and Section 75 of the Northern Ireland Act 1998.

## The Disability Statement/Brochure:

Includes: Assistance; finance; educational guidance; Disability Awareness Officer; JUDE Centre; links with faculties; examinations; access; accommodation; catering; counselling; health; educational services; sports; SU; staff development; student evaluation and future developments.

---

### UMIST (merging with University of Manchester 2004/5)

Sackville Street, Manchester M60 1QD

*General Enquiries:*
Tel: 0161 200 4034
Fax: 0161 200 8765
Email: admissions@umist.ac.uk
Website: www.umist.ac.uk/

Disability Adviser: Gerard Conroy
Tel: 0161 200 3336
Fax: 0161 200 3324
Email: conroy@umist.ac.uk
disability@umist.ac.uk

## Fields of study:
Biomolecular sciences; chemical engineering; chemistry; computation; electrical engineering and electronics; management; materials science; mathematics; mechanical, aerospace and manufacturing engineering; optometry and neuroscience; physics; textiles.

➡ Part-time study: **Under discussion.**
➡ Distance learning: **No.**

## About the university:
UMIST is within Manchester city centre and is easily accessible by public transport or car. The university comprises a relatively small number of buildings on a very compact site, whilst the locality offers a range of accessible shops and banks. A shuttle minibus is provided around the campus and the halls of residence.

| Total number of students: 6,800 | Number of disabled students: 220 |
| --- | --- |

## Learning support staff and services:
Full-time disability adviser and learning support tutor; full-time administrator/assistant registrar.
In addition, each department has a departmental disability coordinator who is the first line of support and advice within each department.

## Home sweet home:
A variety of accommodation is available for students with disabilities, including adaptations made for students who are wheelchair users and flashing alarms for those who are D/deaf or hard of hearing. It is usually possible for a room to be available for personal assistants either next to or close to the disabled student's room if this is required. If special items are needed, e.g. a fridge to store insulin, these can usually be provided but UMIST will require a little notice. Wherever it is feasible, UMIST will try to organise more extensive adaptations. Some residences are self-catering and some kitchens have been adapted for wheelchair users; some halls of residence have catering, with breakfast and dinner provided (although this may not be available at weekends). Many bedrooms, in both self-catering and catered residences, have private bathrooms (most with showers, some with baths) and telephone and Internet points. A number of halls are located on or close to the teaching campus; some have a city-centre location; others are on the large residential campus in Fallowfield. There are 43 study bedrooms in total.

UMIST

Accommodation is guaranteed for duration of student's course.

**Out and about:**
University: Dedicated parking spaces near both accommodation and study areas.

**Taking it easy:**
At university: Facilities exist within the Sugden Support Centre to accommodate people with a disability, and advice on the various sporting facilities available and qualified instruction can be obtained from the UMIST Athletics Union. There is no lift in the Barnes Wallis building (housing the SA), which presents wheelchair users with difficulties in gaining access to some but not all of the amenities. Locally: Manchester City Council has worked extensively with community groups and access groups to take account of the needs of people with disabilities in its city planning. A local guide is available; contact Manchester City Council.

**And another thing ...**
➡ UMIST campus is a very level site and can be negotiated without restriction.
➡ UMIST is a member of the Access Summit Consortium, comprising the four higher education institutions in Manchester and Salford, that is recognised nationally as an example of good practice for disability support within HE.
➡ Disabled students are given priority with hardship funds.
➡ UMIST has a permanent Disability Support Committee with membership drawn from all areas of UMIST that students will come into contact with, including representation by disabled students. The Committee ensures that disability issues remain high on the UMIST agenda.
➡ Full study aids and strategies needs assessments provided. Provision of many types of non-medical helper. Training in use of enabling technology, through the Access Summit Consortium.
➡ While at UMIST, students with a disability will be put in contact with an organisation called Workable that arranges placements for disabled students throughout the UK. There is a mentoring scheme, whereby an industry professional can give guidance and provide a role model for success in that field.

## The Disability Statement/Brochure:
Very thorough and useful document covering: Disability support at UMIST; application process; process of obtaining personal support; accommodation; campus accessibility; occupational health; SA;

academic support; examinations and assessment; welfare support; careers advice; health counselling; disabled student numbers; future activities and developments; visiting UMIST; appendices; specific information for those with a particular disability.

**Local disability public service providers:**
Manchester City Council, Albert Square, Manchester.
Access Summit Consortium, St Peter's House, Precinct Centre, Oxford Road, Manchester M13 9GH; 0161 272 7847; text 0161 272 7847; fax: 01601 272 7001.

| University College Chichester |
| --- |

Bishop Otter Campus, College Lane, Chichester, West Sussex
PO19 4PE

*General Enquiries:*
Tel: 01243 816002
Fax: 01243 816080
Email: admissions@ucc.ac.uk
Website: www.ucc.ac.ukem

**Disability Coordinator: Jenni Gorbold**
**Tel: 01243 816276**
**Email: jgorbold@ucc.ac.uk**
**ccormac@ucc.ac.uk**
**Text: 01243 812013**

**Fields of study:**
Animal care and management; arts, literature and creative studies; humanities; management, business and IT; social care, social studies and health care; sports; teacher education and related courses.

➡ Part-time study: **Yes.**
➡ Distance learning: **No.**

**About the college:**
University College Chichester's history spans more than 160 years. It was formed by the merger in 1977 of two former colleges, Bishop Otter College in Chichester and Bognor Regis College, which are now the two main campuses of the modern university college. The campuses feature modern facilities alongside older buildings of historical interest. Both towns are fairly small, with the campuses only a short distance from the available amenities.

| Total number of students: 4,700 | Number of disabled students: 470 |
| --- | --- |

**Learning support staff and services:**
Disability and Learning Support Service

Full-time staff: Disability and Learning Support Coordinator: Jenni Gorbold.
Part-time staff: Sensory Advisor: Christine Mant; Study Skills Advisor: Maureen Preece; Disability Adviser: Eve McCormac and a team of support staff.
Assistance with DSA applications, Hardship Funds and bursaries; initial assessments for dyslexia and arrangement of formal educational psychologist assessments; individual study skills support; alternative examination, assessment and study arrangements; provision of auxiliary aids and services; advice and guidance; one-to-one/group tuition for students with dyslexia; support service for students with mental health issues; liaison with external organisations and technical assistance with DSA equipment. Students may also be referred to outside agencies for specialist support.

**Home sweet home:**
There are two single en-suite study bedrooms on ground-floor level, suitable for wheelchair access, on both campuses. Accommodation for a carer/personal assistant can also be provided. Rental is at the usual rate paid by students. Shared kitchen facilities do not have adjustable units or appliances. Kitchens are equipped with refrigerator, hob/cooker or microwave. D/deaf and hard of hearing students can be provided with vibrating fire alarms. Wardens are usually third- or fourth-year students. Accessible accommodation is fully integrated within the student residences. Accommodation can be guaranteed for duration of student's course.

**Out and about:**
College: A free transport service is run between the campuses, but it is not accessible for wheelchair users or those with mobility difficulties. Dedicated parking spaces near both accommodation and study areas.
Public transport: Buses, trains, train stations and taxis are accessible to wheelchair users and people with a visual impairment. Samys (accessible taxis) operate in this area. The Disability Learning Support Service can offer advice and information on public transport and provide people to assist students in and out of taxis and cars if required. Needs are met on an individual basis.

**Taking it easy:**
At college: The SU and bar are fully is accessible by lift at Bishop Otter, but not fully accessible at Bognor Regis.
Locally: The city centre is flat and accessible as are the facilities. There is a Shopmobility scheme and the pavements are tactile. The

Disability Learning Support Service provides a number of access guides to local facilities in the Chichester and Bognor Regis areas.

## And another thing ...

➡ The college has a mix of traditional and new buildings on two mainly level campuses, although there are some inaccessible teaching areas for students with mobility difficulties.

➡ There are two learning resource centres, one on each campus. At Bognor Regis campus there are steps up to the building that currently make it inaccessible to wheelchair users; however, there is an integrated computer system that covers all of the library services. For regular assistance to use the library resources contact the Disability Coordinator.

➡ The Information Services building and two teaching buildings are fully accessible by lift.

➡ There are several accessible toilets located on both campuses.

➡ At Bishop Otter campus nearly all ground-floor rooms are accessible, although there are some 'pinch points' for wider motorised wheelchairs.

➡ Not all lecture theatres on either campus are at ground level, and they are inaccessible for wheelchair users or those with mobility difficulties.

➡ At Bognor Regis campus the two main teaching buildings have lifts.

➡ There are no loop systems currently on campus. Some students use portable radio microphones.

➡ The Estates Office will try to address ground-floor access issues for those experiencing difficulties.

➡ Extensive new building work, currently taking place, will incorporate access for disabled students. During redevelopment there will be some temporary disruptions to some pedestrian routes.

➡ Current students use their guide dogs, but a pen is not provided.

➡ There is a no smoking policy within buildings.

## Local disability public service providers:

ICIS, (Independent Combined Information Service), 0800 859929.
West Sussex Association for the Deaf and Hard of Hearing, 01444 415582.
Foresight, 01243 828555.

## University College London
Gower Street, London WC1 6BT

*General Enquiries:*
Tel: 020 7679 3000
Fax: 020 7679 3001
Email: degree-info@ucl.ac.uk
Website: www.ucl.ac.uk

**Disability Coordinator:**
**Alistair Appleby**
**Tel: 020 7679 1343**
**Fax: 020 7916 8530**
**Email: Alistair.Appleby@ucl.ac.uk**

### Fields of study:
Arts and humanities; built environment; engineering; law; life sciences; mathematical and physical sciences; medicine; Slavonic and East European studies; social and historical sciences.

➡ Part-time study: **Yes.**
➡ Distance learning: **No.**

### About the college:
University College London (UCL) was the first university to be founded in England – in 1826 – after Oxford and Cambridge. UCL was also the first to admit students regardless of race, class or religion as well as to admit women students on equal terms with men. It is now the oldest and largest college of the federal University of London, located in the centre of London on a compact site, among the leafy squares of Bloomsbury.

Total number of students: 17,000    Number of disabled students: 378

### Learning support staff and services:
UCL Access Centre – part of the Academic Services Department
Full-time staff: Disability Coordinator: Alistair Appleby; disability IT trainer; dyslexia tutor; PC support.
Needs assessments; IT training and advice; diagnostic assessments for students with/think they have dyslexia; study skills training; organising non-medical support; alternative assessment and examination arrangements; ensuring appropriate library support is available; liaising with staff; practical advice on physical access to UCL and public amenities in the London area (including general information on access to cinemas, theatres, restaurants, etc.); administering payment for amanuenses and sign language interpreters required for examinations; administering the Disability Initiatives Fund; advice on disability-related benefits.

**Home sweet home:**
There are some wheelchair user accessible rooms that include adapted kitchens, bathrooms and bedrooms. For more information contact the UCL Residence Office.
Accommodation can be guaranteed for duration of student's course depending on the degree of the disability.

**Out and about:**
College: Dedicated parking spaces near both accommodation and study areas.
Public transport: Some bus routes and some train terminals are accessible. Underground access depends on nature of disability and station. Contact Access and Mobility for information about London's public transport services (see Directory).

**Taking it easy:**
At college: The SU facilities are accessible. Most shops, banking services and some refectories and snack bars are accessible.
Locally: There are a variety of guides available from the Disability Coordinator concerning accessibility of venues in the area. Artsline publishes a number of guides about access in London (see Directory).

**And another thing ...**
➡ Following the report of a UCL working party on dyslexia, the college decided that the considerable expertise of its Department of Human Communication Science should be harnessed to provide diagnostic assessments to students. The Dyslexia Clinic, based in the department, was set up as a result of a generous donation from the UCL Friends Programme and has been maintained subsequently by internal funding. The Clinic provides diagnostic assessments free of charge to students and literacy and study skills funded for UK students by the DSA.
➡ UCL is a member of Skill, the Adult Dyslexia Organisation, the British Computer Society Disability Group and the Central London Assessment Network.

## The Disability Statement/Brochure:
*UCL Information for Students with Disabilities 2000/2001*
Detailed booklet containing: Introduction; policy statements; UCL Disability Coordinator; assessment of need; enabling technology; UCL IT trainer; support services; information by disability; funding; UCL student charter; student feedback; statistics; disclaimer and contacts.

## Local disability public service provider:

UCL Union Rights and Advice Centre, 1st Floor, Bloomsbury Theatre Building, 15 Gordon Street, London WC1H 0AH; 020 7679 2533/2507.

---

## University College Northampton

Park Campus, Boughton Green Road, Northampton NN2 7AL;

Avenue Campus, St Georges Avenue, Northampton NN4 0BN

*General Enquiries:*
Tel: 0800 358 2232
Fax: 01604 720636
Email: admissions@
northampton.ac.uk
Website: www.northampton.ac.uk

**Additional Needs Administrator:**
**Vicki Robertson**
**Tel: 01604 735500 ext 2390**
**Fax: 01604 792581**
**Email: disability@**
**northampton.ac.uk**

## Fields of study:

Art and design; behavioural studies; business; cultural studies; education; environmental science; health care education; land and the environment; leather technology; social studies; technology and design.

➡ Part-time study: **Yes.**
➡ Distance learning: **No.**

## About the university:

University College Northampton (UCN) is based on two sites, Park and Avenue, which are 2 miles apart. The university is situated in the heart of England in the historic county of 'Spires and Squires'. Almost £65 million has been spent on student facilities, which have included new student residences, shops and library. Northampton is a successful town, combining old and new. It is surrounded by open countryside and close to the M1.

| Total number of students: 9,000 | Number of disabled students: 750 |
|---|---|

## Learning support staff and services:

Full-time staff: Senior Student Guidance Officer: Clare Davies; Disabled Students Officer/Assessor: Graham Sellick; Dyslexia Administrator: Emma Bulavs.
Part-time staff: Student Mental Health Advisor: Joanna Lester; Additional Needs Administrator: Victoria Robertson; plus hourly paid support staff.

Main services provided are: needs assessment; assistance with DSA applications; provision of auxiliary aids and services; advice and guidance; one-to-one tuition for students with dyslexia; alternative examination, assessment and study arrangements; support service for students with mental health issues; information; coordination of priority accommodation reservation; liaison with academic staff; recruitment of support workers and liaison with external agencies.

## Home sweet home:
There are a number of rooms in halls on both campuses, which have been adapted for disabled students, including a few providing access for people who are wheelchair users – including roll-in showers, accessible toilets and wide doors. Additional rooms can be reserved for PAs.

There are Deaf Alerters and refrigerators for storage of medications; minor adaptations can be made to meet individual needs.

Accommodation can be guaranteed for duration of student's course.

## Out and about:
University: Frequent free bus service runs between the two campuses, but this service is not currently accessible to wheelchair users. Dedicated parking spaces near both accommodation and study areas.

Public transport: Trains, train stations and some buses and taxis are accessible to people who are wheelchair users. Trains, train stations, taxis and some buses are accessible to people with visual impairments. Northampton Door to Door Service, an accessible bus service, and Take6, an accessible minibus, operate in the area.

## Taking it easy:
At university: Contact the SU welfare adviser for information. There are no specific services for disabled students.

Locally: Accessibility in the town is variable and the terrain is generally flat, though hilly in places. There is an accessible pedestrianised town centre, accessible sports facilities and a theatre with accessible seating. Some of the pavements are tactile and there is a Shopmobility scheme. A local disability guide is available from the County Access Officer, Northampton Borough Council, or from Ability Northants (Northamptonshire Council of Disabled People – see below).

## And another thing ...
➡ Access maps are available for both campuses.
➡ Alerters for D/deaf and hard of hearing people installed to cover library and one hall of residence at each campus.

➡ There is an assistive technology room in Park Campus library for disabled students, particularly for students who are blind or who have a visual impairment. This has a range of adaptive technology including a scanner with optical character recognition (OCR) software, networked computers with screen reading and enlargement software, and adjustable-height desks. Similar provision is being developed at Avenue Campus.

➡ The Extra Library Support and Assistance (ELSA) Team are on hand to provide support in the library at both campuses, including help to locate and retrieve material and advice on use of the library's range of assistive technology.

**Local disability public service providers:**
County Access Officer, Northampton Borough Council.
Northamptonshire Council for Disabled People (Ability Northants).
Northamptonshire Social Services Sensory Loss Service.

| University College Worcester |
|---|

Henwick Grove, Worcester WR2 6AJ

*General Enquiries:*
Tel: 01905 855000
Fax: 01905 855132
Email: registry@worc.ac.uk
Website: www.worc.ac.uk

**Disability Coordinator:**
**Zena Morton Jones**
**Tel: 01905 855413**
**Fax: 01905 855132**
**Email: Z.morton-jones@worc.ac.uk**

**Fields of study:**
Business, management and IT; education; English, drama and performing arts; environmental science and land management; health and social care; history, sociology and art; nursing; psychology and sport.

➡ Part-time study: **Yes.**
➡ Distance learning: **No.**

**About the college:**
University College Worcester (UCW) is in St John's, known as the 'village in the city' for its atmosphere and good choice of shopping facilities, banks, pubs and places to eat. The college is a self-contained single-site parkland campus close to the city centre. Running through the heart of Worcester is the River Severn and with it a flow of history that has taken the city from its medieval origins to its current status as a thriving multicultural community. Nearby

attractions include the Malvern Hills, Black Mountains, Welsh borders and Stratford-upon-Avon.

Total number of students: 5,000
Number of disabled students: admission target 14%

## Learning support staff and services:
Two full-time disability coordinators and six part-time academic support tutors and pool of 15 part-time notetakers.
Assessment of need; DSA applications; staff development; alternative exam/coursework arrangements; advocacy; arrangements of specialist academic one-to-one support.

## Home sweet home:
One room in each hall of residence has wheelchair access and a wheel-in shower. There are also adapted kitchens that are shared. Additional shelving for Braille users as well as vibrating alarms, etc. Accommodation can usually be guaranteed for duration of student's course.

## Out and about:
College: Dedicated parking spaces near both accommodation and study areas.
Public transport: Contact Public Transport Section, Worcester County Council or Worcester Wheels.

## Taking it easy:
At college: SU bars and sports hall with lift access. UCW has a Shopmobility scheme.
Locally: The local town is accessible and Worcestershire Dial publishes a local guide.

## Local disability public service providers:
Worcestershire Dial, 01905 27790.
Worcestershire Social Services, 01905 772288.
Public Transport Section, Worcester County Council, County Hall, Spetchley Road, Worcester WR5 2NP, 01905 766800.
Worcester Wheels, 01905 724274.

| University of Wales, Bangor |
|---|

Bangor, Gwynedd LL57 2DG

*General Enquiries:*
Tel: 01248 382570
Fax: 01248 370451
Email: admissions@bangor.ac.uk
Website: www.bangor.ac.uk
Text: 01248 383723

**Disability Adviser: Carolyn Donaldson Hughes**
**Tel: 01248 382023**
**Fax: 01248 383588**
**Email: aos020@bangor.ac.uk**
**Text: 01248 371811**

**Fields of study:**
Agriculture and forestry; biological sciences; business, finance, marketing and management; chemistry; computer science, electronics and mathematics; education; environmental sciences; health studies; history, Welsh history and archaeology; leisure; tourism and heritage; literature, linguistics, creative writing and film; modern languages; music; ocean sciences; psychology; social sciences; sports sciences; theology and religious studies.

➡ Part-time study: **Yes.**
➡ Distance learning: **No.**

**About the university:**
The University of Wales, Bangor (UWB) was established in the late 1880s as one of the three original constituent institutions of the national University of Wales. The university is 2 miles from the Snowdonia National Park, and by the shores of the Menai Strait.

| Total number of students: 8,500 Number of disabled students: 400 |
|---|

**Learning support staff and services:**
Disability Support Services
Full-time staff: Disability Adviser: Carolyn Donaldson Huges; Dyslexia Tutor/Counsellor: Liz Du Pre.
Part-time staff: mental health adviser; disability coordinator; access centre manager; five assessors.
Needs assessments; assistance with DSA applications; advice on benefits, grants and allowances; provision of auxiliary aids and services; advice and guidance; one-to-one/group tuition for students with dyslexia; alternative examination, assessment and study arrangements; support service for students with mental health problems and liaison with external organisations.
The Dyslexia Unit offers confidential tutorial and counselling support; preliminary screening; arranges assessments with follow-up guidance;

assistance with study skills; exam preparation and spelling tuition on a one-to-one or group basis; resources include reference books, tape recorders, spellcheckers, etc. A student group meets weekly.
UWB Access Centre
Part-time manager; five part-time assessors; three admin staff for support needs.

## Home sweet home:
There are several en-suite study bedrooms with bathroom and kitchen facilities specially designed for wheelchair users at the Ffriddoedd site. Rooms can be fitted with flashing alarm systems, etc. to meet the needs of individual students. Other halls of residence have adaptations such as ramps, stair lifts and accessible kitchen, bath and toilet facilities in non-en-suite halls.
Accommodation can be guaranteed for duration of student's course, depending on nature of student's disability.

## Out and about:
University: Dedicated parking spaces near study areas.
Public transport: Some buses and trains are accessible to people who are wheelchair users and/or who have visual impairments. A local disability group, Independent Living Centre (ILC), organises accessible transport such as taxis.

## Taking it easy:
At university: The university sports hall has recently been upgraded and includes ramped access, low-level reception desk, lift to the weights room on the upper floor, accessible toilet and changing facilities. The SU, which houses bars, eating and leisure facilities, clubs and societies, is accessible. The SU has an elected student officer.
Locally: Bangor is a small city which nevertheless poses some problems for people with mobility difficulties, mainly because it is difficult to find any long stretch of level ground as it is hilly in nature. The facilities are accessible and the city centre is accessible with tactile pavements. There is no Shopmobility scheme. Disabled people have access to the high street at specified times. *Discovering Accessible Wales* is the local area disability guide (contact the Disability Support Service for further information). The large supermarkets in the Bangor area have facilities for disabled shoppers, and the local Tesco store on the outskirts of town also has a sign language interpreter.

## And another thing ...
➡ The university buildings are a variety of ages and styles. Not all are currently wheelchair user accessible, and within buildings that

are accessible differences in levels can cause additional problems The university is putting into action the findings of a recent equal access audit and has been working to make improvements; to install ramps, automatic doors, lifts; to fit handrails where appropriate; to install accessible toilets, etc. There are students who are wheelchair users studying a wide variety of courses at the university.

➡ The university houses a pioneering Dyslexia Unit, internationally known for its research and teaching. Although it operates within the university, the unit is an independent, self-financing body and is a corporate member of the British Dyslexia Association. Contact Liz Du Pre on tel: 01248 383843, email: pss139@bangor.ac.uk.

➡ The Counselling Service is not wheelchair accessible, but arrangements can be made to see a counsellor in an accessible room.

➡ The university has two multimedia resource bases that provide a range of enabling technology for students. Both are accessible to wheelchair users and they house equipment to support the study needs of students with a range of disabilities. Advice and training is provided in the Access Centre (see Learning support staff and services above); email: d.sapsed@bangor.ac.uk.

➡ The university has links with CSV and the local Social Services departments to provide personal support for students. Student volunteers are also recruited who assist fellow students on an occasional basis.

➡ Equipment includes: CCTVs, PCs with large monitors, scanners, a Braille printer and a Fuser that converts line art into tactile form. Also screen reading software and character enhancement software for enlarging text on screen as well as software for students with dyslexia is available on the university network.

➡ More accessible toilet facilities are planned for next year, but at the moment only some buildings have them. The five main lecture theatres, and busy reception points (including the libraries and computer lab), have induction loop systems. Infrared transmission equipment is installed in the smaller lecture rooms. Students can borrow neck loops or headphones.

➡ The majority of lecture theatres and teaching areas are accessible. Students can be timetabled into appropriate rooms most of the time. The science buildings are not all accessible and in some areas alternative arrangements may have to be made for practical work.

➡ Sign language interpreters can be supplied from the North Wales Deaf Association. Readers, lipspeakers and notetakers are also available.

## The Disability Statement/Brochure:
*Information Guide for Disabled Students*, available on
www.bangor.ac.uk/
Information from the Web included: Additional information for
students; university services; access information; study support
centre; examination arrangements; sports centre; accommodation;
car parking; health; chaplaincy; shop and banking.

## Local disability public service providers:
North Wales Deaf Association.
North Wales Society for the Blind.
RNID.
Independent Living Centre.
Disability Rights Commission.
SCOPE.
ME Support Group.
Mental Health Advocacy Scheme.

---

## University of Wales College Newport (UWCN) – Coleg Prifysgol Cymru, Casnewydd

Caerleon Campus, PO Box 101, Newport NP18 3YH

*General Enquiries:*
Information Centre
Tel: 01633 430088
Fax: 01633 432850
Email: uic@newport.ac.uk
Website: www.newport.ac.uk

**Disability Coordinator: Bruce Davies**
**Tel: 01633 432658**
**Fax: 01633 432063**
**Email: bruce.davies@newport.ac.uk**
**Text: 01633 432657**

## Fields of study:
Accounting; art, media and design; business and management;
community studies; computing and information technology;
counselling and social welfare; engineering; humanities; science and
teacher training.

➡ Part-time study: **Yes.**
➡ Distance learning: **Yes.**

## About the college:
UWCN's Caerleon campus has far-reaching views over rolling Welsh
hills. It is close to the River Usk, and the M4 motorway is minutes
away. The bustling town of Newport – with its road, rail, bus and

coach links – is a short bus ride away whilst Caerleon town is very nearby. UWCN's second campus is Allt-yr-yn.

| Total number of students: 7,000 | Number of disabled students: 500 |

## Learning support staff and services:
Student Support Services (made up of the Chaplaincy, Counselling, Medical and Welfare Services)
Full-time staff: Disability Coordinator: Bruce Davies; Disability Administrator: Ian Hibble.
Needs assessments; assistance with DSA applications and other sources of funding including Access, European Social Fund and SLDD; provision of auxiliary aids and services; advice and guidance; one-to-one/group tuition for students with dyslexia; alternative examination, assessment and study arrangements on request; support service for students with mental health issues; arrange educational psychologist's assessments; arrangement of technological and non-medical helpers; and liaison with external organisations.
The Welfare staff offer financial advice.

## Home sweet home:
Six en-suite rooms, with either shower or bathing facilities, have been adapted and are wheelchair accessible. A room would be made available for a PA. There is a doorbell and phone for students who are D/deaf or hard of hearing. Estates will be adapting some of the kitchens in the future. Further adaptations may be possible if sufficient notice is given.
Accommodation can be guaranteed for duration of student's course.

## Out and about:
College: The college provides accessible transport for its disabled students. Dedicated parking spaces near both accommodation and study areas.
Public transport: Train stations and some trains, buses and taxis are accessible to people who are wheelchair users and/or who have visual impairments. There is a taxi scheme for disabled people operating in the area.

## Taking it easy:
At college: A fully accessible sports centre, Internet café and SU bar.
Locally: Newport is an accessible pedestrianised town with areas that are flat and hilly. The town's facilities are accessible and there is a shopping arcade that provides the Shopmobility scheme. The pavements are tactile.

## And another thing ...

➡ Future plans include improving accessibility to the upper two floors of the library and learning resources on the Caerleon campus and the Harrison building on the Allt-yr-yn campus.

➡ Student Support Services and the Careers Service have established links with a number of external agencies including RNID, RNIB, DGISC (Disabled Graduates Information Sub Committee – Association of Graduate Careers Advisory Services), PACT (Placing Assessment and Counselling Teams), British Dyslexia Association and Cartefi Cymru.

## The Disability Statement/Brochure:

Includes: Policies; procedures; current provision; access; long-term plans; abbreviations and useful telephone numbers.

## Local disability public service provider:

Cartefi Cymru.

---

### UWIC: University of Wales Institute Cardiff

Western Avenue, Cardiff CF5 2SG

*General Enquiries:*
Tel: 029 2041 6070
Fax: 029 2041 6286
Email: uwicinfo@uwic.ac.uk
Website: www.uwic.ac.uk

**Disability Manager: Karen Robson**
**Tel: 029 2041 6170**
**Fax: 029 2041 6950**
**Email: disability@uwic.ac.uk**

## Fields of study:

Applied sciences; art and design; business; education; health and social sciences; history, politics, sociology, broadcast media and popular culture; hospitality; product and engineering design; sport, PE and recreation; tourism and leisure.

➡ Part-time study: **Yes, on some courses.**
➡ Distance learning: **Yes, on some courses.**

## About the university:

UWIC is located at four campuses – Colchester Avenue, Cyncoed, Howard Gardens and Llandaff. There is also a residential campus at Plas Gwyn. The capital city of Wales has seen massive investment with the regeneration of its docks. Cardiff is also home to the National Museum of Wales, the Museum of Welsh Life and the Welsh National Opera.

| Total number of students: 8,000 | Number of disabled students: 700 |

## Learning support staff and services:
Disability Team
Disability service manager; disability adviser; dyslexia tutors; accessible curriculum development adviser; clerical support and freelance support workers.
Needs assessments; assistance with DSA applications and Financial Contingency Fund; provision of auxiliary aids and services; advice, support and guidance; dyslexia assessments; one-to-one/group tuition for students with dyslexia; alternative examination, assessment and study arrangements; support service for students with mental health issues; advice and support to staff and liaison with external organisations.

## Home sweet home:
The Plas Gwyn campus has a room that is suitable for students with mobility disabilities. Certain other units are also adaptable for use by those with physical disabilities. Additional accessible rooms planned. All rooms are fully integrated within the living accommodation. Accommodation can be guaranteed for the duration of the student's course.

## Out and about:
University: Accessible transport for disabled students can be arranged. There are dedicated parking spaces near both the accommodation and study areas.
Public transport: Some buses, trains, train stations and taxis are accessible to people who are wheelchair users. Buses, trains, train stations and taxis are accessible to people with visual impairments.

## Taking it easy:
At university: The Wales Sports Centre for the Disabled (fitness centre), one of only two in the world, offers a whole host of accessible activities.
Locally: Level city centre with some areas accessible. Some of the facilities are accessible and there is a Shopmobility scheme. Some of the pavements are tactile. There is a local area disability access guide; contact the Disability Team for details.

## And another thing ....
➡ The disability team has recently been expanded to address the growing numbers of disabled students choosing UWIC.
➡ Great emphasis is placed on making the curricula accessible.

➡ UWIC are currently involved in carrying out a strategic review of all disability-related provision with the purpose of establishing a plan to ensure that students with disabilities have access to relevant support. Like the access audit, the review will assist UWIC to plan for the future.

## The Disability Statement/Brochure:
*Information for Disabled Students*
Covers: Who to contact; pre-application considerations; applications; facilities; access; accommodation; setting up support; study and examination arrangements; financial support; other support; monitoring; future developments and contacts.

## Local disability public service providers:
Disability Wales – consortium of local organisations.
Social Services, Cardiff County Council, County Hall, Atlantic Wharf; 029 2087 2000.

---

| University of Wales, College of Medicine – Coleg Meddygaeth Prifysgol Cymru |
|---|

Heath Park, Cardiff, CF14 4XN

*General Enquiries:*
Assistant Registrar
Tel: 029 2074 2027
Fax: 029 2074 4170
Email: UWCMAdmissions@cf.ac.uk
Website: www.uwcm.ac.uk

**Disability Coordinator:**
**Christine Werrell**
**Tel: 029 2074 3811**
**Fax: 029 2074 3574**
**Email: dds@cardiff.ac.uk**

## Fields of study:
Dentistry; health care studies; medicine; nursing and midwifery studies.

➡ Part-time study: **Yes, depends on the course.**
➡ Distance learning: **Yes, depends on the course.**

## About the college:
Situated in the city of Cardiff, the University of Wales, College of Medicine became established as a medical school in 1931. The teaching centre, complete with 920-bed hospital, one of the largest in Europe, successfully integrates medical education and patient care with research facilities on a single campus. It is one of six constituent

institutions comprising the federal University of Wales. The college was required to produce a Welsh language scheme, which was approved in 1999. The college shares its 53-acre site with the University Hospital of Wales.

| Total number of students: 3,915 | Number of disabled students: 162 |
| --- | --- |

## Learning support staff and services:
Dyslexia and Disability Service
Full-time staff: Disability Coordinator: Christine Werrell.
Part-time staff: Disability Support Officer: Hugo Cosh.
Annie Blackburn and Menai Jones are available for individual sessions to assist with a range of counselling and welfare issues including advice on any individual support required.
Needs assessments: assistance with DSA applications; provision of auxiliary aids and services; advice and guidance; one-to-one/group tuition for students with dyslexia; alternative examination, assessment and study arrangements; support service for students with mental health issues and liaison with external organisations.
There is a quiet study room with IT equipment which can be loaned to students.

## Home sweet home:
Access to all residential areas will be provided wherever reasonably practicable. Flatlets in Neuadd Merionnydd are available for the use of students with disabilities, including wheelchair access and facilities. However, students at the college often undertake clinical training in other health care settings, and if you have a disability or specific need you will be advised about particular difficulties, and either appropriate local arrangements will be made or alternative placements organised. Accommodation can be guaranteed for the duration of the student's course.

## Out and about:
College: Provides specialist transport for disabled students if required. There are dedicated parking spaces on site, but these are not particularly close to the accommodation or study areas.
Public transport: Some buses, trains, train stations and taxis are accessible to people who are wheelchair users and/or who have visual impairments.

## Taking it easy:
At college: The college has activities at the UWCM SU, which is accessible. Cardiff Medical Centre Sports and Social Club has been

adapted to cater for people with disabilities. However, access to some facilities for wheelchair users is restricted.
Locally: The city centre is flat and some local facilities are accessible. There is a Shopmobility scheme and some pavements are tactile.

## And another thing ...

➡ The college has plans to develop its facilities and access including improving the provision of toilet facilities for wheelchair users in the main lecture theatres and the SU, as well as installing induction loops in the main lecture theatres.
➡ If you choose to register with the Student Learning Support Service you will have 24-hour access to facilities including four dedicated workstations with specialist software for students with visual impairments and learning difficulties.

## The Disability Statement/Brochure:

Covers: Disability staff contacts; admissions; declaration; fitness to practise; referral; support; examination and assessments; disability provision; access; quality assessment, monitoring and evaluation; fianancial assistance and future developments.
Cardiff Institute for the Blind, 029 20485 414
RNID Wales, 029 20333 378
Mind Wales, 029 20395 123

---

| University of Wales, Lampeter |
|---|

Lampeter, Pont Steffan, Ceredigion SA48 7ED

*General Enquiries:*
Tel: 01570 422351
Fax: 01570 423423
Email: admissions@lamp.ac.uk
Website: www.lamp.ac.uk

**Student Support Officer:**
**Victoria Wade**
**Tel: 01570 424876**
**Fax: 01570 424876**
**Email: v.wade@lamp.ac.uk**

## Fields of study:

Anthropology; archaeology; astudiaethau Cymraeg/Welsh studies; classics; culture, film and media; English; environmental management; history; IT; management; philosophy; theology and religious studies.

➡ Part-time study: **Yes.**
➡ Distance learning: **Yes (anthropology and Welsh).**

University of Wales, Lampeter

## About the university:
The University of Wales, Lampeter is situated in a small market town in west Wales. The campus is largely self-contained and is close to the heart of the town, to local shops and to facilities. A small river bisects the campus forming a valley with gently sloping sides. Some buildings are therefore at different elevations, though all are accessible by vehicle, wheelchair and on foot.

| Total number of students: 1,000 |
| :---: |
| Number of disabled students: approx. 100 |

## Learning support staff and services:
Student Support Office
Full-time Student Support Officer: Victoria Wade; part-time IT specialist; 15 one-to-one support tutors with various specialisms ranging from adult dyslexia support to BSL.
Needs assessment; assistance with DSA applications; provision of auxiliary aids and services; advice, guidance and support; one-to-one/group tuition for students with dyslexia; alternative examination, assessment and study arrangements; support service for students with mental health issues; liaises with local authorities, internal support services, departments and individual staff within the university; confidential assessment interview; screening and arrangements for the professional assessment of dyslexia and study needs; post-assessment advice and discussion about learning requirements; arrangement of appropriate individual counselling and learning support; referral to other support agencies both internal and external; group study sessions for disabled students and their learning support; regular contact with the student's learning support tutor to monitor progress; liaising with student's department when requested and liaison with external organisations both local and national including the British Dyslexia Association, Skill, RNID, RNIB and Disability Wales.

## Home sweet home:
Adapted flat with wheelchair accessible kitchen facilities, en-suite bathrooms and extra rooms for PA. Other en-suite rooms for inclusive accommodation (i.e. meals included) are also wheelchair accessible. Accommodation can be guaranteed for duration of student's course.

## Out and about:
University: Specialist transport can be arranged to meet individual needs, e.g. the hire of an accessible minibus to enable a student to go on a trip. Dedicated parking spaces near both accommodation and study areas.

Public transport: There are wheelchair accessible railway stations at Carmarthen and Aberystwyth, with local bus services connecting to Lampeter. There is a through-coast service to Cardiff and Swansea. The trains are accessible but the buses are not. The taxi service will need to be used to access the nearest railway stations at Carmarthen and Aberystwyth. There is a taxi service, Chris Cars, based in Carmarthen, which is wheelchair accessible (ask for Ken). Buses, trains, train stations and taxis are accessible for people with visual impairments.

**Taking it easy:**
At university: All facilities of the SU are accessible by wheelchair users. The union building, Ty Ceredig, is on two floors, with access to the upper floor by means of an external bridge. The sports hall and multi-gym are accessible by wheelchair users, with male and female changing and wheelchair accessible toilet facilities. There is an occasional cinema club and a student buddy scheme (i.e. students can be supported by a volunteer).
Locally: The city centre is flat (but the campus is sloping) and accessible. Some of the town's facilities are accessible, and there is a Shopmobility scheme. The pavements are not tactile. The town of Lampeter is very small and the majority of students, local and business people are supportive of disabled students using local facilities and will assist wherever possible.

**And another thing …**
➡ The campus provides an environment suitable for blind and visually impaired people. Routes are easily learnt, and potential hazards are few.
➡ Portable induction receivers for people who are D/deaf or hard of hearing.
➡ Induction loops have been installed in a selection of teaching rooms of different sizes. Classes will be timetabled accordingly.
➡ All levels of the main library are accessible to wheelchair users.
➡ New ICT equipment in libraries for visually impaired and dyslexic students.
➡ Study skills room for dyslexic students.
➡ Academic Computer Service provides workstation rooms, all accessible to wheelchair users.
➡ All academic services are accessible by wheelchair users. Whilst some academic departments are housed in two- or three-storey buildings without lifts, all departments have some teaching accommodation that is wheelchair accessible, or will arrange ground-floor facilities for wheelchair users.

➡ Accessible toilets are located in all key areas.

➡ Future plans include undertaking a physical access audit (currently under way) to help the university to improve access for those students with physical disabilities and visual impairments.

➡ The student welfare organisation provides non-medical support at all times.

➡ The Media Centre holds equipment for use by students with visual impairments or students who are D/deaf or hard of hearing, and provides information on access to appropriate technology. The TV studio, subtitling suite and video conferencing room in the media building are all accessible by wheelchair users.

➡ Open learning courses are run as franchises with other institutions throughout England and Wales, so students can choose to do one of the university's courses at an institution close to home.

➡ Many of the students at Lampeter choose to attend because it is a local university and they can still live at home.

## The Disability Statement/Brochure:
Available in alternative formats on request: enlarged print, on the Web and on cassette.

## Local disability public service providers:
Disability Wales.
Local authority advises on special facilities for individual students on request. Felin Fach 01545 572735 for occupational therapist and Sight Centre.

---

| University of Wales Swansea – Prifysgol Cymru Abertawe |
| --- |

Swansea SA2 9ZZ

*General Enquiries:*
Tel: 01792 295111
Fax: 01792 295110
Email: admissions@swansea.ac.uk
Website: www.swansea.ac.uk

**Disability Officer: Richard Edwards**
**Tel: 01792 513000**
**Fax: 01792 513200**
**Email: disability@**
**swansea.ac.uk**
**Text: 01792 513100**

## Fields of study:
Arts and social studies; business; economics and law; education and health studies; engineering and science.

## About the university:
The University of Wales, Swansea is located on a fairly flat, compact campus. The university has bars, shops and eating places all in one location and is largely traffic-free. The campus is close to both city and countryside and the beach is within easy reach. Swansea is both a popular centre for tourism and a busy commercial city.

> Total number of students: 10,350   Number of disabled students: 729

## Learning support staff and services:
Disability officer; assistant disability officer; assessment and training officer; IT support officer; dyslexia tutor; mental health coordinator; access to a chartered educational psychologist.
Needs assessments; comprehensive IT and dyslexia tution and support service; arrangements for assessments for dyslexic students, free of charge; managing of mental health casework and direction to the most appropriate support service both within and outside the university; well-equipped Assessment and Training Centre for Students with Disabilities; assistance in obtaining appropriate technical and human support, e.g. PC, specific software and assistance with study skills.

## Home sweet home:
In 1999 £250,000 was spent to extend provision for students with mobility difficulties in campus halls, so there are a large number of rooms. PAs can be accommodated. There is accommodation specifically adapted for blind and visually impaired students, where guide dogs are welcome. Accommodation for D/deaf and hard of hearing students includes vibrating pillows and flashing red-strobe fire alarms. Hearing dogs for the deaf are welcome. Adaptations to accommodation can be arranged in conjunction with the Disability Office, the Halls Manager/Accommodation Office, and Social Services Department/Occupational Therapist (as applicable).
Accommodation can be guaranteed for duration of student's course.

## Out and about:
University: Dedicated parking spaces near both accommodation and study areas.

## And another thing ...
➡ Since almost all undergraduate teaching takes place on the main, Singleton campus it is not too difficult for those with mobility difficulties to get about. The majority of teaching blocks are modern and were built with at least one lift. Following a major

access audit undertaken several years ago the university has been implementing a rolling programme of improving access and upgrading facilities.

➡ There are a large number of ramps, toilet facilities for wheelchair users, automatic entrance doors, several chairlifts and wide doorways.

➡ A large number of seminar rooms have been equipped with infrared sound systems whilst some of the larger lecture theatres have induction loops. The university is committed to increasing the number of lecture theatres having this equipment.

➡ Notetakers are provided for those who require them.

➡ The Recording Centre for the Blind has three broadcast-standard recording studios equipped with specialist tape recorders and microphones. The Centre also offers a Braille and large print service, which can be in English, Welsh or most of the main European languages (detailed leaflet available from the Manager of the Centre – Kathy Williams – tel: 01792 295085; fax: 01792 295901; email: kathy.williams@swansea.ac.uk).

➡ The library has study desks reserved for wheelchair users in the main study areas.

➡ The campus is criss-crossed with a network of tactile paths. Mobility training will be arranged for those who require it.

➡ The university was awarded funding from the Higher Education Funding Council for Wales to develop its Disability Provision Development Plan (DPDP). The DPDP has established the Training and Assessment Centre for Students with Disabilities, which enables in-house assessments of students' needs.

## The Disability Statement/Brochure:
Includes: Policy; admissions; examinations and assessments; complaints and appeals; staff development; non-medical helpers; existing provision by disability and long-term plans.

### Local disability public service provider:
Disability Wales.

---

| **Warrington Collegiate Institute** |
| --- |

Winwick Road, Warrington WA2 8QA

*General Enquiries:*
Tel: 01925 494494
Email: learner.services@warr.ac.uk

**Learning Support Officers:**
**Clare Litherland/**
**Jane Yarwood**

Web: www.warr.ac.uk

**Tel: 01925 494508**
**Text: 01925 494508**

## Fields of study:
Business; child studies; computing; leisure; management; media; nursing and midwifery; psychology; social sciences; social work; sports studies; teacher training.

➡ Part-time study: **Yes.**

## About the institute:
Warrington Collegiate Institute represents a fusion between community, further and higher education. Since October 2002 the former Faculty of Higher Education of the Institute, its staff, students and Padgate Campus have become part of an enlarged Chester College of Higher Education. As a result, £9 million will be spent to enhance the facilities on the Padgate Campus.

## Learning support staff and services:
Two Learning Support Officers: Clare Litherland and Jane Yarwood. Assistance with individual needs; alternative formats of learning materials; loan of equipment; provision of notetakers, communicators for students who are D/deaf or hard of hearing; personal assistance; support workers for students with specific learning difficulties; alternative examination arrangements.

## Out and about:
Institute: Dedicated parking spaces near both accommodation and study areas.

## And another thing ...
➡ The institute has computers with speech output and programmes to assist people with dyslexia.
➡ The institute has a portable induction loop.
➡ There is CCTV to enlarge written material.

---

### University of Warwick
Gibbet Hill Road, Coventry CV4 7AL

*General Enquiries:*
Tel: 024 7652 3523
Fax: 024 7646 1606

**Disability Coordinator:**
**Claire Graham**
**Tel: 024 7655 3761**

University of Warwick

Email: ugadmissions@warwick.ac.uk      **Fax: 024 7652 2433**
Website: www.warwick.ac.uk      **Email: disability@warwick.ac.uk**

## Fields of study:
Arts; education; medicine; science and social studies.

➡ Part-time study: **Yes.**
➡ Distance learning: **PG only.**

## About the university:
The University of Warwick was built on a greenfield site in the 1960s and has been continuously developed ever since. There are lakes and woods on the landscaped campus, with Birmingham, Stratford and major attractions such as the National Exhibition Centre nearby.

| Total number of students: 17,900 | Number of disabled students: 659 |
| --- | --- |

## Learning support staff and services:
Full-time staff: Disability Coordinator, Claire Graham.
Part-time staff: Dyslexia Support Tutor
Assistance with DSA applications; some provision of auxiliary aids and services; support, guidance and advice; putting provision in place to support needs; one-to-one/group tuition for students with dyslexia; alternative examination, assessment and study arrangements; support service for students with mental health issues; offer guidance on purchase of specialist equipment; liaison with individual departments including accommodation and liaison with external organisations.

## Home sweet home:
Warwick has recently invested in major new residential accommodation for students, and has built a number of specially adapted rooms for both undergraduates and postgraduates, all en-suite, which are wheelchair accessible and should be appropriate for most major physical disabilities. Funding is available to cover any further alterations that have to be made to student rooms to meet other specific needs that may arise.
Accommodation can currently be guaranteed for duration of student's course.

## Out and about:
University: Although students are generally not permitted to have cars overnight on campus, the university issues priority parking permits to all students with major disabilities. There are dedicated parking spaces for disabled students near accommodation and study areas.

Public transport: Train stations and some trains and buses are accessible to wheelchair users. There are taxi companies with vehicles that can accommodate wheelchair users.

## Taking it easy:
At university: Recent building work has included installing new lifts in the SU building and upgrading the Arts Centre to make it one of the most disability-friendly regional arts centres in Britain. Further work is planned to improve access to the site. The cinema is accessible. Warwick SU offers a vast range of activities, facilities, entertainments, venues and bars. Access is via lifts and ramps, and some venues are smoke-free. The Sports Centre has a lift to all floors, and a special suite adjacent to the swimming pool with appropriate toilet and shower facilities for people with disabilities. Most catering outlets are accessible.
Locally: The local towns are Coventry (2 miles away) and Leamington (10 miles away). Both offer good access, with Coventry having a flat, pedestrianised shopping centre.
The Disability Coordinator is able to offer information on access in the local towns.

## And another thing ...
➡ The university will adapt physical features of the site as needed.
➡ The pavements on campus are tactile.
➡ The university offers a full range of academic support services to students with disabilities. Library staff can also offer support.
➡ For placements, including international placements, departments and the university will provide support before and during to ensure the placement is accessible.
➡ A comprehensive Web-based register of disability-related resources that can be accessed at university on local, regional and national levels is being assembled.
➡ Every building in the centre of campus is accessible, as are the great majority of buildings on the other two parts of the site (at Westwood and Gibbet Hill).
➡ The library is fully wheelchair accessible and has accessible toilet facilities.
➡ All of the university's central student computing areas have been designed for or adapted to the needs of students with disabilities. The university's IT Services Department can offer advice on IT issues.
➡ Most lecture theatres are fitted with induction loops.
➡ The university has software for students with dyslexia and visual impairments, but most students access their own software via DSA.
➡ The SU has a Students with Disabilities Campaign Committee.

## The Disability Statement/Brochure:
*Information for Students with Disabilities,* available on
www.warwick.ac.uk/info/disability/.
Includes: Welcome; contact; applications; financial support; living at
university; what's available; support with studying; other support;
monitoring and complaints; future plans and additional information.

**Local disability public service provider:**
CSV, Scala House, Queensway, Birmingham B1 1EQ, 0121 643 8080.

---

| **Webber Douglas Academy of Dramatic Art** |
|:---:|

Chanticleer Theatre, 30 Clareville Street, London SW7 5AP

*General Enquiries:*
Tel: 020 7370 4154
Fax: 020 7373 5639
Email: webberdouglas@btclick.com
Amanda Brenan

**Fields of study:**
Acting – physical and classical; musical; showcase and media and
marketing.

➡ Part-time study: **No.**
➡ Distance learning: **No.**

**About the academy:**
The academy was founded in 1926 as a School of Singing in
Clareville Street, London. Facilities at this school have been
substantially developed over the years. In 1980 the accreditation
system devised and executed by the National Council for Drama
Training accredited the two- and three-year diploma courses and in
1985 the postgraduate course was also accredited. The academy is
situated in the pleasant residential area of South Kensington, within a
few minutes' walk of the parks, museums and the main shopping
areas of Knightsbridge and Chelsea; also within easy reach are the
West End theatres.
Applications from people with disabilities welcome. Please call to
discuss your specific needs. Study support is available for students
with dyslexia and dyspraxia. Buildings are not fully accessible.

## University of the West of England

Bristol UWE, Frenchay Campus, Coldharbour Lane, Bristol BS16 1QY

*General Enquiries:*
Tel: 0117 344 3333
Fax: 0117 344 2810
Email: Enquiries@uwe.ac.uk
Website: www.uwe.ac.uk

**Disability Coordinator:**
**Tel: 0117 344 2564**
**Fax: 0117 344 2935**
**Email: drc@uwe.ac.uk**
**Text: 0117 344 3644**
**Text: 0117 344 2233**

### Fields of study:
Accounting; animal science; architecture; art; biochemistry; biological sciences; building; chemistry; design; drama; economics; education; EFL; engineering; English; environment; film studies; geography; health; history; information systems; languages; law; leisure; linguistics; marketing; media; nursing; planning; politics; psychology; real estate; science; sociology; statistics; surveying and transport.

➡ Part-time study: **Yes.**
➡ Distance learning: **PG and a limited number of UG courses.**

### About the university:
Bristol UWE's history goes back as far as 1595, and it has four campuses in and around the city of Bristol, an associate faculty in Gloucestershire, and regional centres in Bath, Gloucester and Swindon. Bristol is a cosmopolitan city, with numerous live arts activities from around the world.

Total number of students: 24,000+
Number of disabled students: approx. 900

### Learning support staff and services:
Disability Resource Centre (DRC) – Frenchay campus.
Full-time staff: disability officer; disability administrator; disability support administrator; disability adviser; study needs assessor/trainer.
Part-time staff: disability adviser; study needs assessor.
Needs assessment; assistance with DSA applications, Hardship and Emergency Fund; provision of auxiliary aids and services; advice and guidance; one-to-one/group tuition for students with dyslexia; alternative examination, assessment and study arrangements; support service for students with mental health issues; liaison with UWE Careers Service; training in the use of assistive technology; accessing

technical and non-medical support; offers range of facilities, including a Braille embosser and liaison with external organisations
A member of the academic and administrative staff in each faculty acts as contact for disability issues. Assistive technology PCs are available in most campus libraries; similar machines are being installed in faculties.

## Home sweet home:

UWE offers places in fully adapted accommodation for up to ten students and their PAs. Adaptations include level taps, handrails and telephone points. There are also visual fire alarms, and sockets for vibrating pad alarms, for students who are D/deaf or hard of hearing. Additional adaptations may be made on an individual basis subject to resources. It is possible to accommodate guide dog users although rooms are somewhat small for this.
Accommodation can be guaranteed for duration of student's course.

## Out and about:

University: There are dedicated parking spaces near both accommodation and study areas, but on a first come, first served basis, so spaces are not guaranteed.
Public transport: Some trains, train stations and taxis are accessible to people who are wheelchair users. Contact FirstBus and train operators for further information.

## Taking it easy:

At university: The SU has an elected Disabled Students' Officer who represents disabled students within the union and university – Nic Baine, tel: 0117 344 2573; email: studentsupport@uwe.ac.uk.
Locally: For information about Bristol and its accessibility, contact Bristol City Council: www.bristol-city.gov.uk/.

## And another thing ...

➡ All parts of the Frenchay campus are wheelchair accessible including the shops, refreshment facilities and the Octagon. The Campus is multi-levelled, and access to different levels is possible from the outside or by the use of lifts on the inside.
➡ Most parts of the other campuses are accessible but there are some local difficulties due to the age of some of the buildings. Arrangements can usually be made, however, so that students can meet, or attend lectures, in accessible rooms.
➡ All upper levels of the libraries at St Matthias and Frenchay are accessible by a lift, and hearing loops have been fitted in the library training rooms at these campuses.

➡ Audit reports to examine access for disabled people have been undertaken and a five-year programme of improvements put in place. Recent work includes the installation of lifts, automatic doors, toilet facilities for disabled people, induction loops in all lecture theatres and a comprehensive programme to improve signage and wayfinding on all campuses.

➡ Students may use the PC laboratory in the DRC by appointment. The PCs have a variety of assistive technology such as Read and Write, Inspiration and voice input technology. The lab also provides access to a Brailler, scanner, CCTV. Campus libraries provide similar technology, with staff on hand to give additional support. The libraries at each of the seven university campuses have a member of staff with a specific brief to provide a service to disabled users.

➡ The DRC offers a linking service to an annual register of non-medical support workers, which includes BSL interpreters, notetakers, lipspeakers and speedtext operators.

## The Disability Statement/Brochure:
*Information for Students with an Impairment, Medical Condition, Mental Health or Specific Learning Difficulty*
Includes: University policies; support for students; other provision at UWE; future plans; sources of advice and evaluation form.

### Local disability public service providers:
West of England Coalition of Disabled People, 6 Somerville Road, Bishopston, Bristol BS7 9AA, 0117 942 0721 (voice or text) Tuesday, Wednesday and Thursday, fax: 0117 942 0722.

Bristol Disability Equality Forum, Equalities Unit, Bristol City Council, Council House, College Green, Bristol BS1 5TR 0117 922 2358; text: 0117 922 2661; fax: 0117 922 2392; email: equality-team@bristol-city.gov.uk.

Disability Information and Advice Service (DIAS) at West of England Centre for Integrated Living, Leinster Avenue, Knowle West, Bristol BS4 1AR; 0117 983 2828 (voice or text).

West of England Centre for Integrated Living, Courtlands, Leinster Avenue, Knowle, Bristol BS4 1AR 0117 965 3651 (voice or text).

Disabled Living Centre (West of England), Vassall Centre, Gill Avenue, Fishponds, Bristol BS16 2QQ 0117 965 3651 (voice or text).

| **West Hertfordshire College** |
| --- |

Cassio Campus, Langley Road, Watford, Hertfordshire WD17 4YH

*General Enquiries:*
Tel: 01923 812000
Fax: 01923 812480
Email: admissions@westherts.ac.uk
Website: www.westherts.ac.uk

**Team Leader of Assessment and Learning Support: Jill Tattle**
**Tel: 01923 812000**
**Fax: 01923 812556**
**Email: jillt@westherts.ac.uk**

## Fields of study:
Art and design; business; early childhood studies; engineering and science; hospitality, leisure and travel; humanities; information technology; media; performing arts; public services; publishing, printing and packaging.

- ➡ Part-time study: **Yes.**
- ➡ Distance learning: **Developing, particularly with disabled students in mind.**

## About the college:
One of the largest colleges in the country, West Herts has been running degree courses since the 1960s and has consequently built major contacts within business and industry. West Herts College is based over four campuses in Watford and Hemel Hempstead. Only 20 minutes from Watford to London by train.

| Total number of students: 30,000 |
| --- |
| Number of disabled students: 500+ |

## Learning support staff and services:
Assessment and Learning Support
Team Leader and Life Skills Service Manager: Jill Tattle; Teacher for D/deaf or hard of hearing students: Sue Holmes; team of communicators for students who are D/deaf or hard of hearing; educational psychologist; specialist teacher assessor.
There are over 100 people in the department offering support across the college.
Assessment of needs; identifying and providing a support programme; grants, finance and DSA application assistance; accommodation; assessing students for dyslexia; study skills in literacy and numeracy.
Each student's needs are addressed individually.

**Home sweet home:**
The college has no accommodation of its own. There is an accommodation officer in Student Services who assists students in finding private accommodation including the local YMCA, which offers rooms that have been adapted.

**Out and about:**
There are dedicated parking areas in front of every campus and the main study blocks. Dial-a-Ride is also available.
Public transport: There is a programme of converting buses so that they are accessible. The nearest train station is Watford Junction, which is served by Silverlink. It is currently working towards improving accessibility by providing ramps and lifts, etc.

**Taking it easy:**
At college: There is a strong SU with a community sports centre with swimming pool attached. These facilities are fully accessible and the staff are keen to encourage students with disabilities to participate.
Locally: The Harlequin Centre in Watford is a very large indoor shopping centre which is almost entirely wheelchair accessible. There are ramps, lifts, automatic doors, toilet facilities and schemes where you can rent wheelchairs. It is very user friendly.

**And another thing ...**
➡ There is a three- to five-year scheme to improve the accessibility of the college.
➡ Two out of the four campuses are accessible for all facilities. The other two campuses are working on achieving this.
➡ The college is investing in a portable induction loop scheme rather than installed induction loop systems.
➡ There is software for students with visual impairments and dyslexia.
➡ At HE level all students are offered a study skills programme or workshops in literacy, numeracy and English for Speakers of Other Languages (ESOL).

**Local disability public service provider:**
DISH Disability Information Service for Hertfordshire, 45 Grosvenor Road, St Albans, Hertfordshire AL1 3AW; 0800 181 067; email: info@dish4info.co.uk.

## University of Westminster

309 Regent Street, London W1B 2UW

*General Enquiries:*
Admissions
Tel: 020 7911 5000
Fax: 020 7911 5858
Email: admissions@wmin.ac.uk
Website: www.wmin.ac.uk

**Disability Adviser:**
**Katy Mann/Audrey Fleming**
**Tel: 020 7915 5456/**
**020 8357 7360**
**Fax: 020 7911 5162**
**Email: k.d.mann@wmin.ac.uk**
**fleminga@wmin.ac.uk**
**Website: www.wmin.ac.uk/ccpd/**
**Text: 020 7915 5456**

**Fields of study:**
Architecture, construction and the built environment; artificial
intelligence; arts; biological studies; business; commercial music;
communications; criminology; economics, finance; English;
environmental sciences; European languages and linguistics; fashion;
health sciences; history and geography; journalism; law; leisure;
media technology and arts; operational research; photography;
physiology; politics; psychology and social sciences; software
engineering; sports and exercise science; surveying; third world
studies; tourism; translation; urban studies; women's studies.

➡ Part-time study: **Yes.**
➡ Distance learning: **Yes.**

**About the university:**
Founded as the Royal Polytechnic Institution in 1838, this became
the University of Westminster in 1992; its patron is Queen Elizabeth
II. In 2000 Westminster won the Queen's Award for Enterprise –
International Trade. The university has three West End campuses and
one campus in Harrow. The Computer Centre for People with
Disabilities is located at this university. It is near the Houses of
Parliament, the BBC, the Stock Exchange and the British Library.

Total number of students: 21,000    Number of disabled students: 677

**Learning support staff and services:**
Access Centre
Disability Advisers: Katy Mann and Audrey Fleming.
Needs assessments; assistance with DSA applications, International
Fund and Special Equipment Allowance; provision of auxiliary aids
and services; advice and guidance; one-to-one/group tuition for

students with dyslexia; support service for students with mental health problems; tours of the university and liaison with relevant staff. There is a 'drop-in' tutorial support service for design and media students with dyslexia on Friday mornings.

**Home sweet home:**
The two centrally based residences in the West End, Marylebone and Wells Street Halls, do not have any rooms accessible to students with disabilities. There are ten rooms, all at ground level, at Old Street; five rooms on the ground floor at Highgate; and seven rooms, one on each of the seven floors (lift to all floors), at Victoria. All these rooms have associated showers/bathrooms and kitchens that are wheelchair accessible. All these halls are off campus. At Harrow there are six rooms, all with en-suite facilities. These rooms are located on the ground floor and have access to kitchen facilities with special adaptations. As opportunities permit, more of the university's halls of residence are being connected to the university network in order that students can work privately when required.
Accommodation can be guaranteed for duration of student's course.

**Out and about:**
University: Obtaining car parking spaces is problematic at some sites, although priority is given to drivers with disabilities. At some sites a limited number of car parking spaces are available, but these are not dedicated for university use. Harrow has 15 spaces designated for disabled drivers.
Public transport: Contact Access and Mobility for information about London's public transport services (see Directory).

**Taking it easy:**
There are outdoor sporting facilities at Chiswick sports grounds but there is no access to buildings or facilities here for wheelchair users. The fitness rooms/multi-gyms at Regent Street and Marylebone Road are not accessible to wheelchair users. However, the gym and changing rooms at Harrow are now accessible to wheelchair users. Locally: Artsline publishes a number of guides about access in London (see Directory).

**And another thing ...**
➡ The Computer Centre for People with Disabilities (CCPD) at the University of Westminster plays a recognised role in the region in providing advice on funding/support for students with disabilities, learning needs or long-term medical conditions that impact upon study. Students may be eligible for specialist funding, and CCPD

can advise on the best type of IT equipment to suit a specific study need. Any student in higher education in the south east may use this service and you do not have to be registered disabled. The Computer Centre for People with Disabilities, which provides an assessment centre for all students in the south east, is round the corner from the university in Great Portland Street.

➡ The university is working hard to improve accessibility, but there are some limitations to access to the buildings in the West End. A special guidance leaflet on physical access is available.

➡ Disability Services Committee meets three times a year.

➡ When course tutors organise placements they are expected to take the student's disability into account.

➡ Each campus library has a disability liaison contact.

➡ There are several first aid/rest rooms for those with a medical condition.

➡ Euston Centre: wheelchair access, lifts to all floors, accessible toilet facilities.

➡ Marylebone campus: concrete ramp provides access to the campus at ground level.

➡ Management block – lift to all floors; environment block – lift to all floors except sixth; communal block – no lift (installation planned). Access to library via environment block. Access to other areas in communal block via door in library, which can be unlocked.

➡ second- and third-floor lecture theatres can only be reached by stairs – ground-floor lecture theatre accessible via an external ramp.

➡ Cavendish Campus: ramp from pavement to site. No access from the basement car park. The tower block houses four lifts, only one of which covers all floors. The library is on two floors with access at third-floor level. Access to the fourth floor is possible by arrangement with the lift lobby via the lift.

➡ Regent Street: access ramp for people with mobility problems. Two lifts go to every floor except basement and sixth floor. Social areas and refectory accessible. Accessible toilet on lower ground floor.

➡ 16 Riding House Street: narrow stairs at front entrance problematic for people with mobility difficulties. Access to campus office at ground-floor level for wheelchair users. No lift.

➡ Wells Street: Lift to all floors. All teaching, computer rooms, refectory and bar accessible. Accessible toilet facilities.

➡ Harrow Campus: has been specially designed to give full access to those with physical disabilities.

➡ Ramp at west entrance – side door. Access to main entrance and reception area via a ramp, but level access to east entrance. Campus map available on request. Ramps provide access to all premises on campus. Lifts provide access to all floors. Accessible toilets. Induction loops in the Learning Resources Centre reception and help desk areas, in the cashier's office on the fifth floor and in the main auditorium.

➡ 4–12 Little Titchfield Street: access via ramp at the rear entrance for wheelchair users. Access to all floors via lifts, except lower student common room/snack bar and administration office at ground-floor level. Student common room/snack bar on fourth floor accessible. Accessible toilet facilities.

➡ Little Titchfield Street (international office) and Medway House have only very partial or no access.

➡ Timetabling can sometimes overcome accessibility problems.

## The Disability Statement/Brochure:
*Provision for Students with Disabilities/Specific Learning Difficulties*
Includes: Staff members; policies and procedures; special assessment arrangements; funding sources; student services; assistive technology; access and the built environment; parking facilities; accommodation; recreational facilities; contacts.

---

| **Wimbledon School of Art** |
| --- |

Merton Hall Road, Wimbledon SW19 3QA

*General Enquiries:*
Tel: 020 8408 5014
Fax: 020 8408 5050
Email: registry@wimbledon.ac.uk
Website: www.wimbledon.ac.uk

**Student Welfare Officer:**
**Liz Holdsworth**
**Tel: 020 8408 5092**
**Fax: 020 8408 5050**
**Email: unoldsworth@**
**wimbledon.ac.uk**

**Fields of study:**
Costume; painting and sculpture; technical arts; theatre design.

➡ Part-time study: **Yes.**
➡ Distance learning: **No.**

**About the school:**
Wimbledon School of Art is a specialist institution of higher education, which was founded as an art class in the Rutlish School for Boys in 1890. The teaching staff are artists, designers and practitioners regularly involved in academic, literary and professional fields.

| Total number of students: 820 |
| --- |

## Learning support staff and services:

There are no specific staff or services for students with disabilities. The school offers support to all students through the School Counselling and Welfare Service. A Student Welfare Officer (Liz Holdsworth) and student counsellor are available by appointment or telephone.

Dyslexia support includes: diagnostic assessment; needs assessment; tutorials and workshops; alternative examination/assessment arrangements.

## Home sweet home:

There is no dedicated student accommodation.

## Out and about:

School: There are dedicated parking spaces near study areas.
Public transport: Contact Merton Council for information regarding accessibility of local transport.

## Taking it easy:

At school: There are no facilities or services for the social support of disabled students.
Locally: Contact Merton Council for information regarding access in the local area.

## And another thing ...

➡ In 1994 the school commissioned a Disabled Access and Facilities Audit. Subsequent action has included the building of ramps and the installation of special audio equipment. Work is currently in progress to secure funding for the physical alterations to the building in conformity with the recommendations of the audit. These include the provision of lifts and further ramps to provide people who are wheelchair users access to all parts of the school buildings.

➡ Wheelchair access is currently possible to the school reception, the foyer exhibition gallery and to the studio theatre. Access for wheelchair users is also provided to several ground-floor painting and sculpture studios. At present, wheelchair users are not able to gain access to any of the upper floors, including access to the lecture theatre and two upper storeys of the Learning Resources Centre.

➡ The MPhil/PhD by research and thesis or portfolio provides for considerable flexibility in the arrangements made with students and thus may be suited to disabled artists and scholars to a greater extent than the taught courses.

➡ Wimbledon School of Art welcomes applications from groups currently under-represented in HE. Student selection criteria are based on the knowledge, skills and motivation required for successful participation in courses, and not solely on academic qualifications.

## The Disability Statement/Brochure:
Includes: Current policies; access and admissions; examinations and assessments; quality assurance; staff development and training; finance; current provision; physical environment; education and research opportunities and future activity. A4, eight pages.

### Local disability public service provider:
Merton Council.

---

| Winchester School of Art |
| --- |

Park Avenue, Winchester SO23 8DL

*General Enquiries:*
Tel: 023 8059 6900
Email: artsrec@soton.ac.uk
Web: www.soton.ac.uk/~wsart

### Fields of study:
Art and design history; fine art; textile and fashion design; textile art; textile conservation.

➡ Part-time study: **Yes.**

### About the school:
The Winchester School of Art, which was founded 120 years ago, has the support and resources of Southampton University, which it joined in 1996. Alongside the school is the world-renowned Textile Conservation Centre, which was formerly at Hampton Court. This Centre is one of the major conservators in its field and also provides postgraduate courses.
Please see the University of Southampton entry for full details.

## University of Wolverhampton
Wulfruna Street, Wolverhampton WV1 1SB

*General Enquiries:*
Tel: 01902 344444
Fax: 01902 322517
Email: enquiries@wlv.ac.uk
Website: www.wlv.ac.uk

**Registry Disabilities Adviser:**
**Jackie Evans**
**Tel: 01902 323727**
**Fax: 01902 323744**
**Email: J.M.Evans3@wlv.ac.uk**
**Text: 01902 323743**

**Fields of study:**
Art and design; business; computing and information technology; education; engineering and the built environment; health; humanities, languages and social sciences; legal studies; live sciences and the environment; sport, performing arts and leisure.

➡ Part-time study: **Yes.**
➡ Distance learning: **No.**

**About the university:**
Wolverhampton gained its university status in 1992, but its roots can be traced back to the opening of the Wolverhampton and Staffordshire Technical College in 1933 and to the Municipal School of Arts and Crafts, which was founded in the nineteenth century. The university has ten academic schools and two new learning centres, the Wolverhampton Science Park and a whole new purpose-built campus at Telford in Shropshire. It also offers the only degree course of its kind in Interpreting (BSL/English).

Total number of students: 23,000
Number of disabled students: approx. 800

**Learning support staff and services:**
Registry
The university has a Disabilities Admissions Unit within the Registry, staffed by a part-time FTE disabilities adviser and a part-time FTE disabilities admissions administrator. These staff support disabled applicants. The Student Enabling Centre (SEC) supports those disabled applicants who convert to students. At present the SEC consists of a manager, a disability administrator, a dyslexia adviser, a disability adviser, a support worker coordinator and the Communication Support Unit (CSU), which is a well-established centre of excellence for supporting deaf students. The CSU has a manager, an assistant manager and three full-time BSL/English interpreters.

Assistance with arranging needs assessments of appropriate equipment and support requirements; assistance with funding applications; liaison with academic staff; provision of support workers; troubleshooting; alternative assessment, study and examination arrangements and pilot employability events for final-year disabled students.

### Home sweet home:
Adapted residential accommodation is available on the Telford and Wolverhampton campuses. A more limited number of units are available at Compton Park Campus.
Accommodation can be guaranteed for duration of student's course.

### Out and about:
University: The university provides a shuttle service linking all campuses, and all vehicles are accessible. If for any reason one of the accessible buses is out of service an institution-wide email is circulated and every effort is made to provide alternative travel arrangements. Dedicated parking spaces near both accommodation and study areas, though parking in general at the City campus is limited to Blue Badge holders.
Public transport: Some of the West Midlands Transport buses are accessible, but these tend to be confined to the more frequent services. Very few of the smaller companies in the area have accessible vehicles, although the new metro is accessible.

### Taking it easy:
At university: The Communication Support Unit is well established, and as a result D/deaf students do meet socially at one of the local pubs. It is hoped that, as the Student Enabling Centre develops, disabled students will begin to form support/social groups and that SEC can make students aware of these.
Locally: The city centre is flat and mostly, but not completely, accessible. The town's facilities are generally accessible and there is a Shopmobility scheme. The pavements are tactile.

### And another thing ...
➡ While the university is striving to improve physical access across its campuses the nature of some of the buildings means it cannot currently promise physical access to all areas.
➡ The New Horizons project has meant that almost £60 million will be spent across the campuses in renovation and rebuilding.
➡ The Student Enabling Centre provides a comprehensive range of disability-related support services to enable disabled students to participate in university life to the full.

➡ The university has a large D/deaf and hard of hearing student population. The Communication Support Unit specialises in supporting deaf and hearing-impaired students and is staffed by experts in various modes of communication.

➡ The university offers BAs in Deaf Studies and Interpreting.

➡ The university founded the Consortium of Higher Education Support Services (CHESS) for D/deaf or hard of hearing students in 1993. The Consortium now comprises 93 universities and HE institutions and is a frequent host and contributor to meetings and conferences. The CSU is a member of the Midlands Inter-agency Forum and acts as the West Midlands representative of the Association of Sign Language Interpreters (ASLI).

## The Disability Statement/Brochure:
*Information for Students with Disabilities 2000–2003*
Includes: Institutional policy and procedures; contacts; facilities and equipment; practical support for people with specific impairments; physical environment and future activity and policy development. The Disability Statement is currently being revised. An updated version should be available by January 2004.

### Local disability public service providers:
Disability West Midlands, tel: 0121 414 1616.
One Voice, Unit 8, Business Development Centre, 21 Temple Street, Wolverhampton, tel: 01902 713563.

| Writtle College |
|---|

Chelmsford, Essex CM1 3RR

*General Enquiries:*
Tel: 01245 424200
Fax: 01245 420456
Email: postmaster@writtle.ac.uk
Website: www.writtle.ac.uk

**Disability Coordinator: Tish Joyce**
**Tel: 01245 424200 ext: 25568**
**Fax: 01245 420456**
**Email: tj@writtle.ac.uk**
**Text: 01245 424254**

### Fields of study:
Agricultural engineering; agriculture; amenity horticulture landscape management; animal science and animal management; business and leisure management; commercial horticulture; equine studies; interior design and floristry; plant resources and biology; rural environment and conservation.

➡ Part-time study: **Yes.**
➡ Distance learning: **Yes.**

## About the college:
Writtle College, established in 1893, is based on a campus surrounded by its own estate, farm and gardens serving as a green laboratory for students. Writtle is a higher education (70 per cent of its courses) and further education (30 per cent) college specialising in what are traditionally known as the land-based industries. Chelmsford is 2 miles away.

| Total number of students: 1,200 | Number of disabled students: 190 |
| --- | --- |

## Learning support staff and services:
Learning Support Unit
Full-time staff: Disability Coordinator/Counsellor: Tish Joyce.
Part-time staff: HE Learning Support Specialist: Jo Cooper; HE Learning Support Assistant: Carol Stevens.
Assistance with DSA applications and other sources of funding including Access to Learning Fund; provision of auxiliary aids and services; advice and guidance; one-to-one/group tuition for students with dyslexia; alternative examination, assessment and study arrangements; initial assessments for dyslexia; support service for students with mental health issues and liaison with external organisations.

## Home sweet home:
Students with disabilities receive priority consideration with regard to accommodation in halls. Four rooms in Tabor Hall and three rooms in Maddison Hall have been designed to accommodate students with mobility disabilities. Some rooms have been equipped for students who are D/deaf or hard of hearing. Other equipment is purchased, and adaptations carried out as necessary. There is a team of resident wardens on call and a group of second- and third-year students who offer general support, particularly in the first few weeks of session. Accommodation can be guaranteed for duration of student's course.

## Out and about:
College: The college can provide accessible transport for students with disabilities if required. Dedicated parking spaces near both accommodation and study areas.
Public transport: Buses, trains, train stations and some taxis are accessible to people who are wheelchair users and/or who have visual impairments. Taxibus vehicles are accessible (01245 350350).

## Taking it easy:
At college: Wardens and the SU offer social support to disabled students. The recreation centre and bar are accessible.
Locally: Writtle centre is flat and accessible. Town facilities are accessible and there is a Shopmobility scheme. Most of the pavements are tactile.

## And another thing ...
➡ Writtle is a Typetalk user.
➡ Wheelchair access to most buildings.
➡ Staff throughout the college, including the library, Registry, Computer Suite, Accommodation Office, Careers and Media Resources, are very willing to help students with individual requirements. Students are treated as individuals and the college aims to respond to needs as they arise.
➡ Writtle College has close links with the Access Centre at Anglia Polytechnic University, the University of Essex and the Dyslexia Instititute in Chelmsford.

## The Disability Statement/Brochure:
Available in large print, on disk or on tape.

## Local disability public service providers:
The Chelmsford Area Access Group, The Highfield Centre, Moulsham Street, Chelmsford CH2 9AF; 01245 225985.
Essex Disabled People's Association, 90 Broomfield Road, Chelmsford; 01245 253400.

---

| University of York |
|---|

Heslington, York YO10 5DD

*General Enquiries:*
Admissions
Tel: 01904 433533
Fax: 01904 433538
Email: admissions@York.ac.uk
Website: www.york.ac.uk

**Manager of Disability Services:**
**Penn Snowden**
**Tel: 01904 432637**
**Email: SpecialNeeds@york.ac.uk**

## Fields of study:
Archaeology; economics and related studies; educational studies, English and related studies; eighteenth-century studies; history; language and linguistics; mathematics; medieval studies; music;

philosophy, politics; science; social policy and social work; sociology.

➡ Part-time study: **Yes.**
➡ Distance learning: **Yes.**

## About the university:

The University of York was founded during the period of university expansion in the early 1960s. York's main campus is at Heslington on the edge of the city, set around a large lake in 200 acres of landscaped parkland. The university occupies a second campus, King's Manor, in the centre of York where the architecture is mostly Grade I listed medieval buildings. The university is based on a college system and there are seven colleges on the main campus. Travel between the two campuses is about 25 minutes by bus. York's major landmark is the Minster, the largest Gothic cathedral in northern Europe.

---

Total number of students: 10,000
Number of disabled students: approx. 900

---

## Learning support staff and services:

Full-time staff: Manager of Disability Services: Penn Snowden; Assistant: Jill Cochrane; Disability Support Coordinator: Deb Taylor; Dyslexia Coordinator: Janet Hatcher.
Assistance with DSA applications; organise support that DSA fund, including recruitment and payment of staff; alternative teaching, assessment and examination arrangements. All matters of welfare are overseen by a Welfare Coordination Committee, to which the Manager reports, including an annual written report.
Dyslexia Support Centre:
Operates weekly during term-time – provides assessments and support for individual students who have (or think they may have) dyslexia or related specific learning difficulties; regular workshops for groups of students; advice to both staff and students on assessment and examinations.

## Home sweet home:

The university has a high proportion of study bedrooms that are designed to be accessible. Most of these rooms are on the ground floor and many of them have en-suite bathroom facilities. The choice of a bath or shower is usually available. It is generally possible to make alterations to rooms to meet the needs of individuals. Meals are not included in the rent. Students can eat in any of the snack bars or dining rooms around campus (some are more accessible than others) or cook in the kitchens in the student accommodation. Additional accommodation can be provided for PAs.

Accommodation can be guaranteed for duration of student's course for those who have an individual need to live on campus.

## Out and about:
University: Dedicated parking spaces near both accommodation and study areas.

Public transport: Some buses are accessible. The accessibility of the trains depends on the service operators.

## Taking it easy:
At university: York does not have an SU social building; social events are centred on colleges.

Locally: York city has mixed access. The centre is closed to traffic during the day, which means that people who are wheelchair users can use the roads, but many of the buildings are old and not accessible. The Adviser can give you further information on the accessibility of the area.

## And another thing …
➡ A road, crossed by three footbridges, bisects the main campus. The land to the north of the road rises, so that the university's main library, computer science building, Alcuin College and chemistry department are on top of a hill.

➡ Most of the university buildings are accessible by means of covered ways and ramps. There are lifts in the library, physics, biology, chemistry and computer science buildings as well as in most of the colleges.

➡ Timetabling and allocation of rooms can usually take account of the needs of individual students.

➡ All of the colleges on the main campus have lifts and a good level of accessibility (though it is not complete; some areas and rooms are not accessible).

➡ The main administration offices are in Heslington Hall, which is a historic building with limited access – but plans are under way for its refurbishment, including accessibility.

➡ Student Services, the Careers and Student Counselling Service are all housed in single-storey buildings and the health centre is on the ground floor.

➡ Induction loops are fitted in most lecture theatres as well as Central Hall. There is also a portable system that can be used in other rooms.

- Most buildings have accessible toilet facilities.
- Access at the King's Manor is difficult and limited. There is no wheelchair access to the library there.
- The Borthwick Institute of Historical Research is housed in a medieval guildhall with limited access.
- Speech-output screen reader, a scanner and Braille embosser and a CCTV enlarger.
- There are two dog toilets on campus for guide dogs.
- The modularity of courses allows some flexibility in the way they are pursued, but the degree to which this is possible varies between departments and courses.
- The university has some specialised equipment available to students.
- York is a member of Skill.

## The Disability Statement/Brochure:
*Meeting Special Educational Needs: Statement of policies and provision for students with disabilities*
Includes: Contact; policy; application; location and access; accommodation; teaching, assessment and examinations; staff development and student welfare support; financial support; complaints and future plans.

### Local disability public service provider:
Disability Rights and Resources, Priory Street, York.

| York St John College |
|---|

Lord Mayor's Walk, York YO31 7EX

*General Enquiries:*
Tel: 01904 624624
Fax: 01904 716653
Website: www.yorksj.ac.uk

**Disability Coordinator: Liz Maynard**
**Tel: 01904 716541**
**Text 01904 716540**
**Email: emaynard@yorksj.ac.uk**

### Fields of study:
Art, design and technology; community studies; English literature; history; languages; leisure and tourism; management studies; media and digital culture; music, drama and dance; occupational therapy; physical education and sports studies; physiotherapy; psychology; teacher training; theology and religious studies.

- Part-time study: **Yes.**
- Distance learning: **Yes.**

## About the college:
York St John College was established in 1841. It is a college of the University of Leeds and is located close to the city centre of York. York is a medieval city, one of the UK's top tourist attractions. The college is ten minutes' walk from the train and bus stations.

| Total number of students: 5,264 | Number of disabled students: 175 |
|---|---|

## Learning support staff and services:
Disability Unit
Full-time staff: Director of Student Affairs: Finlay Coupar; disability officer.
Part-time staff: Disability Coordinator: Liz Maynard; Administrator: Anne Parkin; Dyslexia Tutors: Barbara Hickman and Mary Craine.
Needs assessments; assistance with DSA applications; provision of auxiliary aids and services; advice and guidance; one-to-one/group tuition for students with dyslexia; alternative examination, assessment and study arrangements; informal chats about any disability issues; support service for students with mental health issues; staff training in disability awareness and liaison with external organisations.

## Home sweet home:
Two flats accessible for a wheelchair user on the main site, where there is catering. Rooms can be made available for a PA. There are accessible toilets for disabled students in many of the main blocks and two additional flats on the off-campus site. In addition, room adaptations (e.g. fire alarms for students who are D/deaf or hard of hearing) can be arranged. Adaptations would be made according to demand. Staff and students trained in first aid and counselling are on call in all student residential accommodation. Student wardens are ready to assist at all times. At the start of each term, details of the warden on duty and how to contact them are posted on all residence notice boards. Accommodation guaranteed for duration of student's course.

## Out and about:
College: Dedicated parking areas near both accommodation and study areas.
Public transport: Buses, trains, train stations and taxis are accessible for people who are wheelchair users. A taxi scheme for disabled people operates in the area.

## Taking it easy:
At college: There is access to the ground floor of the Student Union.
Locally: The city is flat and accessible. Its facilities are accessible and there is a Shopmobility scheme. The pavements are *not* tactile.

## And another thing ...

➡ Plans are currently being put in place to build new student accommodation that will allow the college to build and expand upon its current facilities. The requirements of students with disabilities are influential in the design of any new building works at college.

➡ AbilityNet, a national charity, operates in association with the college, offering its facilities and resources specifically for the benefit of disabled students, providing guidance, advice and training in the use of IT.

## The Disability Statement/Brochure:

Covers: College and student support; making your application; interviews and admission to courses; personal and academic support; financial help; accommodation during your course; accessibility and facilities; the Disability Unit and map.

# Useful sources of information

## Directory

**AbilityNet**   Charity offering specialist help for people with a disability to enable them to use computers; tel: 01926 312847; fax: 01926 407425; helpline: 0800 269545; text: 01926 312847; website: www.abilitynet.org.uk; email: enquiries@abilitynet.org.uk.

**Access and Mobility**   Details on low-floor buses, mobility buses, details on local Dial-a-Ride, planned and fully accessible stations and new accessible tube train routes, copies of detailed guide *Access to the Underground*, Taxicard Scheme (subsidised rates for disabled residents – 020 7484 2929), Docklands Light Railway (London's first fully accessible railway – 020 7918 4000) and accessible tram services (020 8760 5729). Transport for London, Windsor House, 42/50 Victoria Street, London SW1H 0TL; tel: 020 7941 4600; fax: 020 7941 4605; website: www.tfl.gov.uk; email: access&mobility@tfl.gov.uk

**Action for Blind People**   14–16 Verney Road, London SE16 3DZ; tel: 020 7635 4800; fax: 020 7635 4900; website: www.afbp.org.uk, email: info@afbp.org

**Adult Dyslexia Organisation**   336 Brixton Road, London SW9 7AA; tel: 020 7924 9559; fax: 020 7207 7796; website: www.futurenet.co.uk/charity/ado/index.html; email: dyslexia.hq@dial.pipex.com

**ADP: Association of Disabled Professionals**   Disability and employment issues, membership open to disabled professionals BCM ADP, London WC1N 3XX; tel: 01924 283253; fax: 020 8778 3599; email: assdisprof@aol.com; www.adp.org.uk

**AGCAS: Association of Graduate Careers Advisory Services**   Administration Office, The University of Sheffield, 8–10 Favell Road, Sheffield S3 7QX; tel/fax: 0870 770 3310; www.agcas.org.uk; sally.west@agcas.org.uk

**Arthritis Care**   18 Stephenson Way, London NW1 2HD; tel: 020 7380 6500; fax: 020 7380 6505; helpline: 020 7380 6555; website: www.arthritiscare.org.uk

**Arts Dyslexia Trust**   Lodge Cottage, Brabourne Lees, Ashford, Kent TN25 6QZ; 01303 813221

**Artsline**   Arts and entertainment information and advice for disabled people 54 Chalton Street, London NW1 1HS; tel: 020 7388 2227; fax: 020 7383 2653; website: www.artsline.org.uk; email: access@artsline.org.uk; text: 020 7388 2227; youth project (14–26 years old) 020 7388 7373

**ASBAH: Association for Spina Bifida and Hydrocephalus**   ASBAH House, 42 Park Road, Peterborough PE1 2UQ; tel: 01733 555988; fax: 01733 555985; website: www.asbah.org; email: postmaster@asbah.org

**Association of Managers of Student Services in Higher Education**   Brings together those who have responsibility for the management and coordination of a range of learner support and guidance services for students. 2 St James Hall, King Alfred's College, Sparkford Road, Winchester SO22 4NR; tel: 01962 827554.

**Autism London**   1 Floral Place, London N1 2FS; tel: 020 7704 0501; helpline: 020 7359 6070; fax: 020 7704 2306; website: www. autismlondon.org.uk; email: info@autismlondon.org.uk

**British Council of Organisations of Disabled People**   National organisation established by and to represent disabled people's interests Litchurch Plaza, Litchurch Lane, Derby DE24 8AA; tel: 01332 295551; text: 01332 295581; fax: 01332 295580; website: www.bcodp.org.uk; email: bcodp@bcodp.org.uk

**British Deaf Association**   1–3 Worship Street, London EC2A 2AB; tel: 020 7588 3520; fax: 020 7588 3527; text: 020 7588 3529; videophone: 020 7496 9539; website: www.bda.org.uk; email: helpline@bda.org.uk

**British Dyslexia Association**   98 London Road, Reading, Berkshire RG1 5AU; tel: 0118 966 2677; fax: 0118 935 1927; helpline: 0118 966 8271; website: www.bda-dyslexia.org.uk; email: info@ dyslexiahelp-bda.demon.co.uk

**British Heart Foundation**   14 Fitzhardinge Street, London W1H 6DH; tel: 020 7935 0185; fax: 020 7486 5820; website: www.bhf.org.uk email: internet@bhf.org.uk

**British Stammering Association**   15 Old Ford Road, London E2 9PJ; tel: 020 8983 1003; helpline: 0845 603 2001; fax: 020 8983 3591; website: www.stammering.org; email: mail@stammering.org

**CACDP: Council for the Advancement of Communication with Deaf People**   Durham University, Science Park, Block 4, Stockton Road, Durham DH1 3UZ; tel: 0191 383 1155; fax: 0191 383 7914; text: 0191 383 7915; www.cacdp.org.uk; email: Durham@cacdp.org.uk

**City Lit Centre for Deaf People**   Connaught Hall, 41 Tavistock Square, London WC1H 9EH; tel: 020 7383 7624; fax: 020 7380 1076; text: 020 7383 7200; website: www.citylit.ac.uk; email: infoline@citylit.ac.uk

**Community Service Volunteers**   Provides opportunity for volunteers to support and assist students with disabilities and volunteers with disabilities to support and assist students with disabilities within suitable placement 237 Pentonville Road, London

N1 9NJ; tel: 020 7278 6601; website: www.csv.org.uk; email: information@csv.org.uk

**Computer Centre for People with Disabilities** University of Westminster, 72 Great Portland Street, London W1W 7NH; tel: 020 7911 5808; fax: 020 7911 5162; text: 020 7911 5163; disability advice: 020 7915 5456; Head of Unit: 020 7911 5161; website: www.wmin.ac.uk/ccpd; email: p.j.dilley@wmin.ac.uk

**Cystic Fibrosis Trust** 11 London Road, Bromley, Kent BR1 1BY; tel: 020 8464 7211; fax: 020 8313 0472; out of hours: 020 8464 0623; website: www.cftrust.org.uk; email: enquiries@cftrust.org.uk

**Department for Education and Skills** DSA information. Student Support Division 1, 2F Area C, Mowden Hall, Staindrop Road, Darlington DL3 9BG; tel: 01325 392822; website: www.dfes.gsi.gov.uk/studentsupport

**Department of Education for Northern Ireland** Rathgael House, 43 Balloo Road, Bangor, County Down BT19 7PR; tel: 028 9127 9279; fax: 028 9127 9100; website: www.deni.gov.uk; email: mail@deni.gov.uk

**Diabetes UK** 10 Parkway, London NW1 7AA; tel: 020 7424 1000; fax: 020 7424 1001; website: www.diabetes.org.uk; email: info@diabetes.org.uk

**Disability Alliance** Publishes the *Disability Rights Handbook* and the *Disability Rights Bulletin* three times a year and various other publications as well as providing information on benefit entitlements and campaigning Universal House, 88–94 Wentworth Street, London E1 7SA; tel: 020 7247 8776 (minicom available); fax: 020 7247 8765; Rights Advice Helpline: 020 7247 8763 (minicom available); website: www.disabilityalliance.org; email: office.da@dial.pipex.com

**Disability Direct** website: www.disabilitynet.co.uk

**Disability Law Service** Provides free legal advice and assistance on education 39–45 Cavell Street, London E1 2BP; tel: 020 7791 9800; minicom: 020 7791 9801; fax: 020 7791 9802; website: www.dlx.org.uk; email: advice@dls.org.uk

**Disability Resource Team** Produces Braille and tape transcriptions of the 1986 Act 2nd floor, 6 Park Road, Teddington, Middlesex TW11 0AA; tel: 020 8943 0022; fax: 020 8943 5162; website: www.disabilityresourceteam.com; email: mauricepress@enterprise.net

**Disability Sports England** 784–788 High Road, Tottenham, London N17 0DA; tel: 020 8801 4466; fax: 020 8801 6644; website: www.disabilitysport.org.uk; email: info@dse.org.uk

**Disabled Living Foundation** Provides expert advice on matters relating to equipment for independent living 380–384 Harrow Road, London W9 2HU; tel: 020 7289 6111; helpline: 0845 130 9177

(1–10pm); text: 020 7432 8009; fax: 020 7266 2922; website: www.dlf.org.uk; email: advice@dlf.org.uk

**Disabled Students Committee**   see National Union of Students below

**Dyslexia Scotland**   Psychological assessment, specialist teaching, short courses and teacher training to postgraduate diploma Stirling Business Centre, Wellgreen, Stirling FK8 2DZ; tel: 01786 446650; website: www.dyslexia-in-scotland.org; email: info@dyslexia-in-scotland.org

**Employment Opportunities for People with Disabilities**   123 Minories, London EC3N 1NT; tel: 020 7481 2727; fax: 020 7481 9797; text: 020 7481 2727; website: www.opportunities.org.uk; email: info@employmentopportunities.org.uk

**Epilepsy Action**   New Anstey House, Gateway Drive, Leeds LS19 7XY; tel: 0113 210 8800/0808 800 5050 (helpline); fax: 0113 391 0300 website: www.epilepsy.org.uk; email: epilepsy@epilepsy.org.uk

**Hoffmand de Visme Foundation**   Services for people with behavioural, learning and communication difficulties resulting from autism or Asperger's syndrome; Unit B, Lynton Road, London N8 8SL; tel: 020 8342 7310; fax: 020 8341 1235; www.hdvfoundation.org.uk; ayanna@hdvfoundation.org.uk

**Hypermobility Syndrome Association**   15 Oakdene, Alton, Hants GU34 2AJ; www.hypermobility.org; email: membership@hypermobility.org

**LEAD Scotland: Linking Education and Disability Scotland**   Provides home-based support and guidance to disabled adult learners across Scotland. HQ, Queen Margaret University College, Clerwood Terrace, Edinburgh EH12 8TS; tel: 0131 317 3439; fax: 0131 339 7198; website: www.lead.org.uk; email: enquiries@lead.org.uk

**LEAP: Local Education Adult Projects**   Adult education, dealing mainly with basic skills, needs and university support 23 Market Place, Barnard Castle, Co Durham DL12 8NE; tel: 01833 69028; fax: 01833 690567; website: www.communigate.co.uk/neadulteducationanddyslexiasupport/contact.phtml; email: leapinteesdale@ukonline.co.uk

**Learning Development Aids**   Leading individual needs education and mail order service Duke Street, Wisbech, Cambridgeshire; tel: 01945 463441; fax: 01945 587361; website: www.lda.learning.com

**Mental Health Foundation**   UK office, 7th Floor, 83 Victoria Street, London SW1H 0HW; tel: 020 7802 0300; fax: 020 7802 0301; email: mhf@mhf.org.uk; Scottish Office, 5th Floor, Merchant's House, 30 George Square, Glasgow G2 1EG; tel: 0141 572 0125; fax: 0141 572 0246; email: scotland@mhf.org.uk

**MIND: National Association for Mental Health**　Granta House, 15–19 Broadway, London E15 4BQ; tel: 020 8519 2122; information line: 020 8522 1728 (Greater London); 0845 766 0163 (outside London); fax: 020 8522 1725; text: 0845 330 1585; website: www.mentalhealth.org.uk; email: contact@mind.org.uk

**Mind Cymru**　3rd Floor, Quebec House, Castlebridge, 5–19 Cowbridge Road East, Cardiff CF11 9AB

**Myalgic Encephalomyelitis (ME) Association**　4 Top Angel, Buckingham Industrial Park, Buckingham MK18 1TH; information line: 0871 222 7824; fax: 01280 821602; website: www.meassociation.org.uk; email: meconnect@meassociation.org.uk

**NAC: National Asthma Campaign**　Providence House, Providence Place, London N1 0NT; tel: 020 7226 2260; helpline: 0845 701 0203; fax: 020 7704 0740; website: www.asthma.org.uk NAC Scotland 2a North Charlotte Street, Edinburgh EH2 4HR; tel: 0131 226 2544; fax: 0131 226 2401

**NACC: National Association for Colitis and Crohn's Disease**　4 Beaumont House, Sutton Road, St Albans AL1 5HH; tel: 01727 844296; information service (10am–1pm): 0845 130 2233; fax: 01727 862550; website: www.nacc.org.uk; email: nacc@nacc.org.uk

**NASEN: National Association for Special Educational Needs**　Professional association for teachers in special education, offers professional development opportunities and publications NASEN House, 4–5 Amber Business Village, Amber Close, Amington, Tamworth B77 4RP; tel: 01827 311500; fax: 01827 313005; website: www.nasen.org.uk; email: welcome@nasen.org.uk

**NATED: National Association for Tertiary Education for Deaf People**　For students and trainees in education and training at further education level and above Derby College for Deaf People, Ashbourne Road, Derby DE22 3BH; tel: 01332 297550; website: www.dcdp.org; email: enquiries@dcdp.org.uk

**National Autistic Society**　393 City Road, London EC1V 1NG; tel: 020 7833 2299; fax: 020 7833 9666; website: www.nas.org.uk; email: nas@nas.org.uk

**National Database DisForum and Mentassist**　see **LEAP**

**National Deaf Children's Society**　Charity extends to young adults 15 Differin Street, London EC1Y 8UR; tel: 020 7490 8650; info and helpline: 0808 8000 8880; fax: 020 7251 5020; text: 020 7250 0123; website: www.ndcs.org.uk; email: helpline@ndcs.org.uk

**NFAC: National Federation of Access Centres**　Hereward College of Further Education, Bramston Crescent, Tile Hill Lane, Coventry CV4 9SW; tel: 024 7646 1231; fax: 024 766 9405; website: www.hereward.ac.uk; email: enquiries@hereward.ac.uk

**NUS: National Union of Students**   Students with Disabilities Committee, Nelson Mandela House, 461 Holloway Road, London N7 6LJ; tel: 020 7272 8900; fax: 020 7263 5713; website: www.nusonline.co.uk; email: barry.jarleigh@nus.org.uk

**Potteries Association for the Blind**   Vauxhall Centre, 108–110 Lichfield Street, Hanley, Stoke-on-Trent ST1 3DS; tel: 01782 215755

**Prospects London**   Studio 8, The Ivories, 6–8 Northampton Street London N1 2HY; tel: 020 7704 7450; fax: 020 7359 9440; website: www.nas.org.uk/nas/prospects/contact.html; email: prospects-london@nas.org.uk

**QAA: Quality Assurance Agency for Higher Education**   Assesses and reviews quality of subjects at universities and identifies strengths and weaknesses Southgate House, Southgate Street, Gloucester GL1 1UB; tel: 01452 557000; fax: 01452 557070; website: www.qaa.ac.uk; email: comms@qaa.ac.uk

**RADAR: Royal Association for Disability and Rehabilitation**   Provides a range of practical services for people with disabilities 12 City Forum, 250 City Road, London EC1V 8AF; tel: 020 7250 3222; minicom 020 7250 4119; fax: 020 7250 0212; website: www.radar.org.uk; email: radar@radar.org.uk

**Rethink**   Head Office, 30 Tabernacle Street, London EC2A 4DD; tel: 020 7330 9100/01; fax: 020 7330 9102; Registered Office 28 Castle Street, Kingston upon Thames, KT1 1SS; tel and membership line: 0845 456 0455; fax: 020 8547 3862; helpline: 0208 974 6814; website: www.rethink.org; email: info@rethink.org

**RNIB: Royal National Institute for the Blind**   Education and Employment Centre, 105 Judd Street, London WC1H 9NE; tel: 020 7388 1266; fax: 020 7388 2034; helpline: 0845 766 9999; text; dial 18001 before the telephone numbers already given; website: www.rnib.org.uk; email: helpline@rnib.org.uk

**RNID: Royal National Institute for Deaf People**   19–23 Featherstone Street, London EC1Y 8SL; tel: 020 7296 8000; fax: 020 7296 8199; information line freephone and text: 0808 808 9000; text: 020 7296 8001; website: www.rnid.org.uk; email: informationline@rnid.org.uk.

**Scope**   Organisation for people with cerebral palsy 6 Market Road, London N7 9PW; tel: 020 7619 7100; helpline: 0808 800 3333; website: www.scope.org.uk; email: cphelpline@scope.org.uk

**Scottish Spina Bifida Association**   National Office, 190 Queensferry Road, Edinburgh EH4 2BW; tel: 0131 332 0743 fax: 0131 343 3651; website: www.ssba.org.uk; email: mail@ssba.org.uk

**SIA: Spinal Injuries Association**   National association for spinal cord injured people 76 St James's Lane, London N10 3DF; tel: 020

8441 2121; helpline 0800 980 0501; fax: 020 8444 3761; website: www.spinal.co.uk; email: sia@spinal.co.uk

**Skill: National Bureau for Students with Disabilities** Chapter House, 18–20 Crucifix Lane, London SE1 3JW; tel and text: 020 7450 0620; information service: 0800 328 5050; text: 0800 068 2422; fax: 020 7450 0650; website: www.skill.org.uk; email: skill@skill.org.uk

**SNAP: Special Needs Advisory Project** (Cymru) Offers support to young people who have or may have individual needs in education 10 Cooper's Yard, Curran Road, Cardiff CF10 5NB; tel: 029 2038 8776; fax: 029 2037 1876; website: www.snapcymru.org; email: centraloffice@snapcymru.org

**Speakability** Charity raising awareness of communication problems caused by aphasia. Information self-help groups around the country 1 Royal Street, London SE1 7LL; tel: 020 7261 9572; helpline: 080 8808 9572; fax: 020 7928 9542; website: www.speakability.org.uk; email: speakability@speakability.org.uk

**Student Awards Agency for Scotland** Provides funding and students' fees Gyleview House, 3 Redheughs Rigg, Edinburgh EH12 9HH; tel: 0131 476 8212; website: www.student-support-saas.gov.uk

**Student Support Agency for Scotland** Gyleview House, 3 Redheughs Rigg, Edinburgh EH12 9HH; tel: 0131 476 8212; fax: 0131 244 5887; website: www.saas.gov.uk; email: saas.geu@scotland.gov.uk

**Surrey Interpreting Agency** CO Deaf Services Team, Rentwood Resource Centre, School Lane, Fetcham, Surrey KT22 9JX; tel: 01372 360718; minicom: 01372 362471; fax: 01372 363239; email: SSD.SIA@surreycc.gov.uk

**Triscope** A nationwide telephone-based travel and transport information service for people with a mobility disability. Offers assistance with any aspect of travel in the UK and abroad The Vassall Centre, Gill Avenue, Bristol BS16 2QQ; tel: 0845 758 5641; fax: 0117 939 7736; www.triscope.org.uk

## Publications

*A Level Playing Field?* A job hunting guide for students and graduates and information on how to challenge discrimination, AGCAS
*Bridging the Gap*
*Careers tape library information sheet/listing*, RNIB
*The Disability Rights Bulletin* (three times a year), Disability Alliance
*The Disability Rights Handbook*, Disability Alliance
*Employment of Deaf People fact sheet for employers*; *Basic survival signs in BSL*, both RNID

*Employment Update* newsletter; *A practical guide to adjustments in employment*, both Employers Forum on Disability
*Epilepsy and Employment*, British Epilepsy Association
*Guidelines on Mental Health*, University of Stirling,
www.registry.stir.ac.uk/MentalHealth/index.html
*Hobsons Disabled Graduates Casebook*
*Hobsons Guide to Careers for Disabled Students* Freepost CB 264,
Airfield Industrial Estate, Warboys, Huntingdon, Cambridgeshire PE28
2SH; tel: 01487 823546; fax: 01487 822781; website:
www.hobsons.com
*Into Higher Education*, Skill
*Student Mental Health Planning, Guidance and Training Manual*,
produced by Lancaster University, www.studentmentalhealth.org.uk